UNLIKELY

a true love story

UNLIKELY

PRODUCTION DESIGN BY PAUL HORNSCHEMEIER AND JEFFREY BROWN

PUBLISHED BY TOP SHELF PRODUCTIONS
PO BOX 1282
MARIETTA GA
30061-1282
www.topshelfcomix.com
TOP SHELF PRODUCTIONS AND THE TOP SHELF LOGO
ARE ® AND ©2007 BY TOP SHELF PRODUCTIONS INC.

ISBN-13 9781891830419
ISBN-10 1891830414
3rd PRINTING SPring 2007
PRINTED IN CANADA

JEFFREY BROWN WOULD LIKE TO THANK ALL OF
HIS FRIENDS AND FAMILY, ESPECIALLY PAUL FOR
FRIENDSHIP, THE HOLY CONSUMPTION AND PUTTING BOOKS
TOGETHER, CHRIS AND BRETT FOR PUBLISHING, MY MOM
AND DAD, CHRIS WARE, DAN CLOWES, JAMES KOCHALKA,
ADRIAN TOMINE AND ALL THE OTHER CARTOONISTS WHO
HAVE GIVEN ME SUPPORT AND INSPIRATION, DANIEL D., JOSH,
SAMMY FOR MY FIRST ANTHOLOGY INVITE, MIKE AND
CHRISTINE FOR GIVING ME A HOME AND TO JONATHAN
GOLDSTEIN AND IRA GLASS FOR PUTTING ME ON THE
RADIO, TO FANS FOR BUYING BOOKS AND GIVING
ME ENCOURAGEMENT, AND TO HER, FOR BEING FIRST.

To everyone who ends up
looking at the sky.

LONGING

WHEN WE MET

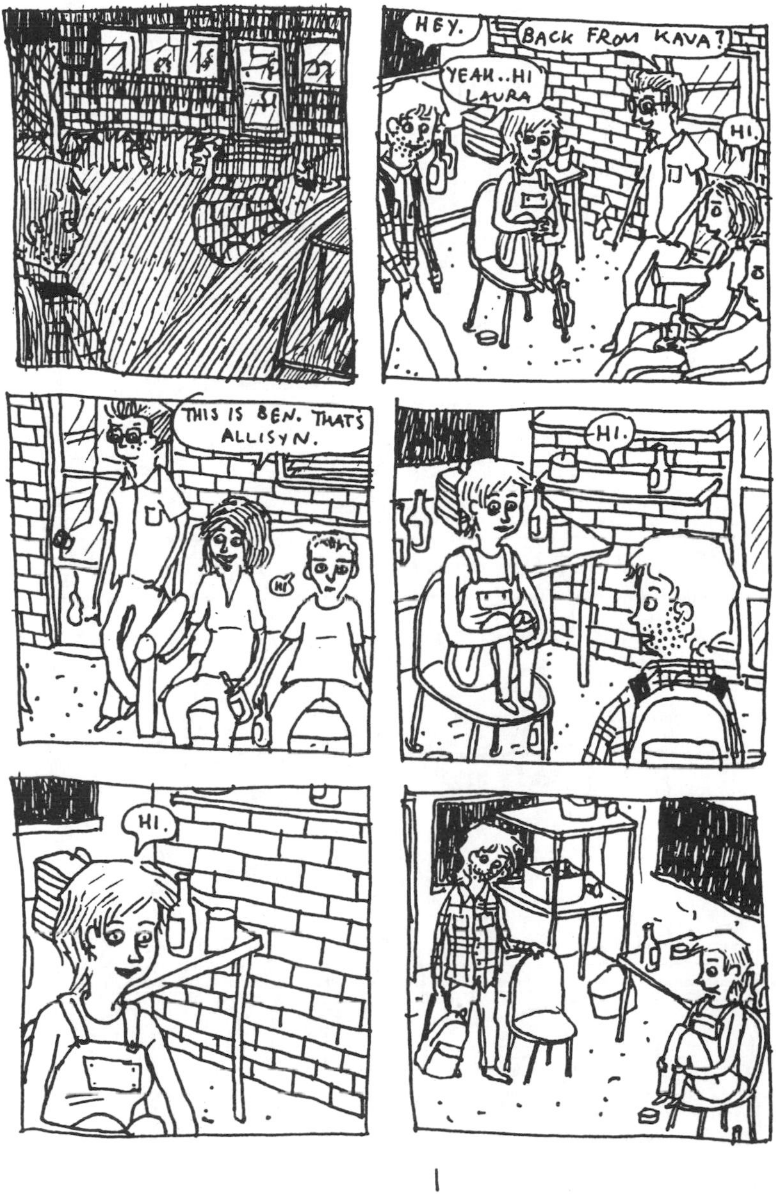
HEY.
BACK FROM KAVA?
YEAH..HI LAURA
HI.
THIS IS BEN. THATS ALLISYN.
HI
HI.
HI.

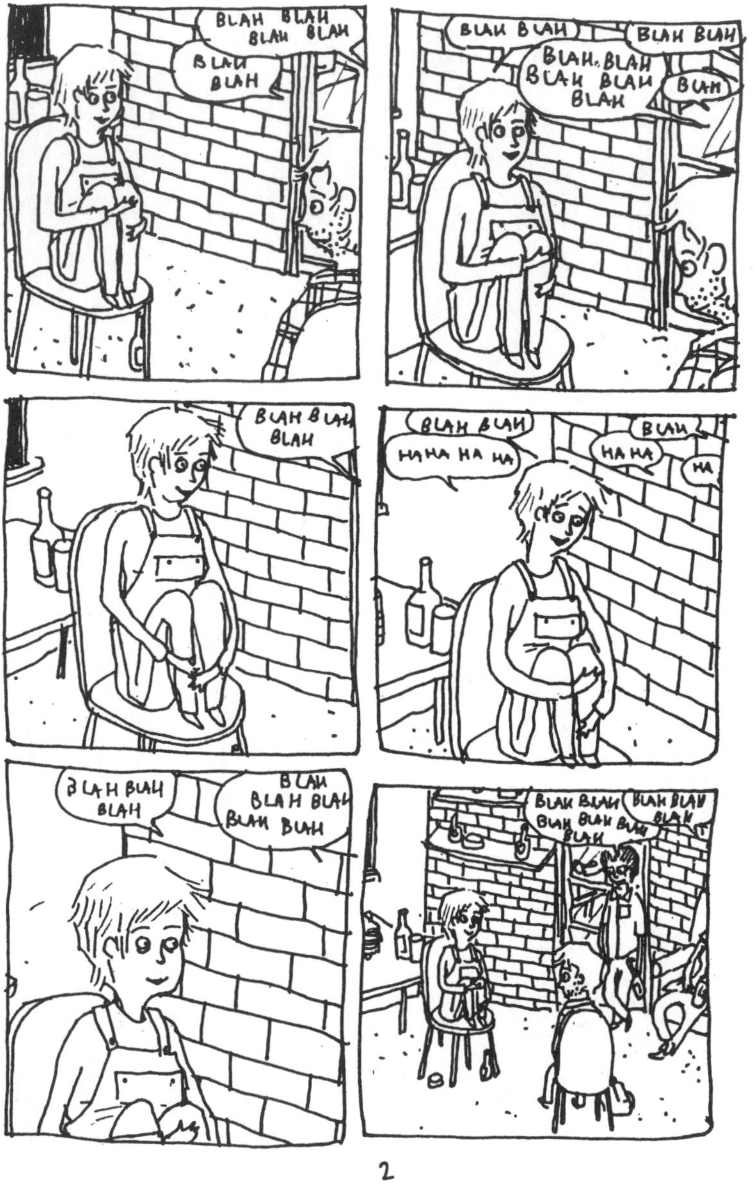
BLAH BLAH BLAH BLAH
BLAH BLAH
BLAH BLAH
BLAH BLAH
BLAH, BLAH BLAH BLAH BLAH
BLAH
BLAH BLAH BLAH
BLAH BLAH
HAHA HA HA
BLAH
HAHA
HA
BLAH BLAH BLAH
BLAH BLAH BLAH BLAH BLAH
BLAH BLAH BLAH BLAH BLAH BLAH
BLAH BLAH BLAH

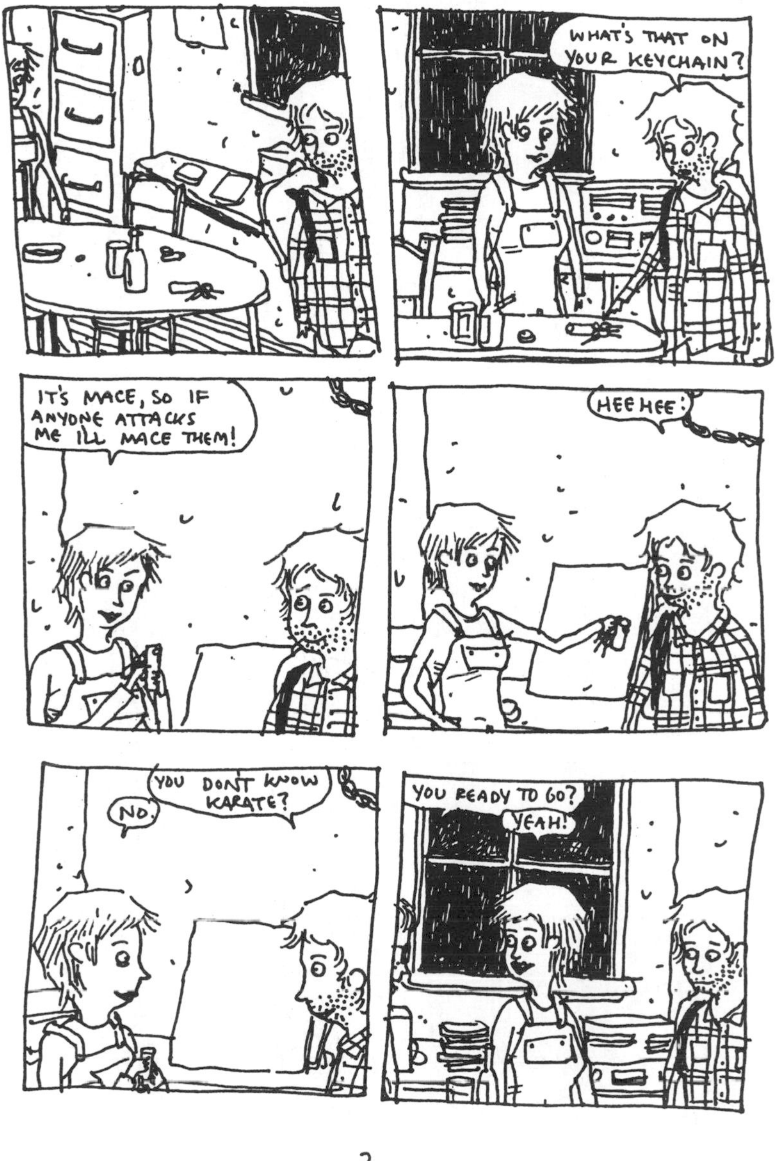
WHAT'S THAT ON YOUR KEYCHAIN?
IT'S MACE, SO IF ANYONE ATTACKS ME I'LL MACE THEM!
HEE HEE!
YOU DONT KNOW KARATE?
NO.
YOU READY TO GO?
YEAH!

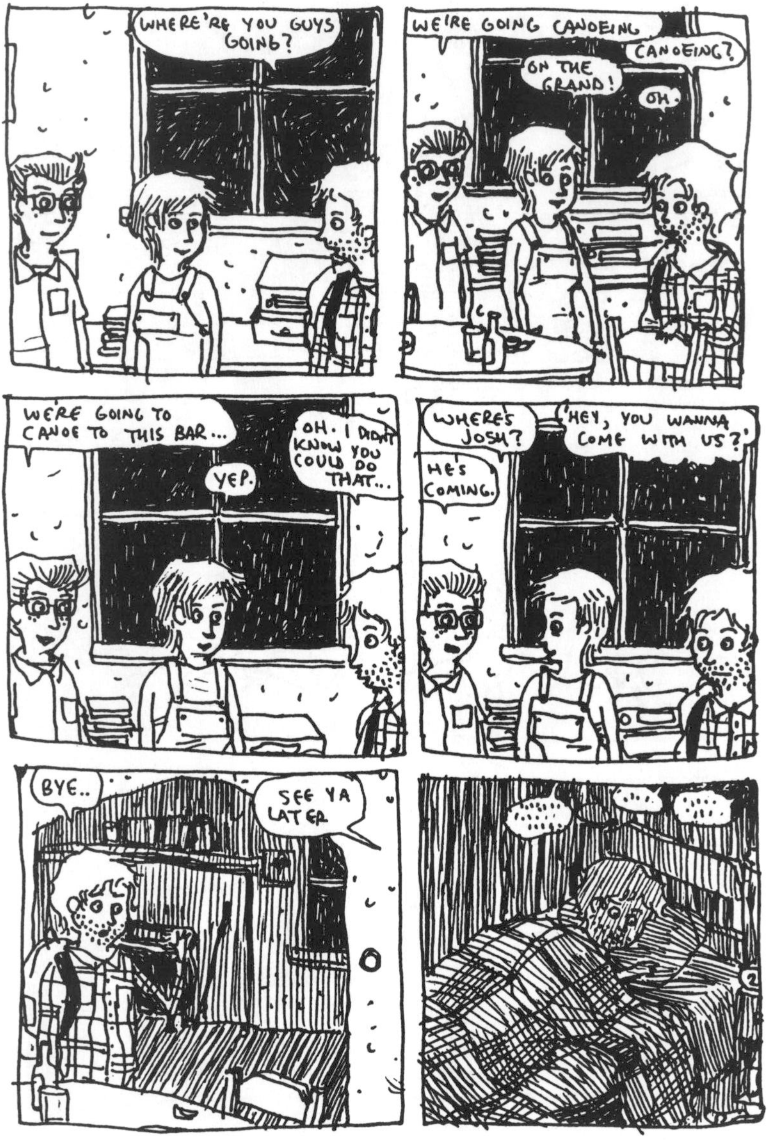
WHERE'RE YOU GUYS GOING?
WE'RE GOING CANOEING
CANOEING?
ON THE GRAND!
OH.
WE'RE GOING TO CANOE TO THIS BAR...
YEP.
OH. I DIDN'T KNOW YOU COULD DO THAT...
WHERE'S JOSH?
HE'S COMING.
HEY, YOU WANNA COME WITH US?
BYE..
SEE YA LATER

I'D DO HER

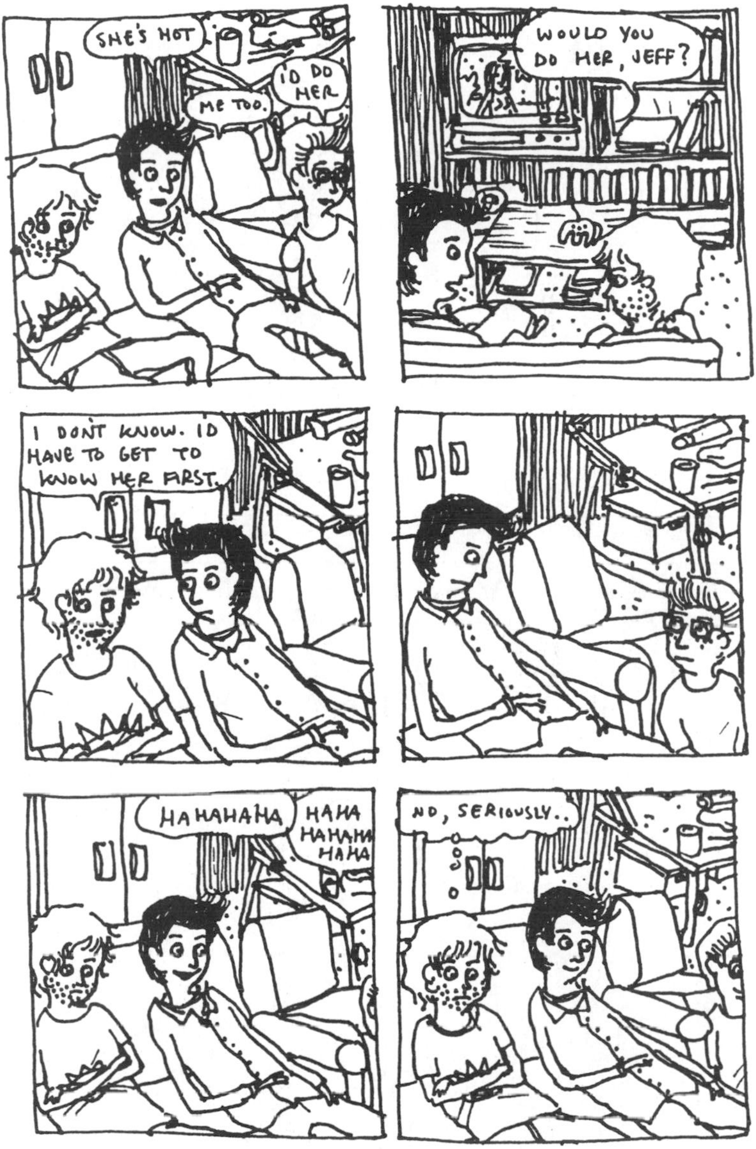
SHE'S HOT
I'D DO HER
ME TOO.
WOULD YOU DO HER, JEFF?
I DON'T KNOW. I'D HAVE TO GET TO KNOW HER FIRST.
HAHAHAHA
HAHA HAHAHA HAHA
NO, SERIOUSLY..

CUTE

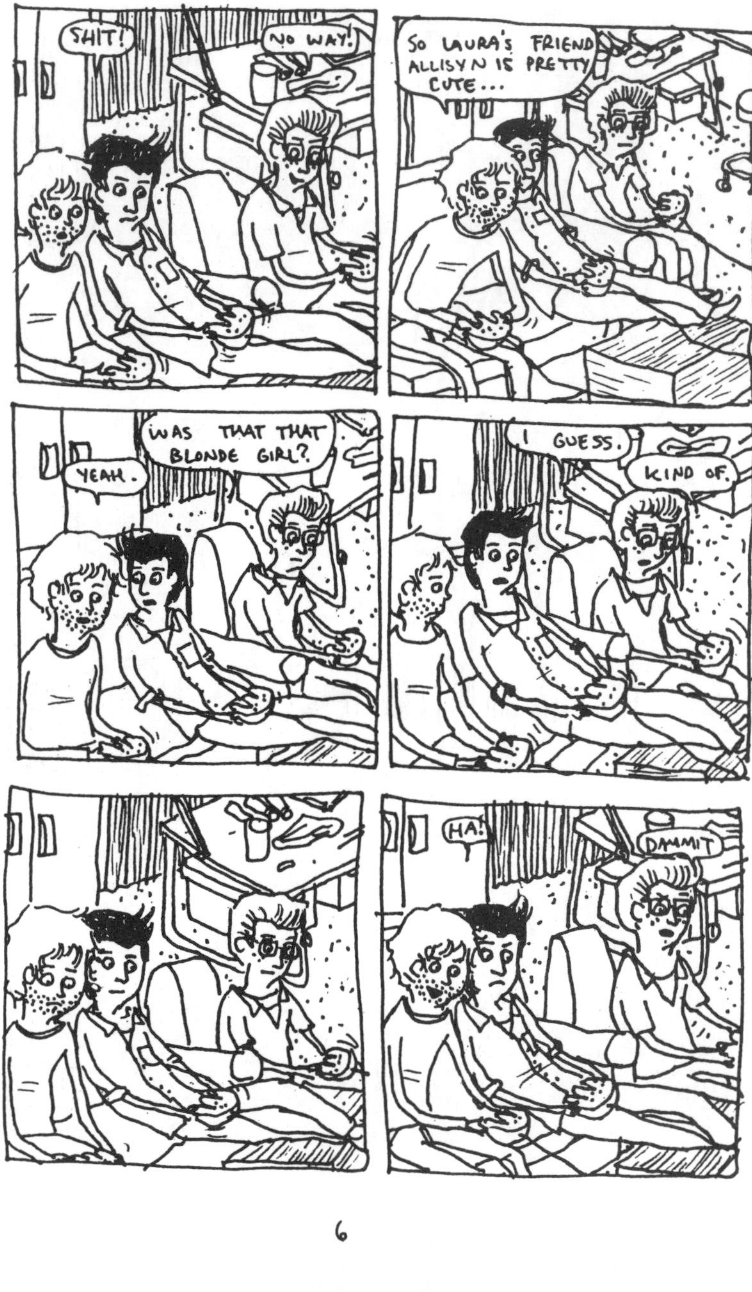
SHIT!
NO WAY!
SO LAURA'S FRIEND ALLISYN IS PRETTY CUTE...
WAS THAT THAT BLONDE GIRL?
YEAH.
I GUESS.
KIND OF.
HA!
DAMMIT

SHE STOPS BY SOMETIME

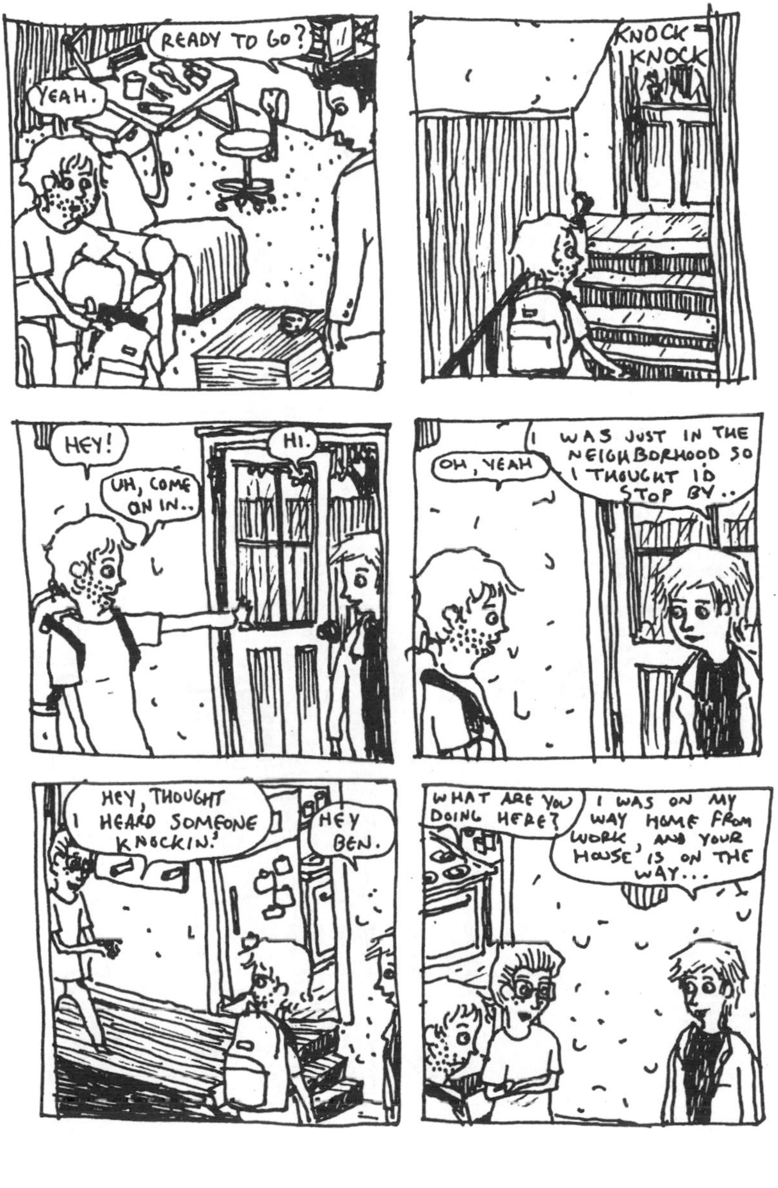

READY TO GO?
YEAH.
KNOCK KNOCK
HEY!
UH, COME ON IN..
HI.
OH, YEAH
I WAS JUST IN THE NEIGHBORHOOD SO I THOUGHT I'D STOP BY..
HEY, THOUGHT I HEARD SOMEONE KNOCKIN'.
HEY BEN.
WHAT ARE YOU DOING HERE?
I WAS ON MY WAY HOME FROM WORK, AND YOUR HOUSE IS ON THE WAY...

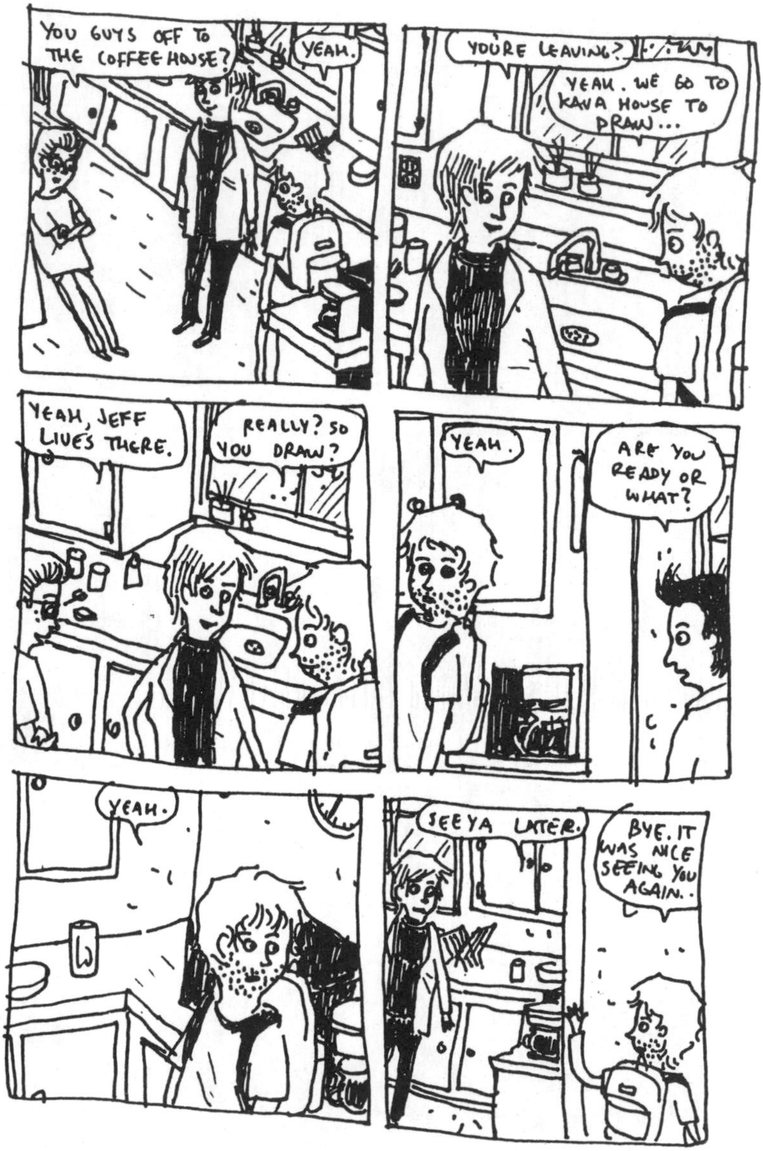
YOU GUYS OFF TO THE COFFEE HOUSE?
YEAH.
YOU'RE LEAVING?
YEAH. WE GO TO KAVA HOUSE TO DRAW...
YEAH, JEFF LIVES THERE.
REALLY? SO YOU DRAW?
YEAH.
ARE YOU READY OR WHAT?
YEAH.
SEEYA LATER.
BYE. IT WAS NICE SEEING YOU AGAIN..

NO, THIS IS JEFF

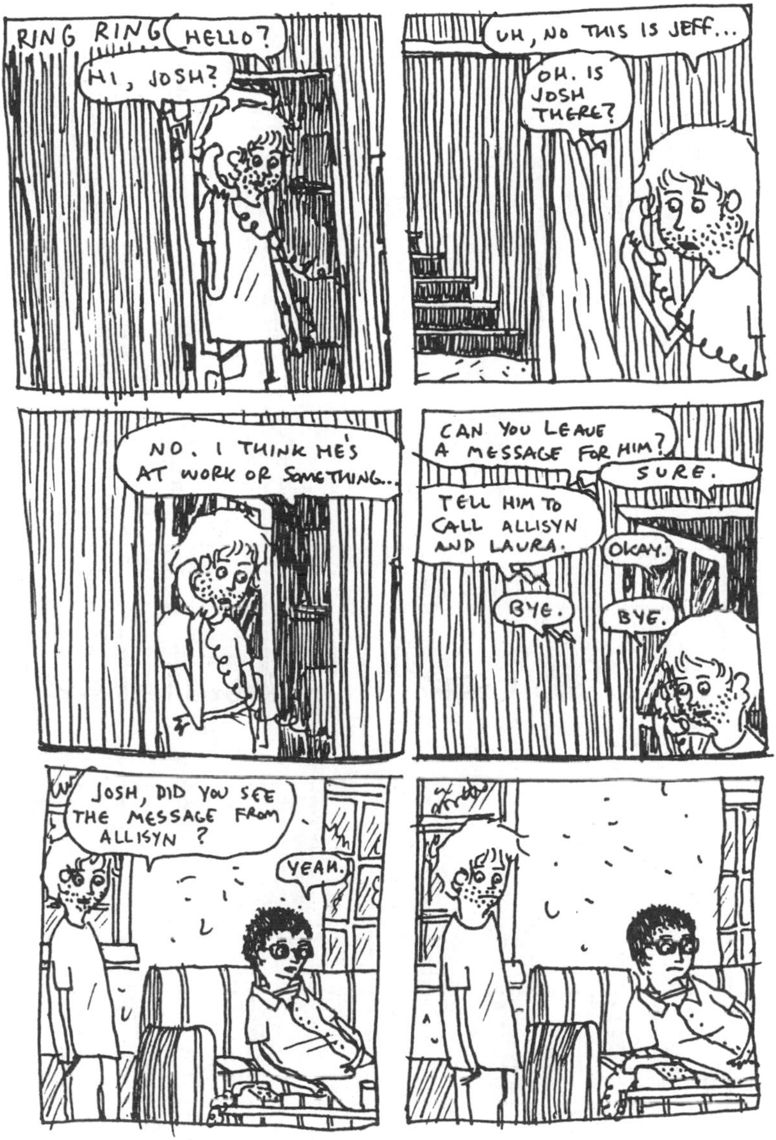
RING RING
HELLO?
HI, JOSH?
UH, NO THIS IS JEFF...
OH. IS JOSH THERE?
NO. I THINK HE'S AT WORK OR SOMETHING...
CAN YOU LEAVE A MESSAGE FOR HIM?
SURE.
TELL HIM TO CALL ALLISYN AND LAURA.
OKAY.
BYE.
BYE.
JOSH, DID YOU SEE THE MESSAGE FROM ALLISYN ?
YEAH.

INTERSECTING

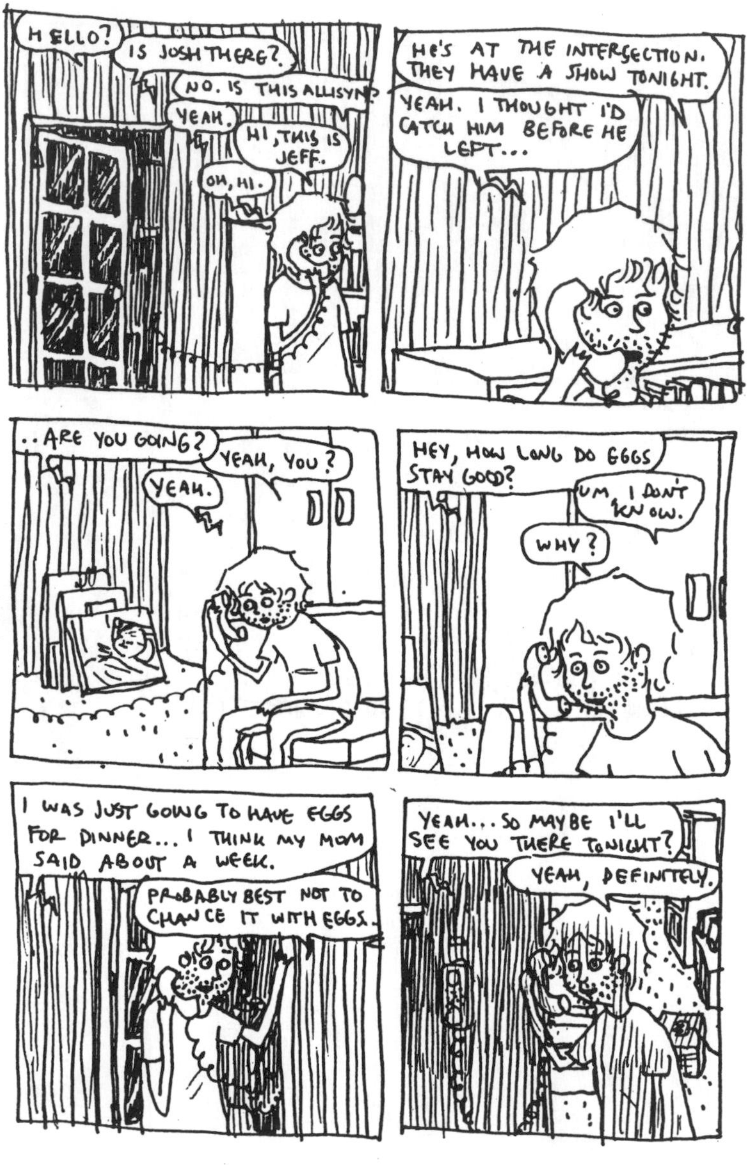
HELLO?
IS JOSH THERE?
NO. IS THIS ALLISYN?
YEAH.
HI, THIS IS JEFF.
OH, HI.
HE'S AT THE INTERSECTION. THEY HAVE A SHOW TONIGHT.
YEAH. I THOUGHT I'D CATCH HIM BEFORE HE LEFT...
..ARE YOU GOING?
YEAH, YOU?
YEAH.
HEY, HOW LONG DO EGGS STAY GOOD?
UM, I DON'T KNOW.
WHY?
I WAS JUST GOING TO HAVE EGGS FOR DINNER... I THINK MY MOM SAID ABOUT A WEEK.
PROBABLY BEST NOT TO CHANCE IT WITH EGGS.
YEAH... SO MAYBE I'LL SEE YOU THERE TONIGHT?
YEAH, DEFINITELY.

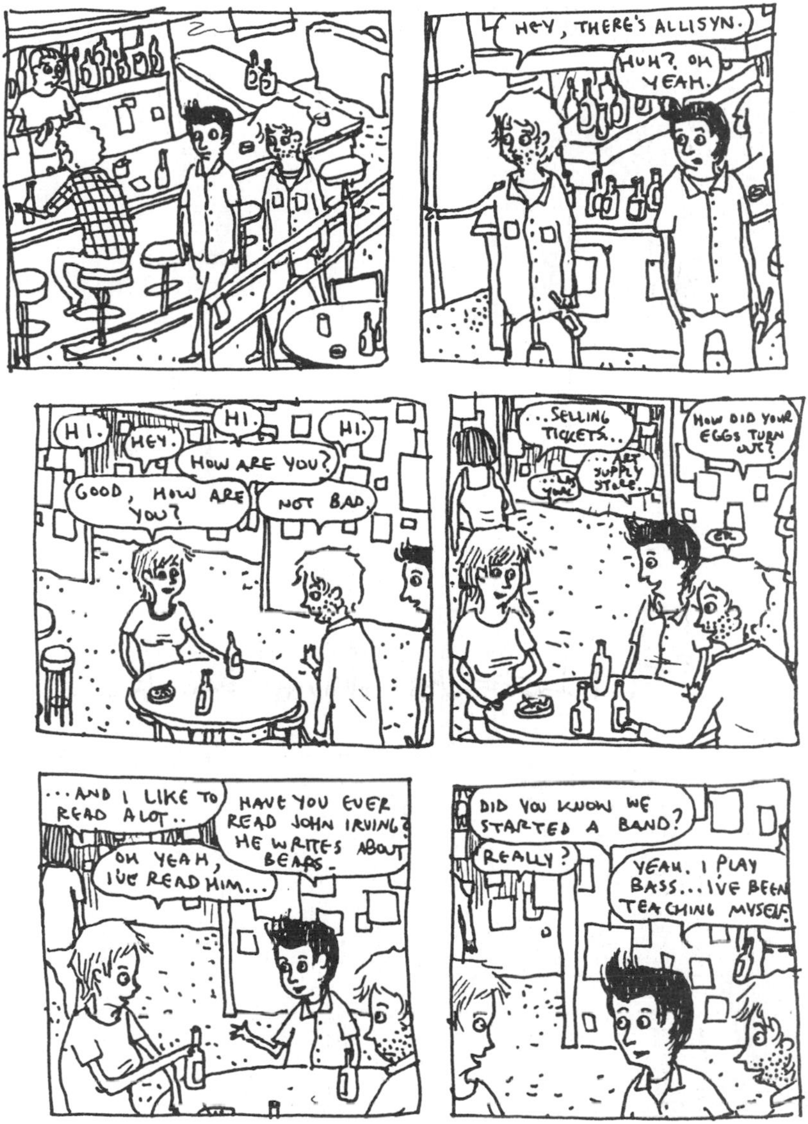
HEY, THERE'S ALLISYN.
HUH? OH YEAH.
HI.
HEY.
HI.
HI.
HOW ARE YOU?
GOOD, HOW ARE YOU?
NOT BAD.
...SELLING TICKETS...
...ART SUPPLY STORE...
HOW DID YOUR EGGS TURN OUT?
ER.
...AND I LIKE TO READ ALOT..
HAVE YOU EVER READ JOHN IRVING? HE WRITES ABOUT BEARS.
OH YEAH, I'VE READ HIM...
DID YOU KNOW WE STARTED A BAND?
REALLY?
YEAH. I PLAY BASS... I'VE BEEN TEACHING MYSELF.

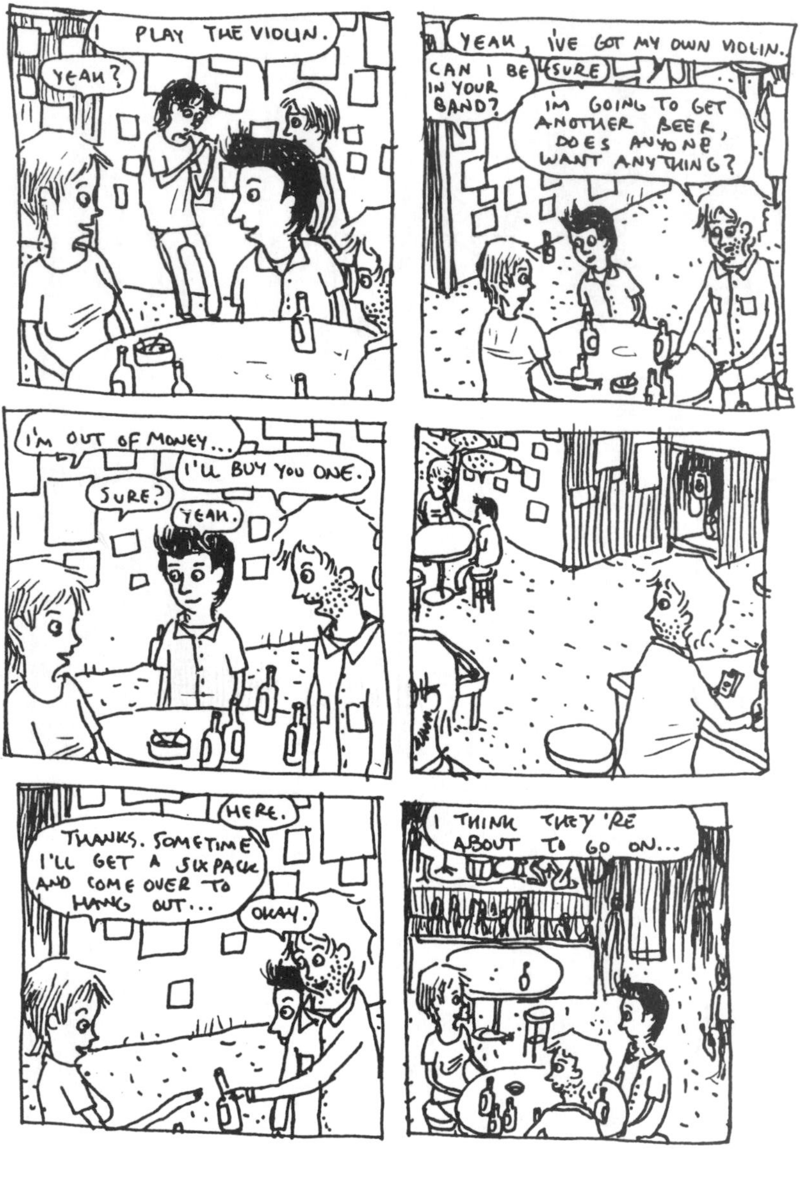
I PLAY THE VIOLIN.
YEAH?
YEAH, I'VE GOT MY OWN VIOLIN.
CAN I BE IN YOUR BAND?
SURE
I'M GOING TO GET ANOTHER BEER, DOES ANYONE WANT ANYTHING?
I'M OUT OF MONEY...
I'LL BUY YOU ONE.
SURE?
YEAH.
HERE.
THANKS. SOMETIME I'LL GET A SIXPACK AND COME OVER TO HANG OUT...
OKAY.
I THINK THEY'RE ABOUT TO GO ON...

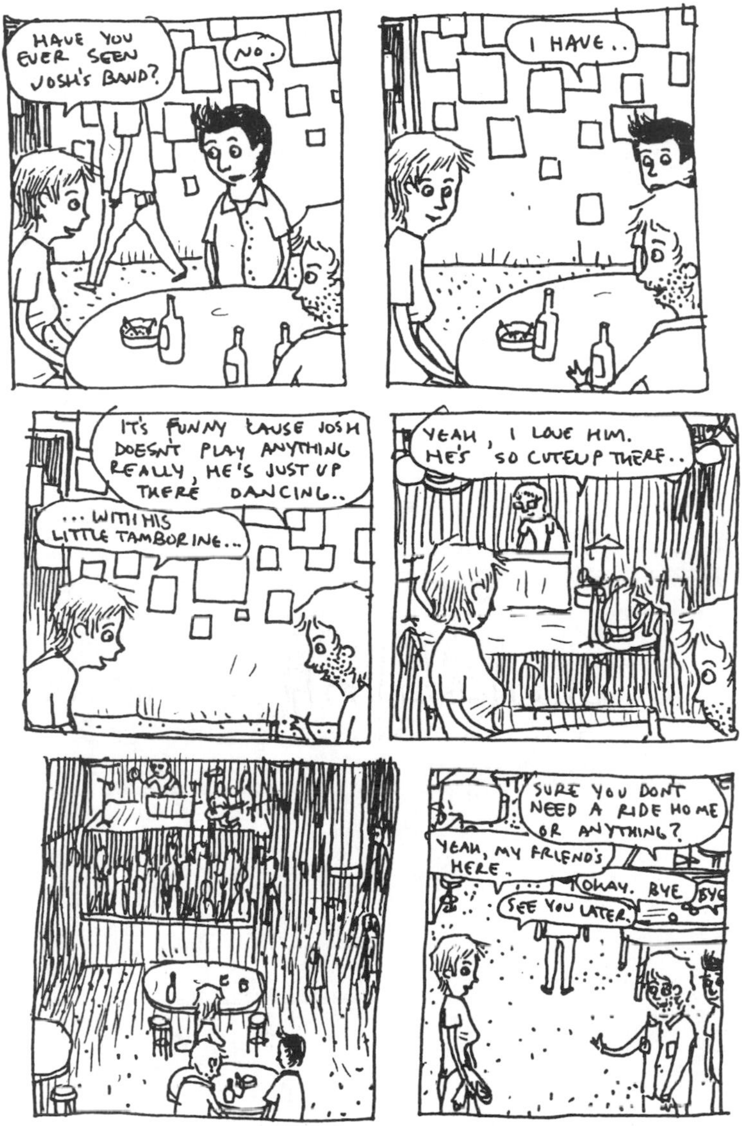
HAVE YOU EVER SEEN JOSH'S BAND?
NO.
I HAVE..
IT'S FUNNY CAUSE JOSH DOESN'T PLAY ANYTHING REALLY, HE'S JUST UP THERE DANCING..
...WITH HIS LITTLE TAMBORINE...
YEAH, I LOVE HIM. HE'S SO CUTE UP THERE..
SURE YOU DON'T NEED A RIDE HOME OR ANYTHING?
YEAH, MY FRIEND'S HERE.
OKAY. BYE.
BYE
SEE YOU LATER.

FANTASY LIFE

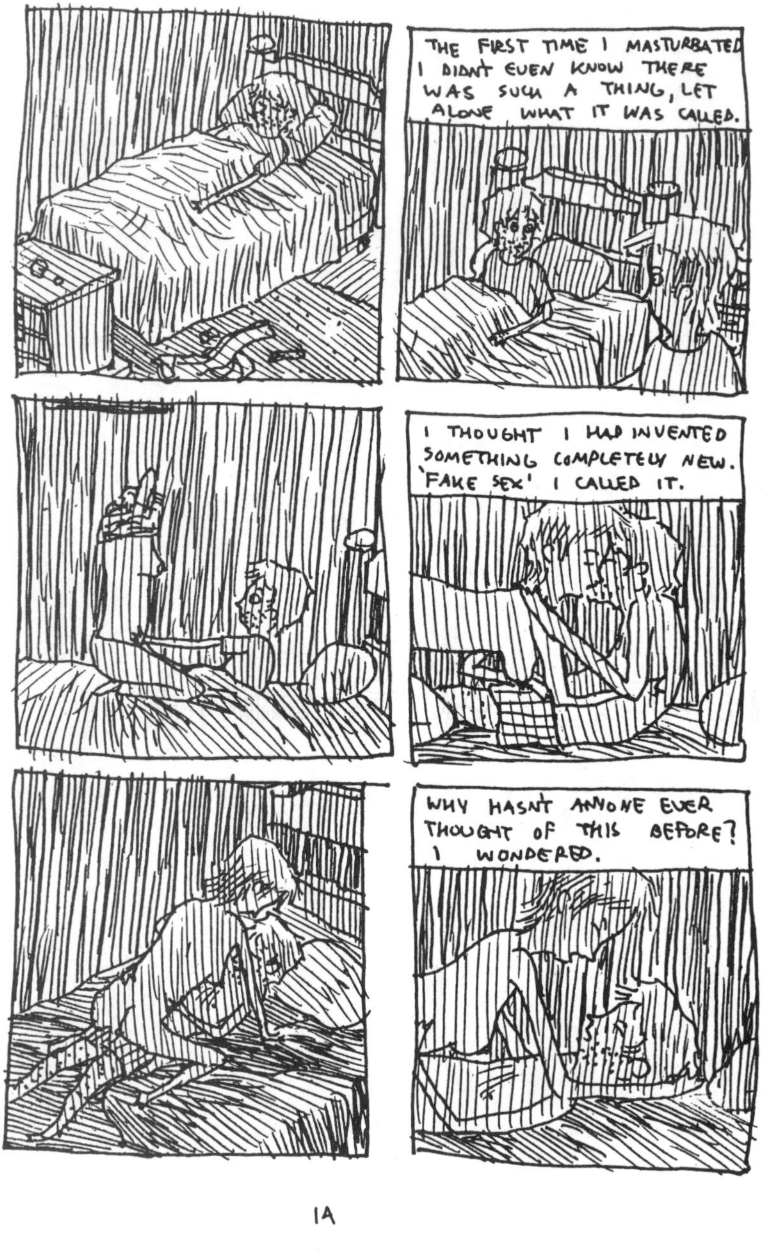
THE FIRST TIME I MASTURBATED I DIDN'T EVEN KNOW THERE WAS SUCH A THING, LET ALONE WHAT IT WAS CALLED.
I THOUGHT I HAD INVENTED SOMETHING COMPLETELY NEW. 'FAKE SEX' I CALLED IT.
WHY HASN'T ANYONE EVER THOUGHT OF THIS BEFORE? I WONDERED.

VIRGIN ALERT

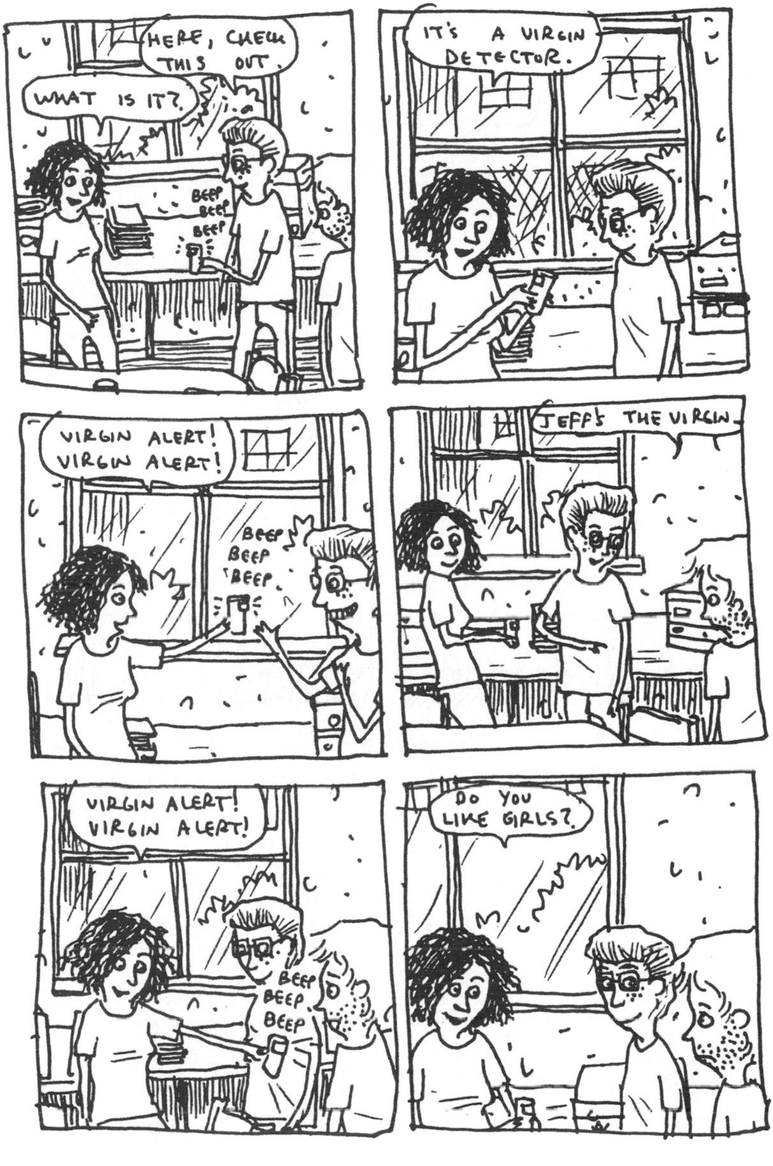
HERE, CHECK THIS OUT.
WHAT IS IT?
BEEP BEEP BEEP
IT'S A VIRGIN DETECTOR.
VIRGIN ALERT! VIRGIN ALERT!
BEEP BEEP BEEP
JEFF'S THE VIRGIN
VIRGIN ALERT! VIRGIN ALERT!
BEEP BEEP BEEP
DO YOU LIKE GIRLS?

BOOGIE NIGHTS

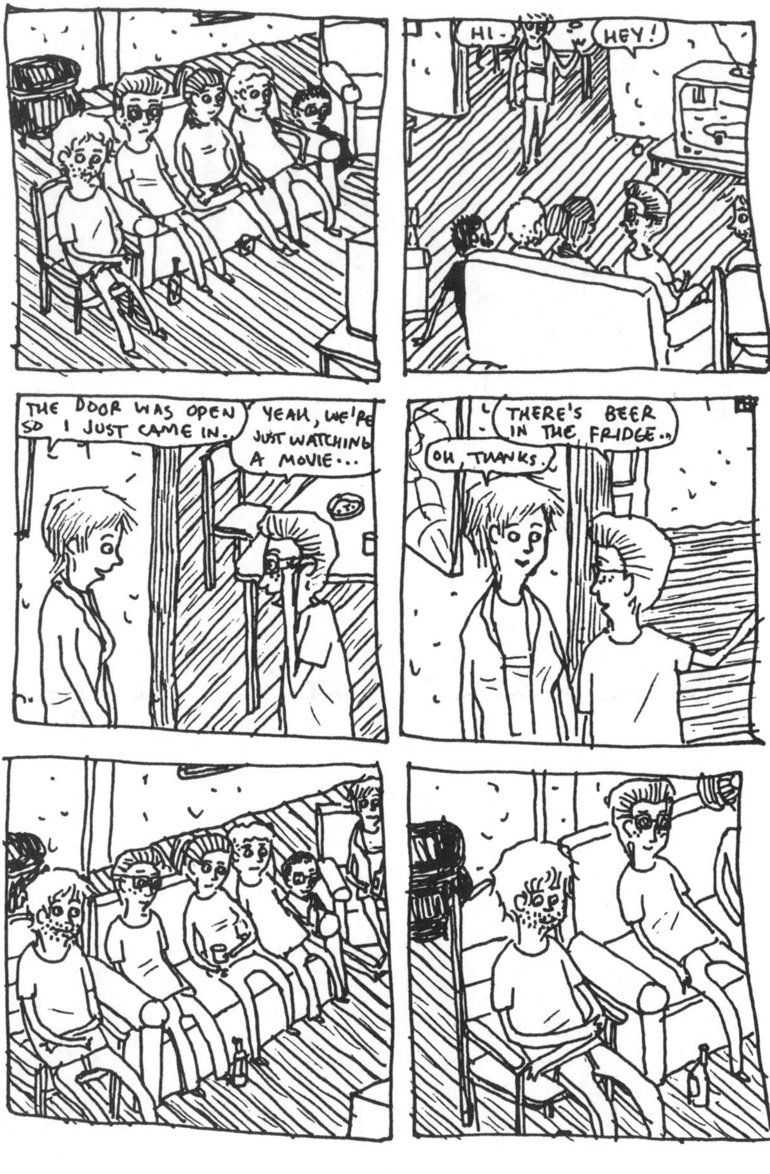
HI-
HEY!
THE DOOR WAS OPEN SO I JUST CAME IN..
YEAH, WE'RE JUST WATCHING A MOVIE...
THERE'S BEER IN THE FRIDGE..
OH, THANKS.

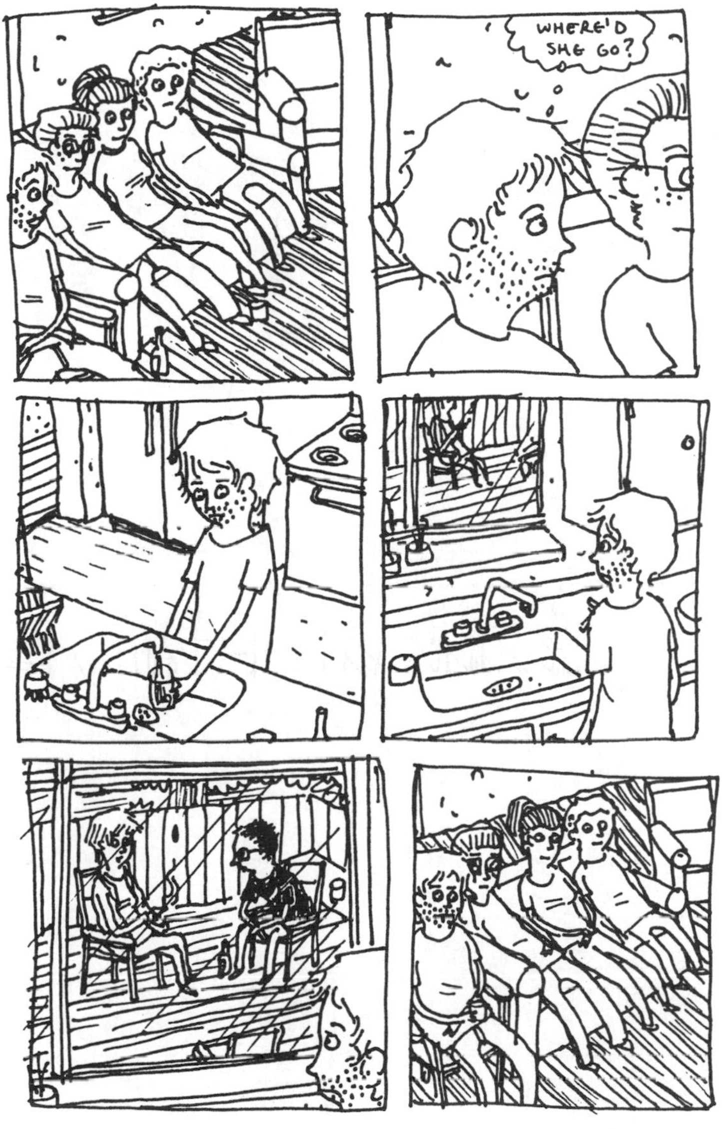
WHERE'D SHE GO?

HAPPY BIRTHDAY

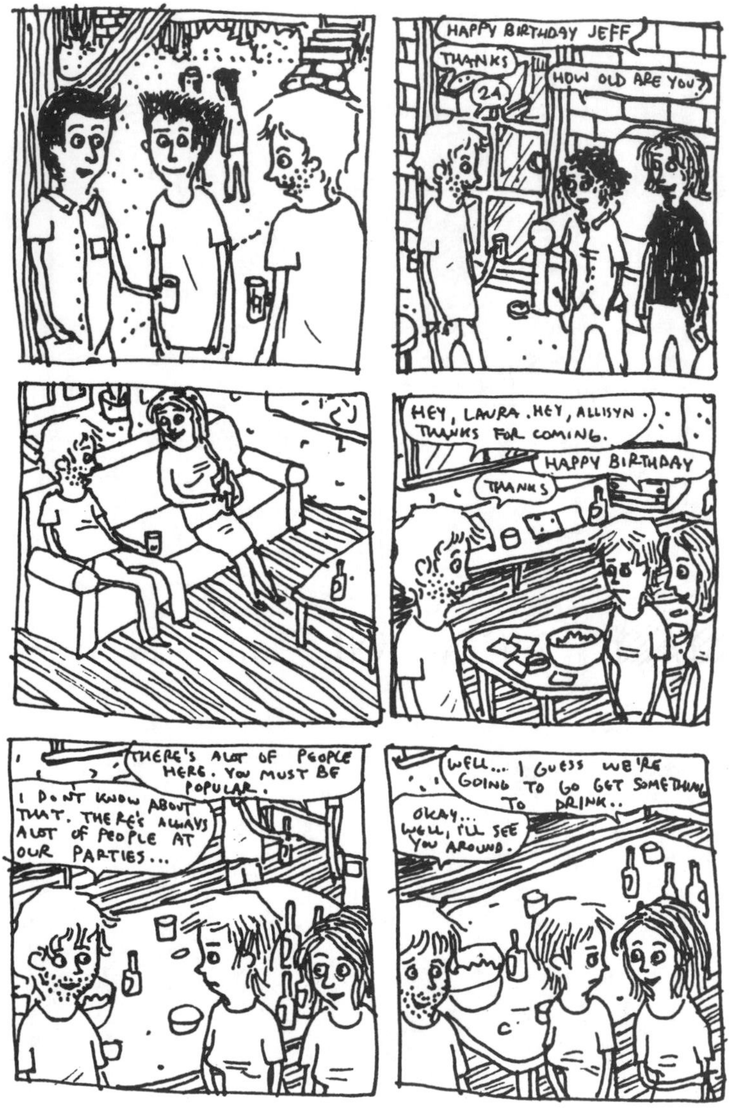
HAPPY BIRTHDAY JEFF
THANKS
HOW OLD ARE YOU?
21
HEY, LAURA. HEY, ALLISYN. THANKS FOR COMING.
HAPPY BIRTHDAY
THANKS
THERE'S ALOT OF PEOPLE HERE. YOU MUST BE POPULAR.
I DON'T KNOW ABOUT THAT. THERE'S ALWAYS ALOT OF PEOPLE AT OUR PARTIES...
WELL... I GUESS WE'RE GOING TO GO GET SOMETHING TO DRINK..
OKAY... WELL, I'LL SEE YOU AROUND.

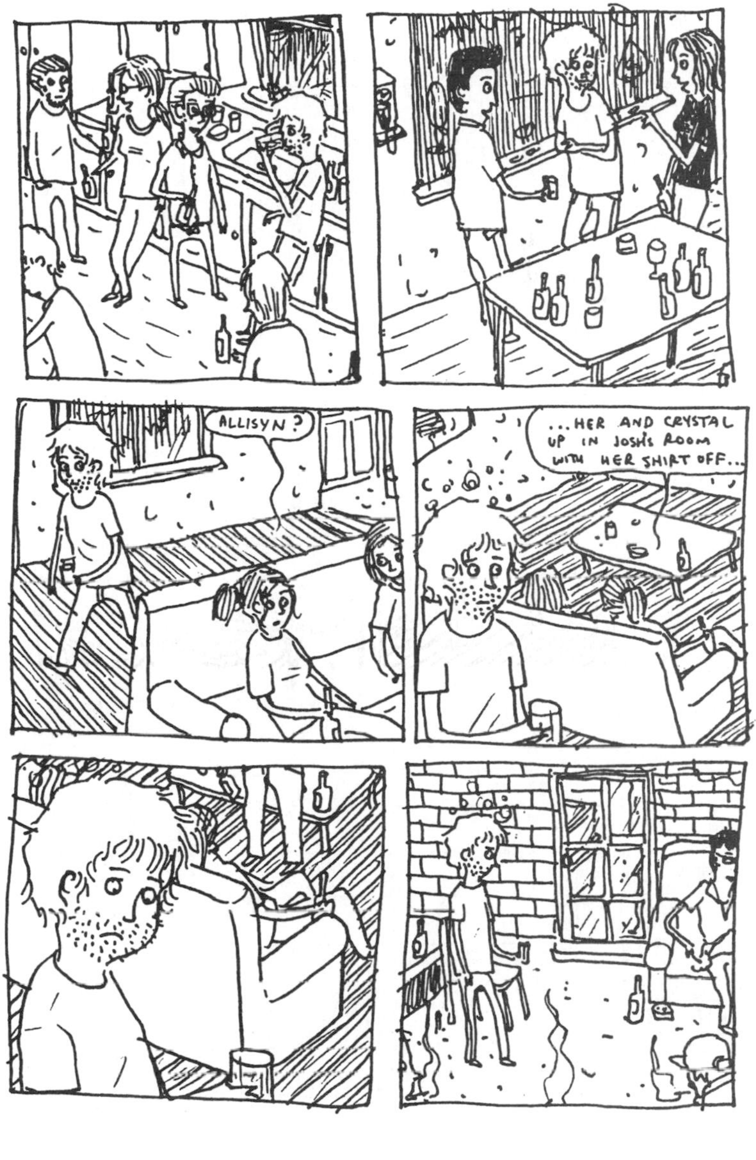
ALLISYN?
...HER AND CRYSTAL UP IN JOSH'S ROOM WITH HER SHIRT OFF...

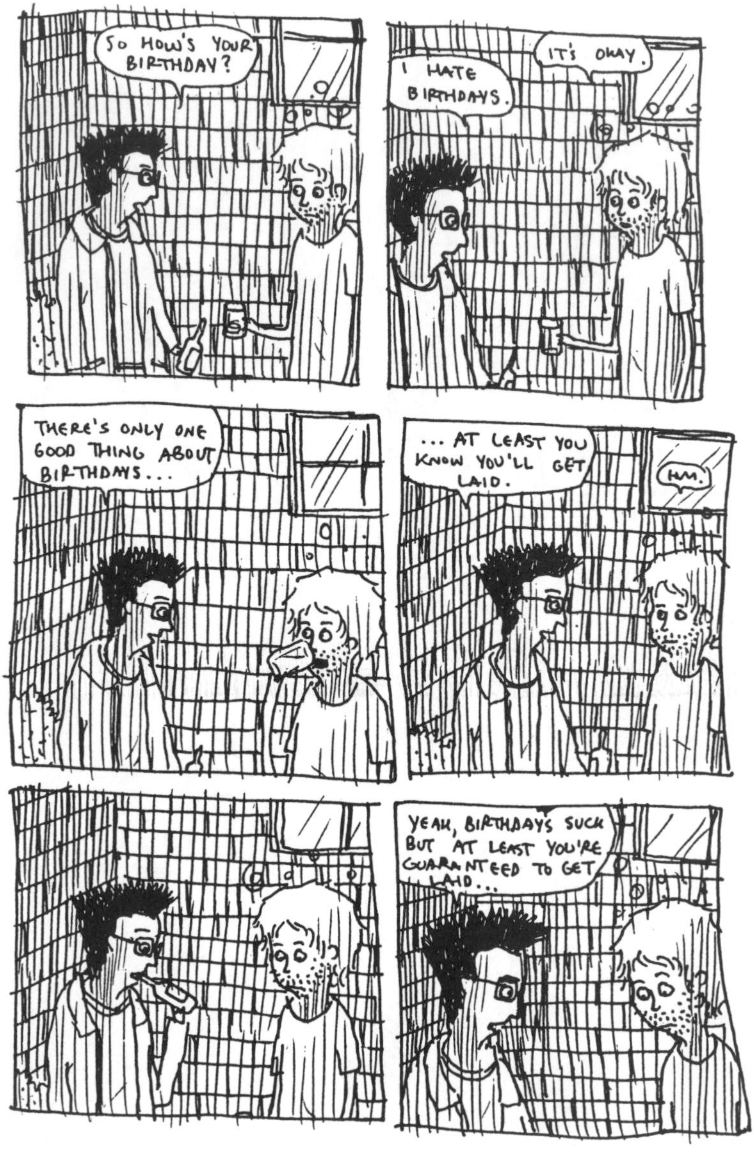
SO HOW'S YOUR BIRTHDAY?
IT'S OKAY.
I HATE BIRTHDAYS.
THERE'S ONLY ONE GOOD THING ABOUT BIRTHDAYS...
... AT LEAST YOU KNOW YOU'LL GET LAID.
HM.
YEAH, BIRTHDAYS SUCK BUT AT LEAST YOU'RE GUARANTEED TO GET LAID...

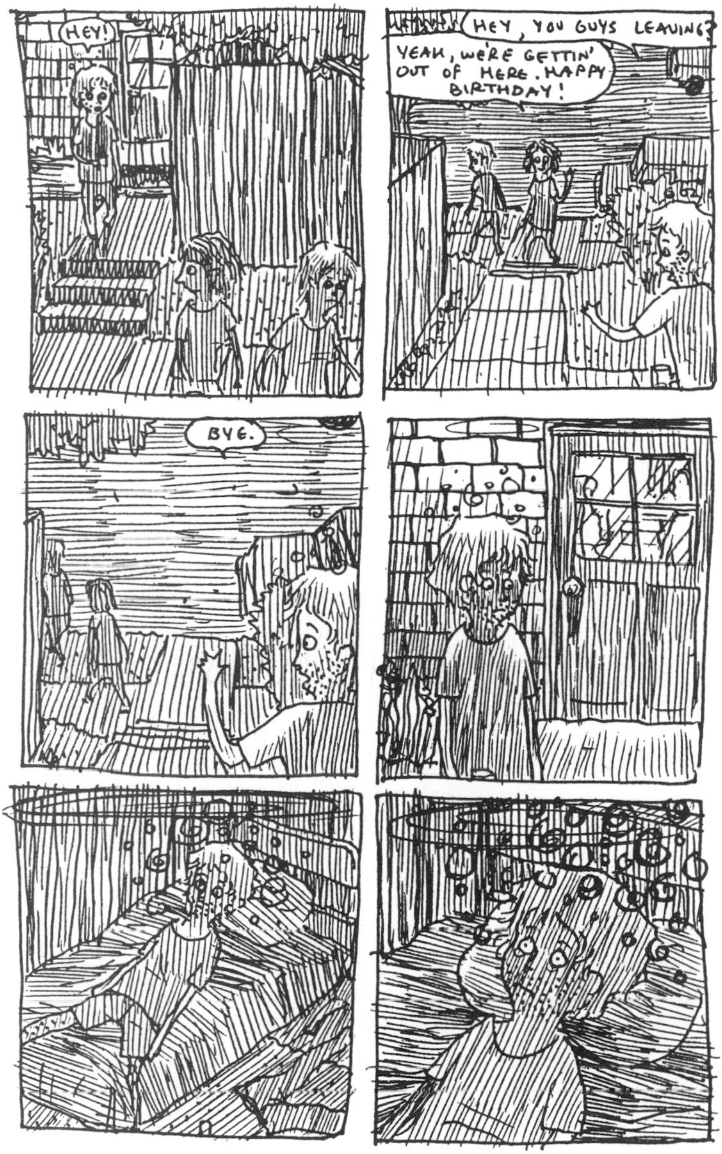
HEY!
HEY, YOU GUYS LEAVING?
YEAH, WE'RE GETTIN' OUT OF HERE. HAPPY BIRTHDAY!
BYE.

VERGE

FROM NOWHERE

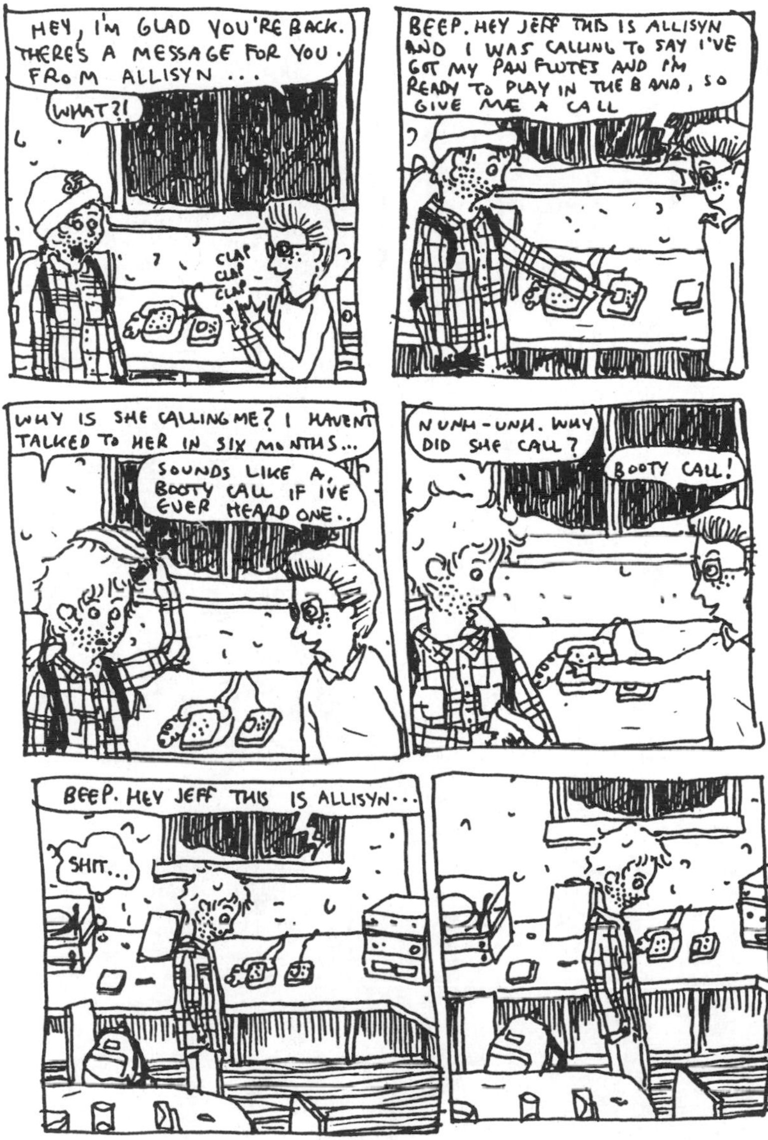
HEY, I'M GLAD YOU'RE BACK. THERE'S A MESSAGE FOR YOU. FROM ALLISYN ...
WHAT?!
CLAP CLAP CLAP
BEEP. HEY JEFF THIS IS ALLISYN AND I WAS CALLING TO SAY I'VE GOT MY PAN FLUTES AND I'M READY TO PLAY IN THE BAND, SO GIVE ME A CALL
WHY IS SHE CALLING ME? I HAVENT TALKED TO HER IN SIX MONTHS...
SOUNDS LIKE A, BOOTY CALL IF IVE EVER HEARD ONE..
NUNH-UNH. WHY DID SHE CALL?
BOOTY CALL!
BEEP. HEY JEFF THIS IS ALLISYN...
SHIT...

TALK

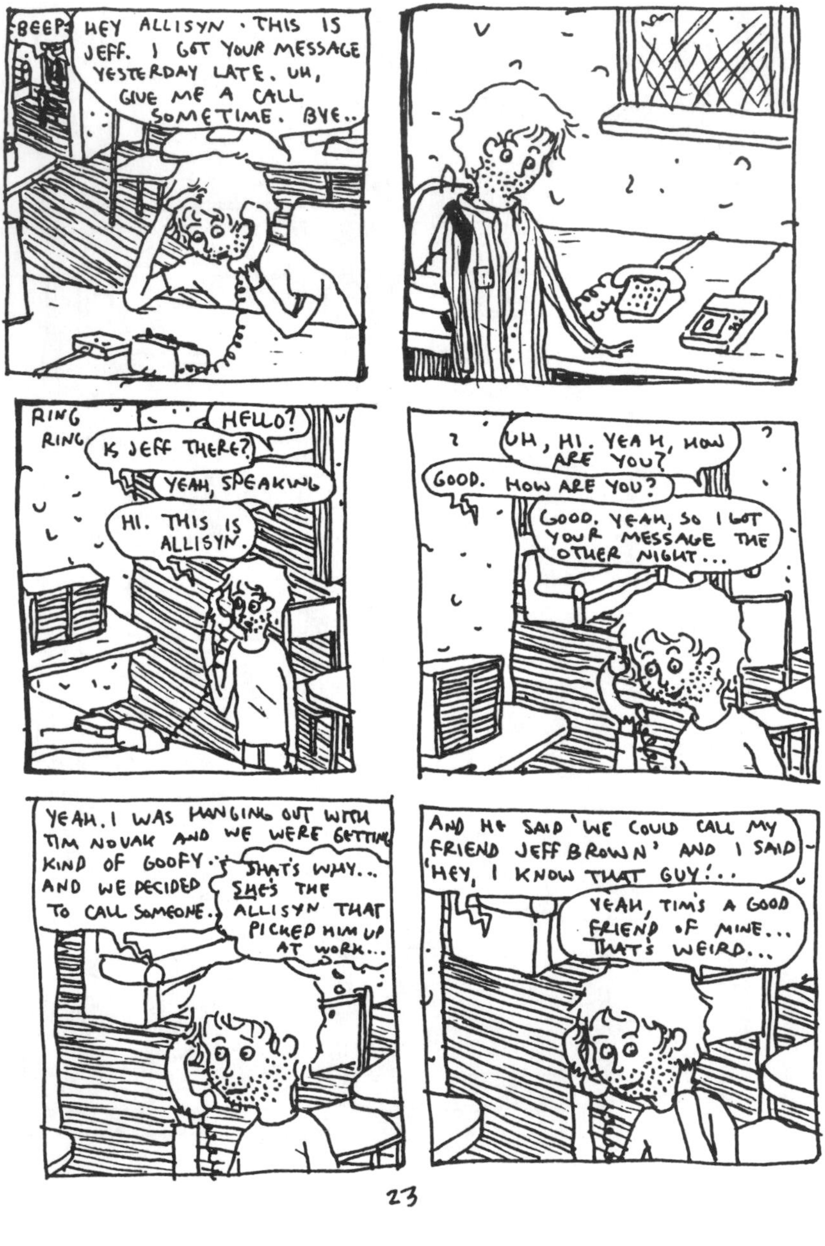
BEEP
HEY ALLISYN. THIS IS JEFF. I GOT YOUR MESSAGE YESTERDAY LATE. UH, GIVE ME A CALL SOMETIME. BYE..
RING RING
HELLO?
IS JEFF THERE?
YEAH, SPEAKING
HI. THIS IS ALLISYN.
UH, HI. YEAH, HOW ARE YOU?
GOOD. HOW ARE YOU?
GOOD. YEAH, SO I GOT YOUR MESSAGE THE OTHER NIGHT...
YEAH. I WAS HANGING OUT WITH TIM NOVAK AND WE WERE GETTING KIND OF GOOFY.. AND WE DECIDED TO CALL SOMEONE..
THAT'S WHY... SHE'S THE ALLISYN THAT PICKED HIM UP AT WORK...
AND HE SAID 'WE COULD CALL MY FRIEND JEFF BROWN' AND I SAID 'HEY, I KNOW THAT GUY!..
YEAH, TIM'S A GOOD FRIEND OF MINE... THAT'S WEIRD...

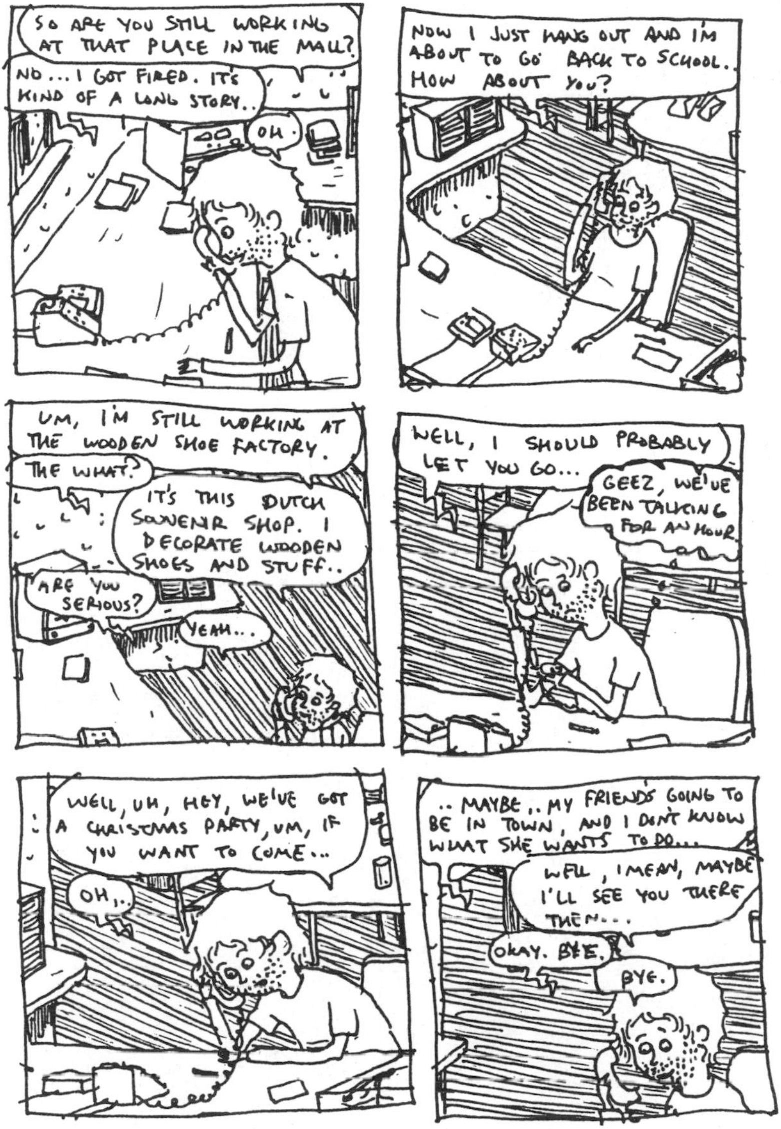
SO ARE YOU STILL WORKING AT THAT PLACE IN THE MALL?
NO... I GOT FIRED. IT'S KIND OF A LONG STORY..
OH.
NOW I JUST HANG OUT AND I'M ABOUT TO GO BACK TO SCHOOL.. HOW ABOUT YOU?
UM, I'M STILL WORKING AT THE WOODEN SHOE FACTORY.
THE WHAT?
IT'S THIS DUTCH SOUVENIR SHOP. I DECORATE WOODEN SHOES AND STUFF..
ARE YOU SERIOUS?
YEAH...
WELL, I SHOULD PROBABLY LET YOU GO...
GEEZ, WE'VE BEEN TALKING FOR AN HOUR
WELL, UH, HEY, WE'VE GOT A CHRISTMAS PARTY, UM, IF YOU WANT TO COME...
OH,..
.. MAYBE .. MY FRIEND'S GOING TO BE IN TOWN, AND I DON'T KNOW WHAT SHE WANTS TO DO...
WELL, I MEAN, MAYBE I'LL SEE YOU THERE THEN...
OKAY. BYE.
BYE.

MESSAGE

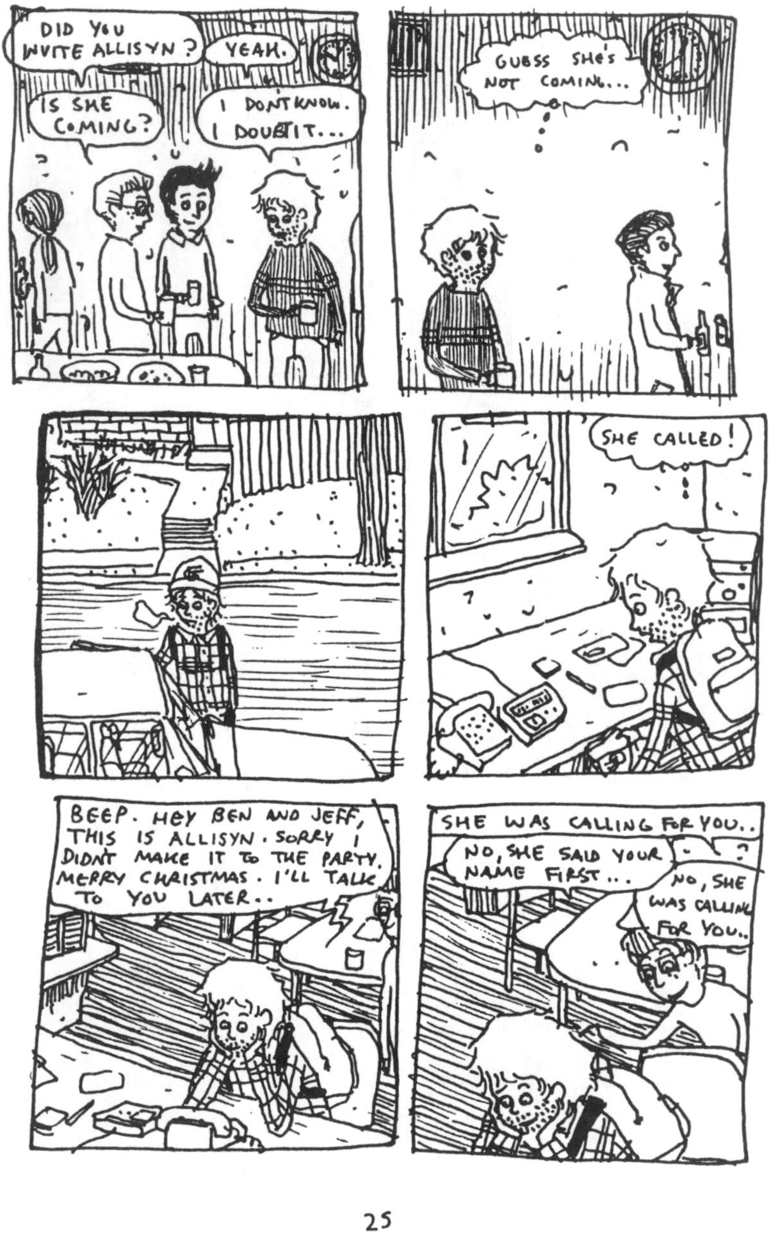
DID YOU WRITE ALLISYN?
YEAH.
IS SHE COMING?
I DONT KNOW. I DOUBT IT...
GUESS SHE'S NOT COMING...
SHE CALLED!
BEEP. HEY BEN AND JEFF, THIS IS ALLISYN. SORRY I DIDN'T MAKE IT TO THE PARTY. MERRY CHRISTMAS. I'LL TALK TO YOU LATER..
SHE WAS CALLING FOR YOU..
NO, SHE SAID YOUR NAME FIRST...
NO, SHE WAS CALLING FOR YOU..

CALL AGAIN

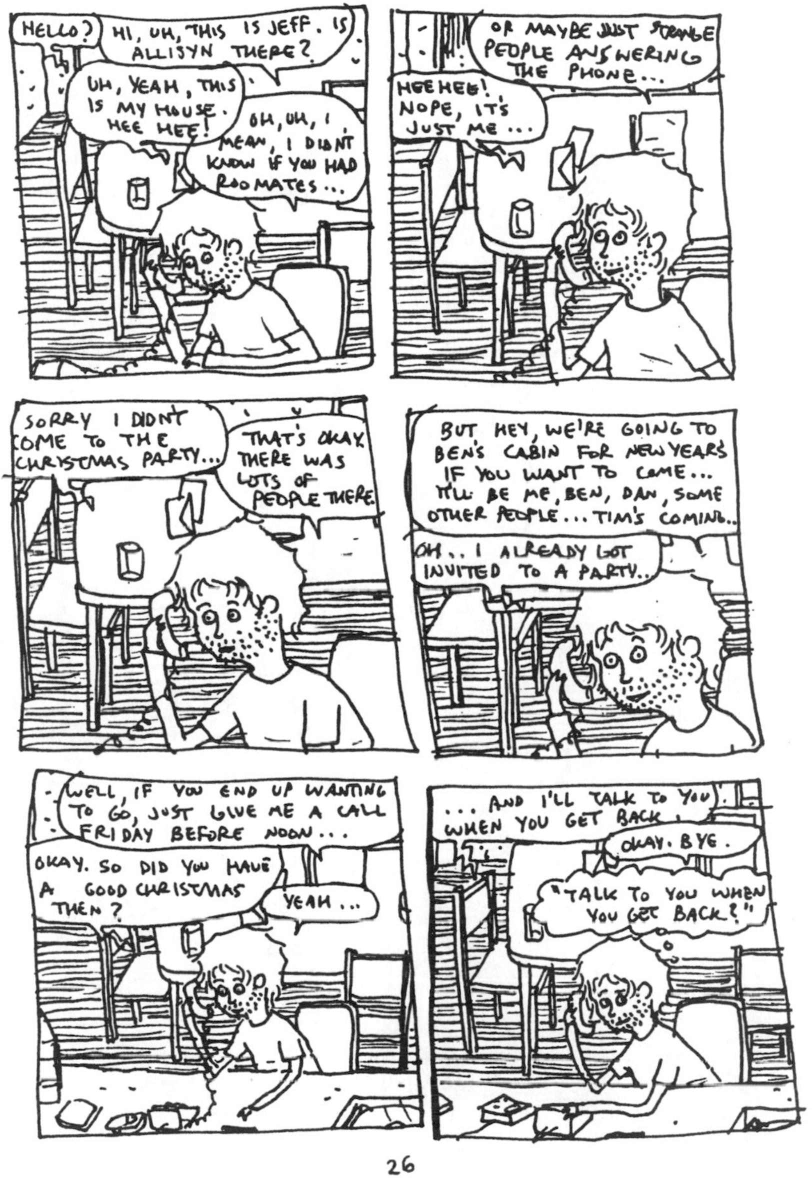
HELLO?
HI, UH, THIS IS JEFF. IS ALLISYN THERE?
UH, YEAH, THIS IS MY HOUSE. HEE HEE!
OH, UH, I MEAN, I DIDNT KNOW IF YOU HAD ROOMATES...
OR MAYBE JUST STRANGE PEOPLE ANSWERING THE PHONE...
HEE HEE! NOPE, IT'S JUST ME...
SORRY I DIDN'T COME TO THE CHRISTMAS PARTY...
THAT'S OKAY. THERE WAS LOTS OF PEOPLE THERE.
BUT HEY, WE'RE GOING TO BEN'S CABIN FOR NEW YEARS IF YOU WANT TO COME... IT'LL BE ME, BEN, DAN, SOME OTHER PEOPLE... TIM'S COMING..
OH.. I ALREADY GOT INVITED TO A PARTY..
WELL, IF YOU END UP WANTING TO GO, JUST GIVE ME A CALL FRIDAY BEFORE NOON...
OKAY. SO DID YOU HAVE A GOOD CHRISTMAS THEN?
YEAH...
... AND I'LL TALK TO YOU WHEN YOU GET BACK.
OKAY. BYE.
"TALK TO YOU WHEN YOU GET BACK?"

NEW YEAR

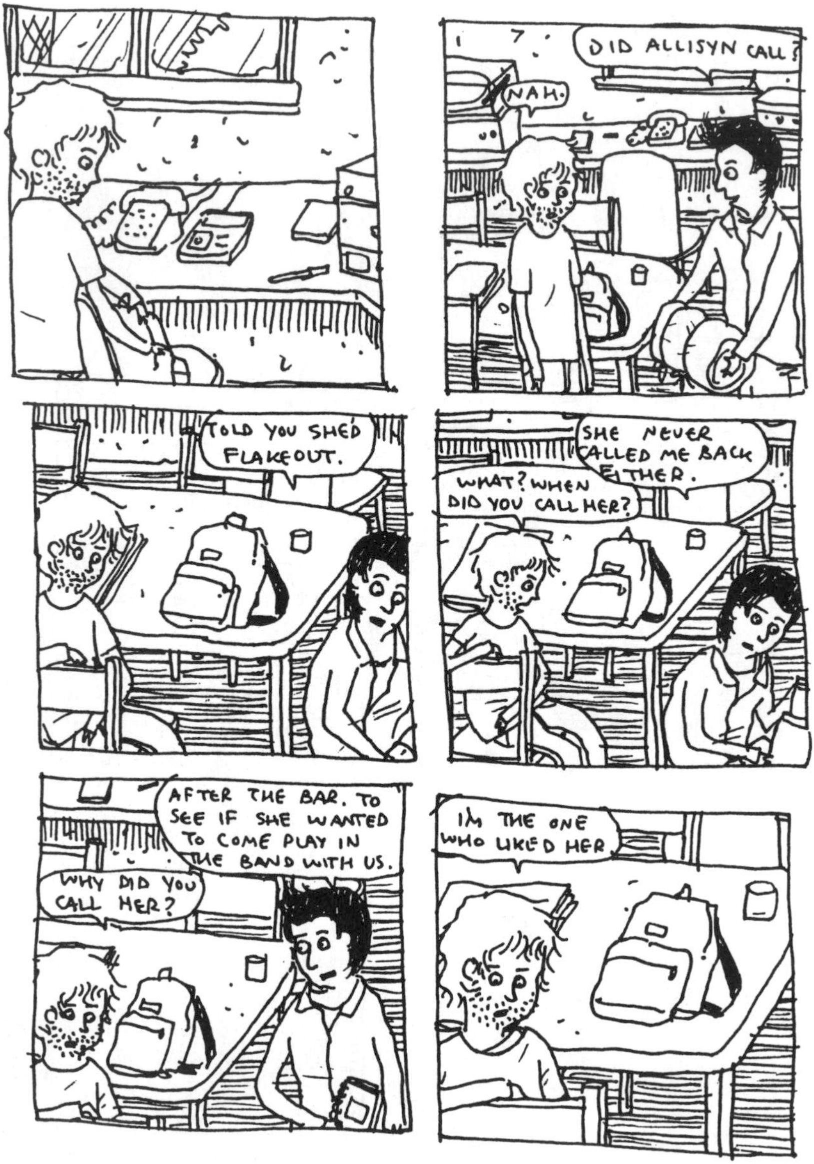

DID ALLISYN CALL?
NAH.
TOLD YOU SHE'D FLAKEOUT.
SHE NEVER CALLED ME BACK EITHER.
WHAT? WHEN DID YOU CALL HER?
AFTER THE BAR. TO SEE IF SHE WANTED TO COME PLAY IN THE BAND WITH US.
WHY DID YOU CALL HER?
I'M THE ONE WHO LIKED HER

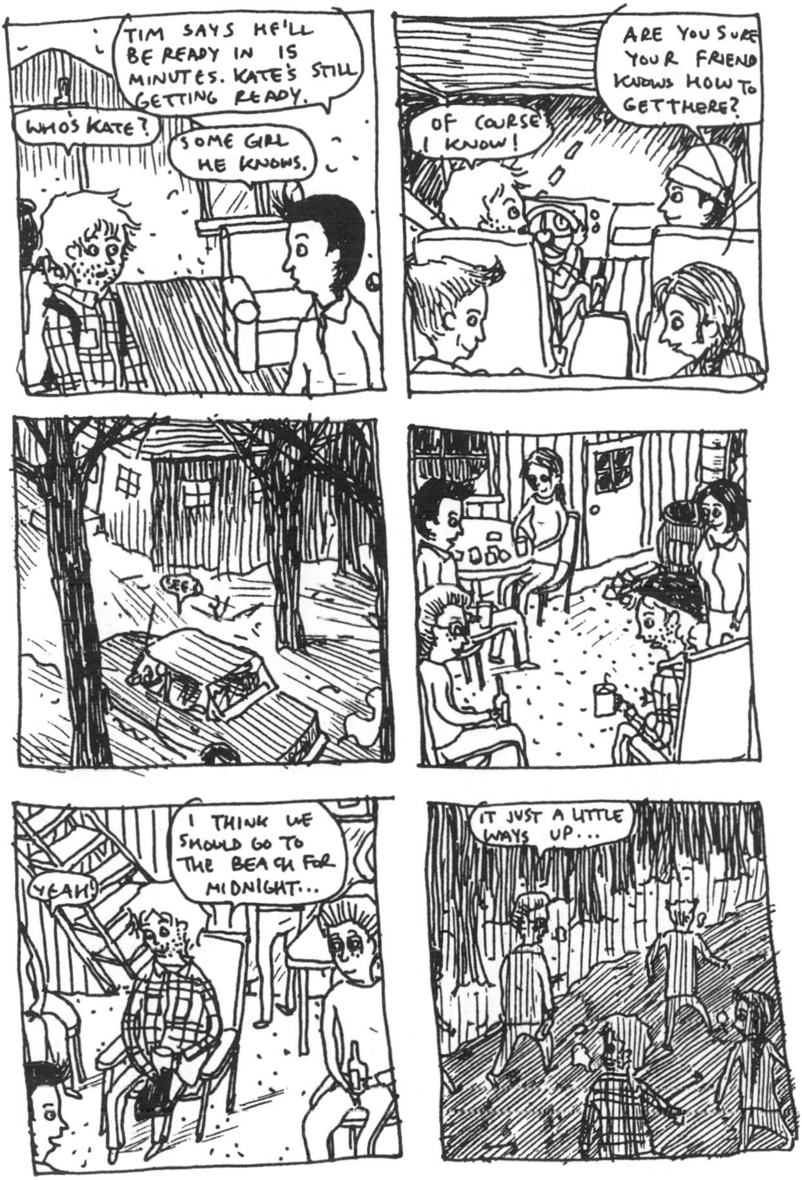
TIM SAYS HE'LL BE READY IN 15 MINUTES. KATE'S STILL GETTING READY.
WHO'S KATE?
SOME GIRL HE KNOWS.
ARE YOU SURE YOUR FRIEND KNOWS HOW TO GET THERE?
OF COURSE I KNOW!
SEE?
I THINK WE SHOULD GO TO THE BEACH FOR MIDNIGHT...
YEAH!
IT JUST A LITTLE WAYS UP...

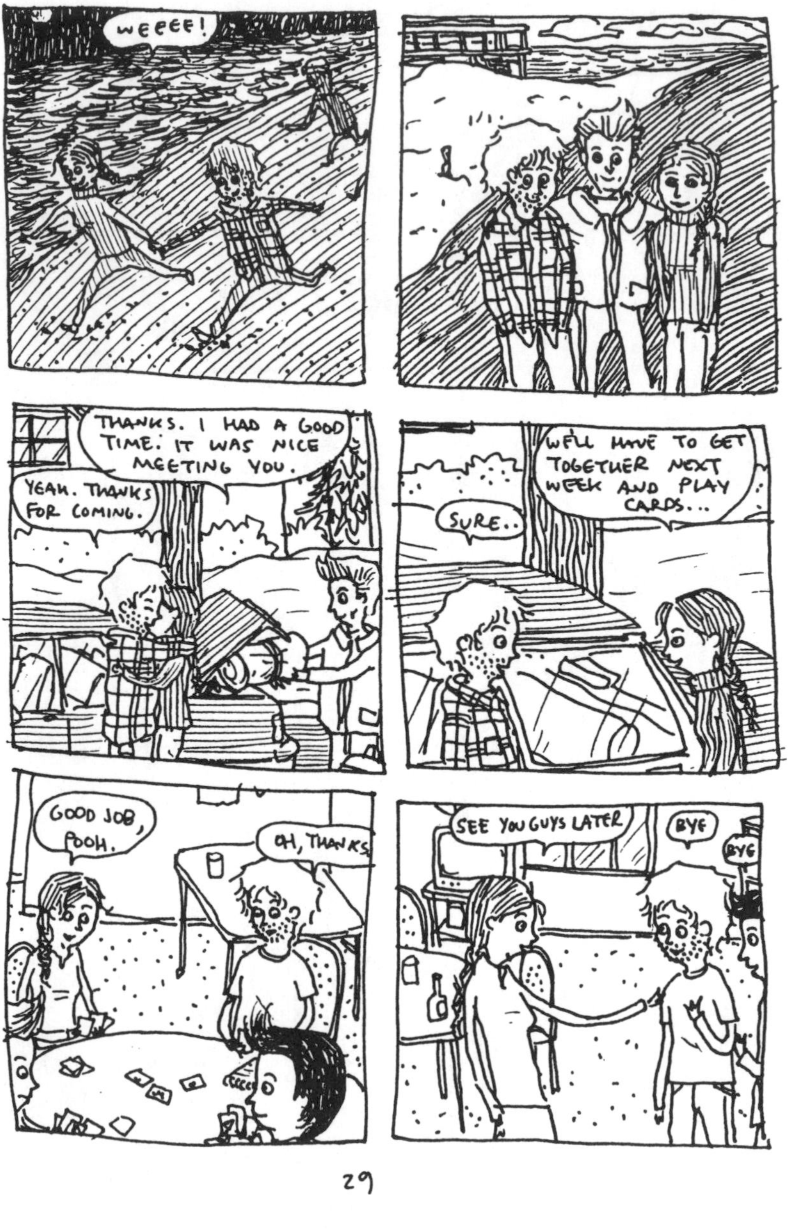
WEEEE!
THANKS. I HAD A GOOD TIME. IT WAS NICE MEETING YOU.
YEAH. THANKS FOR COMING.
WE'LL HAVE TO GET TOGETHER NEXT WEEK AND PLAY CARDS...
SURE..
GOOD JOB, POOH.
OH, THANKS
SEE YOU GUYS LATER
BYE
BYE

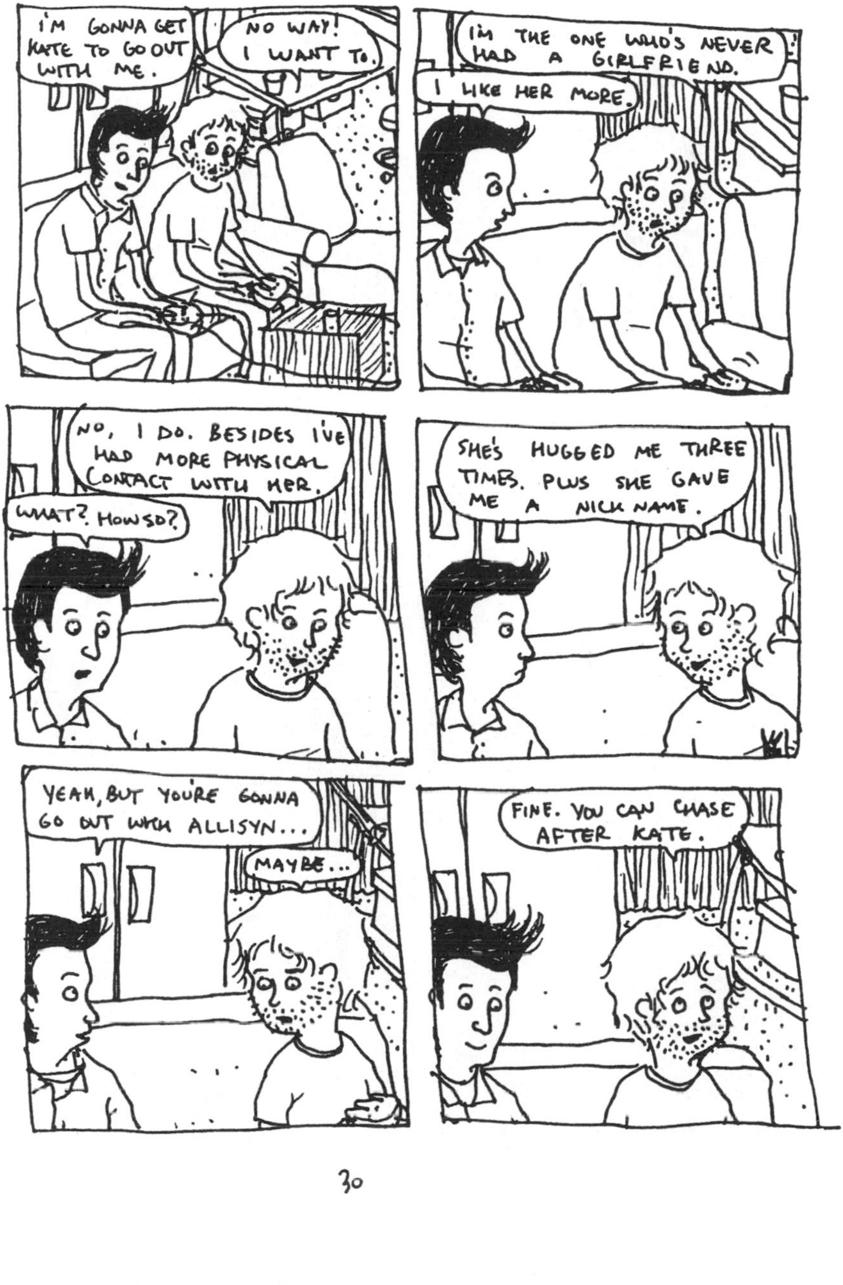
I'M GONNA GET KATE TO GO OUT WITH ME.
NO WAY! I WANT TO.
I'M THE ONE WHO'S NEVER HAD A GIRLFRIEND!
I LIKE HER MORE.
NO, I DO. BESIDES I'VE HAD MORE PHYSICAL CONTACT WITH HER.
WHAT? HOW SO?
SHE'S HUGGED ME THREE TIMES. PLUS SHE GAVE ME A NICK NAME.
YEAH, BUT YOU'RE GONNA GO OUT WITH ALLISYN...
MAYBE...
FINE. YOU CAN CHASE AFTER KATE.

YOU'RE IT

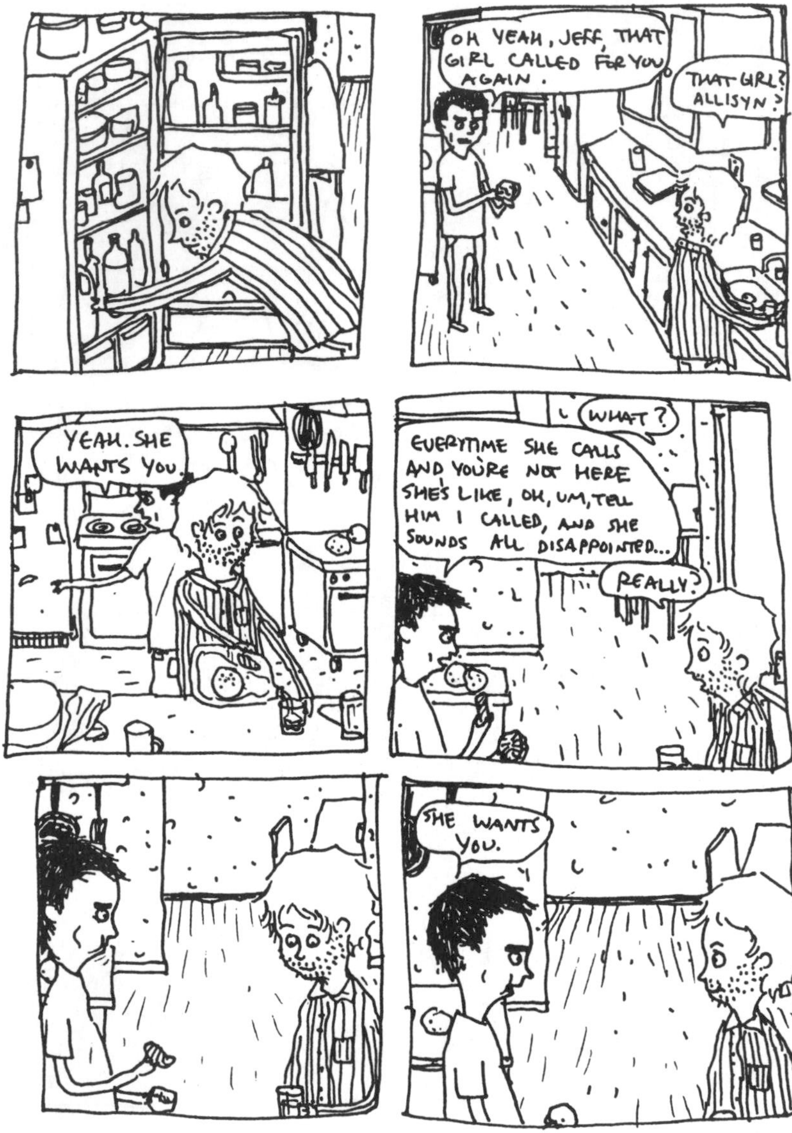
OH YEAH, JEFF, THAT GIRL CALLED FOR YOU AGAIN.
THAT GIRL? ALLISYN?
YEAH. SHE WANTS YOU.
WHAT?
EVERYTIME SHE CALLS AND YOU'RE NOT HERE SHE'S LIKE, OH, UM, TELL HIM I CALLED, AND SHE SOUNDS ALL DISAPPOINTED...
REALLY?
SHE WANTS YOU.

KARAOKE

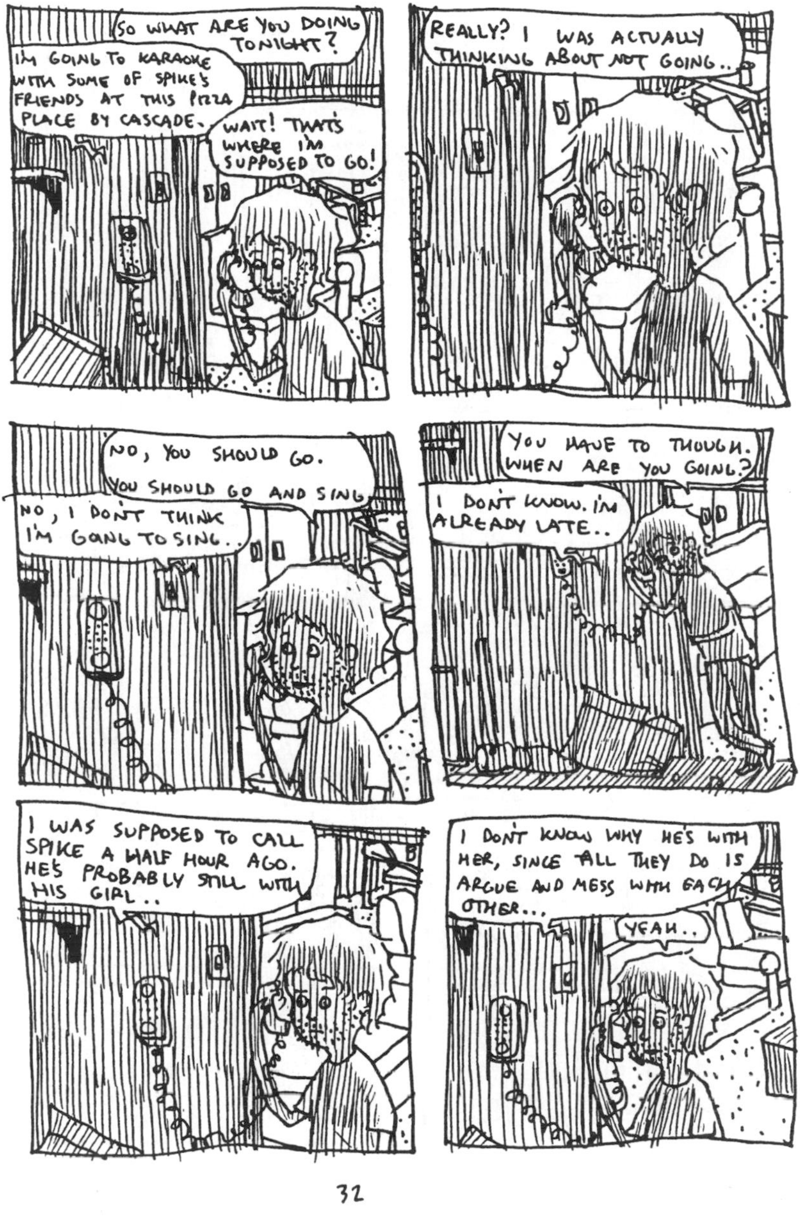

SO WHAT ARE YOU DOING TONIGHT?
I'M GOING TO KARAOKE WITH SOME OF SPIKE'S FRIENDS AT THIS PIZZA PLACE BY CASCADE.
WAIT! THAT'S WHERE I'M SUPPOSED TO GO!
REALLY? I WAS ACTUALLY THINKING ABOUT NOT GOING..
NO, YOU SHOULD GO. YOU SHOULD GO AND SING
NO, I DON'T THINK I'M GOING TO SING..
YOU HAVE TO THOUGH. WHEN ARE YOU GOING?
I DON'T KNOW. I'M ALREADY LATE..
I WAS SUPPOSED TO CALL SPIKE A HALF HOUR AGO. HE'S PROBABLY STILL WITH HIS GIRL..
I DON'T KNOW WHY HE'S WITH HER, SINCE ALL THEY DO IS ARGUE AND MESS WITH EACH OTHER...
YEAH..

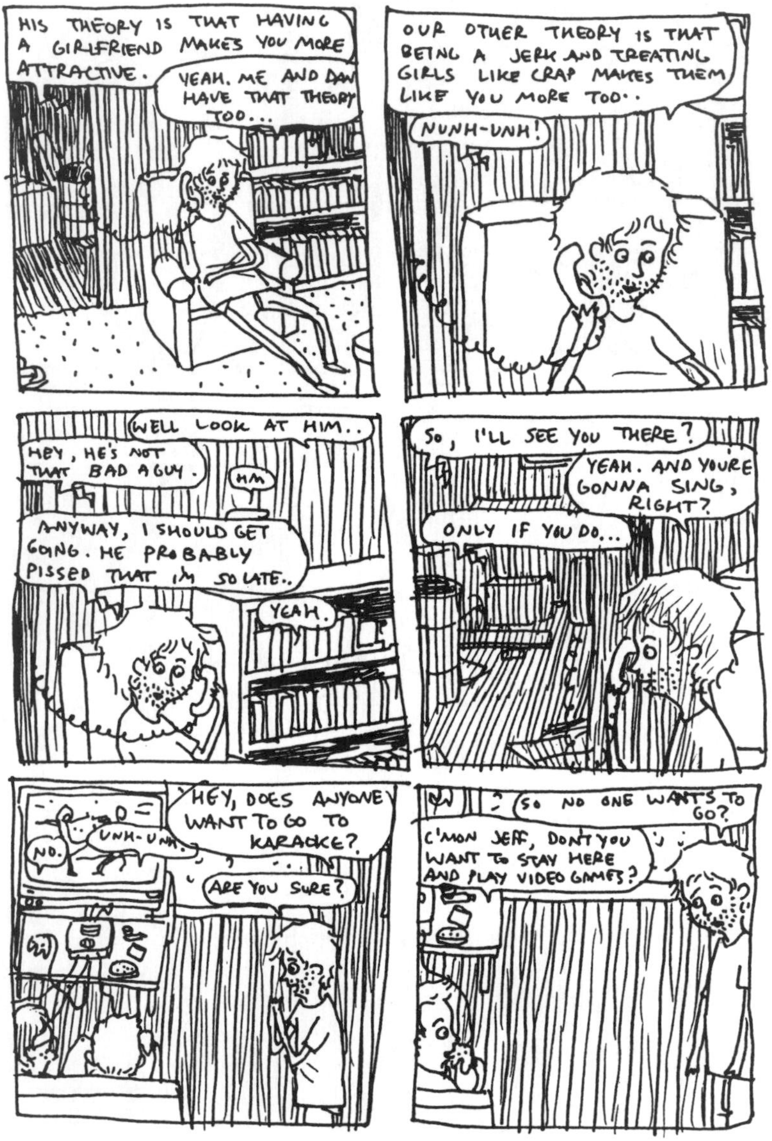
HIS THEORY IS THAT HAVING A GIRLFRIEND MAKES YOU MORE ATTRACTIVE.
YEAH. ME AND DAN HAVE THAT THEORY TOO...
OUR OTHER THEORY IS THAT BEING A JERK AND TREATING GIRLS LIKE CRAP MAKES THEM LIKE YOU MORE TOO..
NUNH-UNH!
WELL LOOK AT HIM..
HEY, HE'S NOT THAT BAD A GUY.
HM
ANYWAY, I SHOULD GET GOING. HE PROBABLY PISSED THAT I'M SO LATE..
YEAH.
SO, I'LL SEE YOU THERE?
YEAH. AND YOU'RE GONNA SING, RIGHT?
ONLY IF YOU DO...
HEY, DOES ANYONE WANT TO GO TO KARAOKE?
UNH-UNH.
NO.
ARE YOU SURE?
SO NO ONE WANTS TO GO?
C'MON JEFF, DON'T YOU WANT TO STAY HERE AND PLAY VIDEO GAMES?

TALKING AND, TALKING

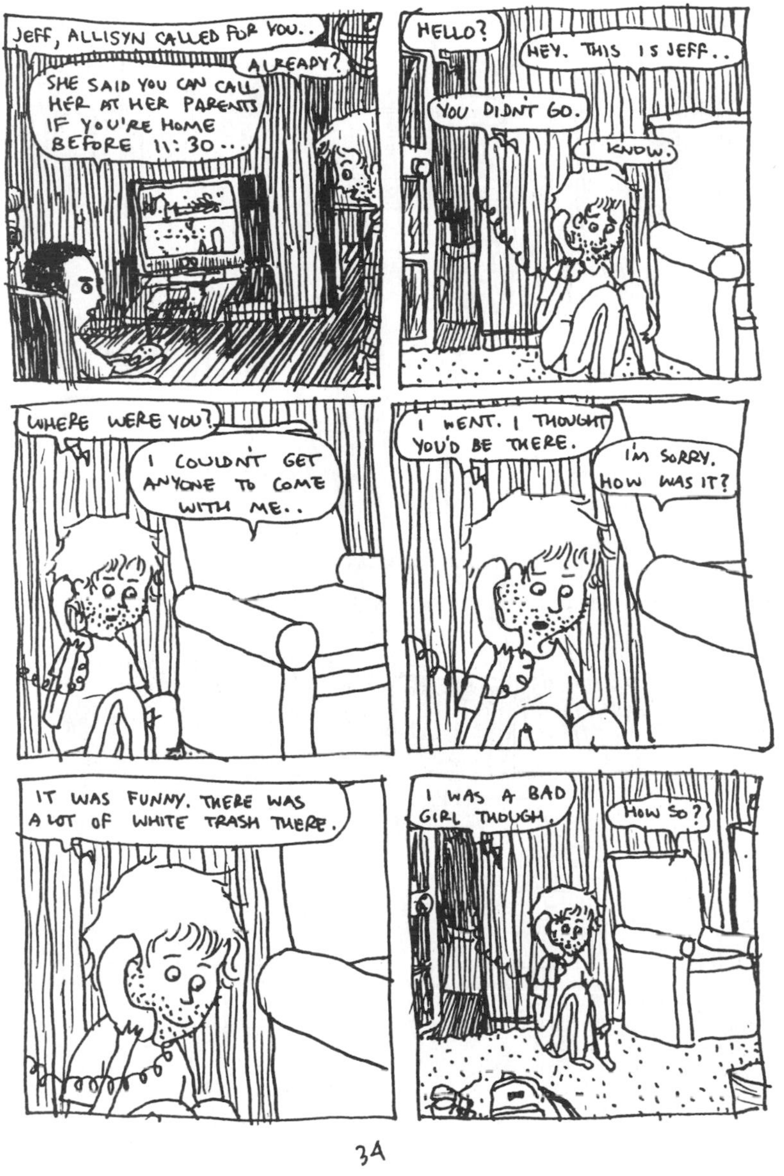
JEFF, ALLISYN CALLED FOR YOU..
ALREADY?
SHE SAID YOU CAN CALL HER AT HER PARENTS IF YOU'RE HOME BEFORE 11:30..
HELLO?
HEY. THIS IS JEFF..
YOU DIDN'T GO.
I KNOW.
WHERE WERE YOU?
I COULDN'T GET ANYONE TO COME WITH ME..
I WENT. I THOUGHT YOU'D BE THERE.
I'M SORRY. HOW WAS IT?
IT WAS FUNNY. THERE WAS A LOT OF WHITE TRASH THERE.
I WAS A BAD GIRL THOUGH.
HOW SO?

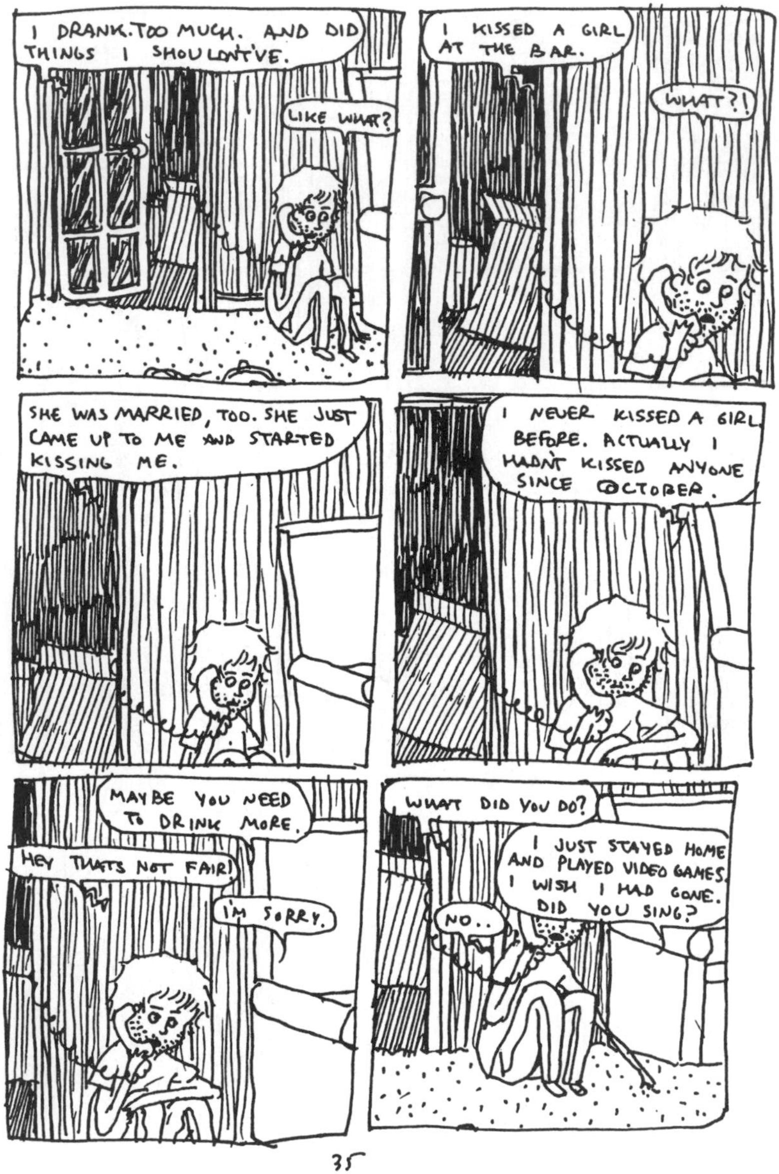
I DRANK TOO MUCH. AND DID THINGS I SHOULDN'T'VE.
LIKE WHAT?
I KISSED A GIRL AT THE BAR.
WHAT?!
SHE WAS MARRIED, TOO. SHE JUST CAME UP TO ME AND STARTED KISSING ME.
I NEVER KISSED A GIRL BEFORE. ACTUALLY I HADN'T KISSED ANYONE SINCE OCTOBER.
MAYBE YOU NEED TO DRINK MORE.
HEY THATS NOT FAIR!
I'M SORRY.
WHAT DID YOU DO?
I JUST STAYED HOME AND PLAYED VIDEO GAMES. I WISH I HAD GONE. DID YOU SING?
NO..

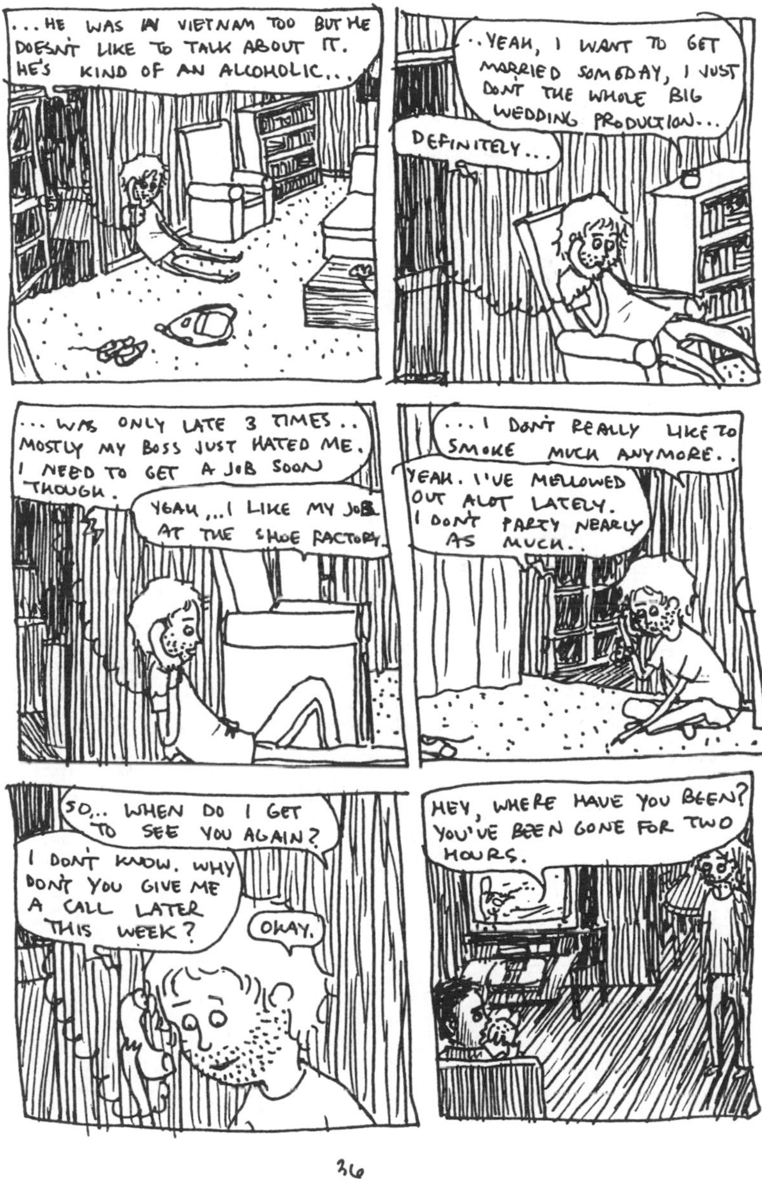
...HE WAS IN VIETNAM TOO BUT HE DOESN'T LIKE TO TALK ABOUT IT. HE'S KIND OF AN ALCOHOLIC...
..YEAH, I WANT TO GET MARRIED SOMEDAY, I JUST DONT THE WHOLE BIG WEDDING PRODUCTION...
DEFINITELY...
...WAS ONLY LATE 3 TIMES.. MOSTLY MY BOSS JUST HATED ME. I NEED TO GET A JOB SOON THOUGH.
YEAH,..I LIKE MY JOB AT THE SHOE FACTORY.
...I DON'T REALLY LIKE TO SMOKE MUCH ANYMORE..
YEAH. I'VE MELLOWED OUT ALOT LATELY. I DONT PARTY NEARLY AS MUCH..
SO... WHEN DO I GET TO SEE YOU AGAIN?
I DON'T KNOW. WHY DON'T YOU GIVE ME A CALL LATER THIS WEEK?
OKAY.
HEY, WHERE HAVE YOU BEEN? YOU'VE BEEN GONE FOR TWO HOURS.

SOUTH PARK

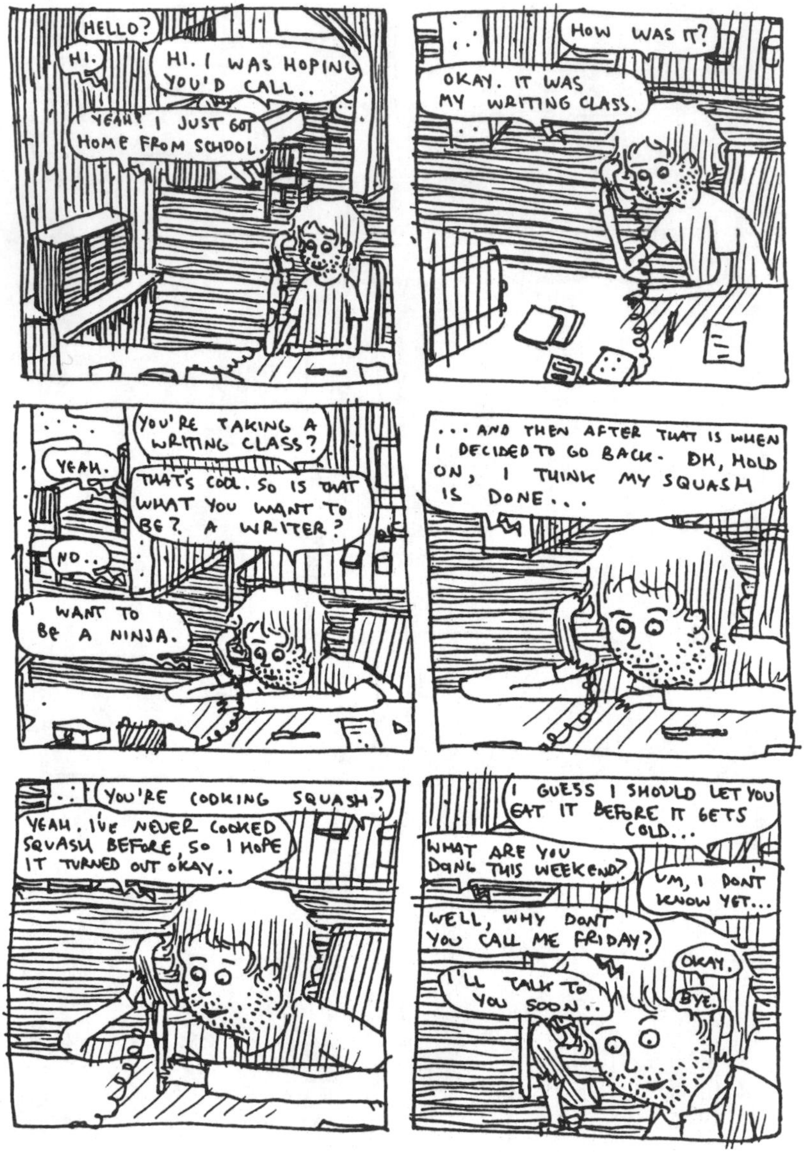
HELLO?
HI.
HI. I WAS HOPING YOU'D CALL..
YEAH! I JUST GOT HOME FROM SCHOOL.
HOW WAS IT?
OKAY. IT WAS MY WRITING CLASS.
YOU'RE TAKING A WRITING CLASS?
YEAH.
THAT'S COOL. SO IS THAT WHAT YOU WANT TO BE? A WRITER?
NO..
I WANT TO BE A NINJA.
...AND THEN AFTER THAT IS WHEN I DECIDED TO GO BACK- OH, HOLD ON, I THINK MY SQUASH IS DONE...
YOU'RE COOKING SQUASH?
YEAH. I'VE NEVER COOKED SQUASH BEFORE, SO I HOPE IT TURNED OUT OKAY..
I GUESS I SHOULD LET YOU EAT IT BEFORE IT GETS COLD...
WHAT ARE YOU DOING THIS WEEKEND?
UM, I DON'T KNOW YET...
WELL, WHY DON'T YOU CALL ME FRIDAY?
OKAY.
I'LL TALK TO YOU SOON..
BYE.

WONDER

DUNE

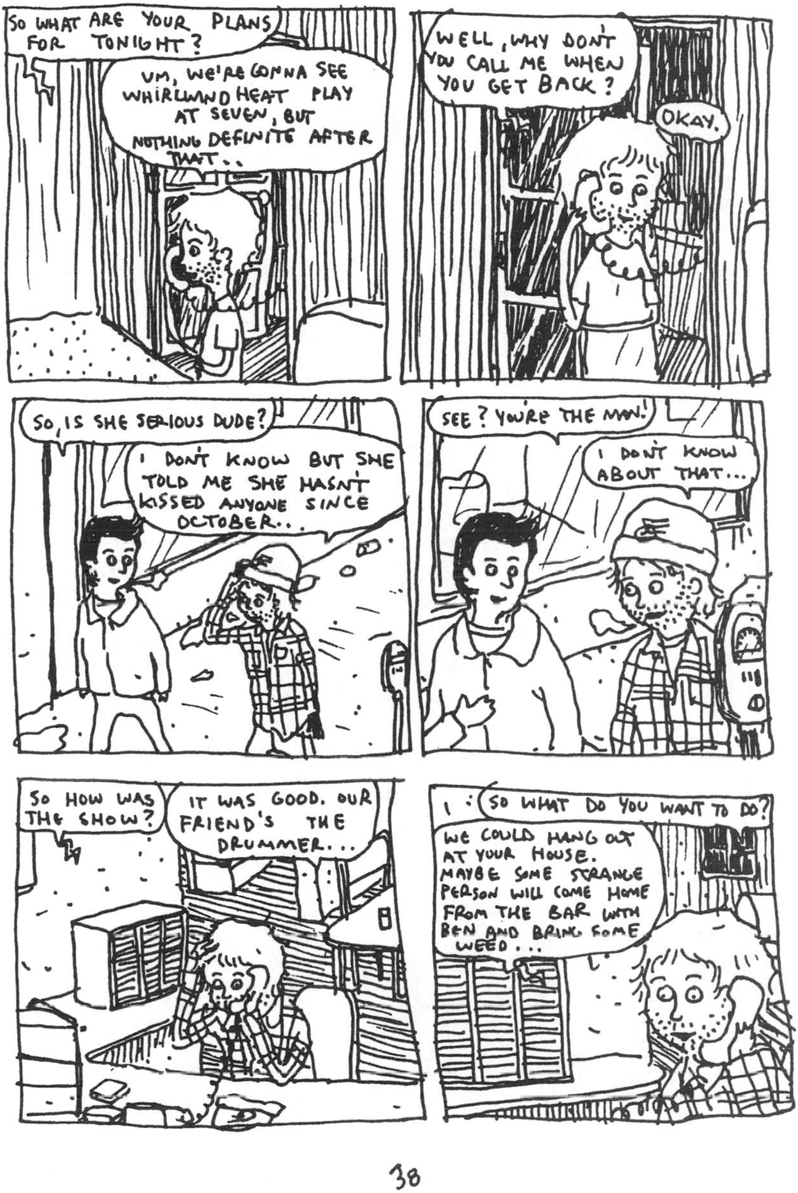
SO WHAT ARE YOUR PLANS FOR TONIGHT?
UM, WE'RE GONNA SEE WHIRLWIND HEAT PLAY AT SEVEN, BUT NOTHING DEFINITE AFTER THAT..
WELL, WHY DON'T YOU CALL ME WHEN YOU GET BACK?
OKAY.
SO, IS SHE SERIOUS DUDE?
I DON'T KNOW BUT SHE TOLD ME SHE HASN'T KISSED ANYONE SINCE OCTOBER..
SEE? YOU'RE THE MAN!
I DON'T KNOW ABOUT THAT...
SO HOW WAS THE SHOW?
IT WAS GOOD. OUR FRIEND'S THE DRUMMER...
SO WHAT DO YOU WANT TO DO?
WE COULD HANG OUT AT YOUR HOUSE. MAYBE SOME STRANGE PERSON WILL COME HOME FROM THE BAR WITH BEN AND BRING SOME WEED...

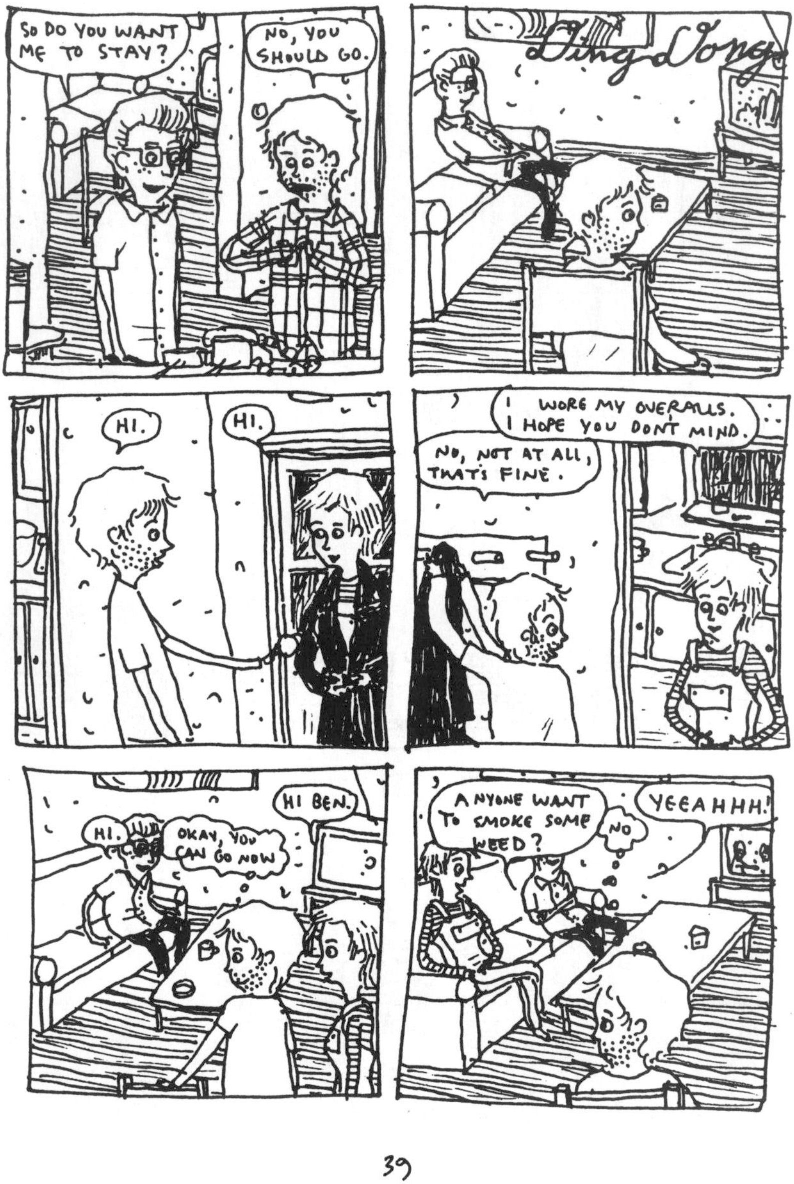
SO DO YOU WANT ME TO STAY?
NO, YOU SHOULD GO.
Ding Dong
HI.
HI.
I WORE MY OVERALLS. I HOPE YOU DON'T MIND.
NO, NOT AT ALL, THAT'S FINE.
HI BEN.
HI.
OKAY, YOU CAN GO NOW
ANYONE WANT TO SMOKE SOME WEED?
NO
YEEAHHH!

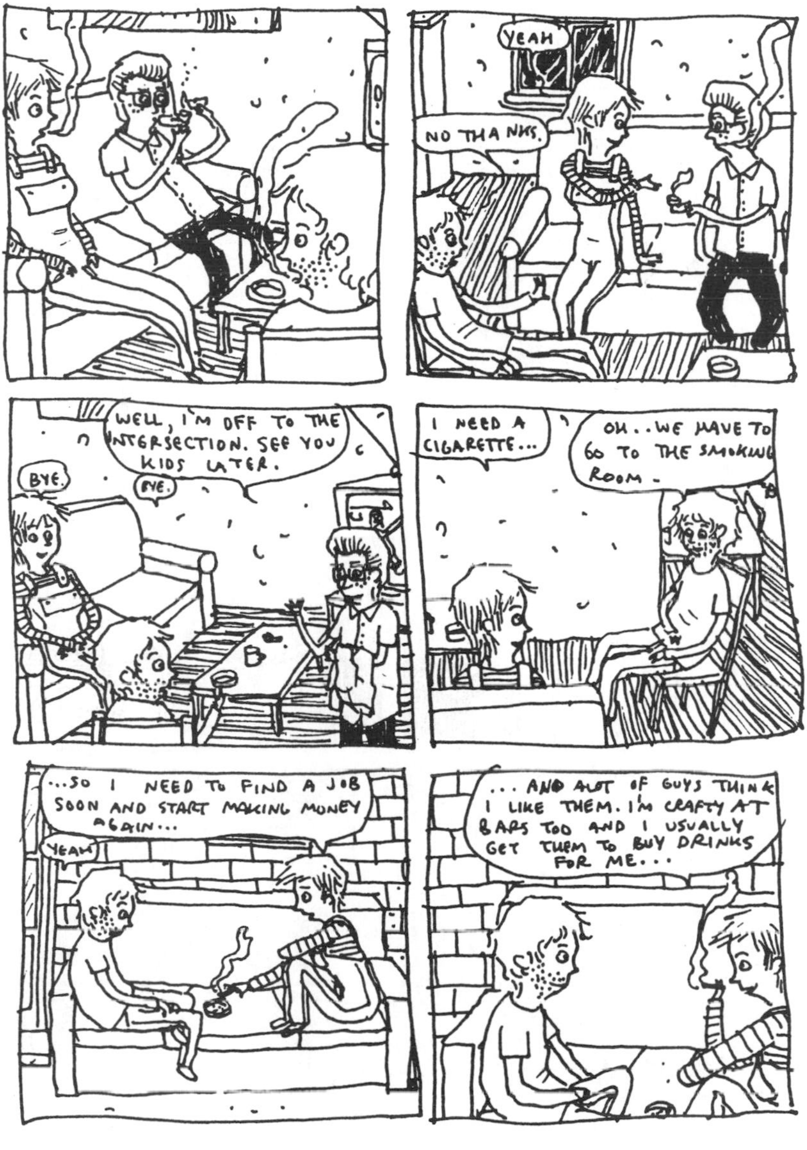
YEAH
NO THANKS.
WELL, I'M OFF TO THE INTERSECTION. SEE YOU KIDS LATER.
BYE.
BYE.
I NEED A CIGARETTE...
OH..WE HAVE TO GO TO THE SMOKING ROOM.
...SO I NEED TO FIND A JOB SOON AND START MAKING MONEY AGAIN...
YEAH
...AND ALOT OF GUYS THINK I LIKE THEM. I'M CRAFTY AT BARS TOO AND I USUALLY GET THEM TO BUY DRINKS FOR ME...

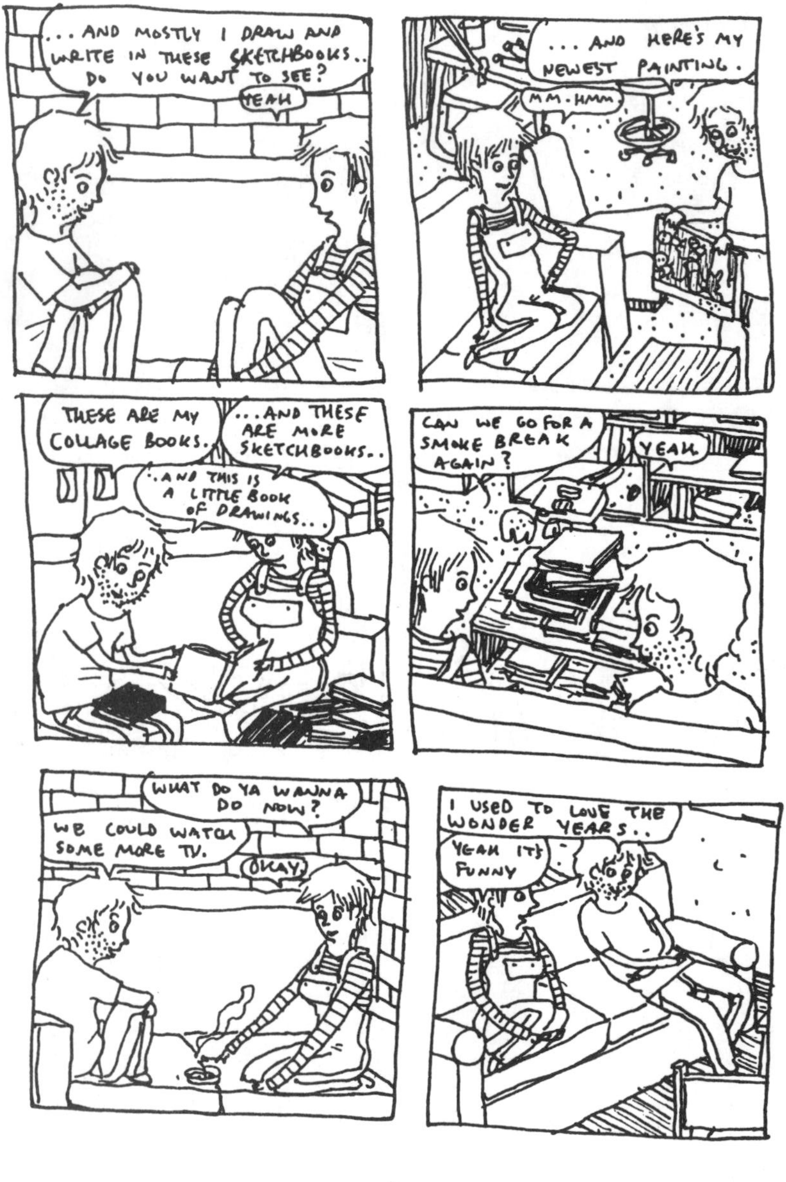
...AND MOSTLY I DRAW AND WRITE IN THESE SKETCHBOOKS.. DO YOU WANT TO SEE?
YEAH
...AND HERE'S MY NEWEST PAINTING.
MM.HMM
THESE ARE MY COLLAGE BOOKS..
...AND THESE ARE MORE SKETCHBOOKS..
..AND THIS IS A LITTLE BOOK OF DRAWINGS...
CAN WE GO FOR A SMOKE BREAK AGAIN?
YEAH
WHAT DO YA WANNA DO NOW?
WE COULD WATCH SOME MORE TV.
OKAY
I USED TO LOVE THE WONDER YEARS..
YEAH IT'S FUNNY

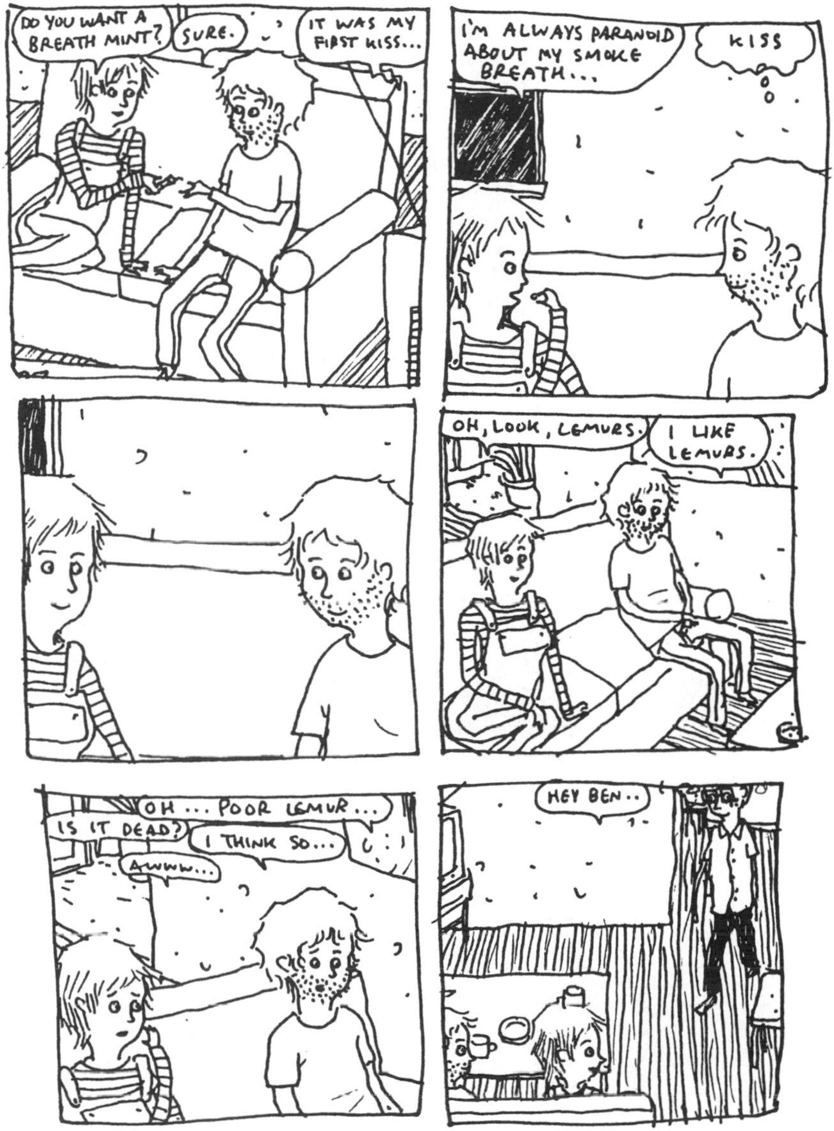
DO YOU WANT A BREATH MINT?
SURE.
IT WAS MY FIRST KISS...
I'M ALWAYS PARANOID ABOUT MY SMOKE BREATH...
KISS
OH, LOOK, LEMURS.
I LIKE LEMURS.
OH... POOR LEMUR...
IS IT DEAD?
I THINK SO...
AWWW...
HEY BEN..

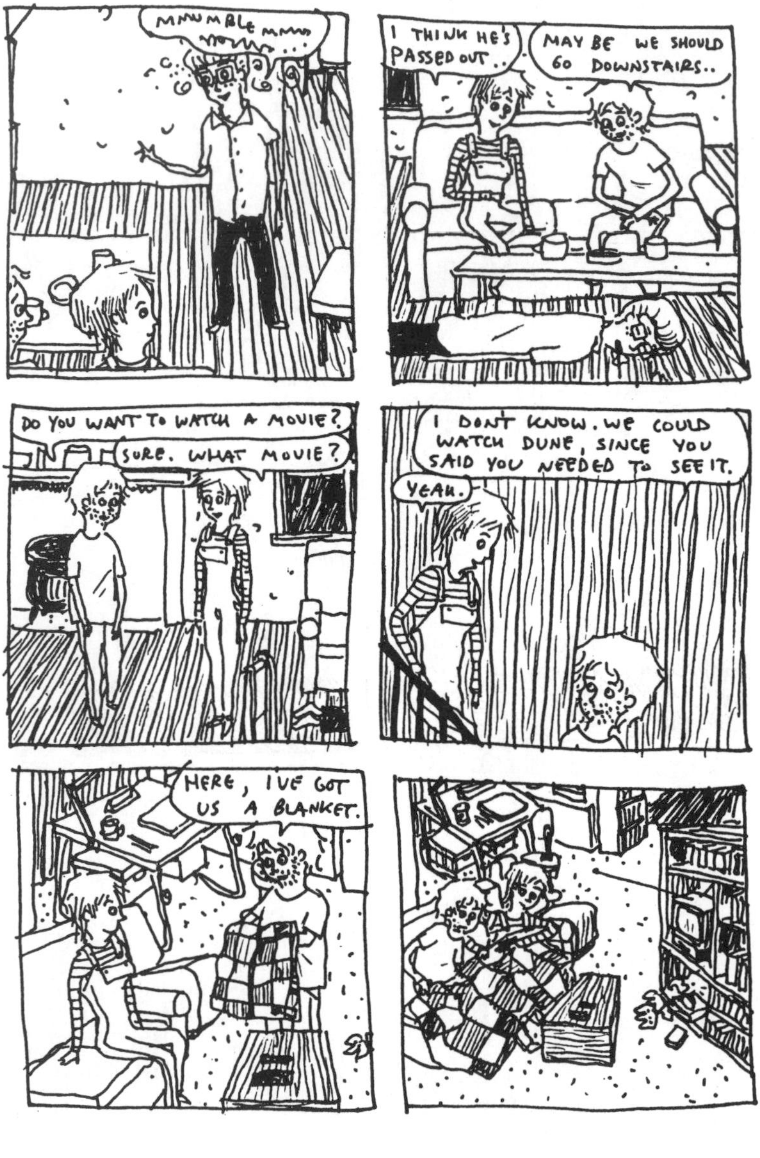
MNUMBLE MNNN
I THINK HE'S PASSED OUT..
MAY BE WE SHOULD GO DOWNSTAIRS..
DO YOU WANT TO WATCH A MOVIE?
SURE. WHAT MOVIE?
I DON'T KNOW. WE COULD WATCH DUNE, SINCE YOU SAID YOU NEEDED TO SEE IT.
YEAH.
HERE, I'VE GOT US A BLANKET.

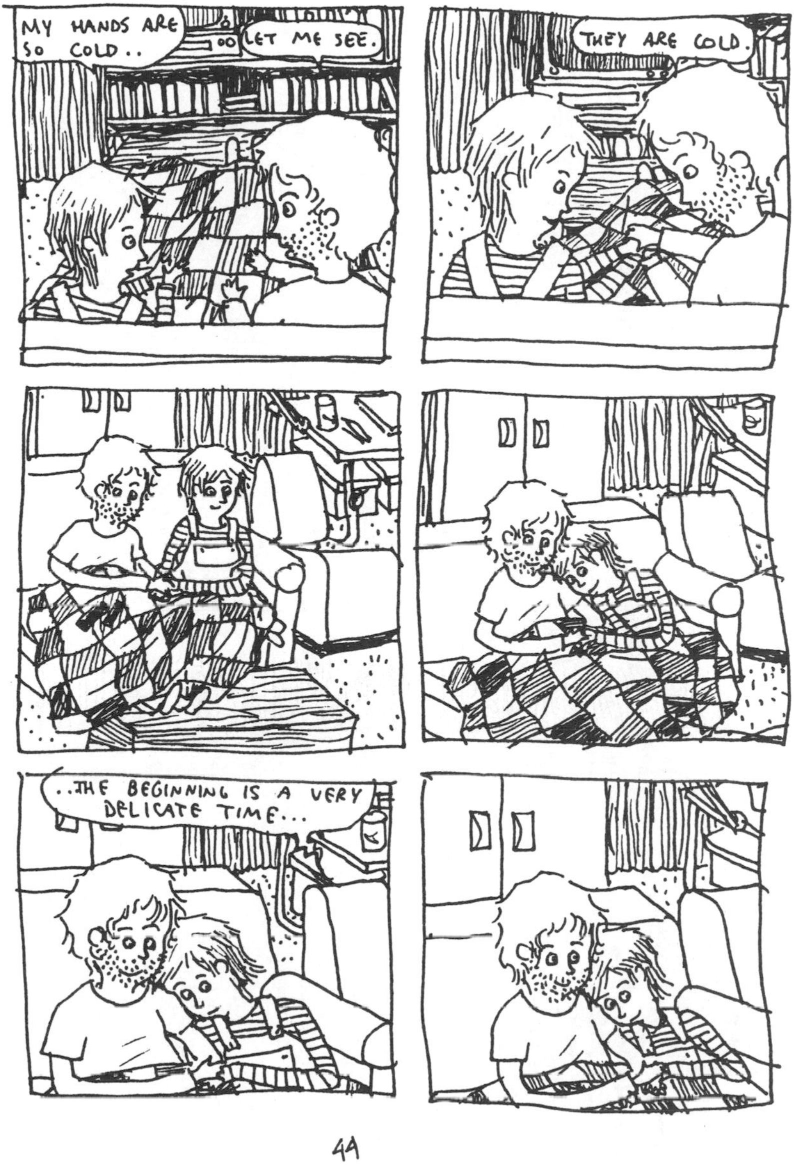
MY HANDS ARE SO COLD..
LET ME SEE.
THEY ARE COLD.
..THE BEGINNING IS A VERY DELICATE TIME...

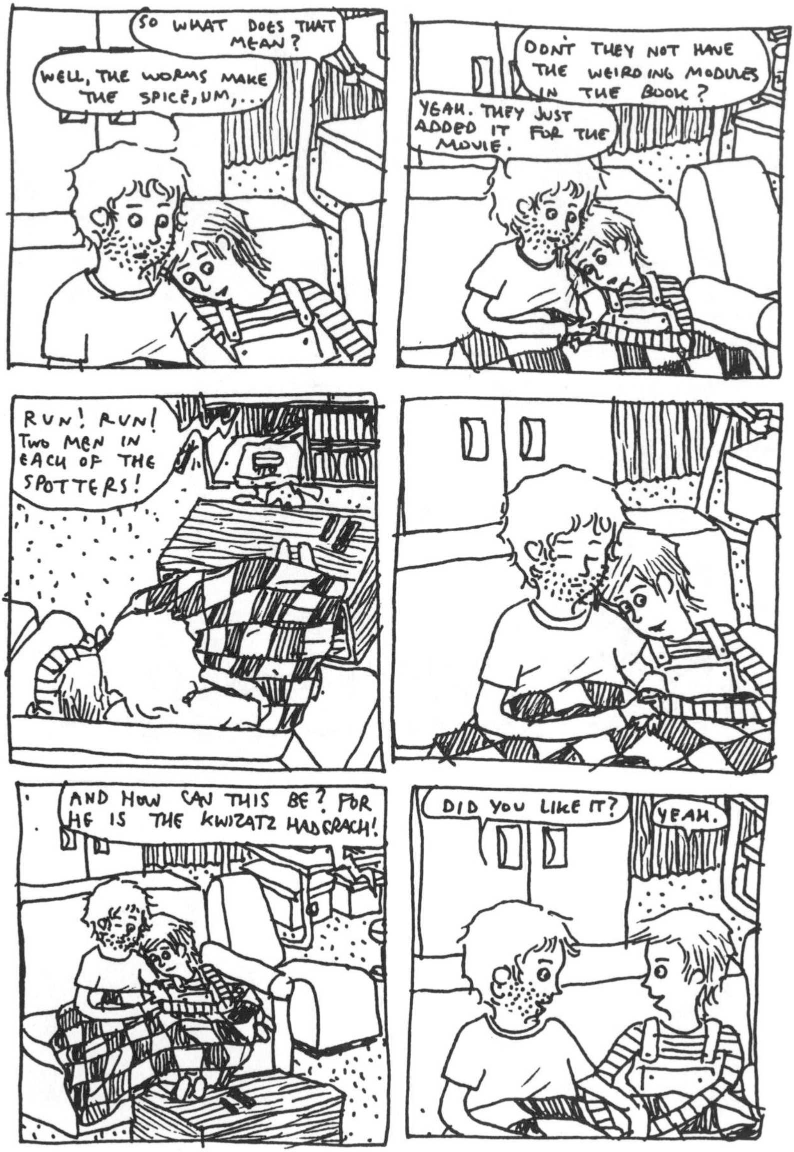
SO WHAT DOES THAT MEAN?
WELL, THE WORMS MAKE THE SPICE, UM,...
DONT THEY NOT HAVE THE WEIRDING MODULES IN THE BOOK?
YEAH. THEY JUST ADDED IT FOR THE MOVIE.
RUN! RUN! TWO MEN IN EACH OF THE SPOTTERS!
AND HOW CAN THIS BE? FOR HE IS THE KWIZATZ HADERACH!
DID YOU LIKE IT?
YEAH.

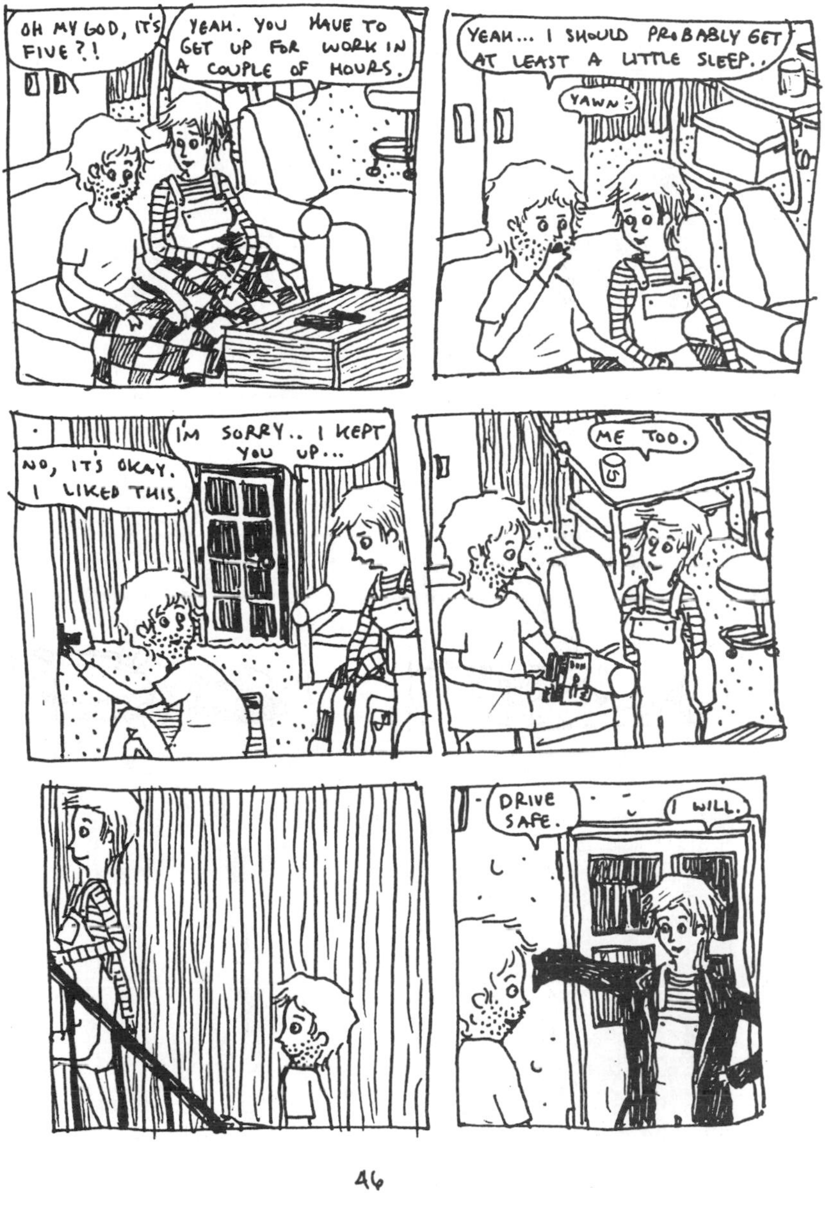
OH MY GOD, IT'S FIVE?!
YEAH. YOU HAVE TO GET UP FOR WORK IN A COUPLE OF HOURS.
YEAH... I SHOULD PROBABLY GET AT LEAST A LITTLE SLEEP..
YAWN
I'M SORRY.. I KEPT YOU UP...
NO, IT'S OKAY. I LIKED THIS.
ME TOO.
DRIVE SAFE.
I WILL.

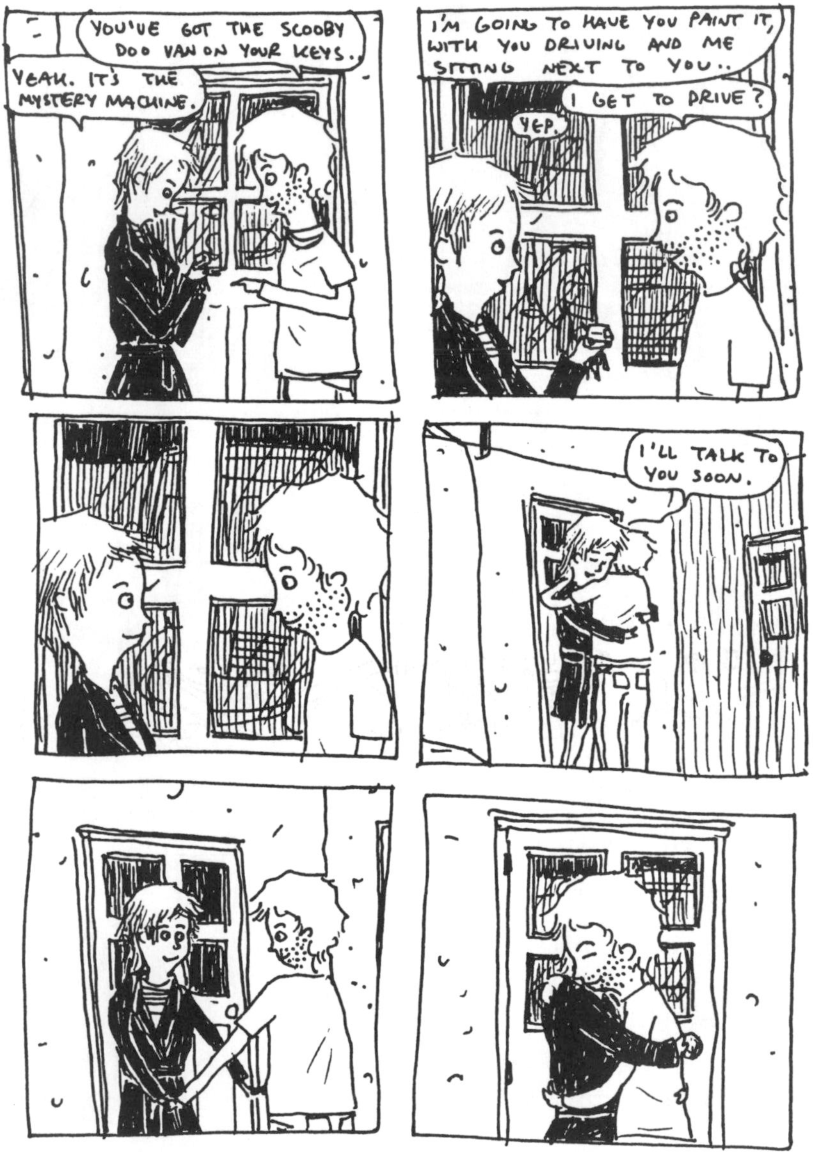
YOU'VE GOT THE SCOOBY DOO VAN ON YOUR KEYS..
YEAH. IT'S THE MYSTERY MACHINE.
I'M GOING TO HAVE YOU PAINT IT, WITH YOU DRIVING AND ME SITTING NEXT TO YOU..
I GET TO DRIVE?
YEP.
I'LL TALK TO YOU SOON.

KISS

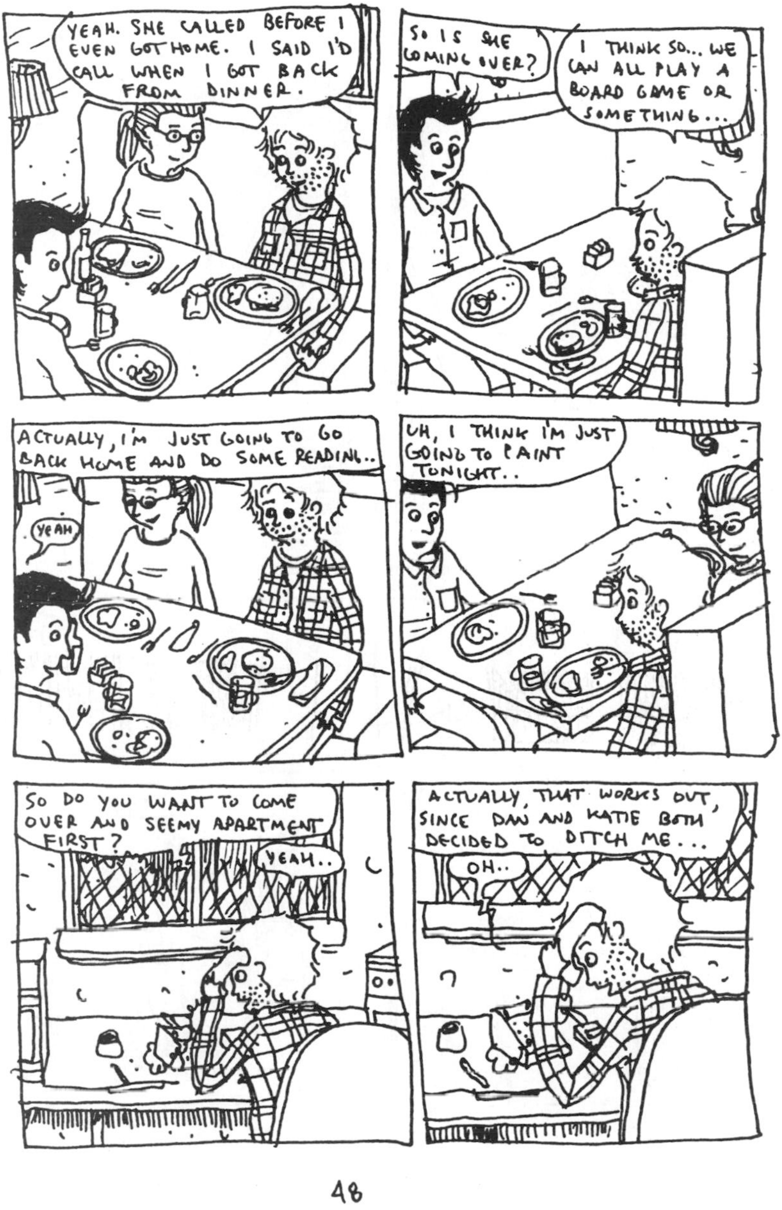
YEAH. SHE CALLED BEFORE I EVEN GOT HOME. I SAID I'D CALL WHEN I GOT BACK FROM DINNER.
SO IS SHE COMING OVER?
I THINK SO... WE CAN ALL PLAY A BOARD GAME OR SOMETHING...
ACTUALLY, I'M JUST GOING TO GO BACK HOME AND DO SOME READING..
YEAH
UH, I THINK I'M JUST GOING TO PAINT TONIGHT..
SO DO YOU WANT TO COME OVER AND SEEMY APARTMENT FIRST?
YEAH..
ACTUALLY, THAT WORKS OUT, SINCE DAN AND KATIE BOTH DECIDED TO DITCH ME...
OH..

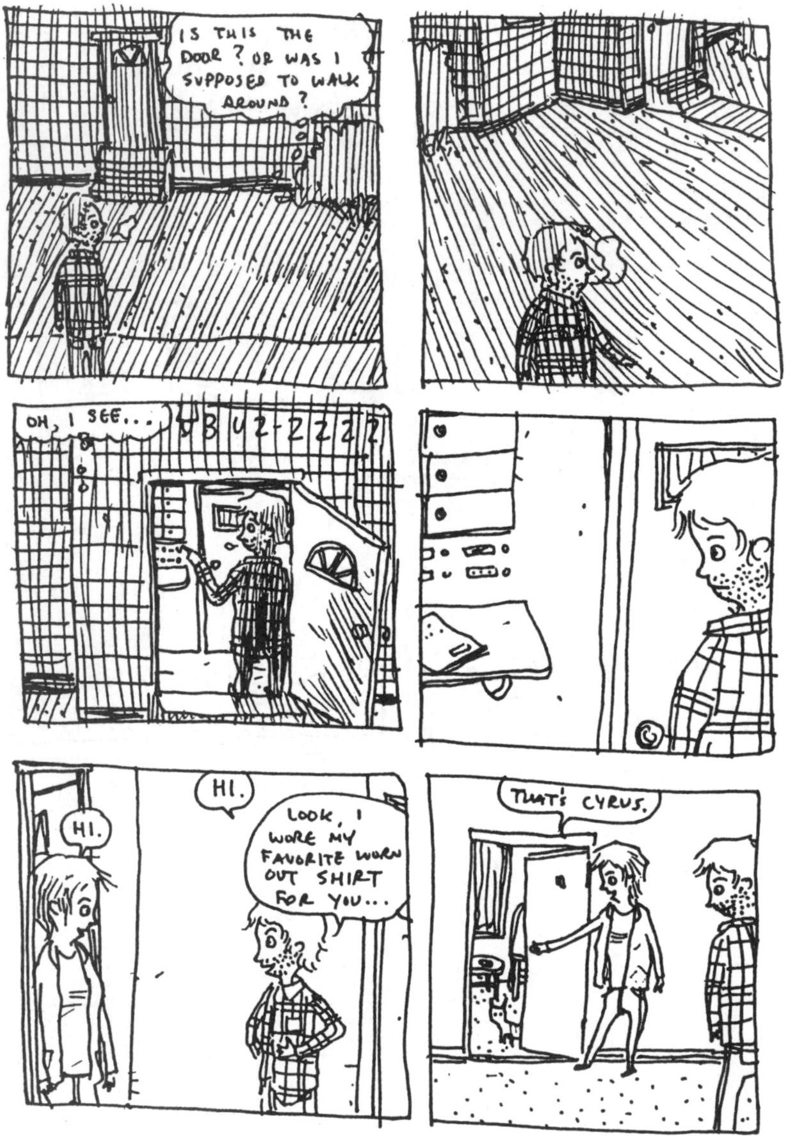
IS THIS THE DOOR? OR WAS I SUPPOSED TO WALK AROUND?
OH, I SEE...
HI.
HI.
LOOK, I WORE MY FAVORITE WORN OUT SHIRT FOR YOU...
THAT'S CYRUS.

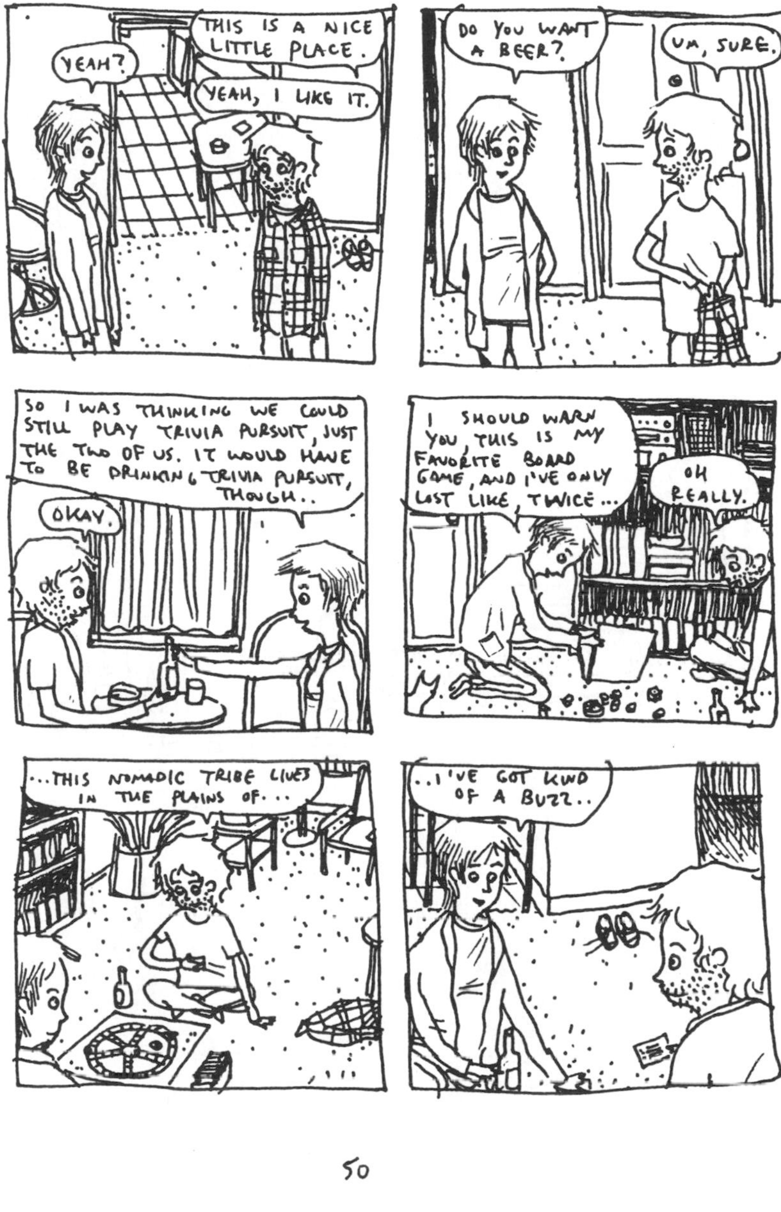
THIS IS A NICE LITTLE PLACE.
YEAH?
YEAH, I LIKE IT.
DO YOU WANT A BEER?
UM, SURE.
SO I WAS THINKING WE COULD STILL PLAY TRIVIA PURSUIT, JUST THE TWO OF US. IT WOULD HAVE TO BE DRINKING TRIVIA PURSUIT, THOUGH..
OKAY.
I SHOULD WARN YOU, THIS IS MY FAVORITE BOARD GAME, AND I'VE ONLY LOST LIKE, TWICE...
OH REALLY.
...THIS NOMADIC TRIBE LIVES IN THE PLAINS OF...
..I'VE GOT KIND OF A BUZZ..

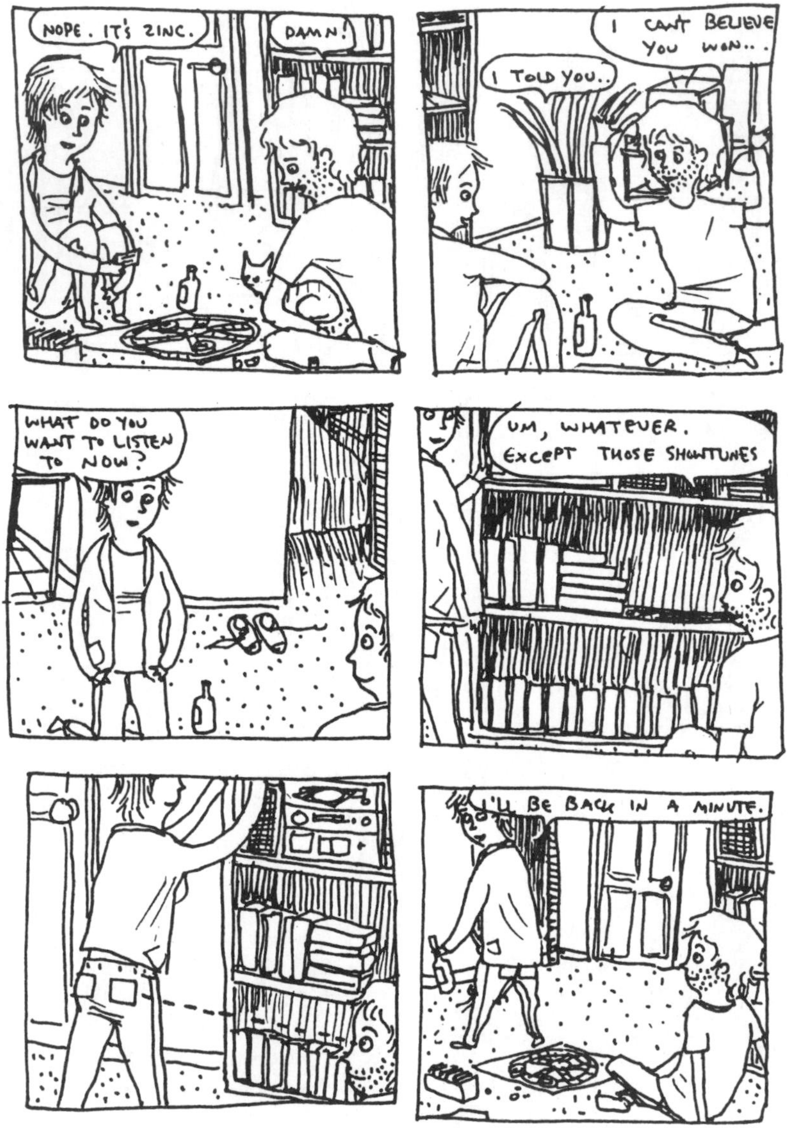
NOPE. IT'S ZINC.
DAMN!
I CAN'T BELIEVE YOU WON...
I TOLD YOU..
WHAT DO YOU WANT TO LISTEN TO NOW?
UM, WHATEVER. EXCEPT THOSE SHOWTUNES
I'LL BE BACK IN A MINUTE.

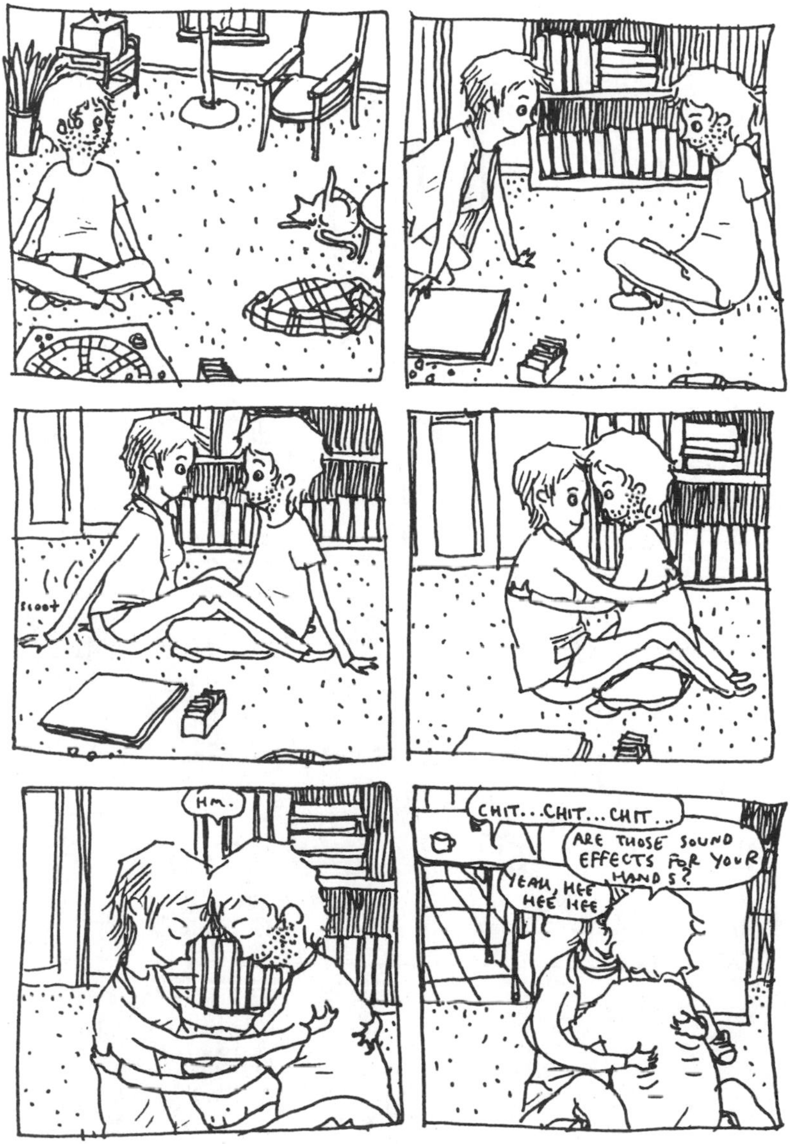
scoot
HM.
CHIT... CHIT... CHIT...
ARE THOSE SOUND EFFECTS FOR YOUR HANDS?
YEAH, HEE HEE HEE

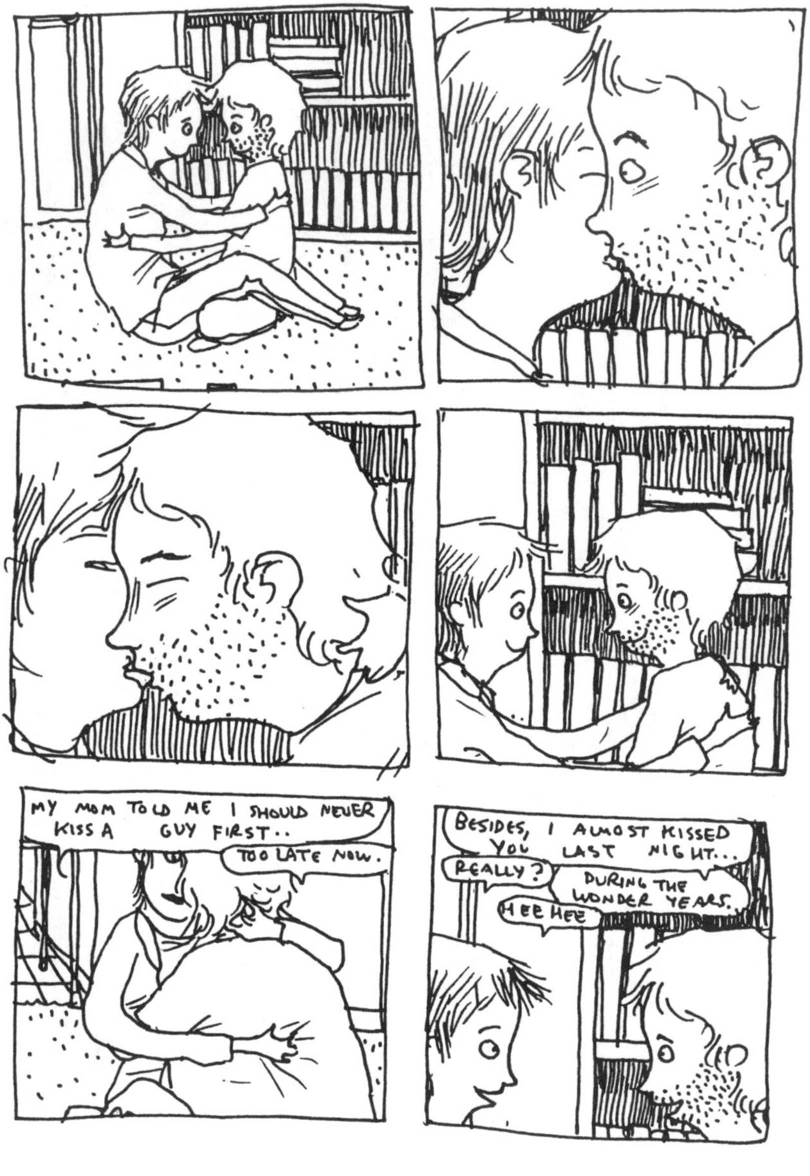
MY MOM TOLD ME I SHOULD NEVER KISS A GUY FIRST..
TOO LATE NOW.
BESIDES, I ALMOST KISSED YOU LAST NIGHT...
REALLY?
DURING THE WONDER YEARS.
HEE HEE

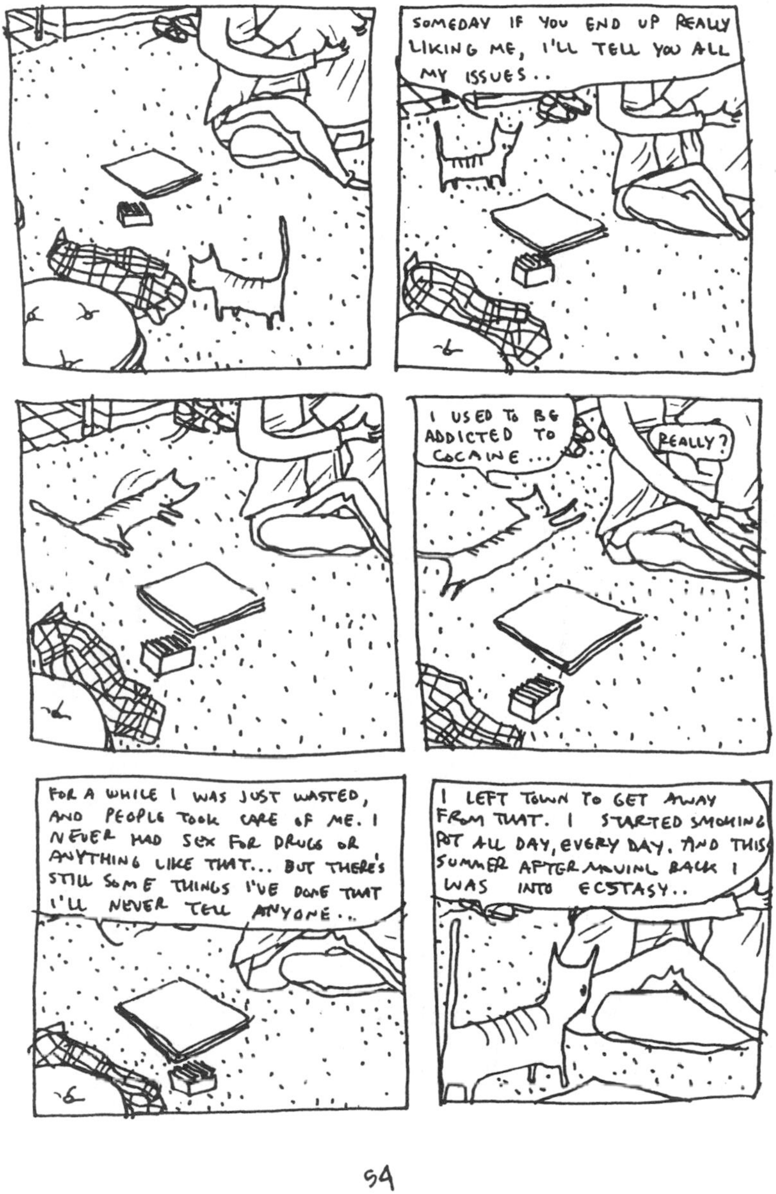
SOMEDAY IF YOU END UP REALLY LIKING ME, I'LL TELL YOU ALL MY ISSUES..
I USED TO BE ADDICTED TO COCAINE...
REALLY?
FOR A WHILE I WAS JUST WASTED, AND PEOPLE TOOK CARE OF ME. I NEVER HAD SEX FOR DRUGS OR ANYTHING LIKE THAT... BUT THERE'S STILL SOME THINGS I'VE DONE THAT I'LL NEVER TELL ANYONE..
I LEFT TOWN TO GET AWAY FROM THAT. I STARTED SMOKING POT ALL DAY, EVERY DAY. AND THIS SUMMER AFTER MOVING BACK I WAS INTO ECSTASY..

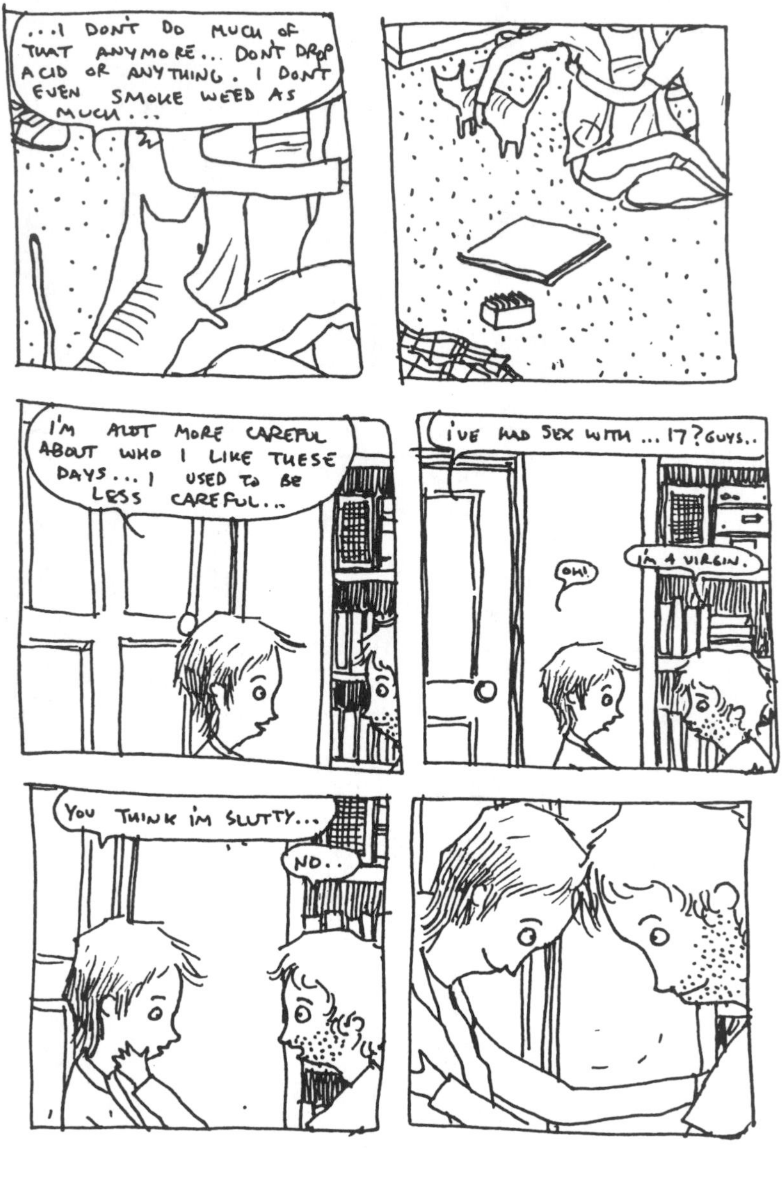
...I DON'T DO MUCH OF THAT ANYMORE... DON'T DROP ACID OR ANYTHING. I DON'T EVEN SMOKE WEED AS MUCH...
I'M ALOT MORE CAREFUL ABOUT WHO I LIKE THESE DAYS... I USED TO BE LESS CAREFUL...
I'VE HAD SEX WITH ...17? GUYS..
OH!
I'M A VIRGIN.
YOU THINK I'M SLUTTY...
NO..

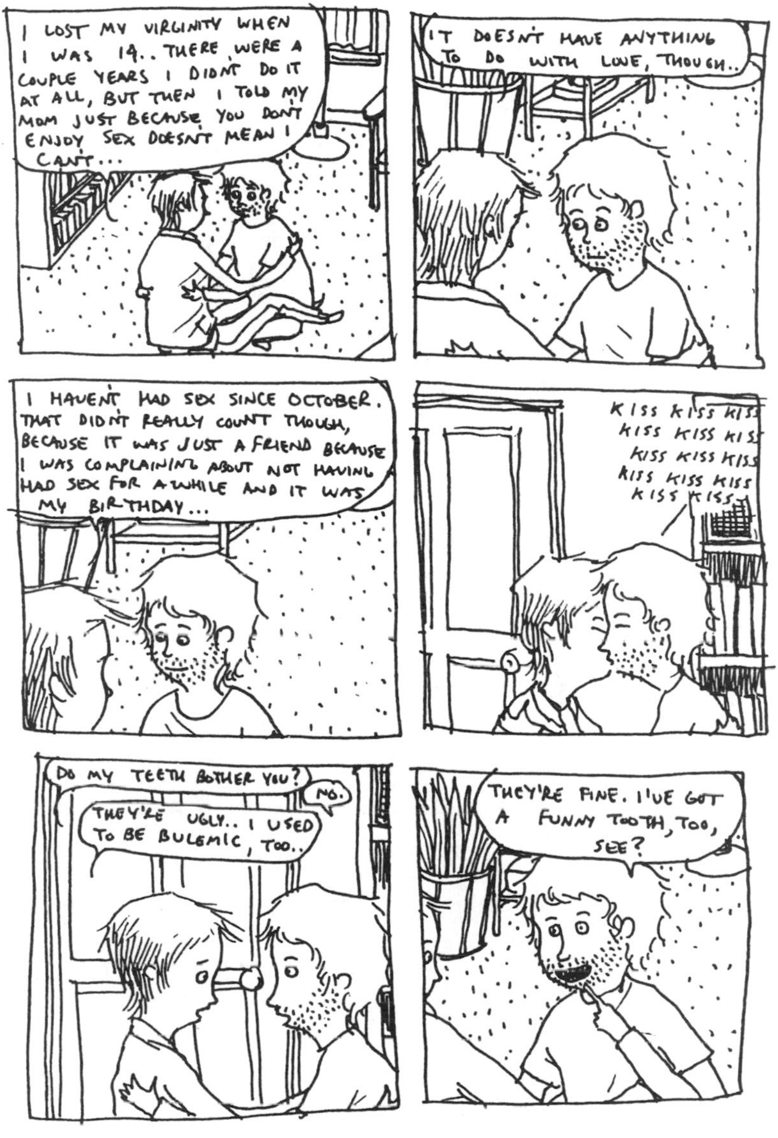
I LOST MY VIRGINITY WHEN I WAS 14.. THERE WERE A COUPLE YEARS I DIDN'T DO IT AT ALL, BUT THEN I TOLD MY MOM JUST BECAUSE YOU DON'T ENJOY SEX DOESN'T MEAN I CAN'T...
IT DOESN'T HAVE ANYTHING TO DO WITH LOVE, THOUGH..
I HAVEN'T HAD SEX SINCE OCTOBER. THAT DIDN'T REALLY COUNT THOUGH, BECAUSE IT WAS JUST A FRIEND BECAUSE I WAS COMPLAINING ABOUT NOT HAVING HAD SEX FOR A WHILE AND IT WAS MY BIRTHDAY...
KISS KISS KISS KISS KISS KISS KISS KISS KISS KISS KISS KISS KISS KISS
DO MY TEETH BOTHER YOU?
NO.
THEY'RE UGLY.. I USED TO BE BULEMIC, TOO..
THEY'RE FINE. I'VE GOT A FUNNY TOOTH, TOO, SEE?

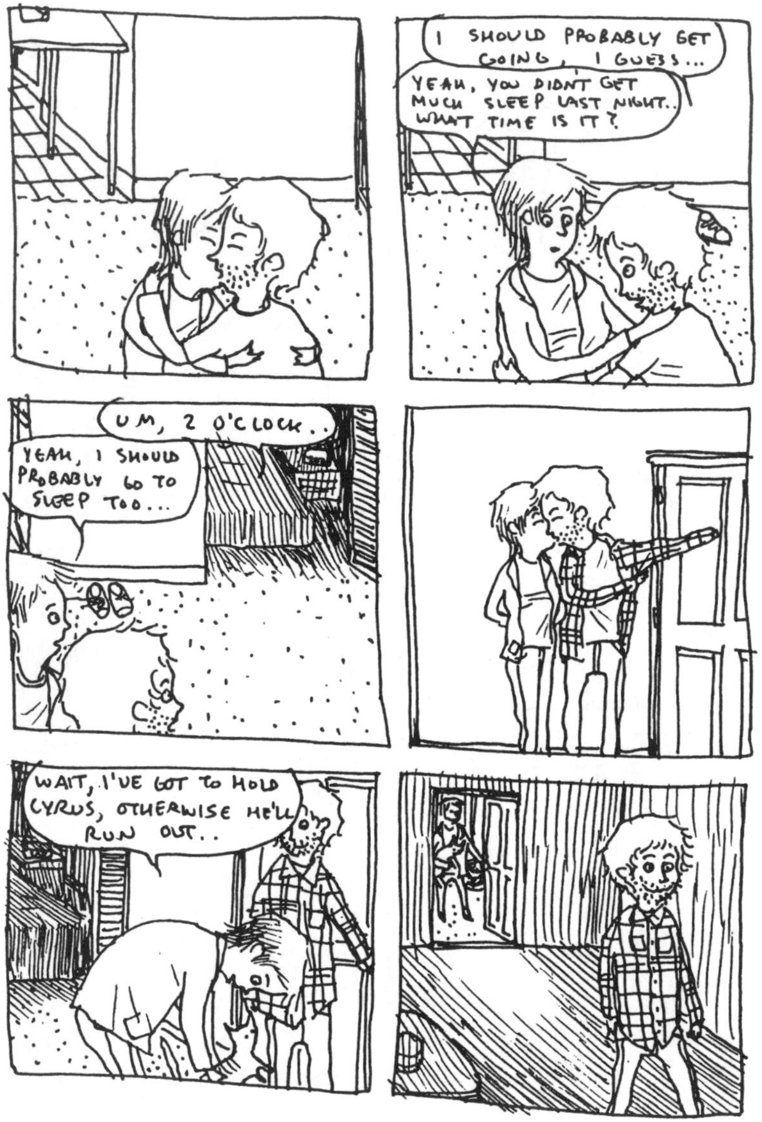
I SHOULD PROBABLY GET GOING, I GUESS...
YEAH, YOU DIDN'T GET MUCH SLEEP LAST NIGHT.. WHAT TIME IS IT?
UM, 2 O'CLOCK..
YEAH, I SHOULD PROBABLY GO TO SLEEP TOO...
WAIT, I'VE GOT TO HOLD CYRUS, OTHERWISE HE'LL RUN OUT..

LUNCH DATE

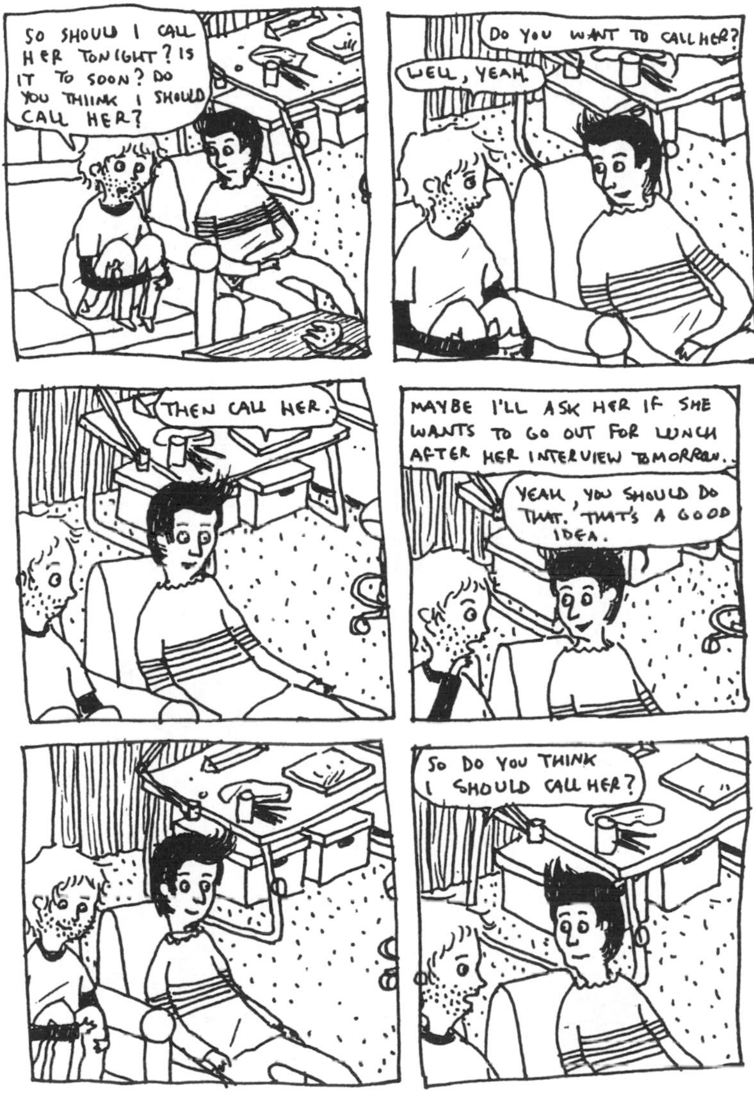
SO SHOULD I CALL HER TONIGHT? IS IT TO SOON? DO YOU THIIINK I SHOULD CALL HER?
DO YOU WANT TO CALL HER?
WELL, YEAH.
THEN CALL HER.
MAYBE I'LL ASK HER IF SHE WANTS TO GO OUT FOR LUNCH AFTER HER INTERVIEW TOMORROW.
YEAH, YOU SHOULD DO THAT. THAT'S A GOOD IDEA.
SO DO YOU THINK I SHOULD CALL HER?

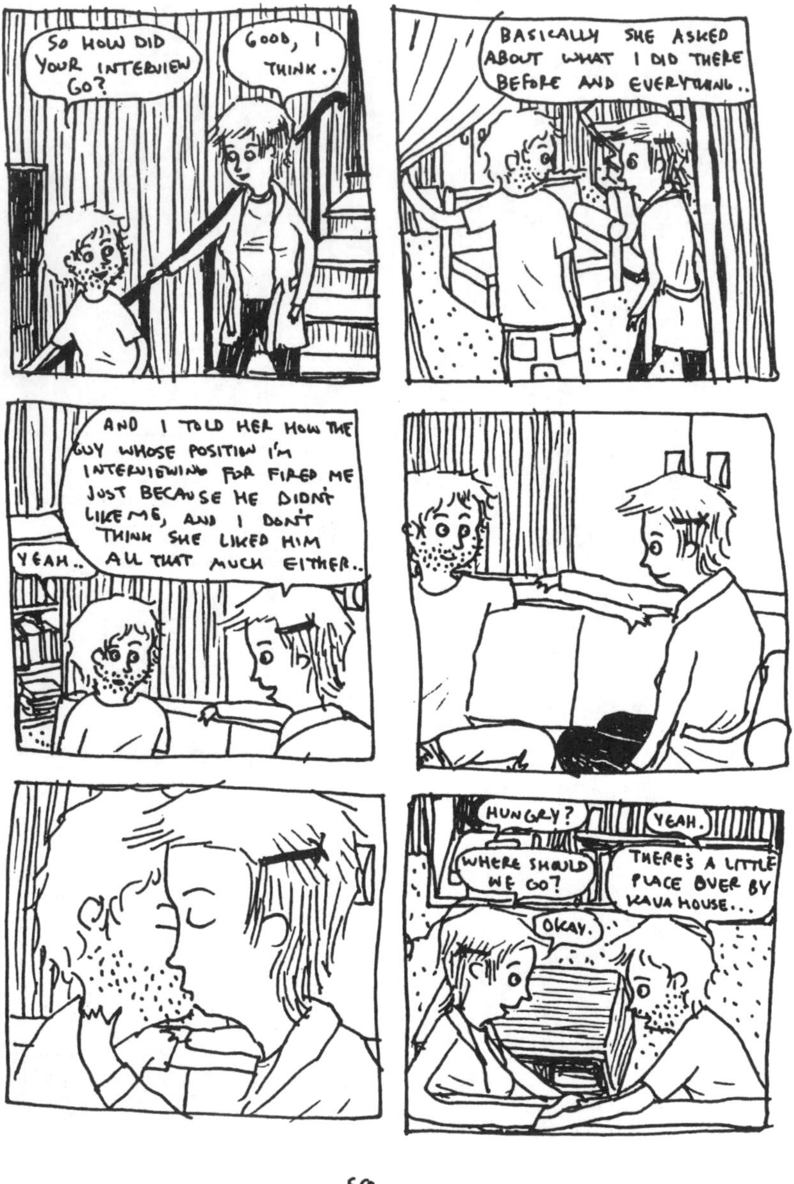
SO HOW DID YOUR INTERVIEW GO?
GOOD, I THINK..
BASICALLY SHE ASKED ABOUT WHAT I DID THERE BEFORE AND EVERYTHING..
AND I TOLD HER HOW THE GUY WHOSE POSITION I'M INTERVIEWING FOR FIRED ME JUST BECAUSE HE DIDN'T LIKE ME, AND I DON'T THINK SHE LIKED HIM ALL THAT MUCH EITHER..
YEAH..
HUNGRY?
YEAH.
WHERE SHOULD WE GO?
THERE'S A LITTLE PLACE OVER BY KAVA HOUSE...
OKAY.

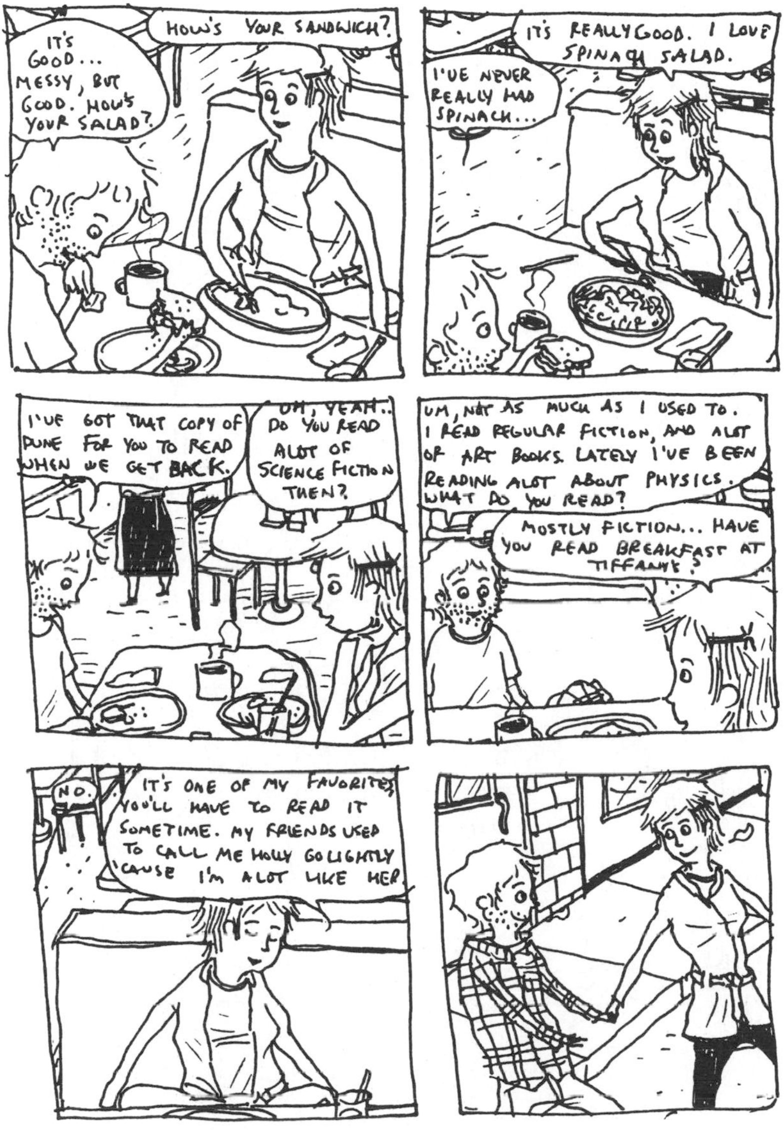
HOW'S YOUR SANDWICH?
IT'S GOOD... MESSY, BUT GOOD. HOW'S YOUR SALAD?
IT'S REALLY GOOD. I LOVE SPINACH SALAD.
I'VE NEVER REALLY HAD SPINACH...
I'VE GOT THAT COPY OF DUNE FOR YOU TO READ WHEN WE GET BACK.
UM, YEAH.. DO YOU READ ALOT OF SCIENCE FICTION THEN?
UM, NOT AS MUCH AS I USED TO. I READ REGULAR FICTION, AND ALOT OF ART BOOKS. LATELY I'VE BEEN READING ALOT ABOUT PHYSICS. WHAT DO YOU READ?
MOSTLY FICTION... HAVE YOU READ BREAKFAST AT TIFFANY'S?
NO.
IT'S ONE OF MY FAVORITES, YOU'LL HAVE TO READ IT SOMETIME. MY FRIENDS USED TO CALL ME HOLLY GOLIGHTLY 'CAUSE I'M ALOT LIKE HER.

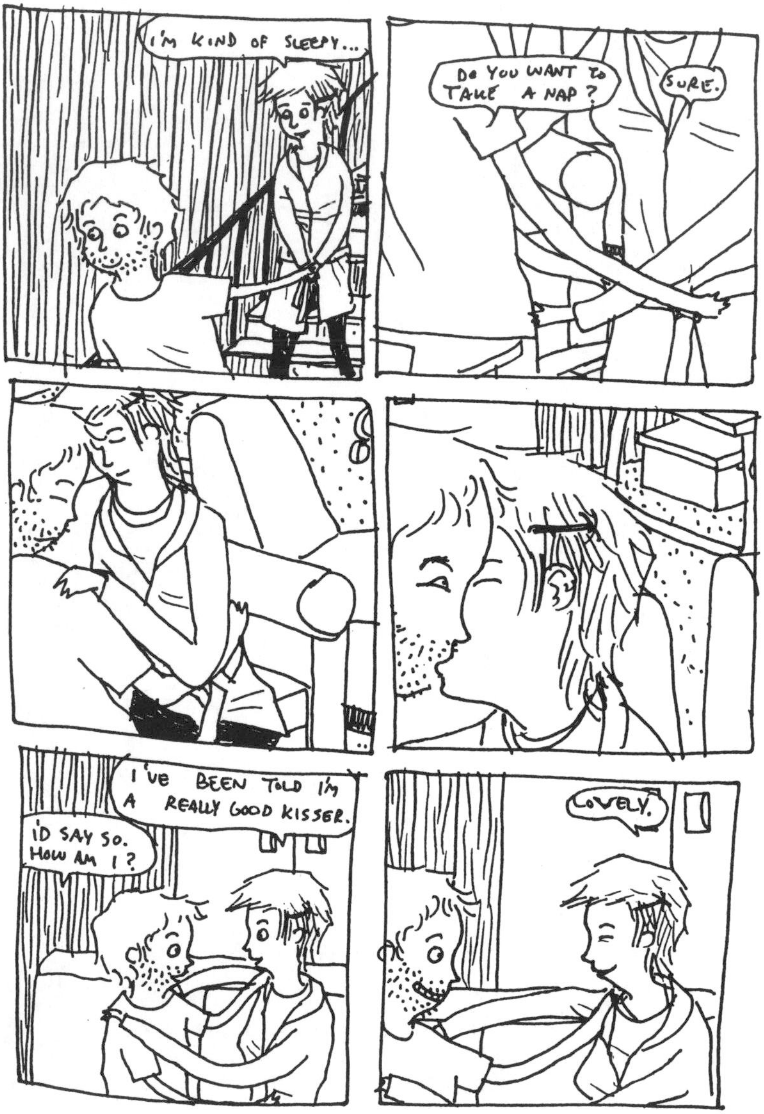
I'M KIND OF SLEEPY...
DO YOU WANT TO TAKE A NAP?
SURE.
I'VE BEEN TOLD I'M A REALLY GOOD KISSER.
I'D SAY SO. HOW AM I?
LOVELY.

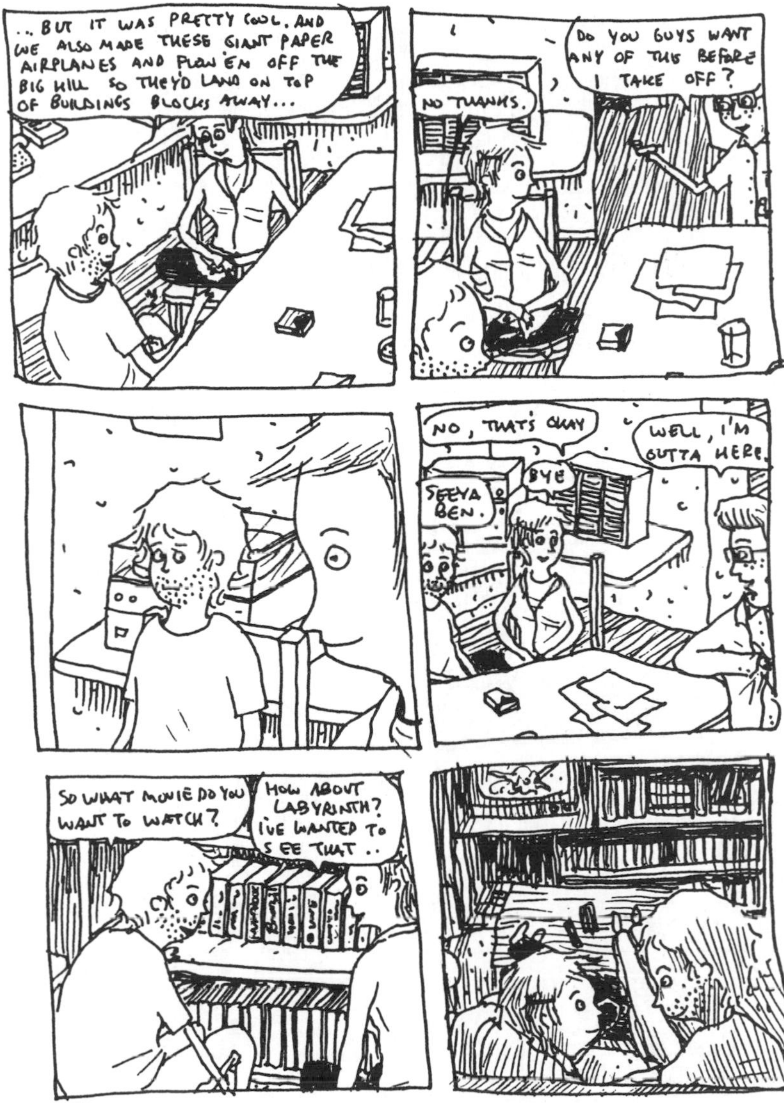
... BUT IT WAS PRETTY COOL. AND WE ALSO MADE THESE GIANT PAPER AIRPLANES AND FLEW 'EM OFF THE BIG HILL SO THEY'D LAND ON TOP OF BUILDINGS BLOCKS AWAY...
DO YOU GUYS WANT ANY OF THIS BEFORE I TAKE OFF?
NO THANKS.
NO, THAT'S OKAY
WELL, I'M OUTTA HERE.
BYE
SEEYA BEN.
SO WHAT MOVIE DO YOU WANT TO WATCH?
HOW ABOUT LABYRINTH? I'VE WANTED TO SEE THAT ..

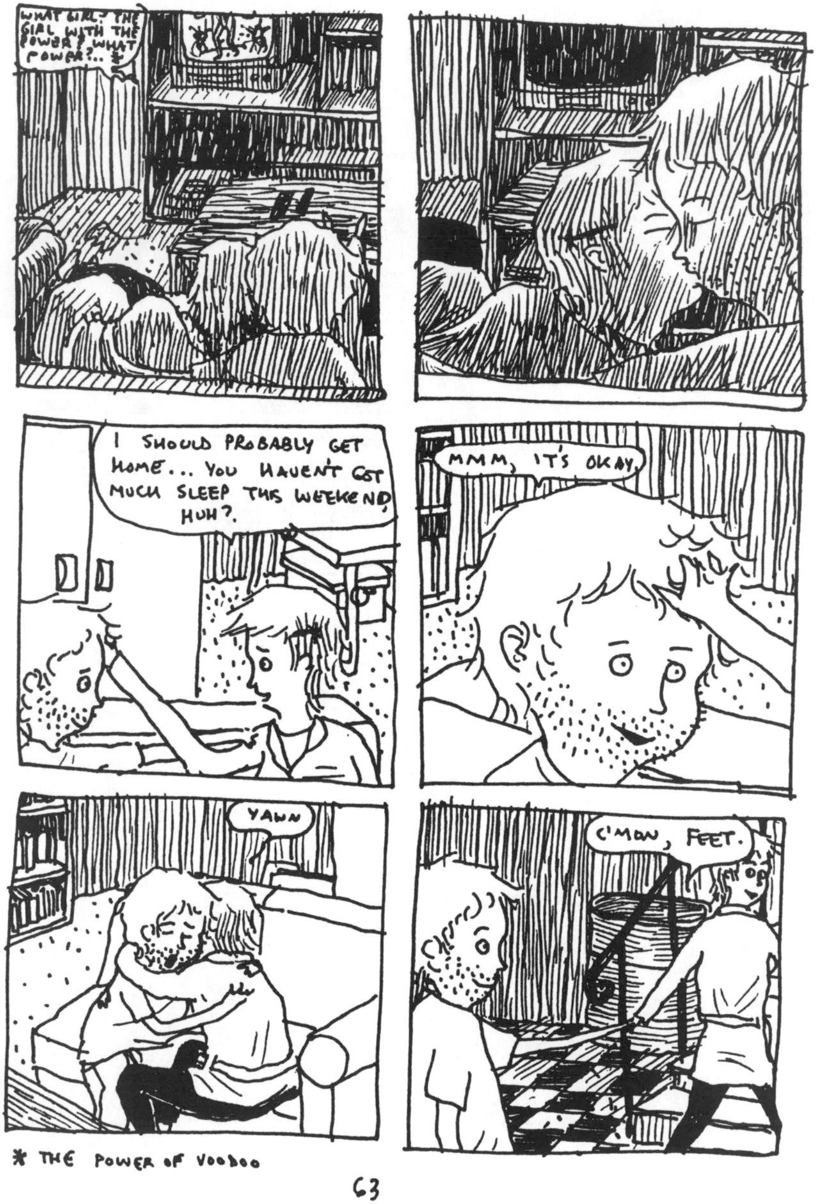
WHAT GIRL? THE GIRL WITH THE POWER? WHAT POWER?... *
I SHOULD PROBABLY GET HOME... YOU HAVEN'T GOT MUCH SLEEP THIS WEEKEND, HUH?
MMM, IT'S OKAY.
YAWN
C'MON, FEET.

* THE POWER OF VOODOO

ALL NIGHTer

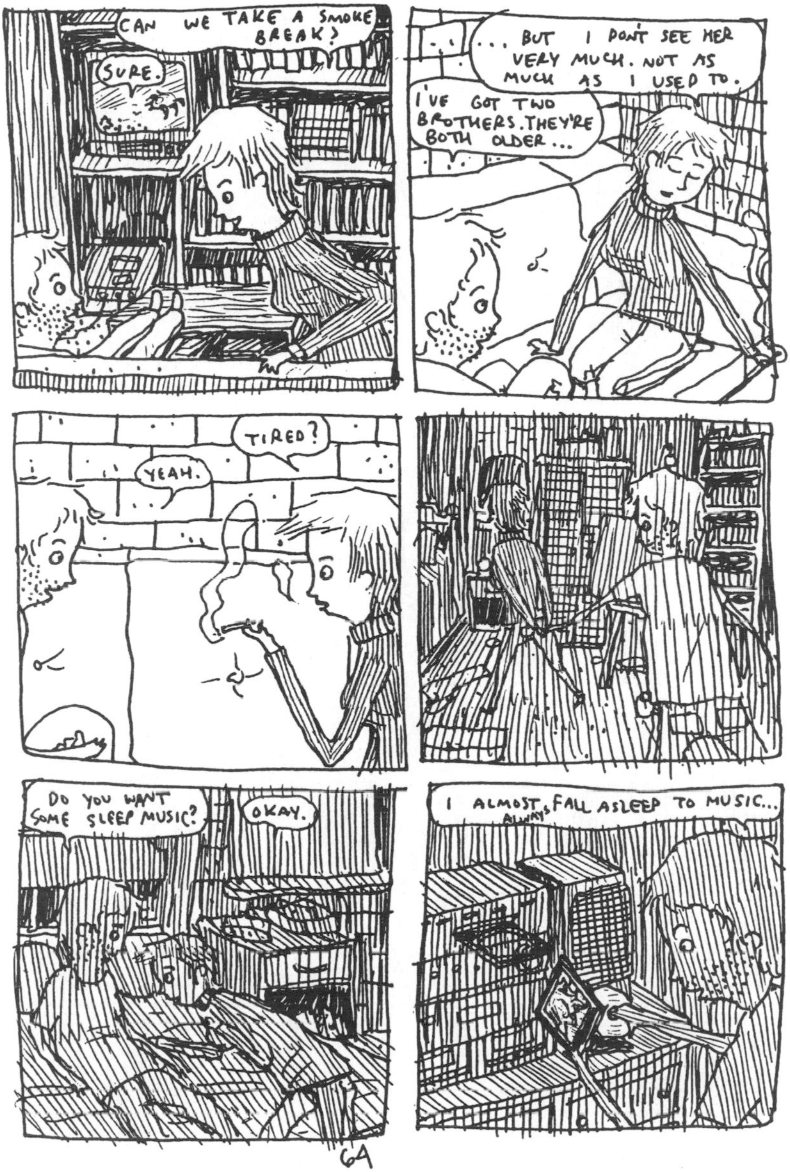
CAN WE TAKE A SMOKE BREAK?
SURE.
...BUT I DON'T SEE HER VERY MUCH. NOT AS MUCH AS I USED TO.
I'VE GOT TWO BROTHERS. THEY'RE BOTH OLDER...
TIRED?
YEAH.
DO YOU WANT SOME SLEEP MUSIC?
OKAY.
I ALMOST ALWAYS FALL ASLEEP TO MUSIC...

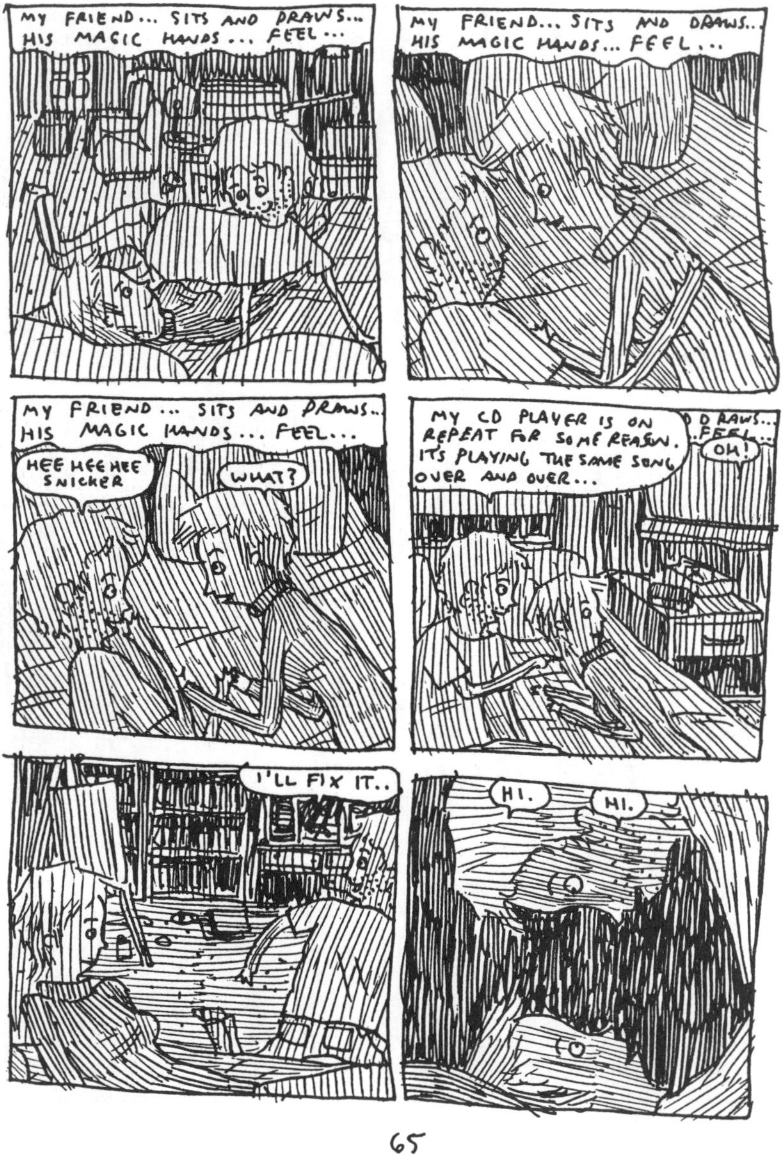
MY FRIEND... SITS AND DRAWS... HIS MAGIC HANDS... FEEL...
MY FRIEND... SITS AND DRAWS... HIS MAGIC HANDS... FEEL...
MY FRIEND... SITS AND DRAWS... HIS MAGIC HANDS... FEEL...
HEE HEE HEE SNICKER
WHAT?
MY CD PLAYER IS ON REPEAT FOR SOME REASON. IT'S PLAYING THE SAME SONG OVER AND OVER...
OH!
I'LL FIX IT..
HI.
HI.

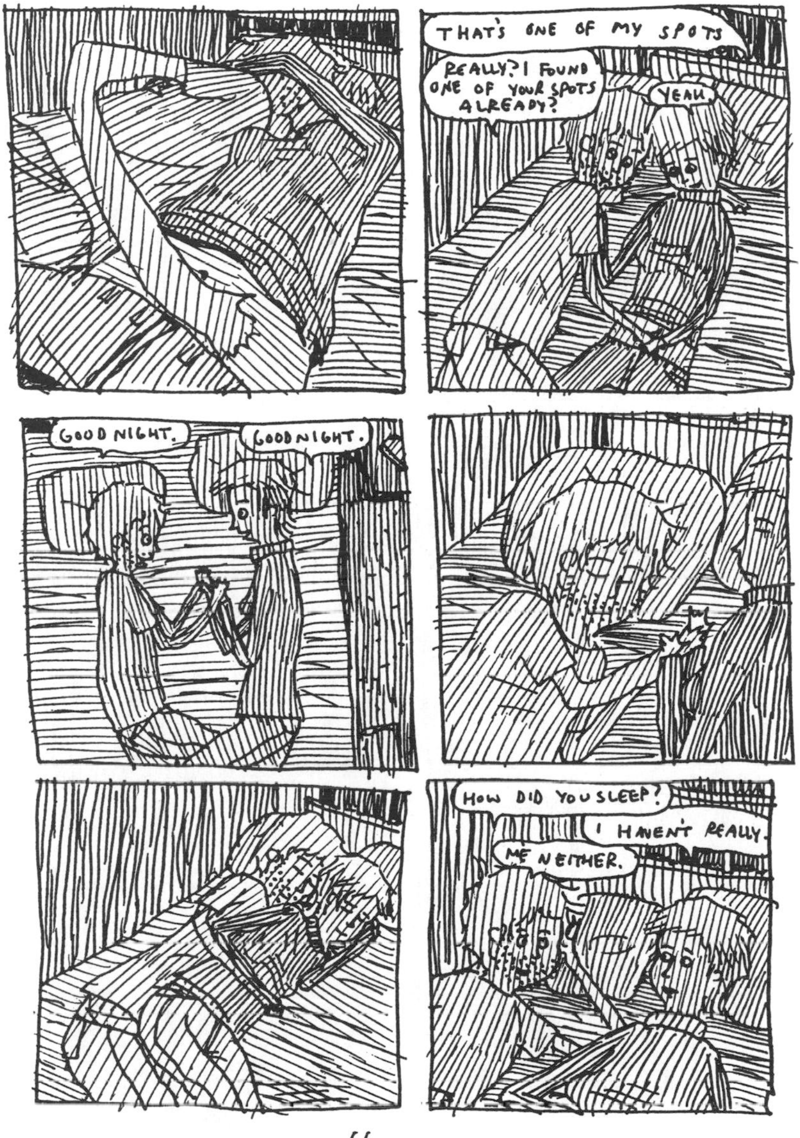
THAT'S ONE OF MY SPOTS
REALLY? I FOUND ONE OF YOUR SPOTS ALREADY?
YEAH.
GOOD NIGHT.
GOODNIGHT.
HOW DID YOU SLEEP?
I HAVEN'T REALLY.
ME NEITHER.

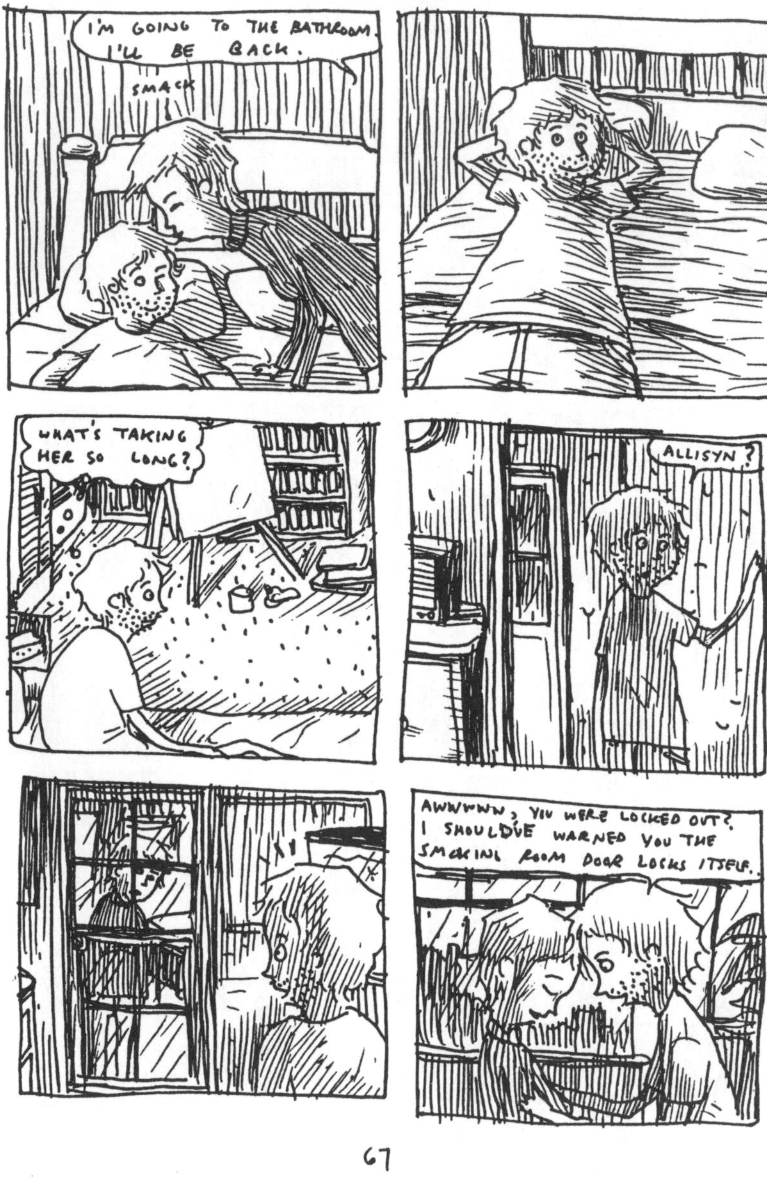
I'M GOING TO THE BATHROOM. I'LL BE BACK.
SMACK
WHAT'S TAKING HER SO LONG?
ALLISYN?
AWWWWN, YOU WERE LOCKED OUT? I SHOULD'VE WARNED YOU THE SMOKING ROOM DOOR LOCKS ITSELF.

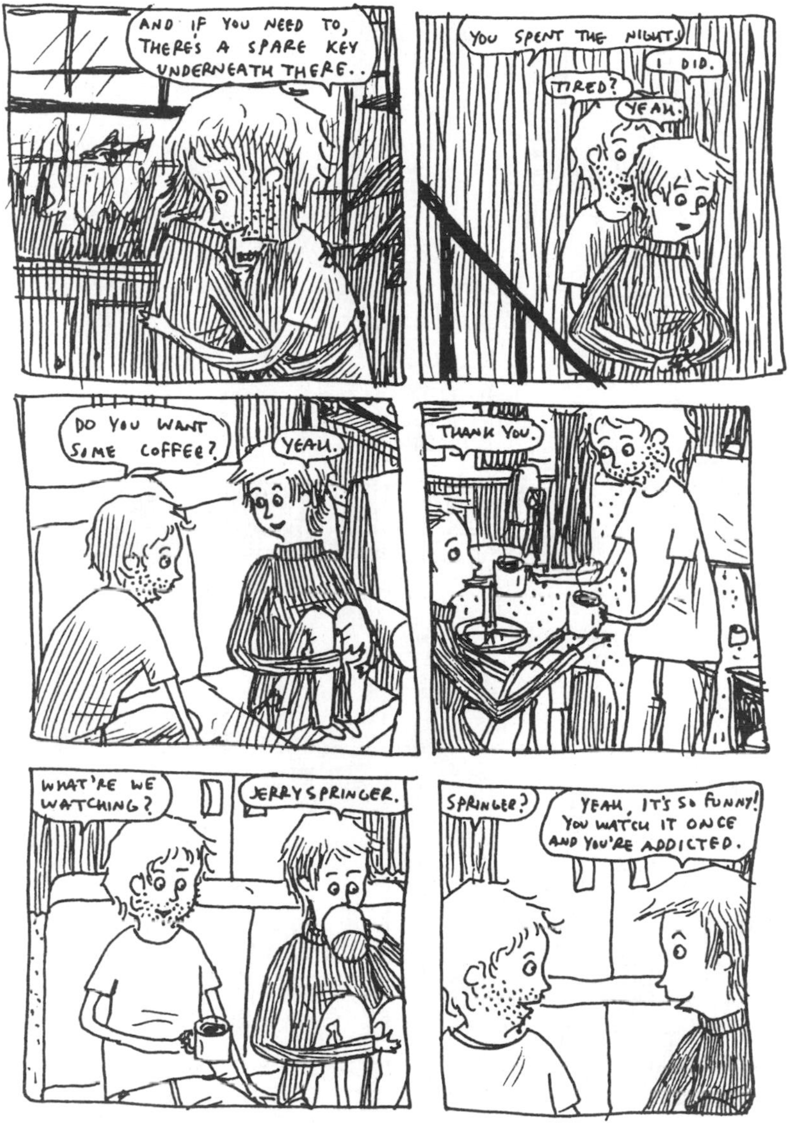
AND IF YOU NEED TO, THERE'S A SPARE KEY UNDERNEATH THERE..
YOU SPENT THE NIGHT.
I DID.
TIRED?
YEAH.
DO YOU WANT SOME COFFEE?
YEAH.
THANK YOU.
WHAT'RE WE WATCHING?
JERRY SPRINGER.
SPRINGER?
YEAH, IT'S SO FUNNY! YOU WATCH IT ONCE AND YOU'RE ADDICTED.

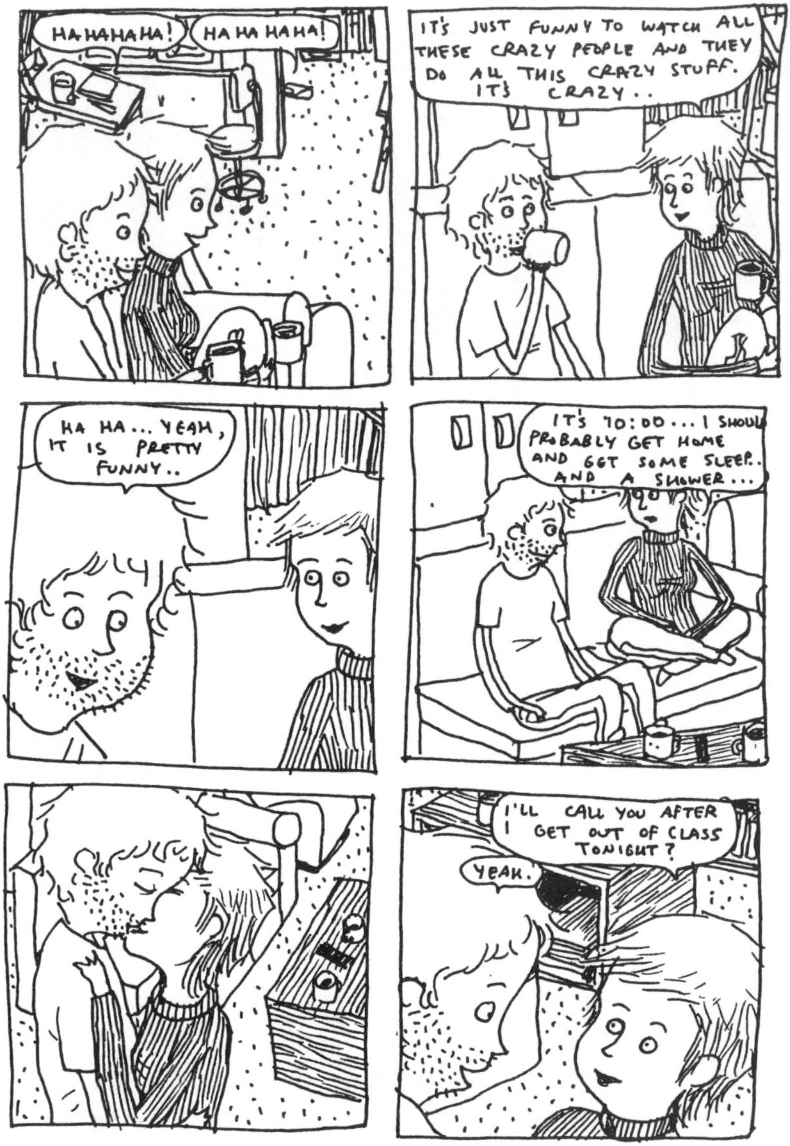
HAHAHAHA!
HA HA HA HA!
IT'S JUST FUNNY TO WATCH ALL THESE CRAZY PEOPLE AND THEY DO ALL THIS CRAZY STUFF. IT'S CRAZY..
HA HA... YEAH, IT IS PRETTY FUNNY..
IT'S 10:00... I SHOULD PROBABLY GET HOME AND GET SOME SLEEP.. AND A SHOWER...
I'LL CALL YOU AFTER I GET OUT OF CLASS TONIGHT?
YEAH.

CLASS

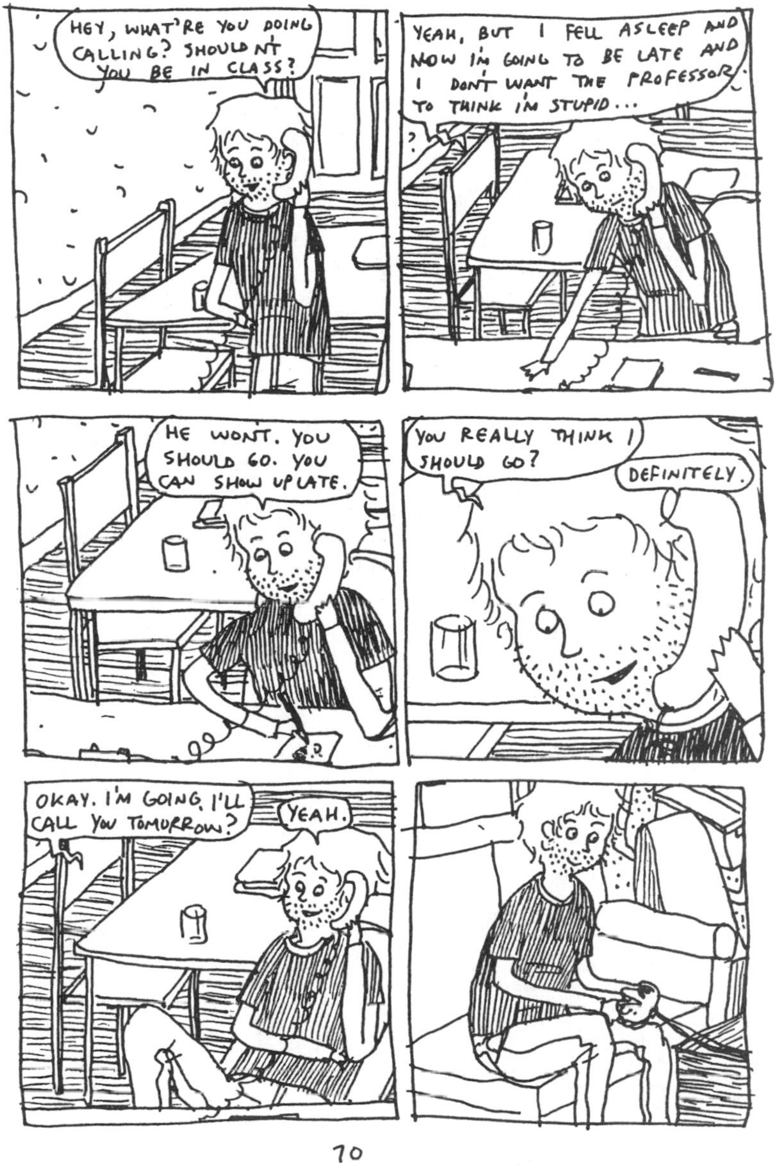
HEY, WHAT'RE YOU DOING CALLING? SHOULDN'T YOU BE IN CLASS?
YEAH, BUT I FELL ASLEEP AND NOW I'M GOING TO BE LATE AND I DON'T WANT THE PROFESSOR TO THINK I'M STUPID...
HE WON'T. YOU SHOULD GO. YOU CAN SHOW UP LATE.
YOU REALLY THINK I SHOULD GO?
DEFINITELY.
OKAY. I'M GOING. I'LL CALL YOU TOMORROW?
YEAH.

DROP OUT

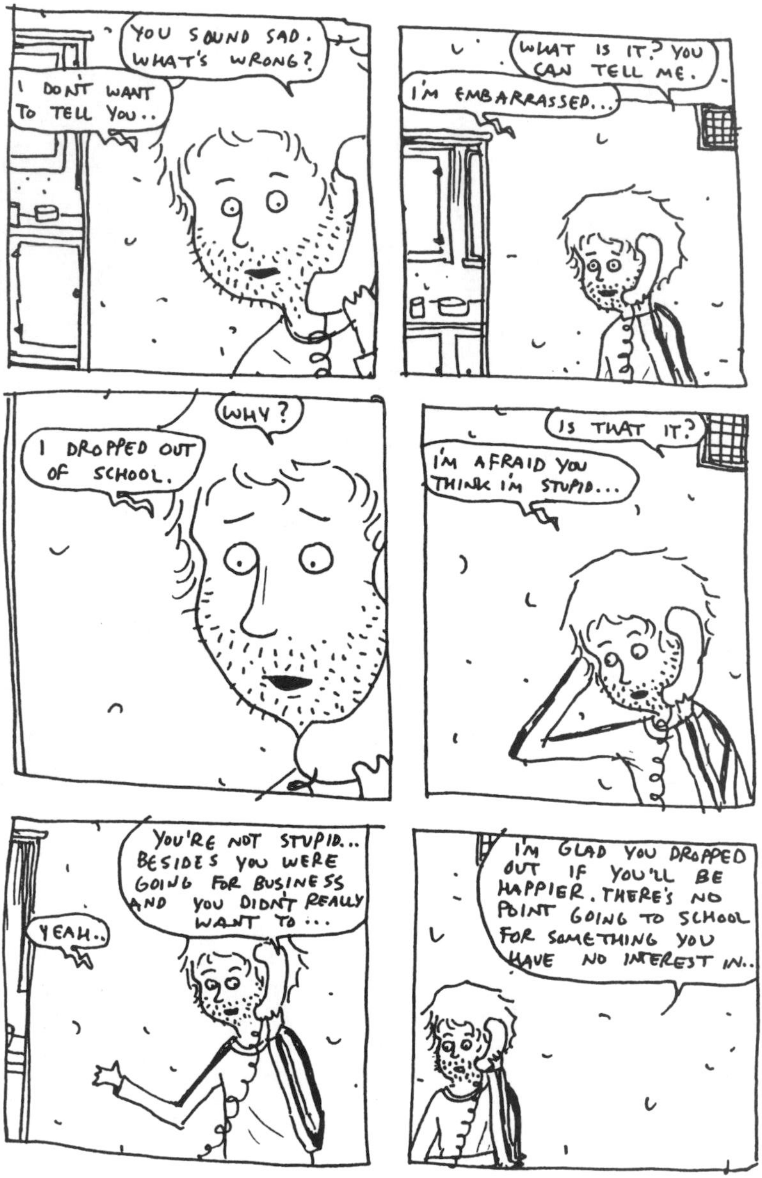
YOU SOUND SAD. WHAT'S WRONG?
I DON'T WANT TO TELL YOU..
WHAT IS IT? YOU CAN TELL ME.
I'M EMBARRASSED...
WHY?
I DROPPED OUT OF SCHOOL.
IS THAT IT?
I'M AFRAID YOU THINK I'M STUPID...
YOU'RE NOT STUPID... BESIDES YOU WERE GOING FOR BUSINESS AND YOU DIDN'T REALLY WANT TO...
YEAH..
I'M GLAD YOU DROPPED OUT IF YOU'LL BE HAPPIER. THERE'S NO POINT GOING TO SCHOOL FOR SOMETHING YOU HAVE NO INTEREST IN..

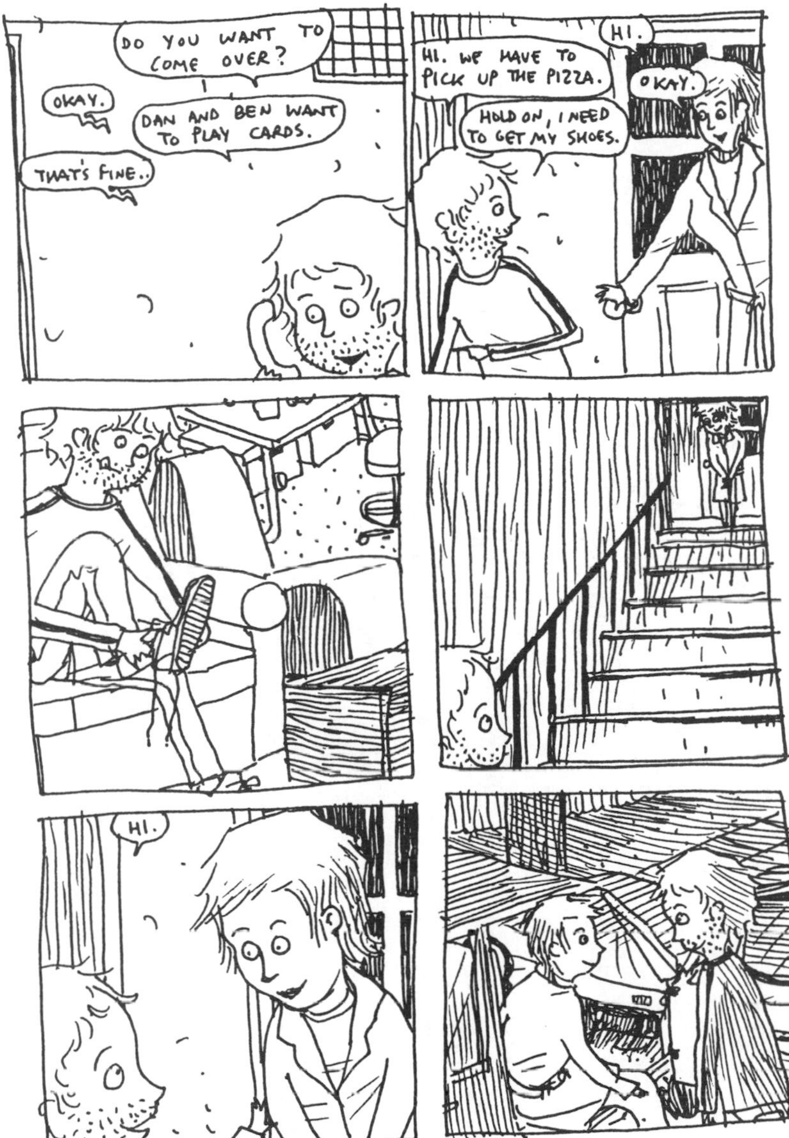
DO YOU WANT TO COME OVER?
OKAY.
DAN AND BEN WANT TO PLAY CARDS.
THAT'S FINE..
HI.
HI. WE HAVE TO PICK UP THE PIZZA.
OKAY.
HOLD ON, I NEED TO GET MY SHOES.
HI.

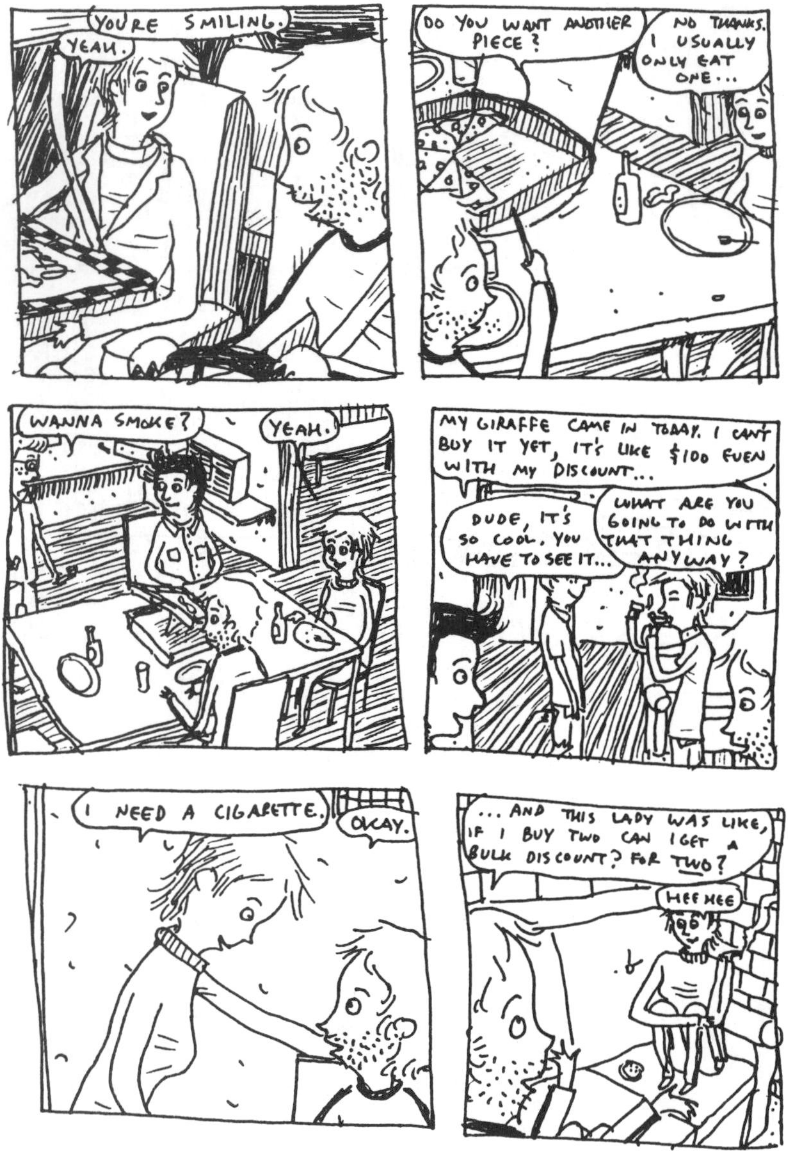
YOU'RE SMILING.
YEAH.
DO YOU WANT ANOTHER PIECE?
NO THANKS. I USUALLY ONLY EAT ONE...
WANNA SMOKE?
YEAH.
MY GIRAFFE CAME IN TODAY. I CAN'T BUY IT YET, IT'S LIKE $100 EVEN WITH MY DISCOUNT...
DUDE, IT'S SO COOL. YOU HAVE TO SEE IT...
WHAT ARE YOU GOING TO DO WITH THAT THING ANYWAY?
I NEED A CIGARETTE.
OKAY.
...AND THIS LADY WAS LIKE, IF I BUY TWO CAN I GET A BULK DISCOUNT? FOR TWO?
HEE HEE

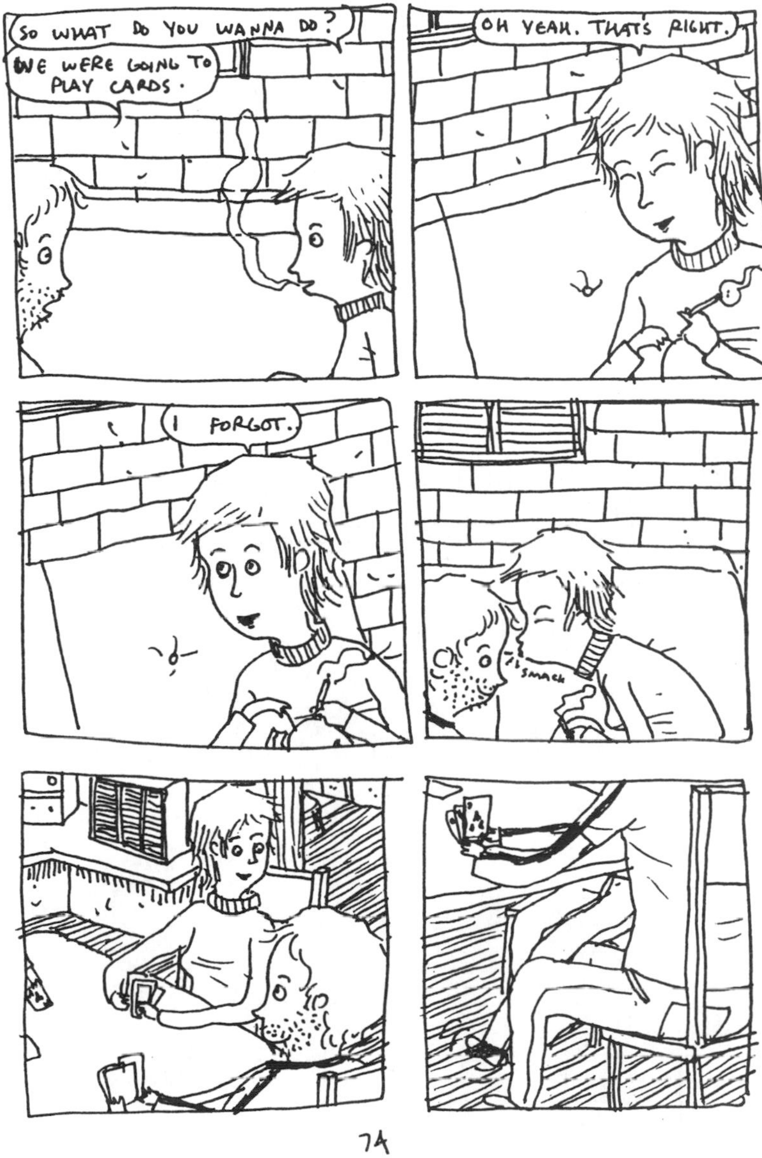
SO WHAT DO YOU WANNA DO?
WE WERE GOING TO PLAY CARDS.
OH YEAH. THAT'S RIGHT.
I FORGOT.
SMACK

BAD NEWS

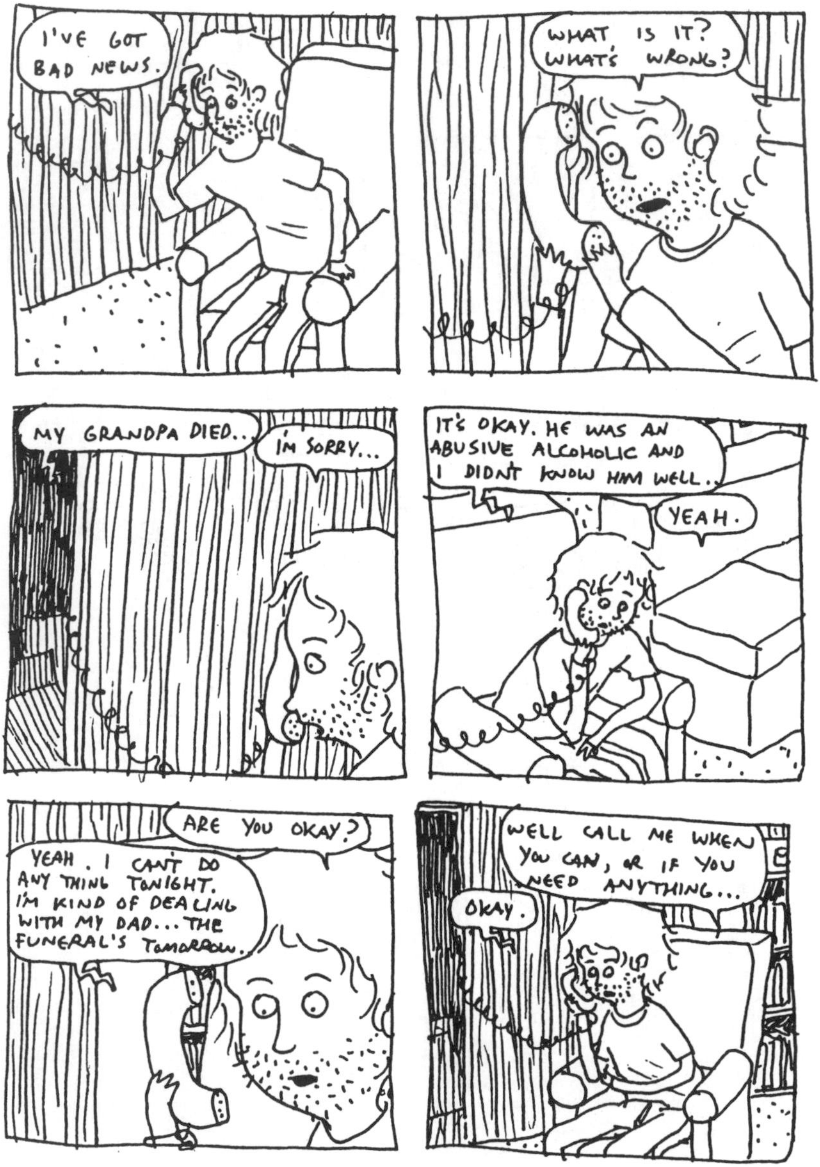
I'VE GOT BAD NEWS.
WHAT IS IT? WHAT'S WRONG?
MY GRANDPA DIED...
I'M SORRY...
IT'S OKAY. HE WAS AN ABUSIVE ALCOHOLIC AND I DIDN'T KNOW HIM WELL...
YEAH.
ARE YOU OKAY?
YEAH. I CAN'T DO ANYTHING TONIGHT. I'M KIND OF DEALING WITH MY DAD... THE FUNERAL'S TOMORROW.
WELL CALL ME WHEN YOU CAN, OR IF YOU NEED ANYTHING...
OKAY.

FUNERAL

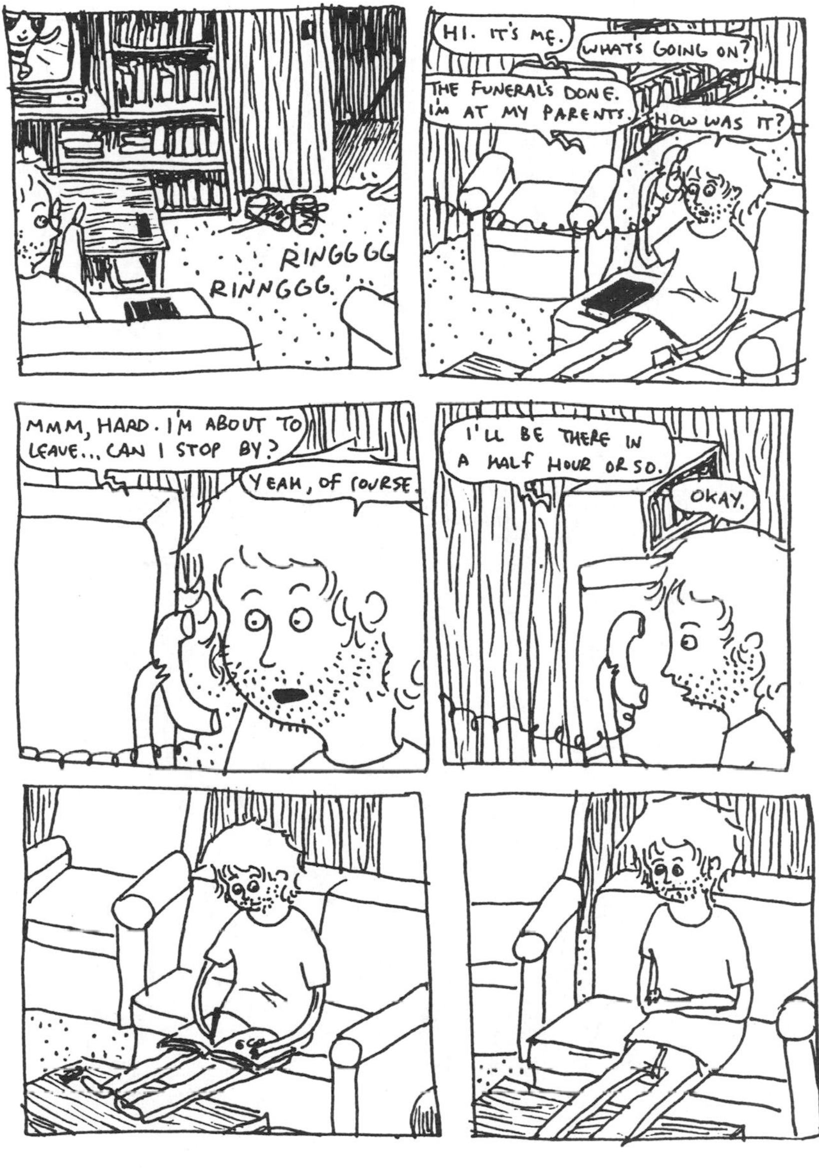

RINGGGG
RINNGGG.
HI. IT'S ME.
WHATS GOING ON?
THE FUNERAL'S DONE. I'M AT MY PARENTS.
HOW WAS IT?
MMM, HARD. I'M ABOUT TO LEAVE... CAN I STOP BY?
YEAH, OF COURSE.
I'LL BE THERE IN A HALF HOUR OR SO.
OKAY.

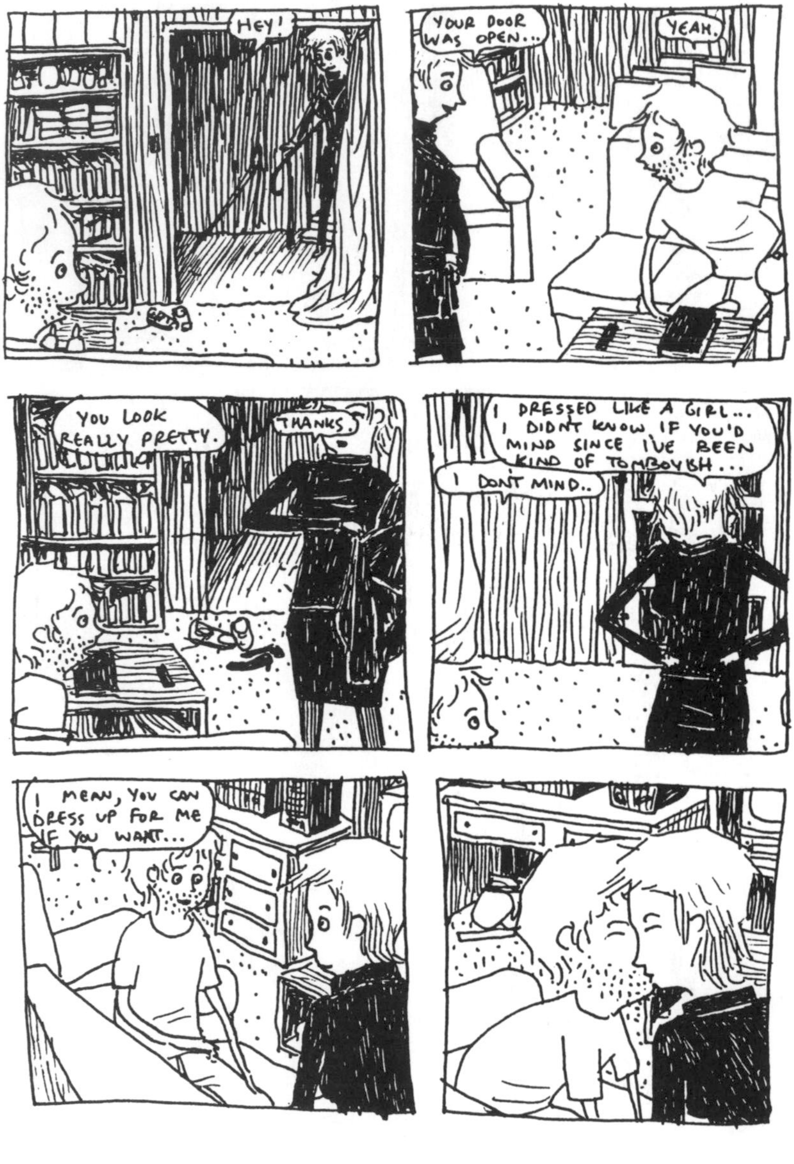
HEY!
YOUR DOOR WAS OPEN...
YEAH.
YOU LOOK REALLY PRETTY.
THANKS.
I DRESSED LIKE A GIRL... I DIDN'T KNOW IF YOU'D MIND SINCE I'VE BEEN KIND OF TOMBOYISH...
I DON'T MIND..
I MEAN, YOU CAN DRESS UP FOR ME IF YOU WANT...

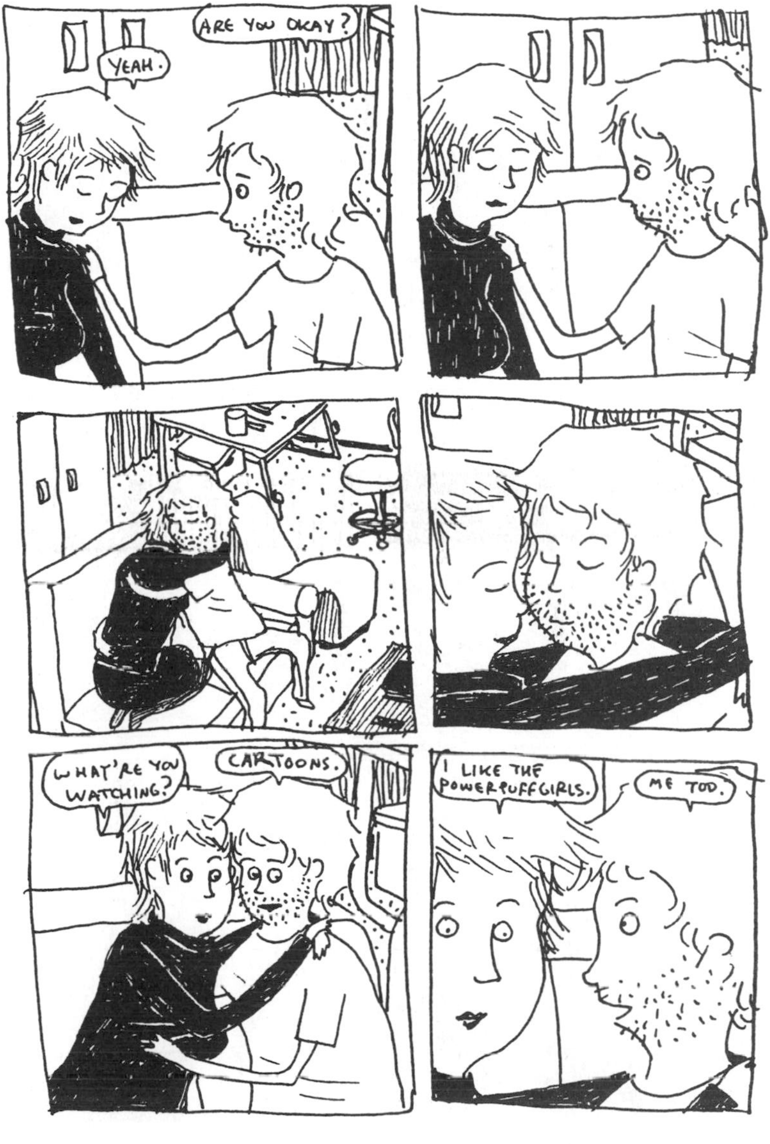
ARE YOU OKAY?
YEAH.
WHAT'RE YOU WATCHING?
CARTOONS.
I LIKE THE POWERPUFFGIRLS.
ME TOO.

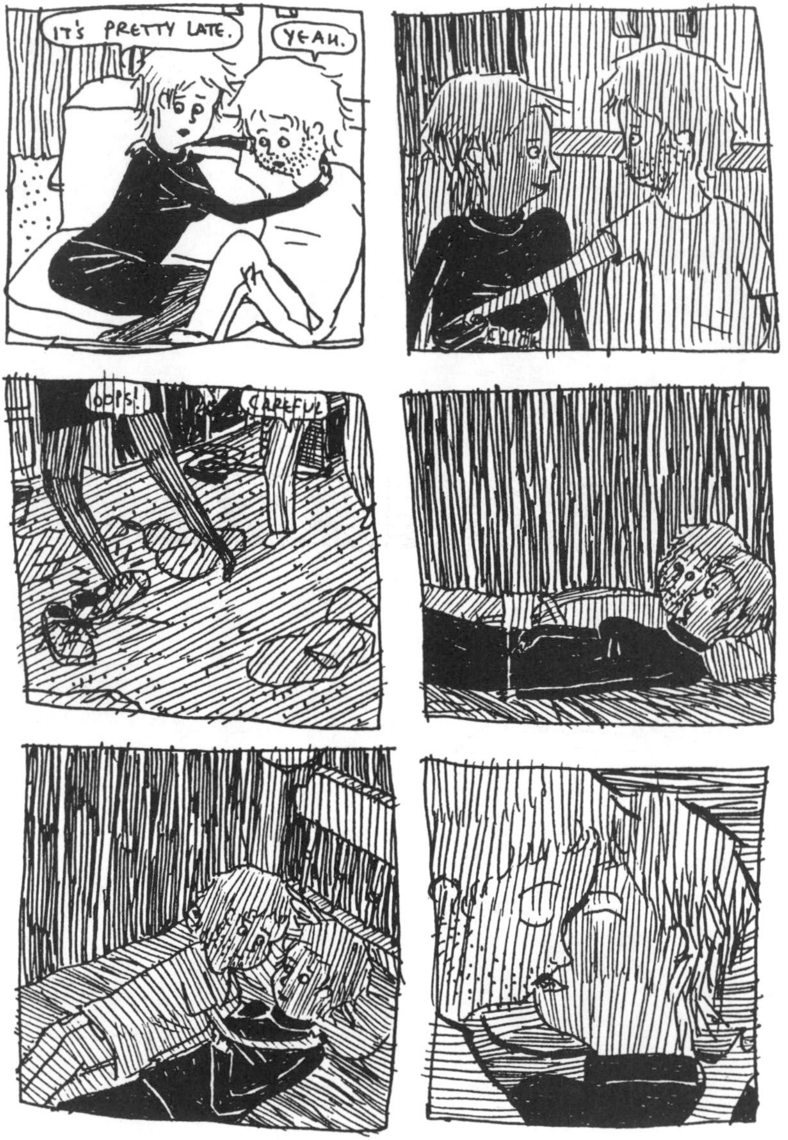
IT'S PRETTY LATE.
YEAH.
OOPS!
CAREFUL

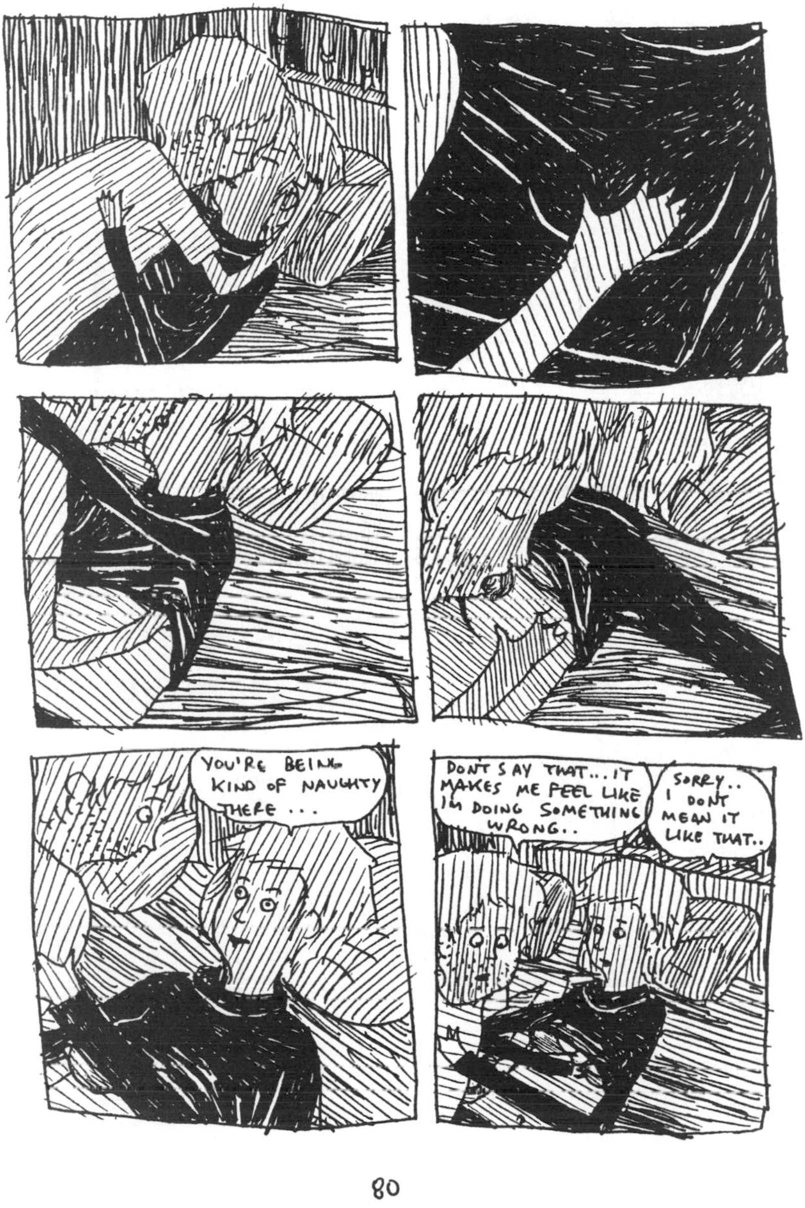
YOU'RE BEING KIND OF NAUGHTY THERE . . .
DON'T SAY THAT... IT MAKES ME FEEL LIKE IM DOING SOMETHING WRONG..
SORRY.. I DONT MEAN IT LIKE THAT..

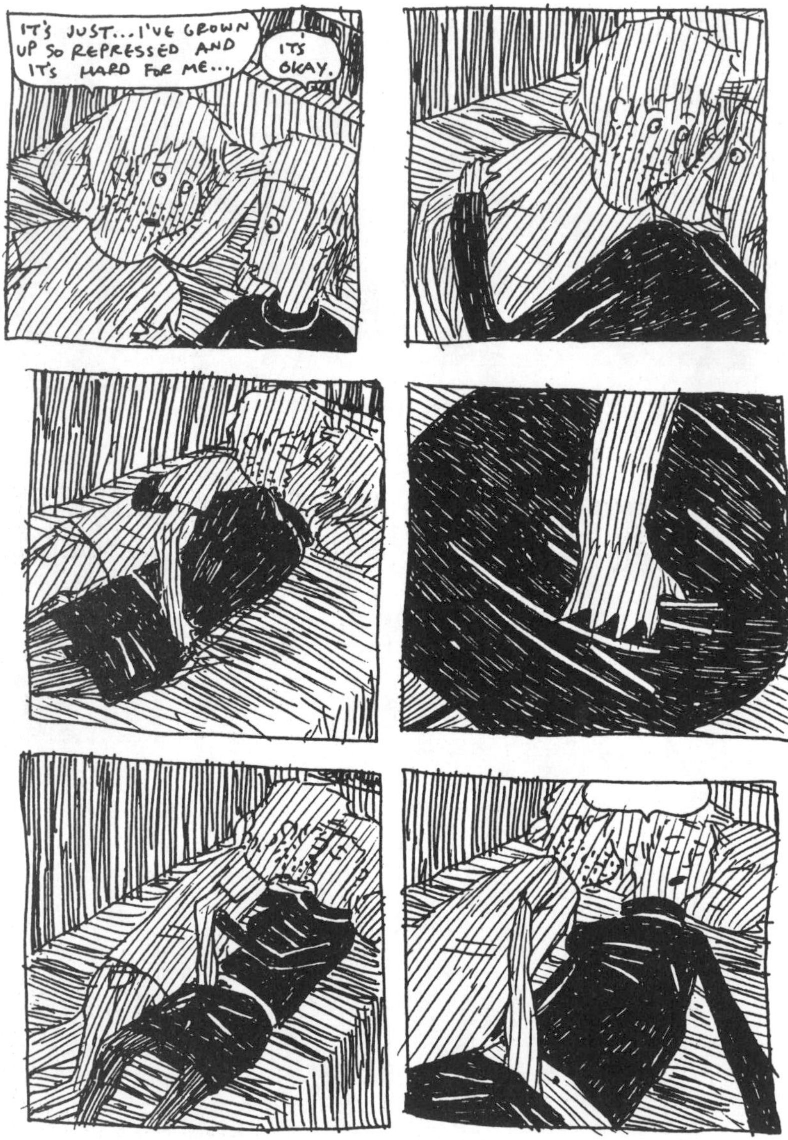
IT'S JUST...I'VE GROWN UP SO REPRESSED AND IT'S HARD FOR ME...
IT'S OKAY.

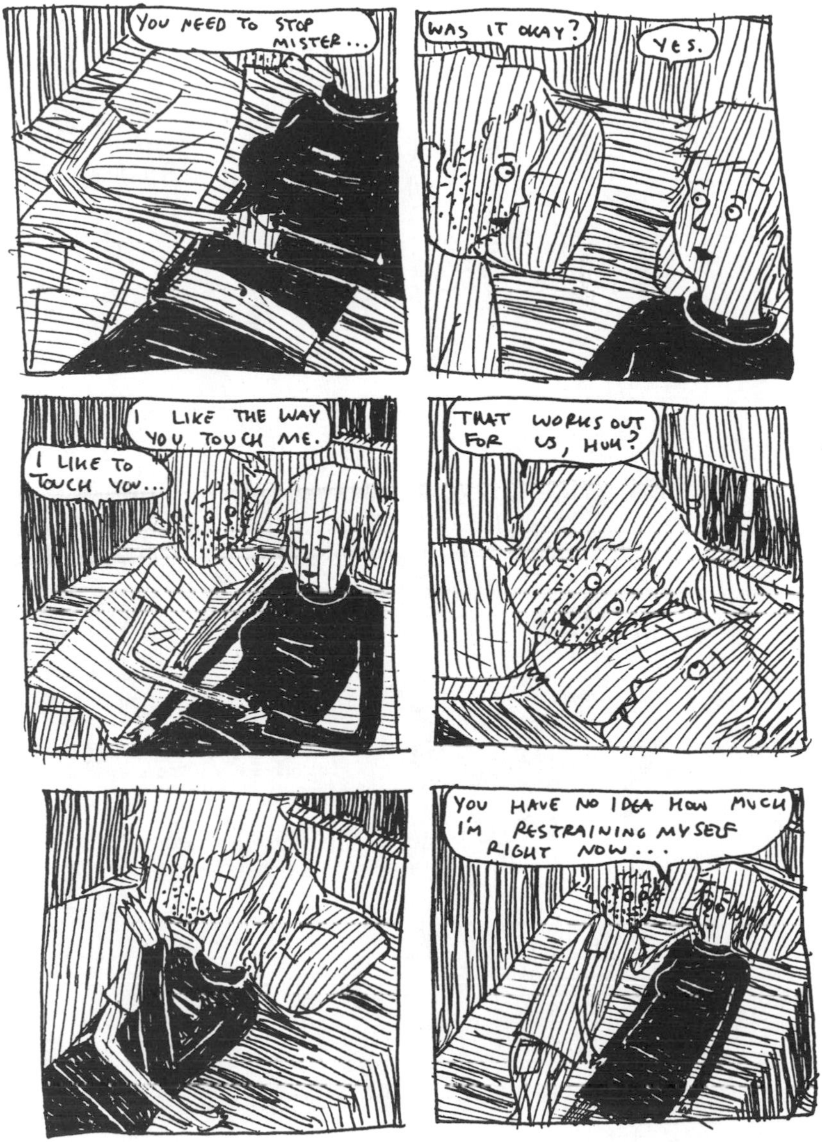
YOU NEED TO STOP MISTER...
WAS IT OKAY?
YES.
I LIKE THE WAY YOU TOUCH ME.
I LIKE TO TOUCH YOU...
THAT WORKS OUT FOR US, HUH?
YOU HAVE NO IDEA HOW MUCH I'M RESTRAINING MYSELF RIGHT NOW...

I WANT TO SO BAD. I JUST WANT TO MAKE SURE FIRST. I WANT YOU TO BE SURE...

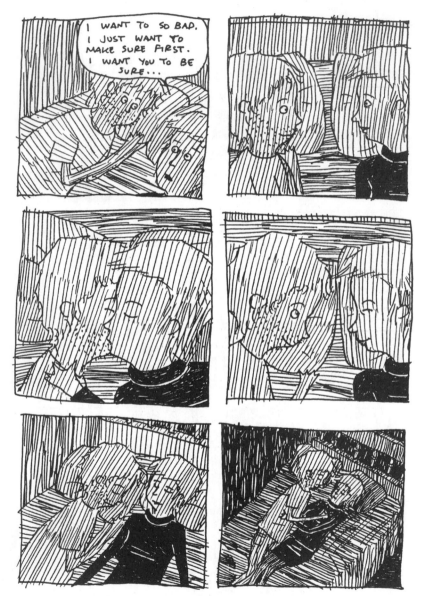

SMOKE BREAK

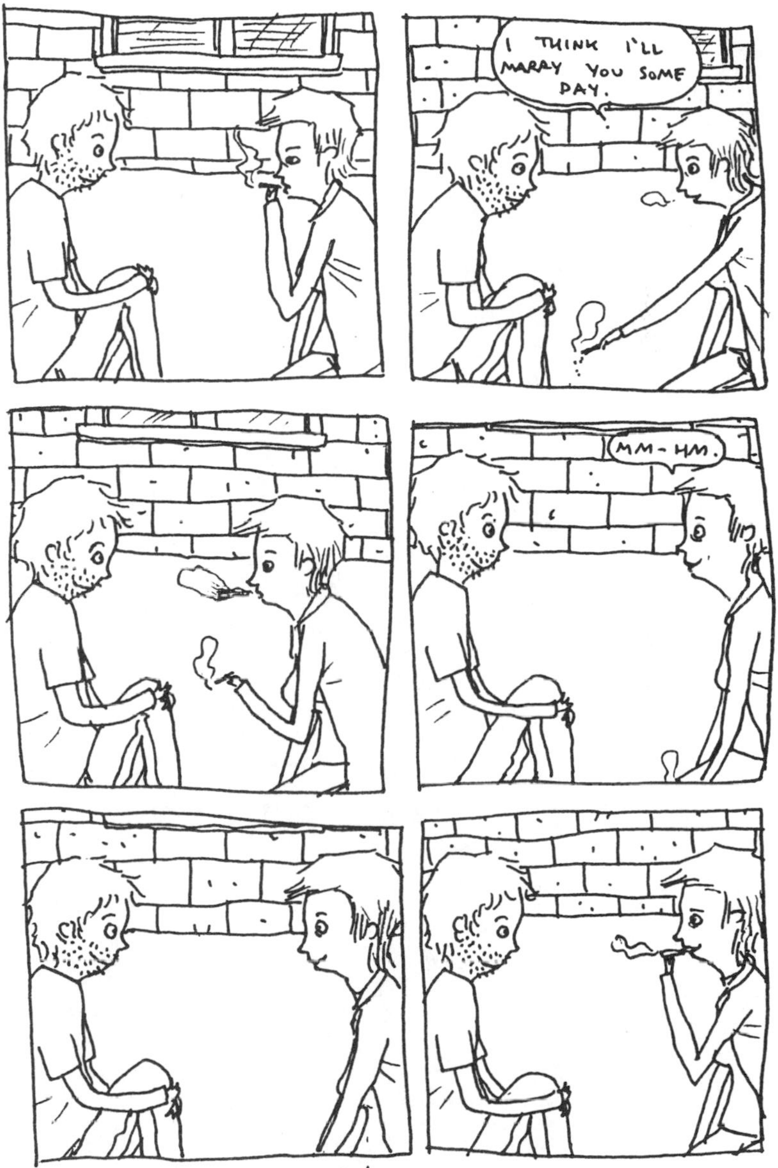
I THINK I'LL MARRY YOU SOME DAY.
MM-HM.

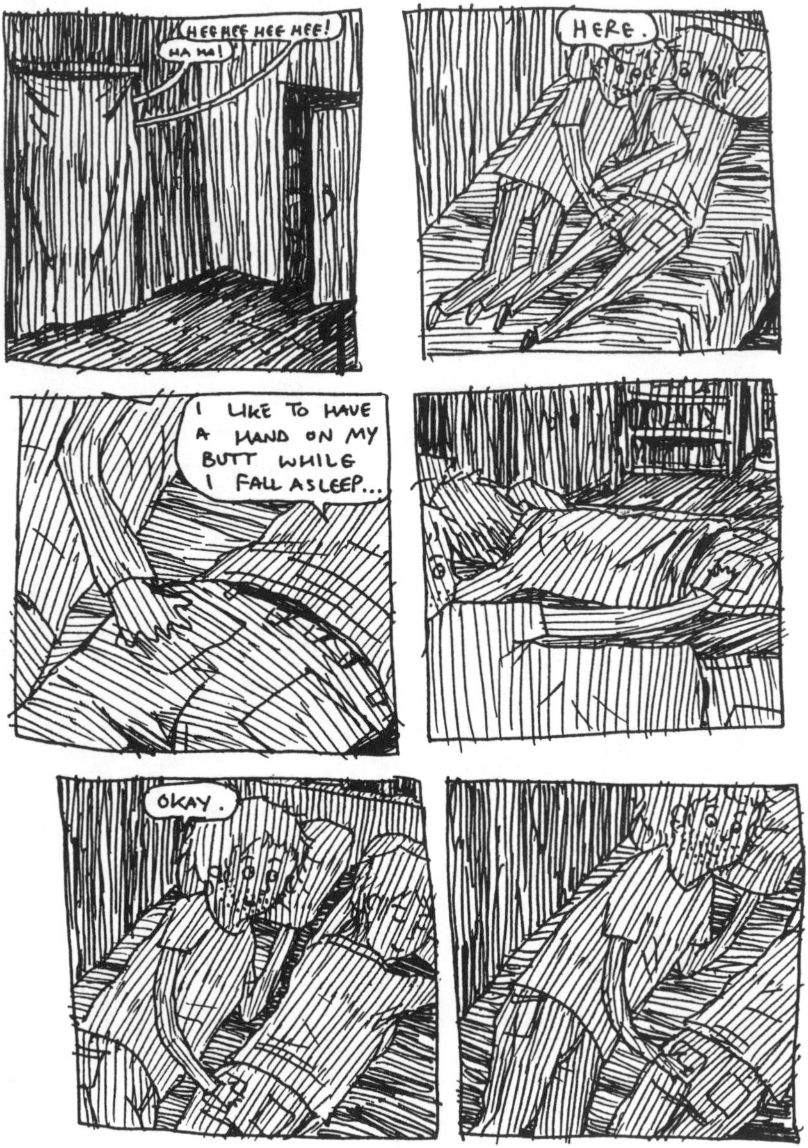
HEE HEE HEE HEE!
HA HA!
HERE.
I LIKE TO HAVE A HAND ON MY BUTT WHILE I FALL ASLEEP...
OKAY.

SOCKS

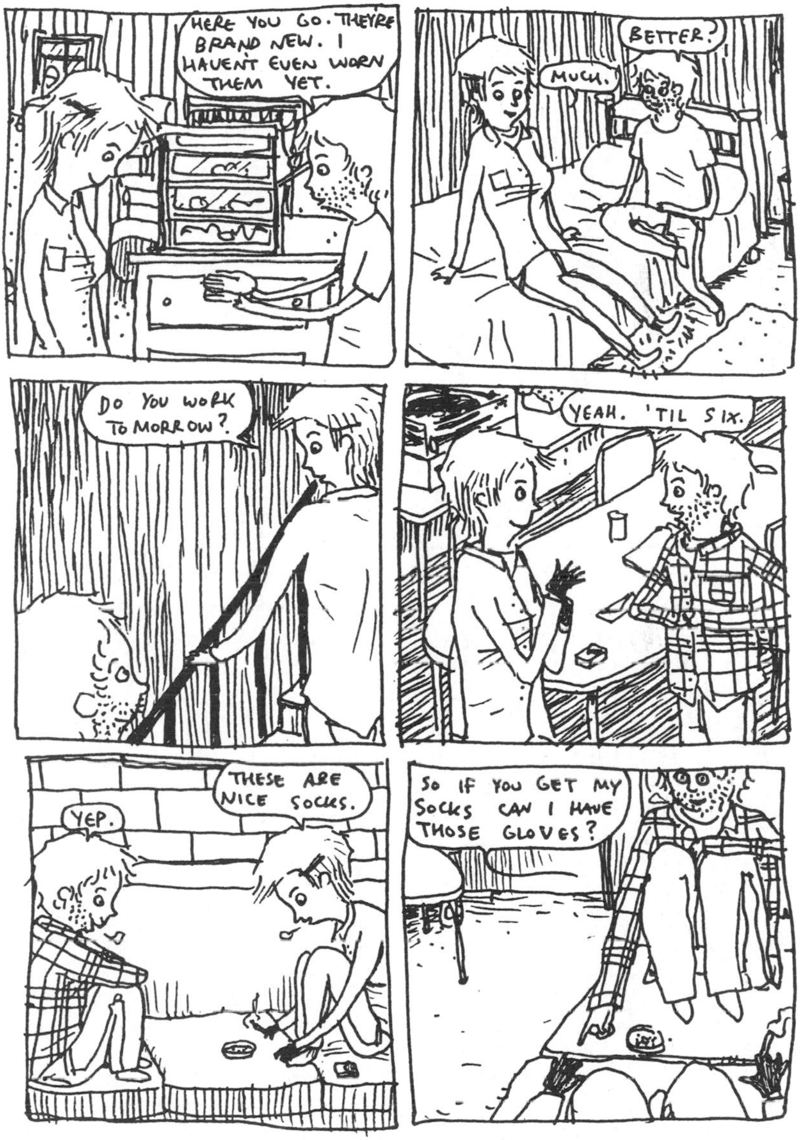
HERE YOU GO. THEY'RE BRAND NEW. I HAVEN'T EVEN WORN THEM YET.
BETTER?
MUCH.
DO YOU WORK TOMORROW?
YEAH. 'TIL SIX.
THESE ARE NICE SOCKS.
YEP.
SO IF YOU GET MY SOCKS CAN I HAVE THOSE GLOVES?

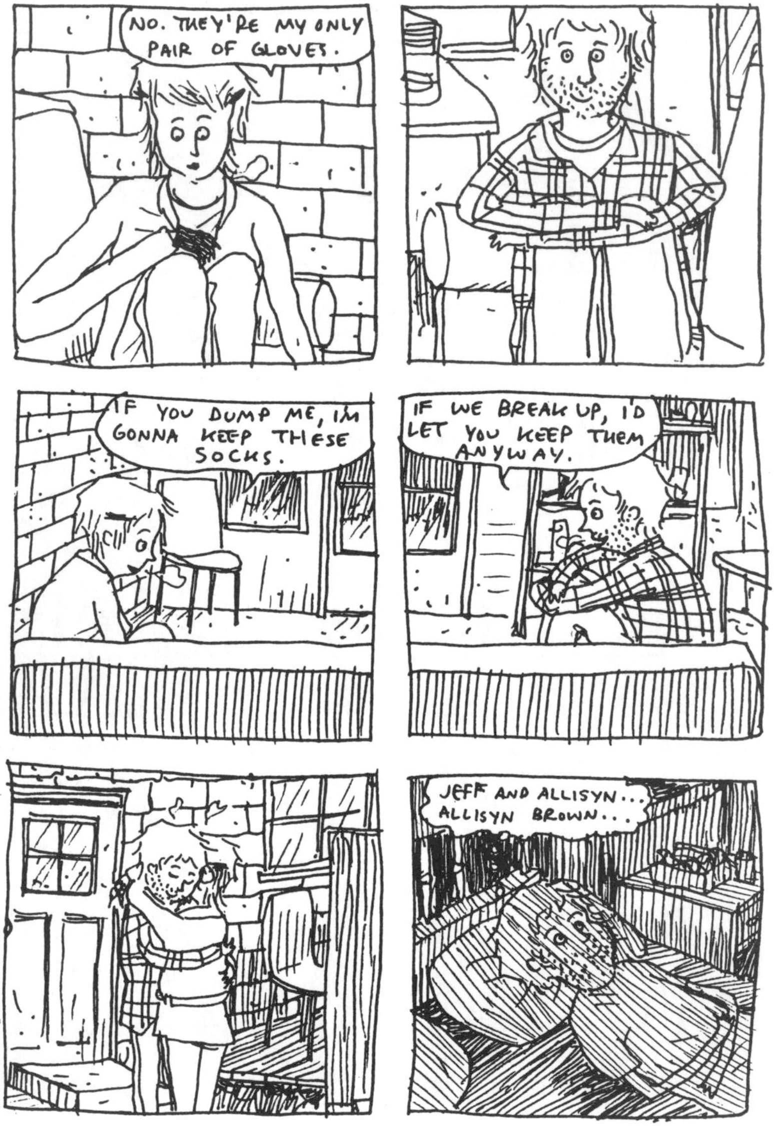
NO. THEY'RE MY ONLY PAIR OF GLOVES.
IF YOU DUMP ME, I'M GONNA KEEP THESE SOCKS.
IF WE BREAK UP, I'D LET YOU KEEP THEM ANYWAY.
JEFF AND ALLISYN... ALLISYN BROWN...

CIDERHOUSE RULES

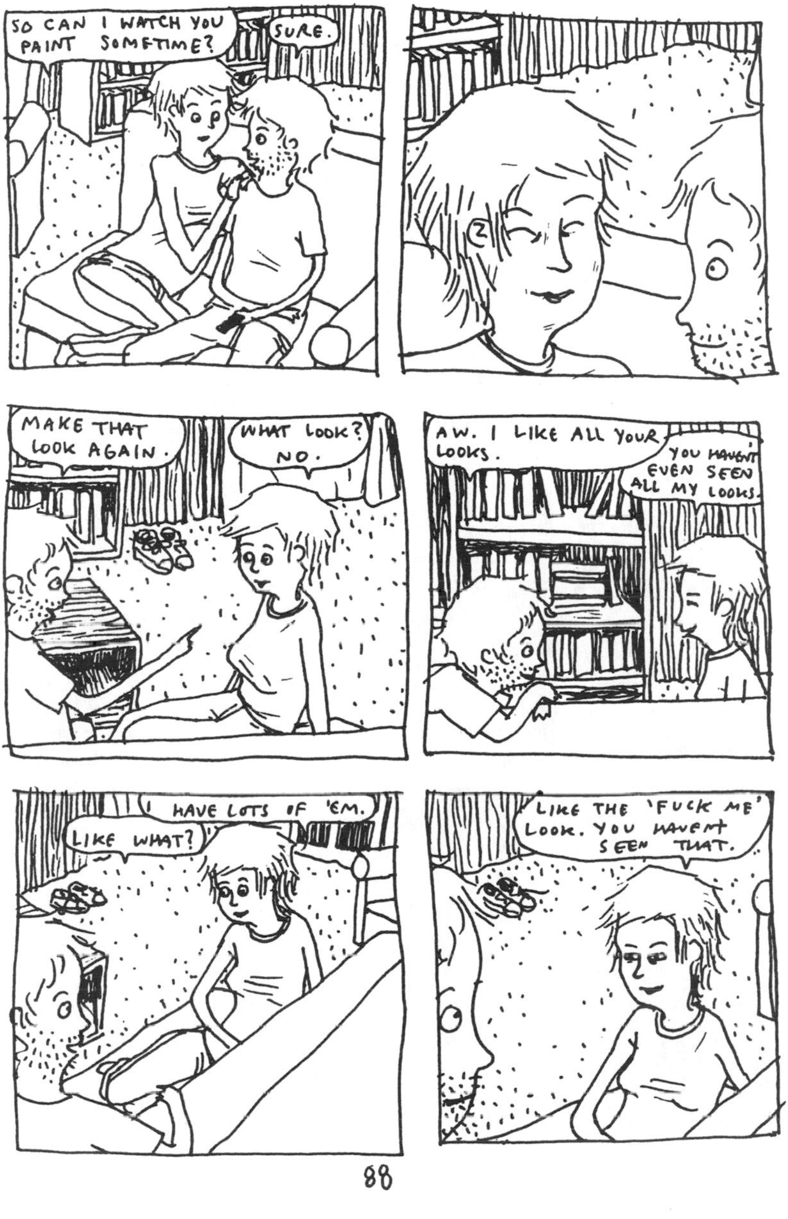
SO CAN I WATCH YOU PAINT SOMETIME?
SURE.
MAKE THAT LOOK AGAIN.
WHAT LOOK? NO.
AW. I LIKE ALL YOUR LOOKS.
YOU HAVEN'T EVEN SEEN ALL MY LOOKS.
I HAVE LOTS OF 'EM.
LIKE WHAT?
LIKE THE 'FUCK ME' LOOK. YOU HAVENT SEEN THAT.

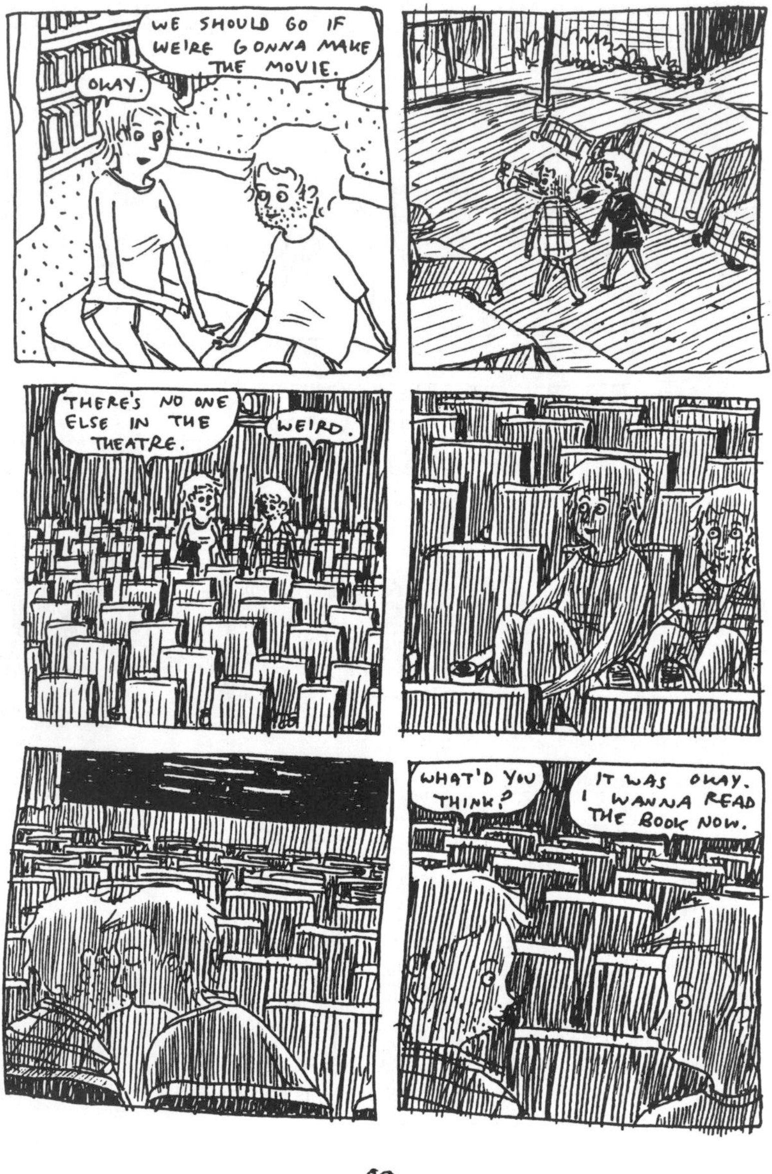
WE SHOULD GO IF WE'RE GONNA MAKE THE MOVIE.
OKAY.
THERE'S NO ONE ELSE IN THE THEATRE.
WEIRD.
WHAT'D YOU THINK?
IT WAS OKAY. I WANNA READ THE BOOK NOW.

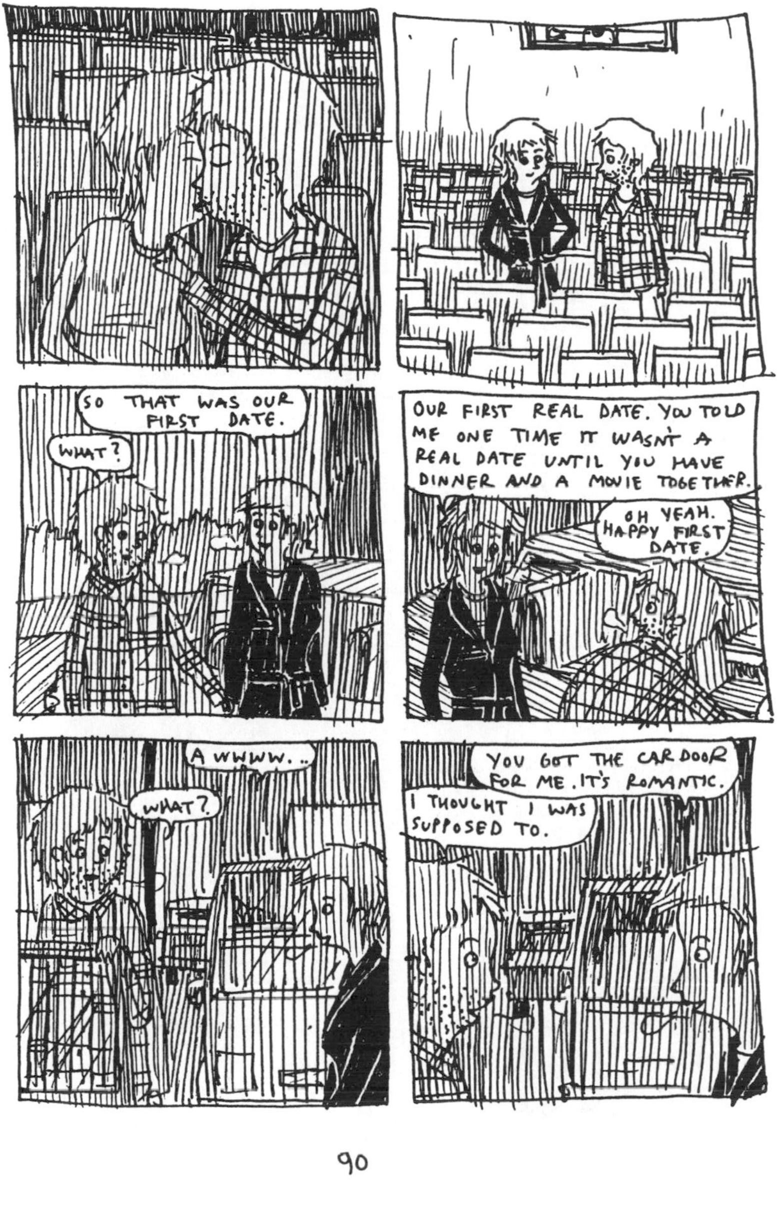
SO THAT WAS OUR FIRST DATE.
WHAT?
OUR FIRST REAL DATE. YOU TOLD ME ONE TIME IT WASN'T A REAL DATE UNTIL YOU HAVE DINNER AND A MOVIE TOGETHER.
OH YEAH. HAPPY FIRST DATE.
AWWWW...
WHAT?
YOU GOT THE CAR DOOR FOR ME. IT'S ROMANTIC.
I THOUGHT I WAS SUPPOSED TO.

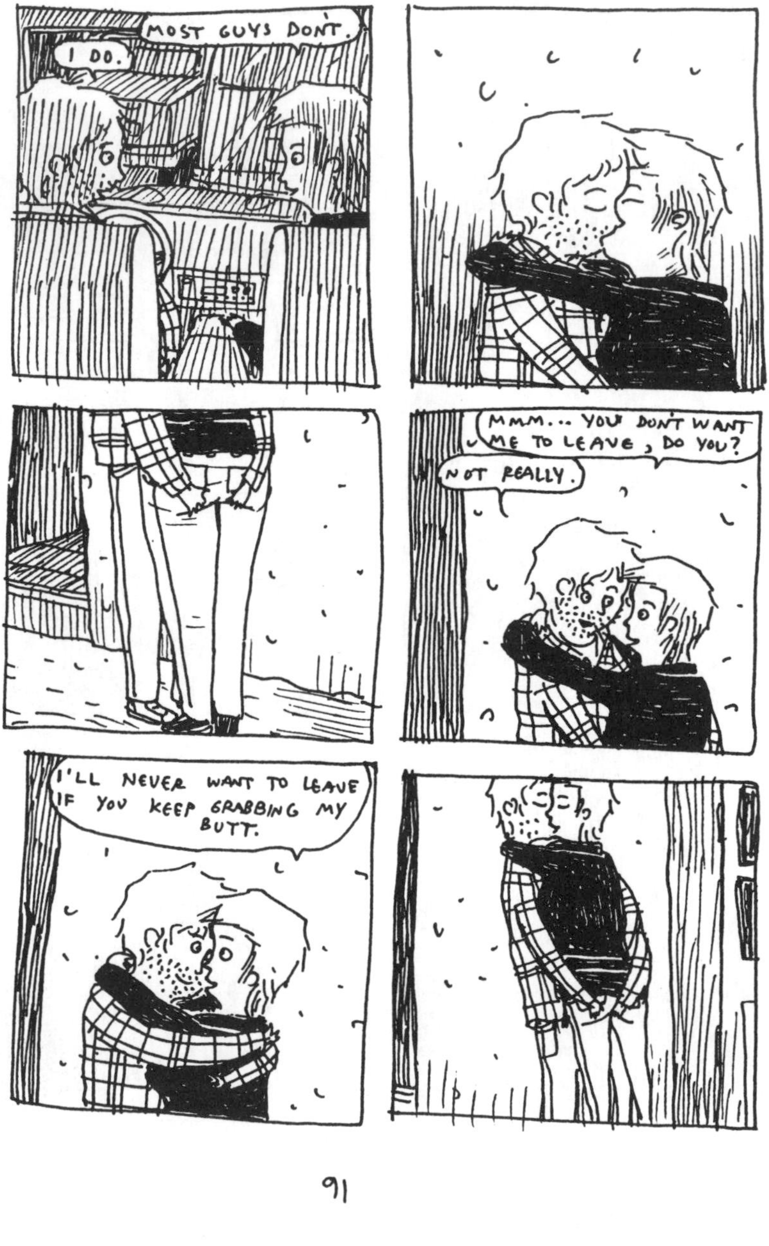
MOST GUYS DON'T.
I DO.
MMM... YOU DON'T WANT ME TO LEAVE, DO YOU?
NOT REALLY.
I'LL NEVER WANT TO LEAVE IF YOU KEEP GRABBING MY BUTT.

PHOTOS

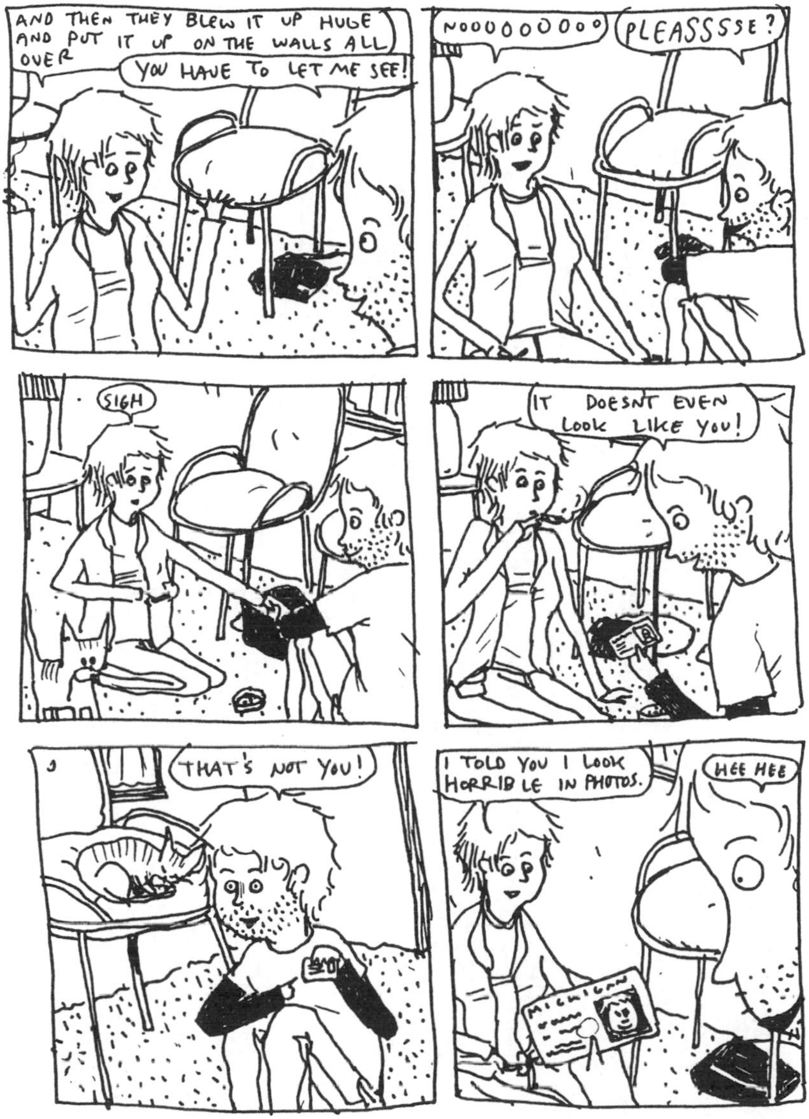
AND THEN THEY BLEW IT UP HUGE AND PUT IT UP ON THE WALLS ALL OVER
YOU HAVE TO LET ME SEE!
NOOOOOOOOOO
PLEASSSSE?
SIGH
IT DOESNT EVEN LOOK LIKE YOU!
THAT'S NOT YOU!
I TOLD YOU I LOOK HORRIBLE IN PHOTOS.
HEE HEE
MICHIGAN

SCRUBS

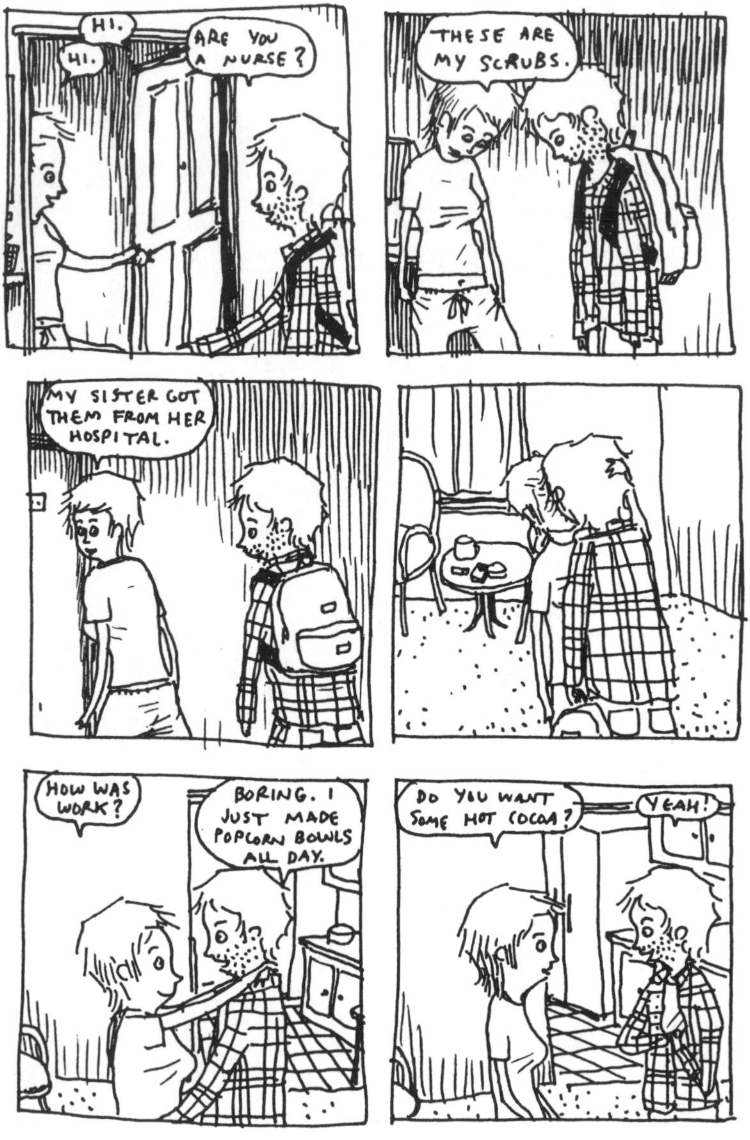
HI.
HI.
ARE YOU A NURSE?
THESE ARE MY SCRUBS.
MY SISTER GOT THEM FROM HER HOSPITAL.
HOW WAS WORK?
BORING. I JUST MADE POPCORN BOWLS ALL DAY.
DO YOU WANT SOME HOT COCOA?
YEAH!

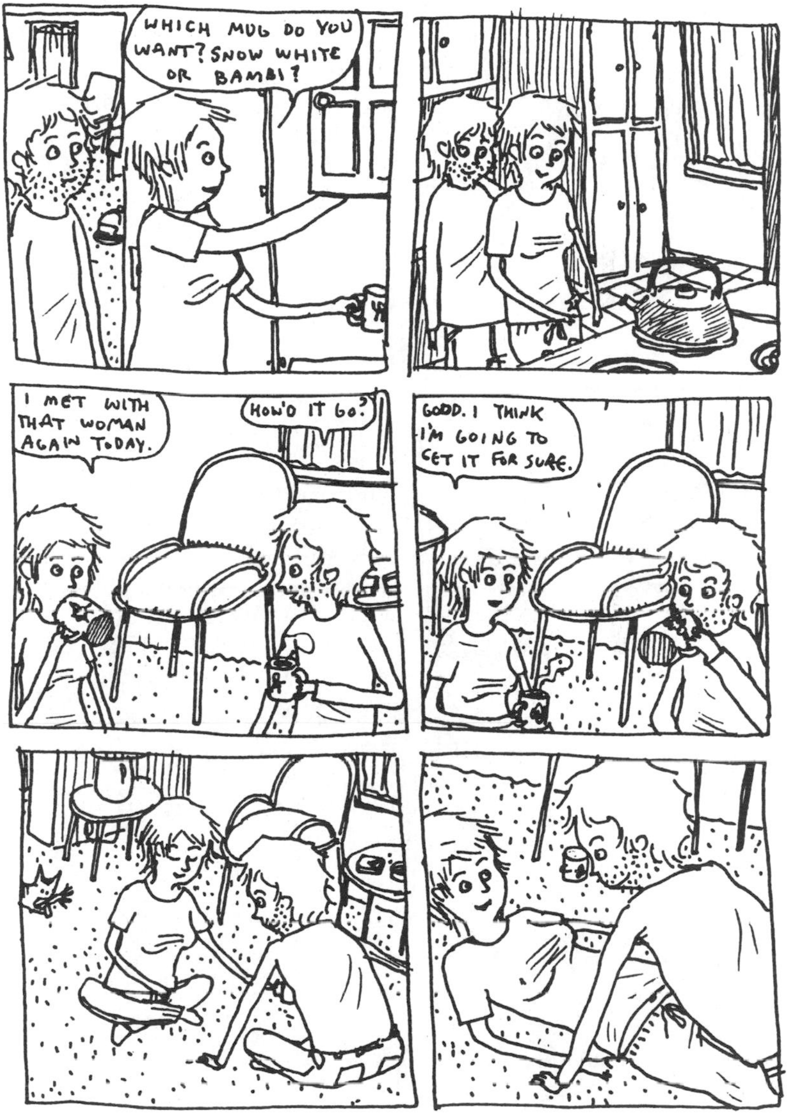
WHICH MUG DO YOU WANT? SNOW WHITE OR BAMBI?
I MET WITH THAT WOMAN AGAIN TODAY.
HOW'D IT GO?
GOOD. I THINK I'M GOING TO GET IT FOR SURE.

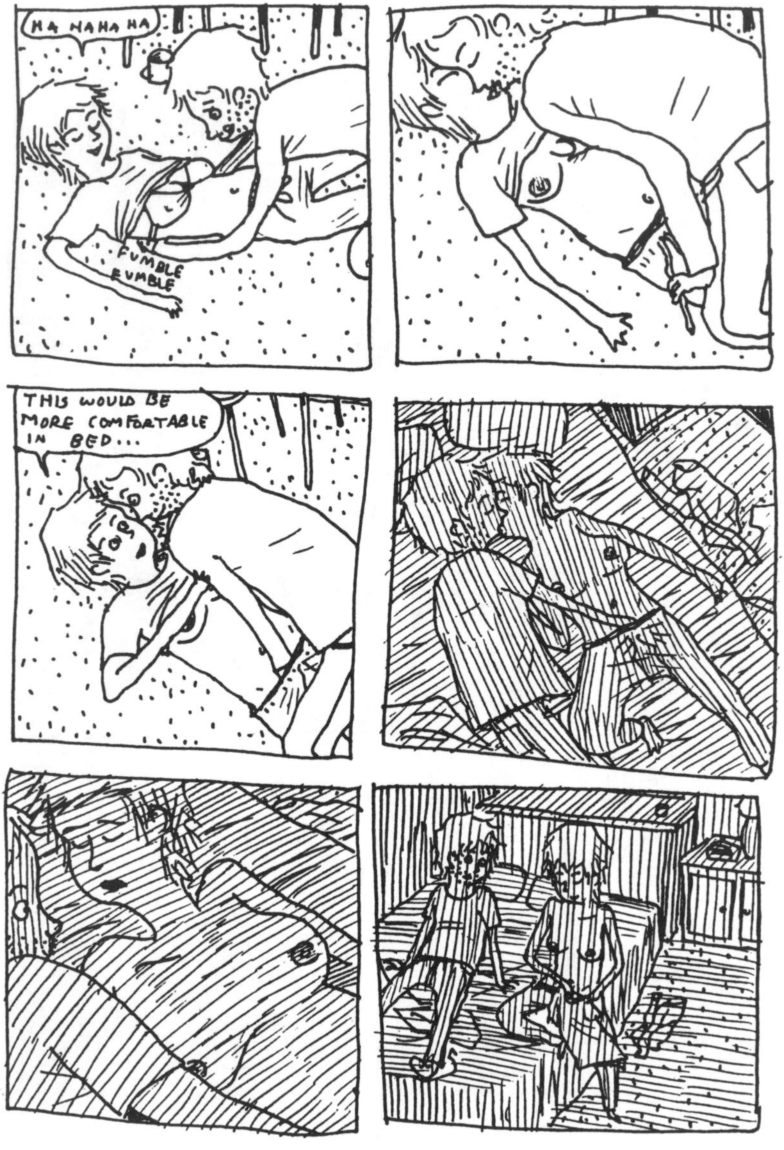
HA HAHAHA
FUMBLE
FUMBLE
THIS WOULD BE MORE COMFORTABLE IN BED...

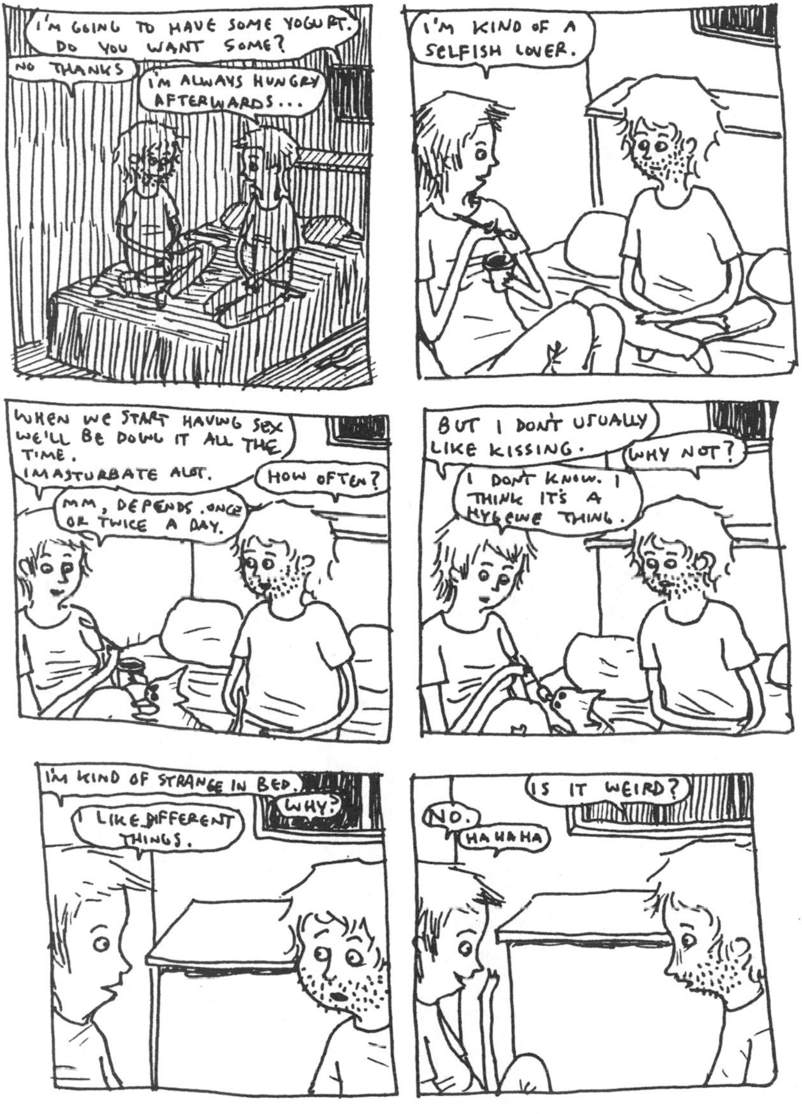
I'M GOING TO HAVE SOME YOGURT. DO YOU WANT SOME?
NO THANKS
I'M ALWAYS HUNGRY AFTERWARDS...
I'M KIND OF A SELFISH LOVER.
WHEN WE START HAVING SEX WE'LL BE DOING IT ALL THE TIME. I MASTURBATE ALOT.
HOW OFTEN?
MM, DEPENDS. ONCE OR TWICE A DAY.
BUT I DON'T USUALLY LIKE KISSING.
WHY NOT?
I DON'T KNOW. I THINK IT'S A HYGIENE THING.
I'M KIND OF STRANGE IN BED.
WHY?
I LIKE DIFFERENT THINGS.
IS IT WEIRD?
NO.
HAHAHA

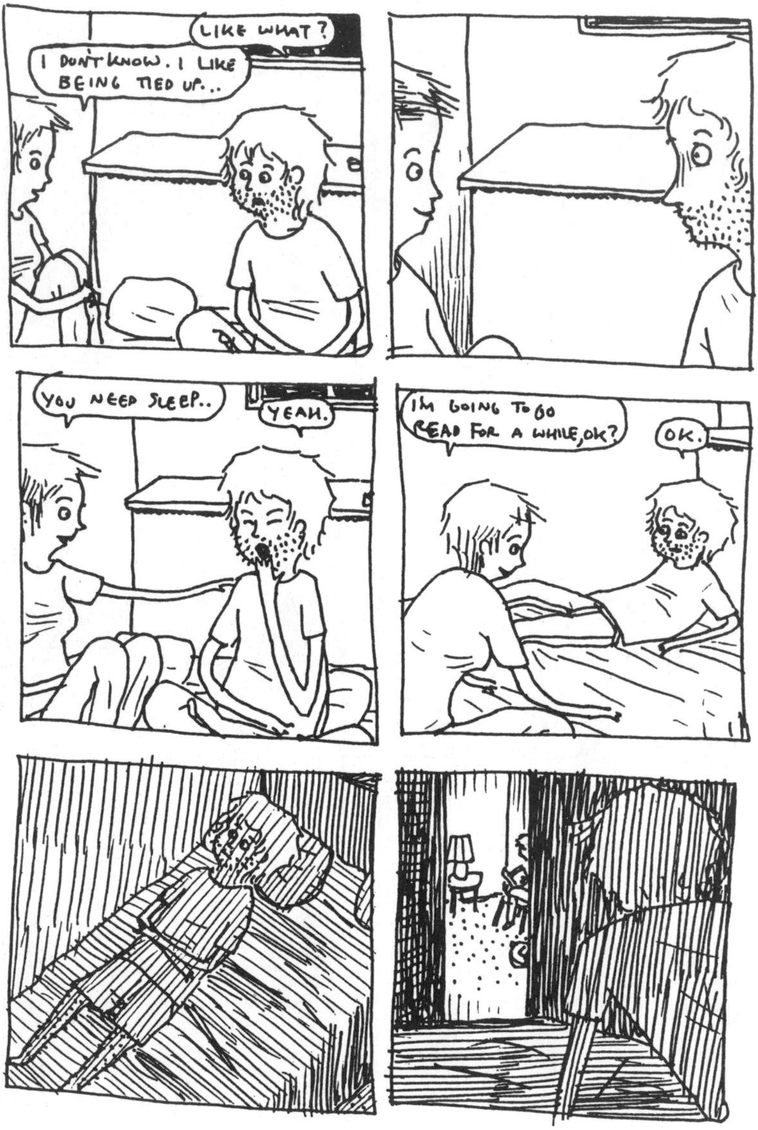
LIKE WHAT?
I DON'T KNOW. I LIKE BEING TIED UP..
YOU NEED SLEEP..
YEAH.
I'M GOING TO GO READ FOR A WHILE, OK?
OK.

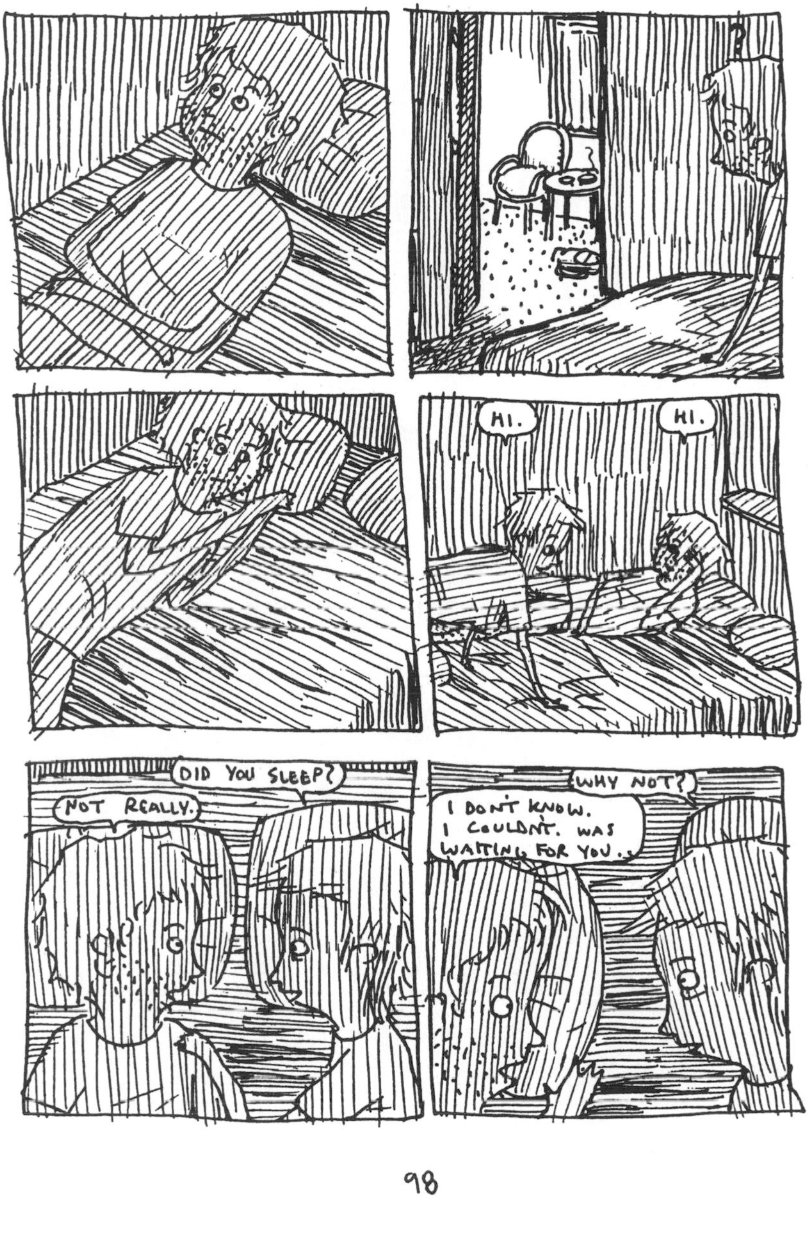
?
HI.
HI.
DID YOU SLEEP?
NOT REALLY.
WHY NOT?
I DON'T KNOW.
I COULDN'T. WAS
WAITING FOR YOU..

SWALLOW

PURSUIT

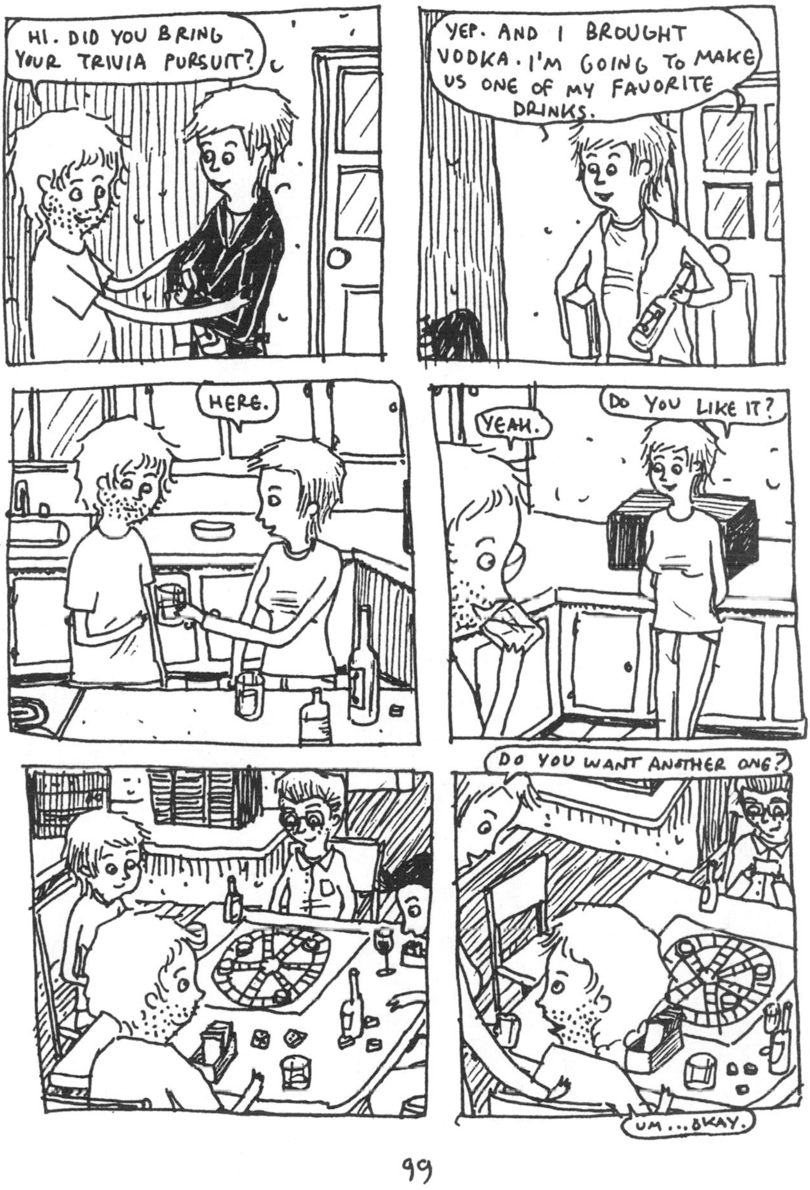
HI. DID YOU BRING YOUR TRIVIA PURSUIT?
YEP. AND I BROUGHT VODKA. I'M GOING TO MAKE US ONE OF MY FAVORITE DRINKS.
HERE.
DO YOU LIKE IT?
YEAH.
DO YOU WANT ANOTHER ONE?
UM...OKAY.

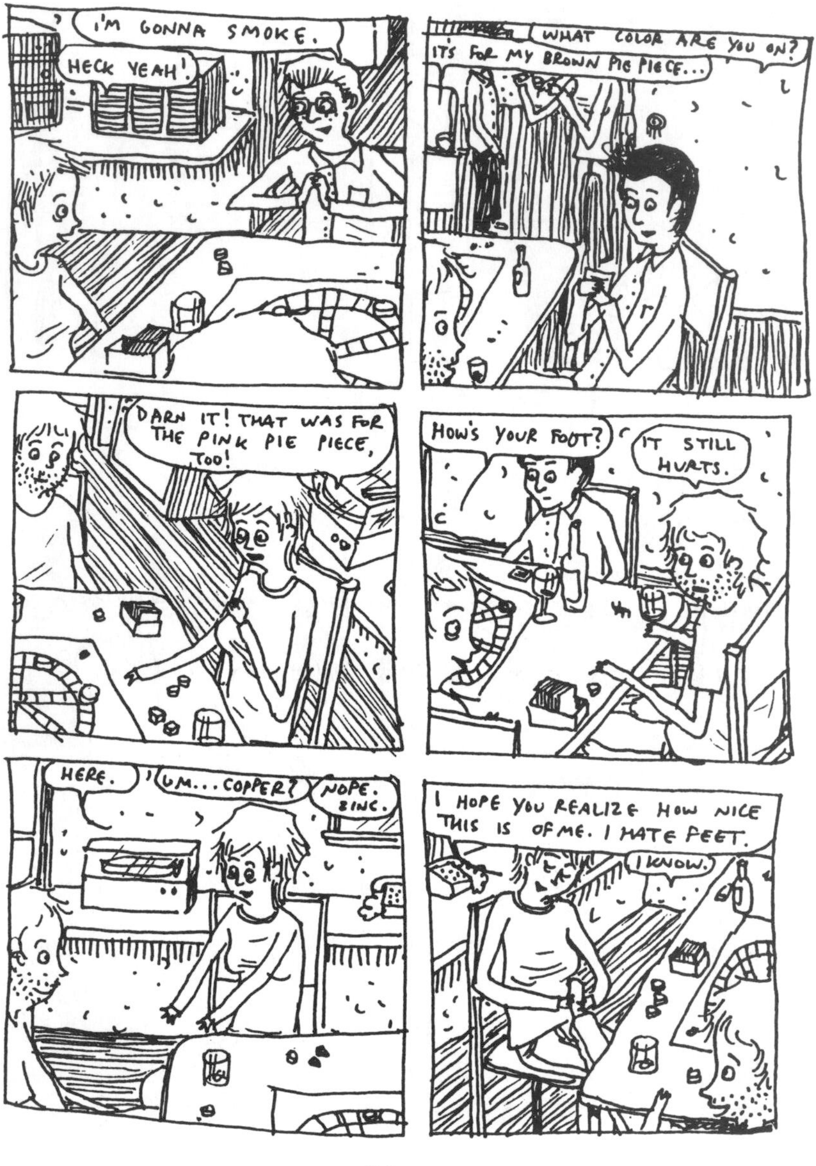
I'M GONNA SMOKE.
HECK YEAH!
WHAT COLOR ARE YOU ON?
IT'S FOR MY BROWN PIE PIECE...
DARN IT! THAT WAS FOR THE PINK PIE PIECE, TOO!
HOW'S YOUR FOOT?
IT STILL HURTS.
HERE.
UM... COPPER?
NOPE. ZINC.
I HOPE YOU REALIZE HOW NICE THIS IS OF ME. I HATE FEET.
I KNOW.

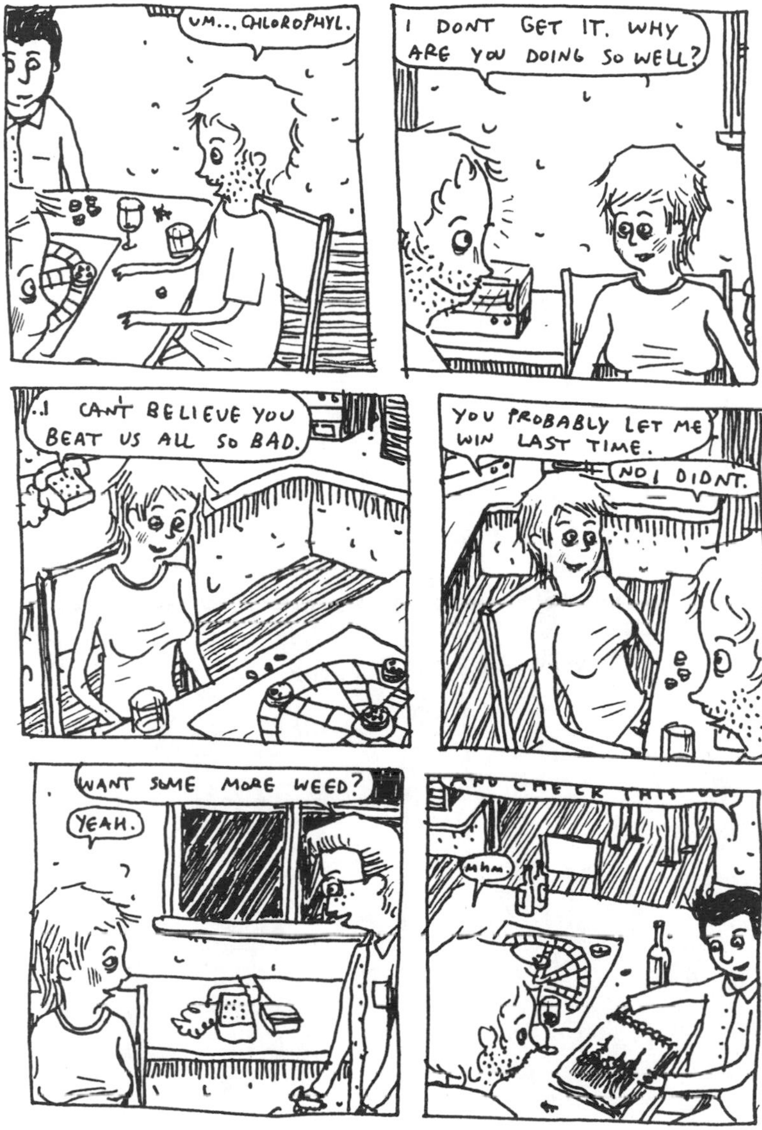
UM... CHLOROPHYL.
I DONT GET IT. WHY ARE YOU DOING SO WELL?
..I CAN'T BELIEVE YOU BEAT US ALL SO BAD.
YOU PROBABLY LET ME WIN LAST TIME.
NO I DIDNT.
WANT SOME MORE WEED?
YEAH.
Mhm.

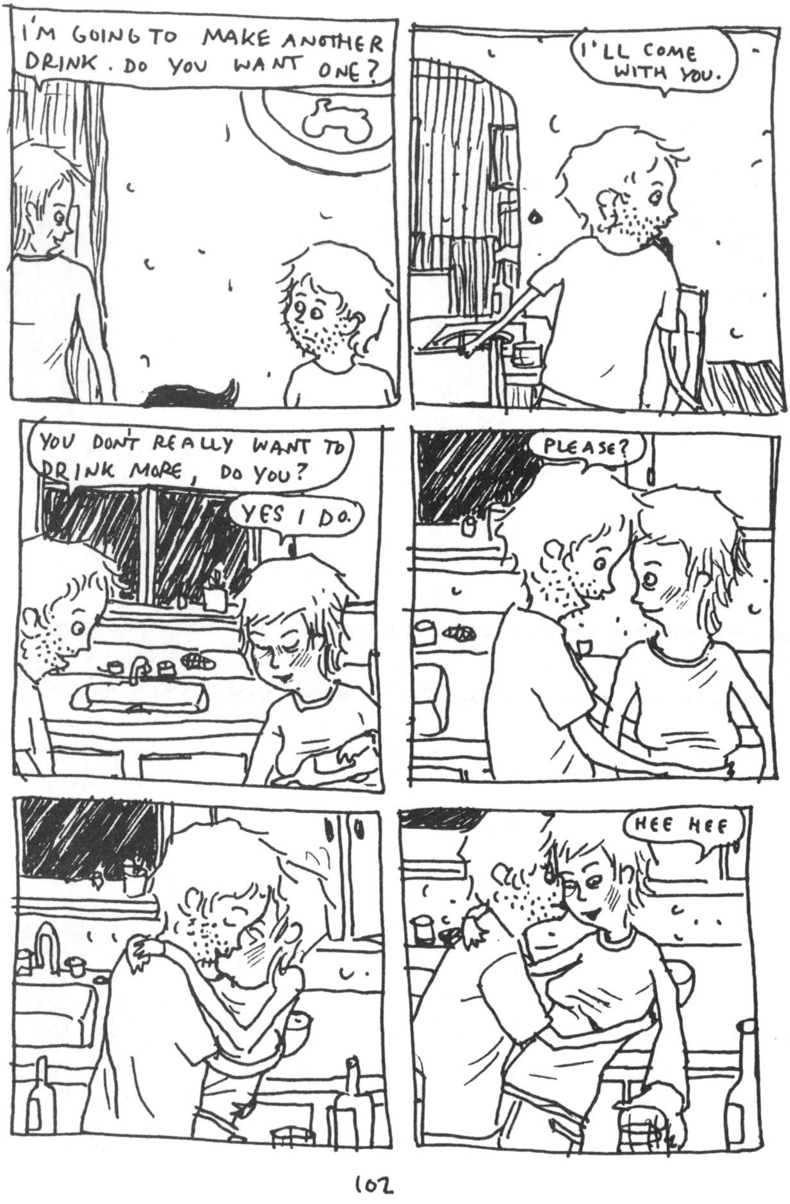
I'M GOING TO MAKE ANOTHER DRINK. DO YOU WANT ONE?
I'LL COME WITH YOU.
YOU DON'T REALLY WANT TO DRINK MORE, DO YOU?
YES I DO.
PLEASE?
HEE HEE

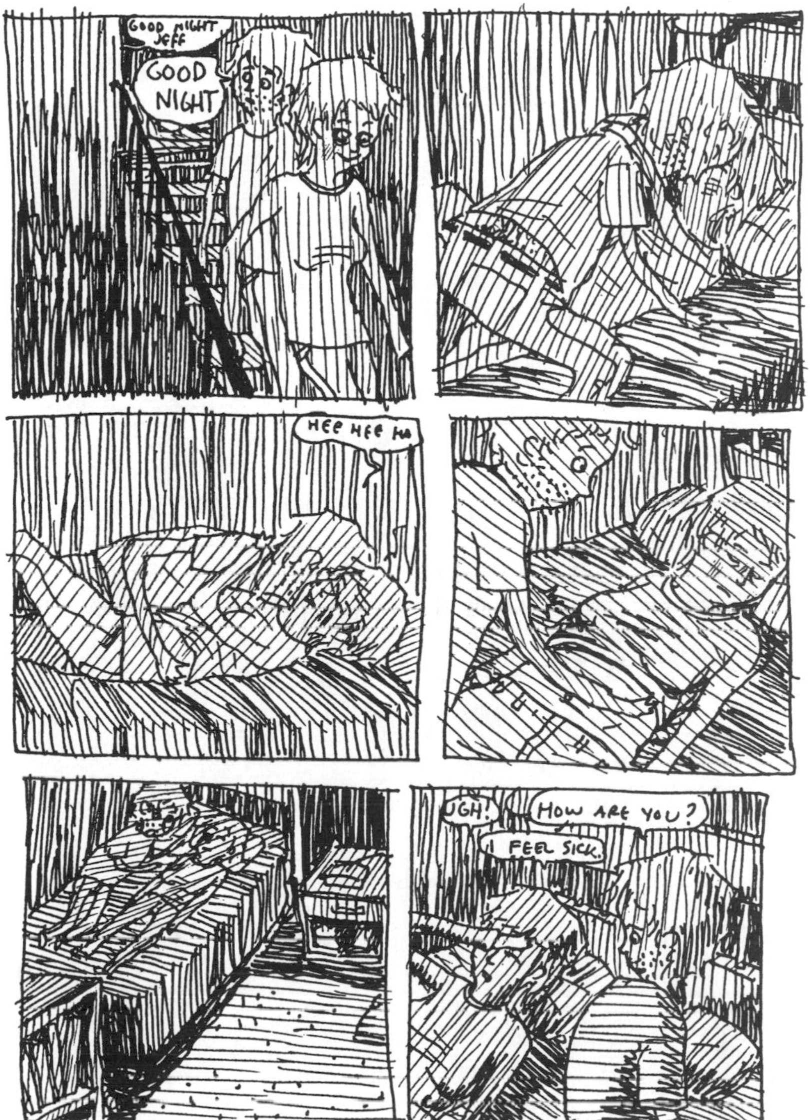
GOOD NIGHT JEFF
GOOD NIGHT
HEE HEE HA
UGH!
HOW ARE YOU?
I FEEL SICK.

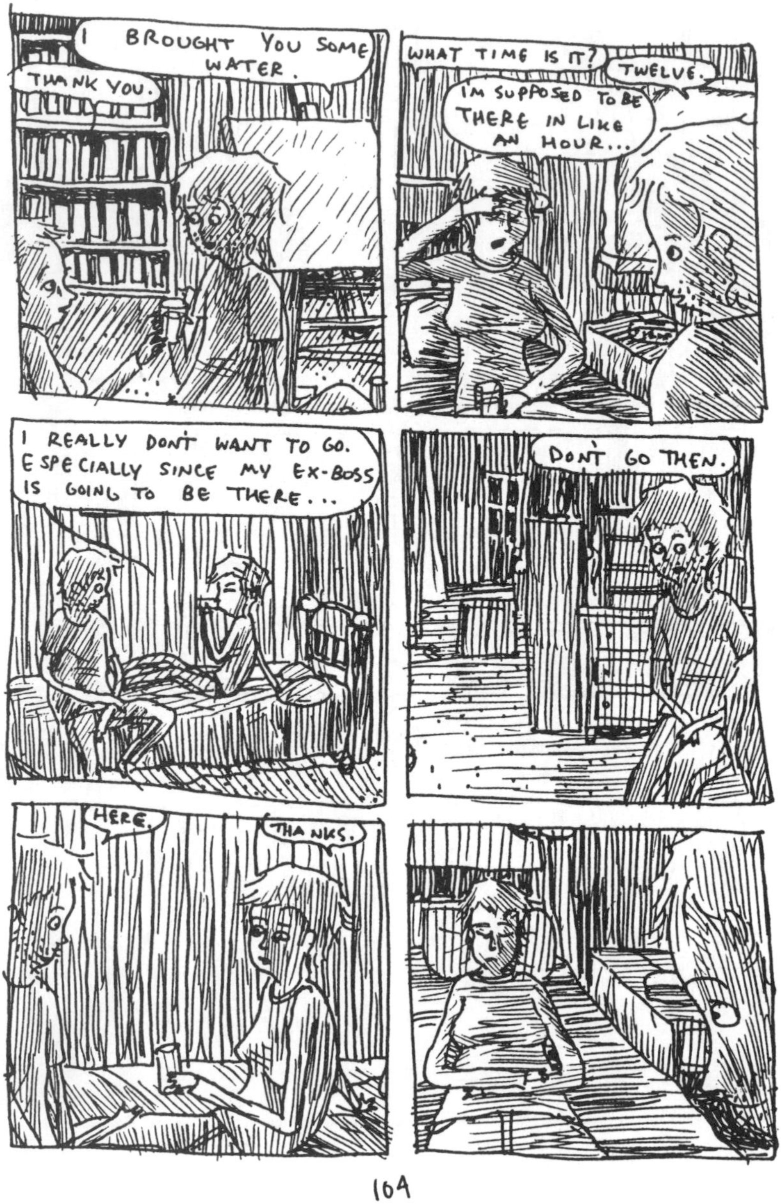
I BROUGHT YOU SOME WATER.
THANK YOU.
WHAT TIME IS IT?
TWELVE.
I'M SUPPOSED TO BE THERE IN LIKE AN HOUR...
I REALLY DON'T WANT TO GO. ESPECIALLY SINCE MY EX-BOSS IS GOING TO BE THERE...
DON'T GO THEN.
HERE.
THANKS.

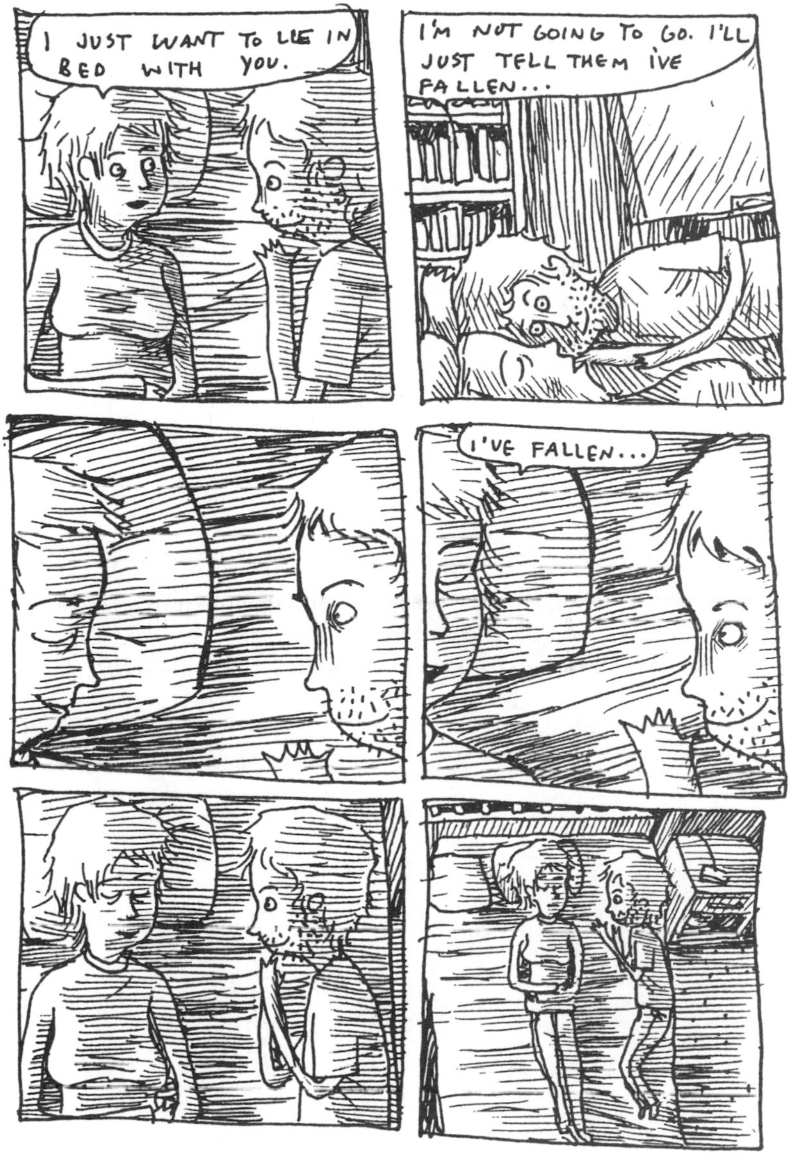
I JUST WANT TO LIE IN BED WITH YOU.
I'M NOT GOING TO GO. I'LL JUST TELL THEM I'VE FALLEN...
I'VE FALLEN...

ANGEL

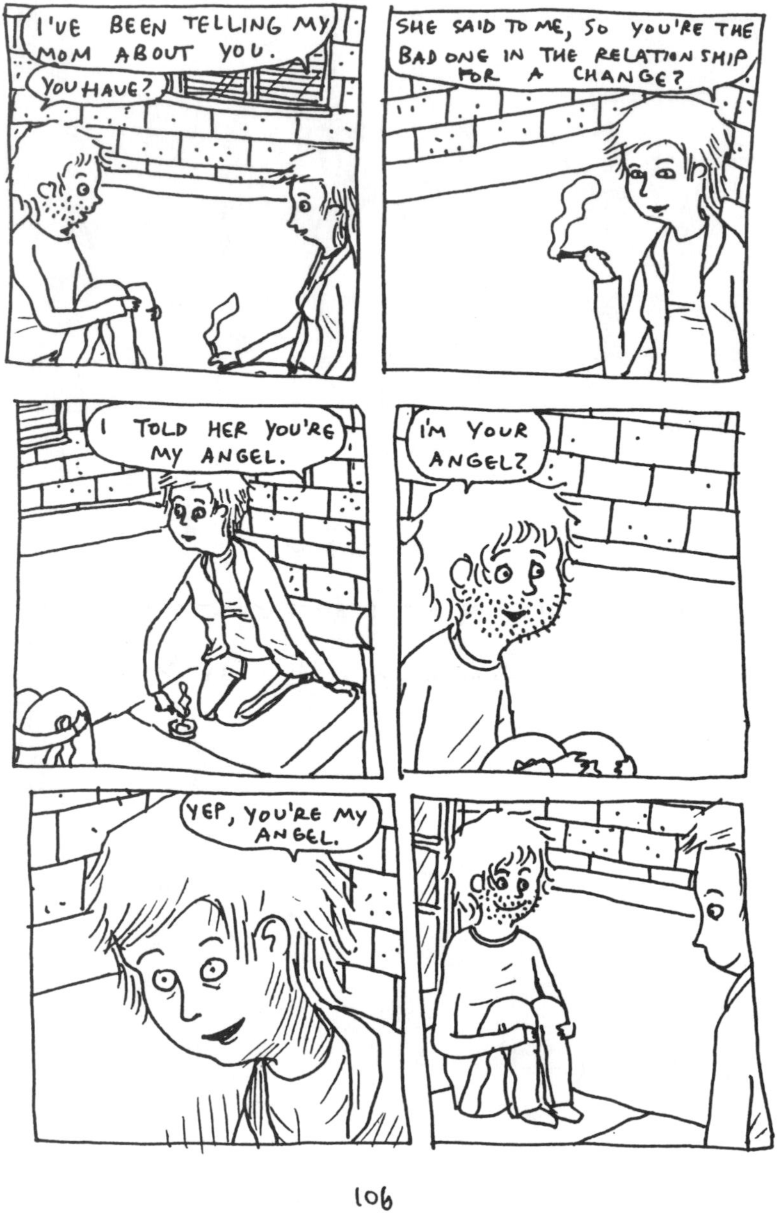

I'VE BEEN TELLING MY MOM ABOUT YOU.
YOU HAVE?
SHE SAID TO ME, SO YOU'RE THE BAD ONE IN THE RELATIONSHIP FOR A CHANGE?
I TOLD HER YOU'RE MY ANGEL.
I'M YOUR ANGEL?
YEP, YOU'RE MY ANGEL.

SURE

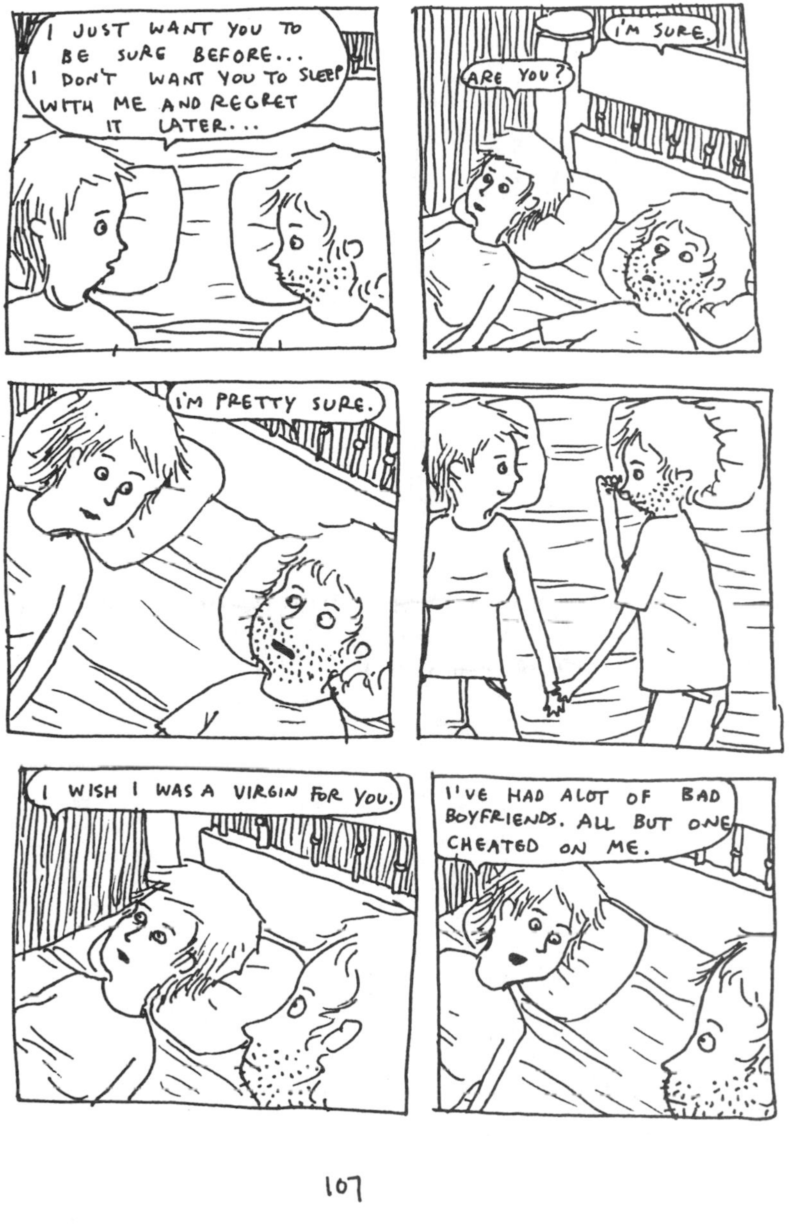

I JUST WANT YOU TO BE SURE BEFORE... I DON'T WANT YOU TO SLEEP WITH ME AND REGRET IT LATER...
ARE YOU?
I'M SURE.
I'M PRETTY SURE.
I WISH I WAS A VIRGIN FOR YOU.
I'VE HAD ALOT OF BAD BOYFRIENDS. ALL BUT ONE CHEATED ON ME.

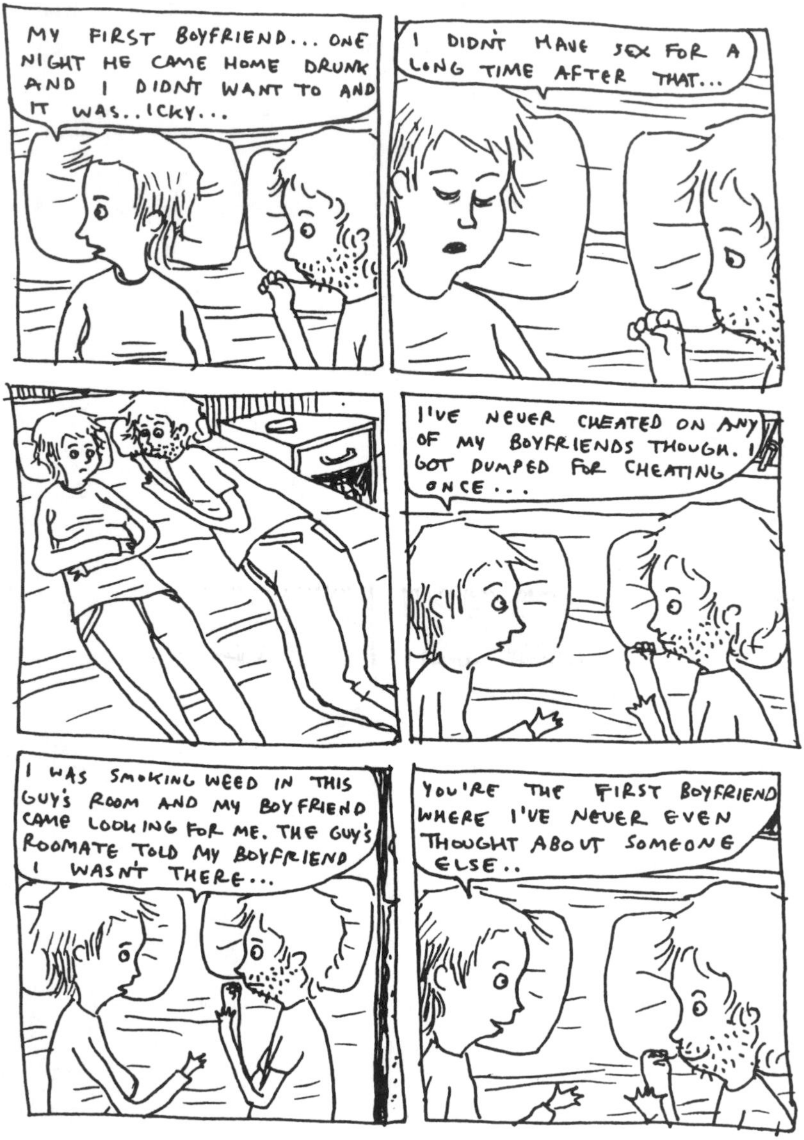
MY FIRST BOYFRIEND... ONE NIGHT HE CAME HOME DRUNK AND I DIDN'T WANT TO AND IT WAS..ICKY...
I DIDN'T HAVE SEX FOR A LONG TIME AFTER THAT...
I'VE NEVER CHEATED ON ANY OF MY BOYFRIENDS THOUGH. I GOT DUMPED FOR CHEATING ONCE...
I WAS SMOKING WEED IN THIS GUY'S ROOM AND MY BOYFRIEND CAME LOOKING FOR ME. THE GUY'S ROOMATE TOLD MY BOYFRIEND I WASN'T THERE...
YOU'RE THE FIRST BOYFRIEND WHERE I'VE NEVER EVEN THOUGHT ABOUT SOMEONE ELSE..

QUIT

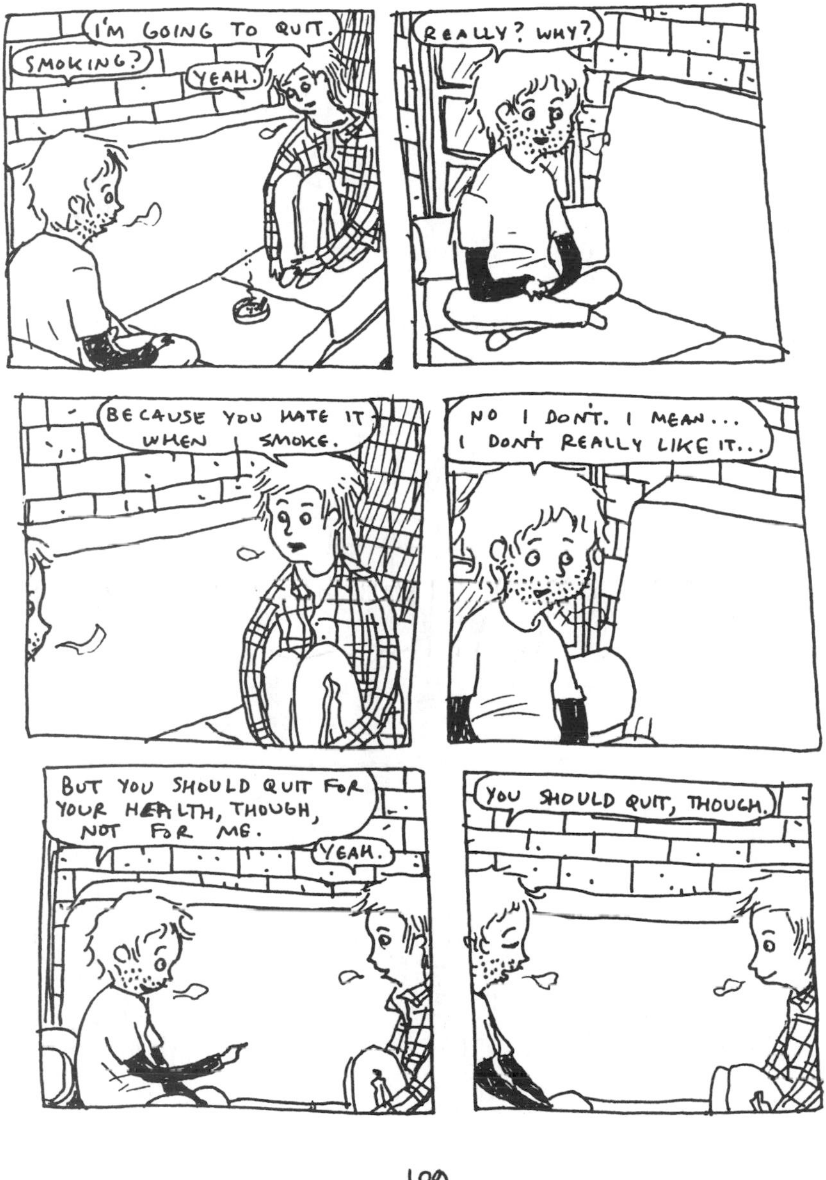
I'M GOING TO QUIT.
SMOKING?
YEAH.
REALLY? WHY?
BECAUSE YOU HATE IT WHEN I SMOKE.
NO I DON'T. I MEAN... I DON'T REALLY LIKE IT...
BUT YOU SHOULD QUIT FOR YOUR HEALTH, THOUGH, NOT FOR ME.
YEAH.
YOU SHOULD QUIT, THOUGH.

I HAD A WEIRD DREAM

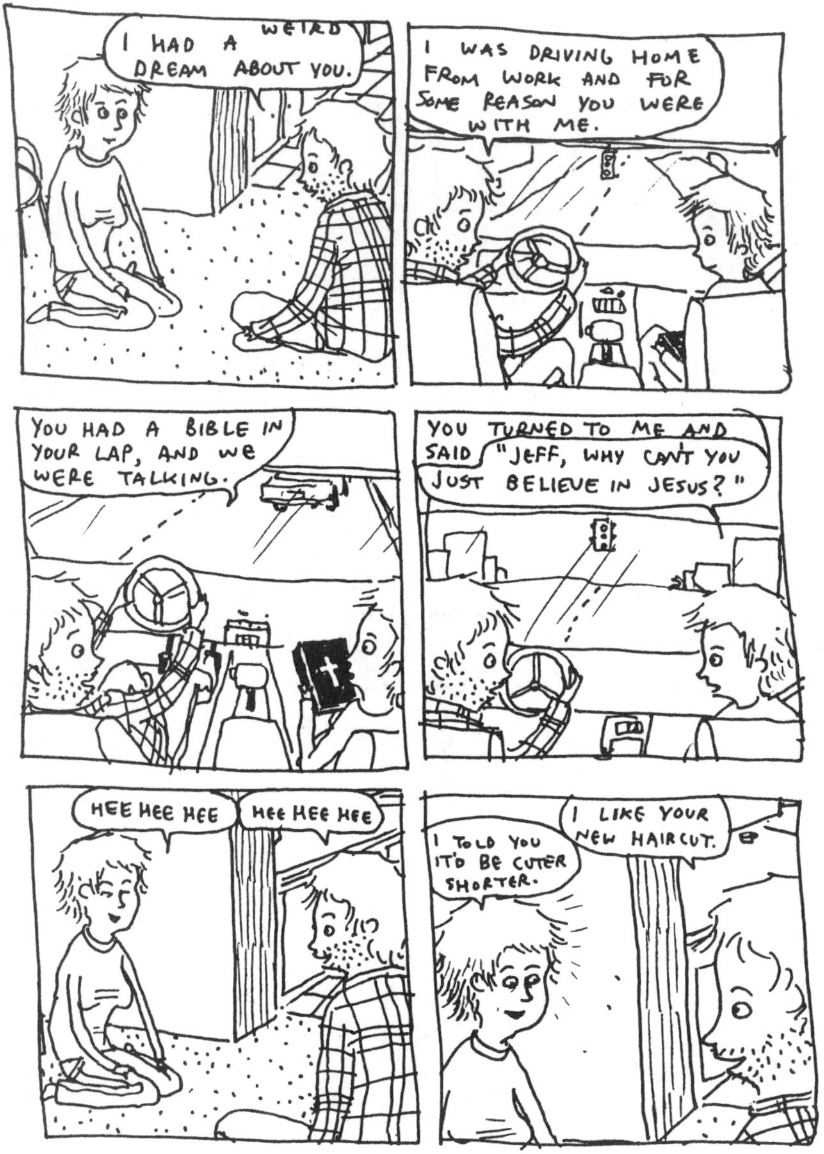
I HAD A WEIRD DREAM ABOUT YOU.
I WAS DRIVING HOME FROM WORK AND FOR SOME REASON YOU WERE WITH ME.
YOU HAD A BIBLE IN YOUR LAP, AND WE WERE TALKING.
YOU TURNED TO ME AND SAID "JEFF, WHY CAN'T YOU JUST BELIEVE IN JESUS?"
HEE HEE HEE
HEE HEE HEE
I LIKE YOUR NEW HAIRCUT.
I TOLD YOU IT'D BE CUTER SHORTER.

HOT COCOA

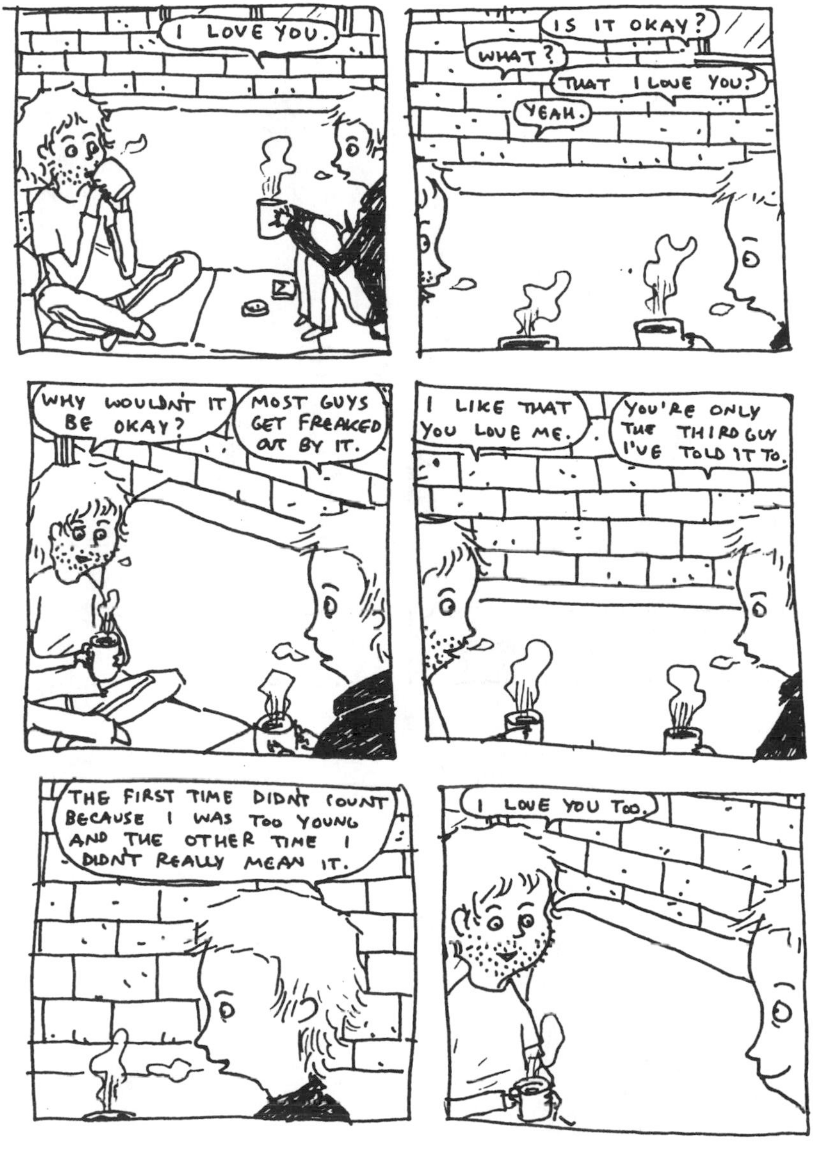
I LOVE YOU.
IS IT OKAY?
WHAT?
THAT I LOVE YOU?
YEAH.
WHY WOULDN'T IT BE OKAY?
MOST GUYS GET FREAKED OUT BY IT.
I LIKE THAT YOU LOVE ME.
YOU'RE ONLY THE THIRD GUY I'VE TOLD IT TO.
THE FIRST TIME DIDN'T COUNT BECAUSE I WAS TOO YOUNG AND THE OTHER TIME I DIDN'T REALLY MEAN IT.
I LOVE YOU TOO.

GARDENS

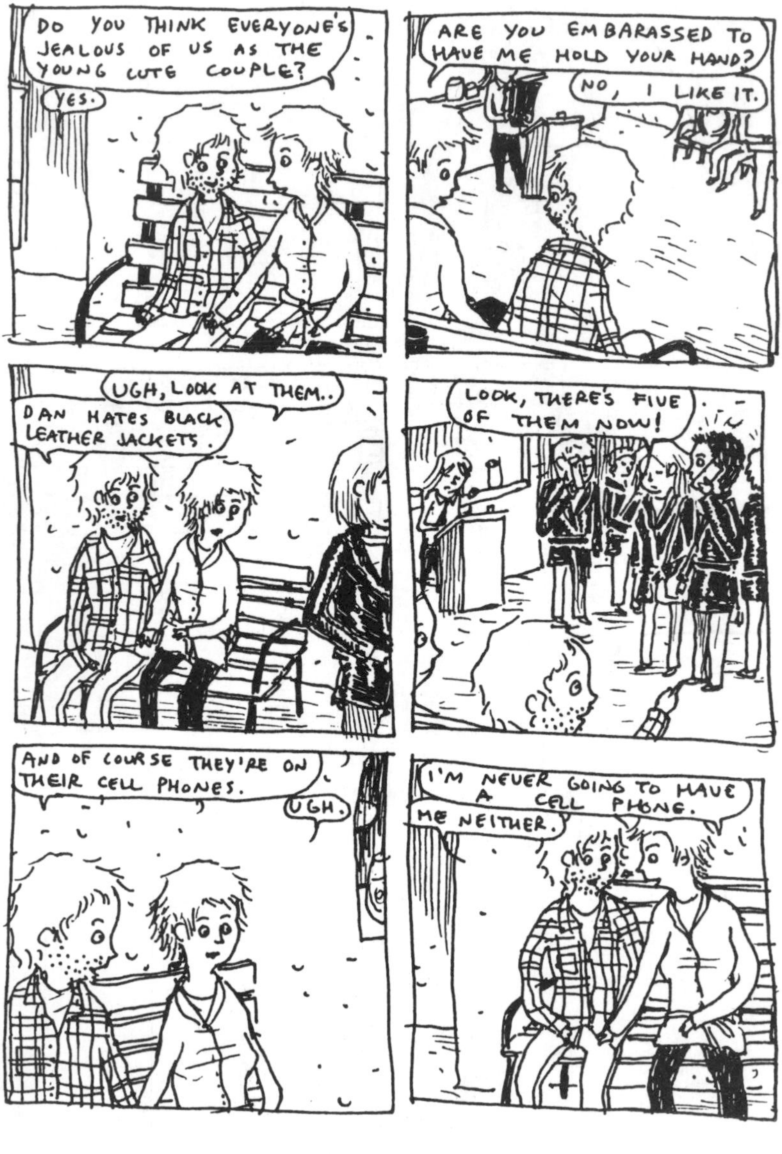
DO YOU THINK EVERYONE'S JEALOUS OF US AS THE YOUNG CUTE COUPLE?
YES.
ARE YOU EMBARASSED TO HAVE ME HOLD YOUR HAND?
NO, I LIKE IT.
UGH, LOOK AT THEM..
DAN HATES BLACK LEATHER JACKETS.
LOOK, THERE'S FIVE OF THEM NOW!
AND OF COURSE THEY'RE ON THEIR CELL PHONES.
UGH.
I'M NEVER GOING TO HAVE A CELL PHONE.
ME NEITHER.

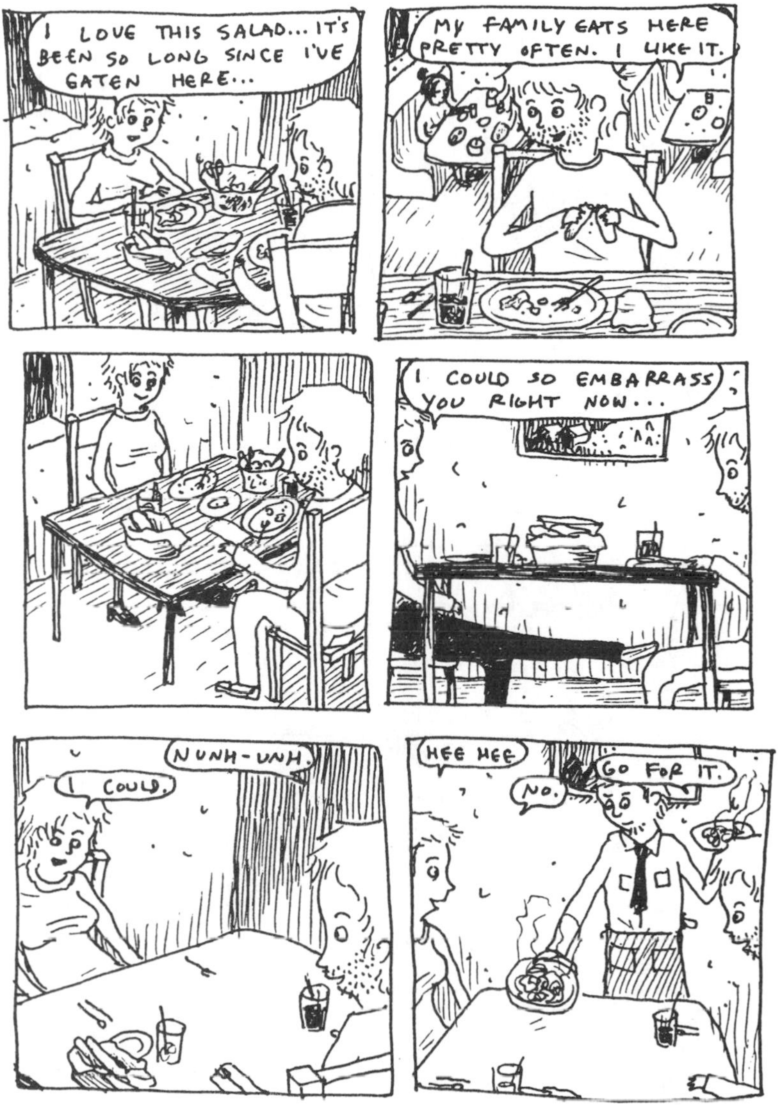
I LOVE THIS SALAD... IT'S BEEN SO LONG SINCE I'VE EATEN HERE...
MY FAMILY EATS HERE PRETTY OFTEN. I LIKE IT.
I COULD SO EMBARRASS YOU RIGHT NOW...
I COULD.
NUNH-UNH.
HEE HEE
NO.
GO FOR IT.

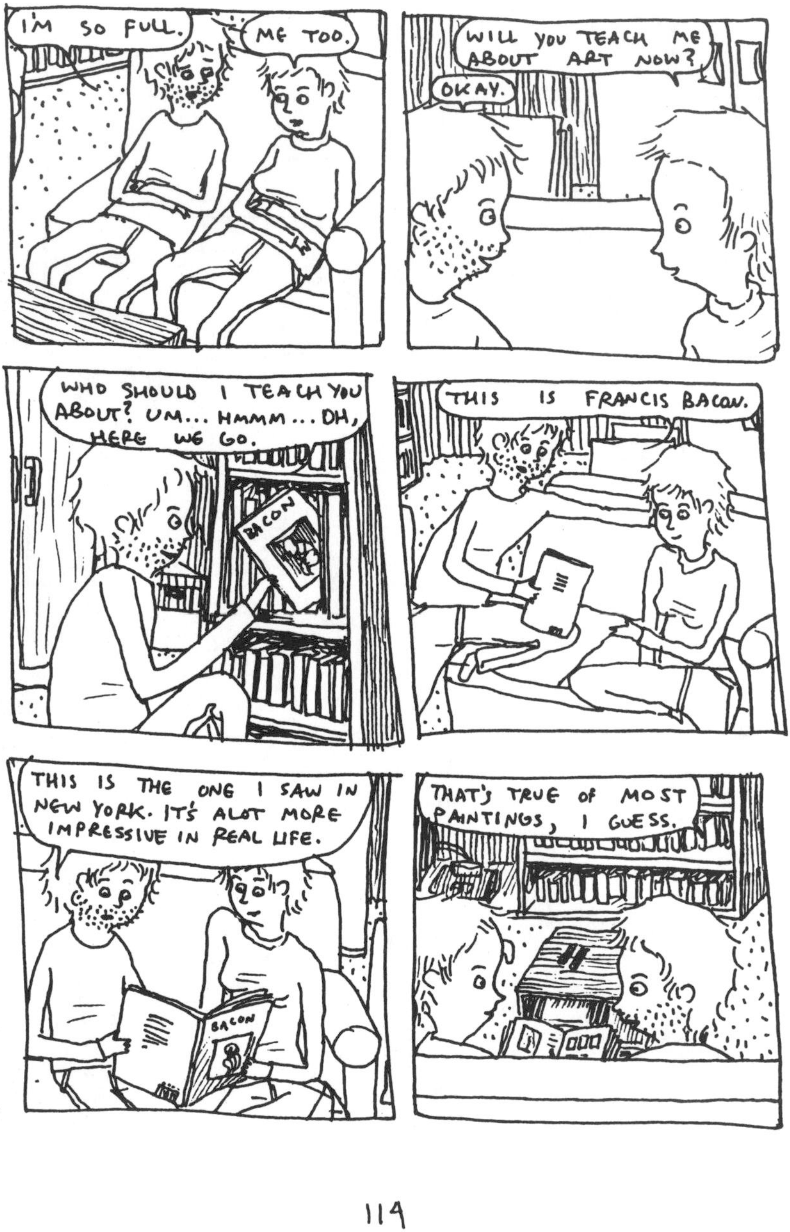
I'M SO FULL.
ME TOO.
WILL YOU TEACH ME ABOUT ART NOW?
OKAY.
WHO SHOULD I TEACH YOU ABOUT? UM... HMMM... OH, HERE WE GO.
BACON
THIS IS FRANCIS BACON.
THIS IS THE ONE I SAW IN NEW YORK. IT'S ALOT MORE IMPRESSIVE IN REAL LIFE.
BACON
THAT'S TRUE OF MOST PAINTINGS, I GUESS.

WRITING

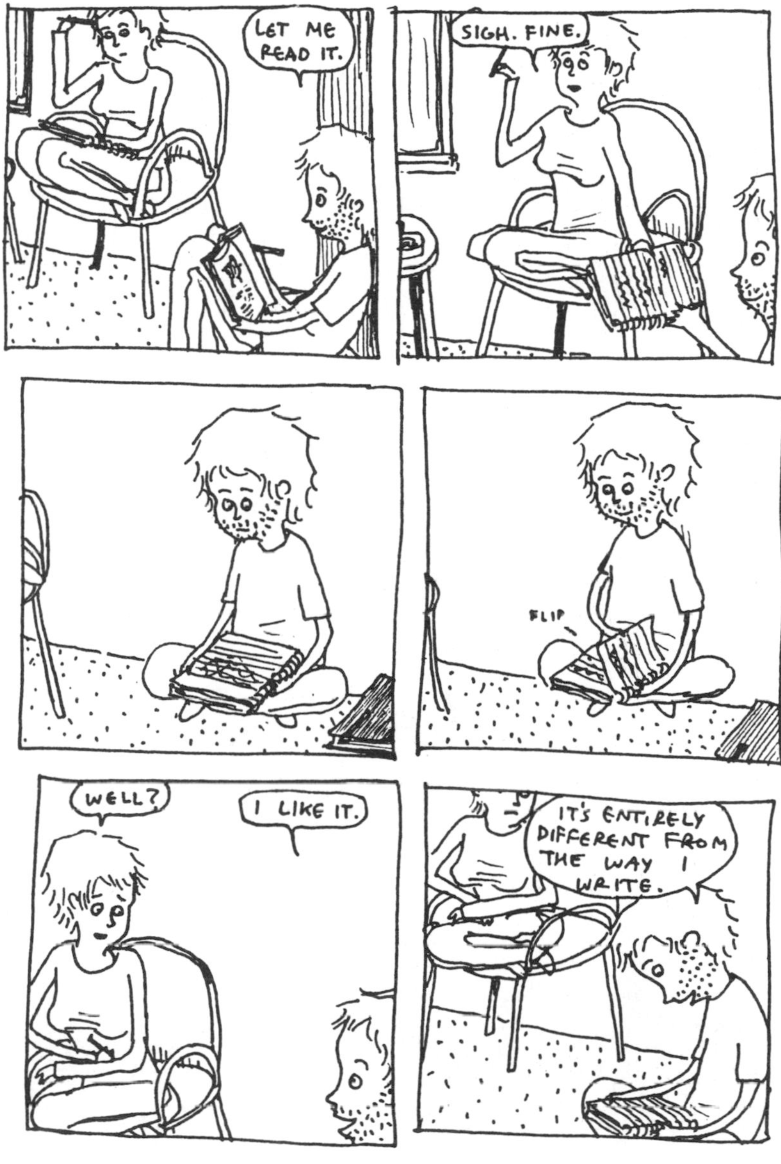
LET ME READ IT.
SIGH. FINE.
FLIP
WELL?
I LIKE IT.
IT'S ENTIRELY DIFFERENT FROM THE WAY I WRITE.

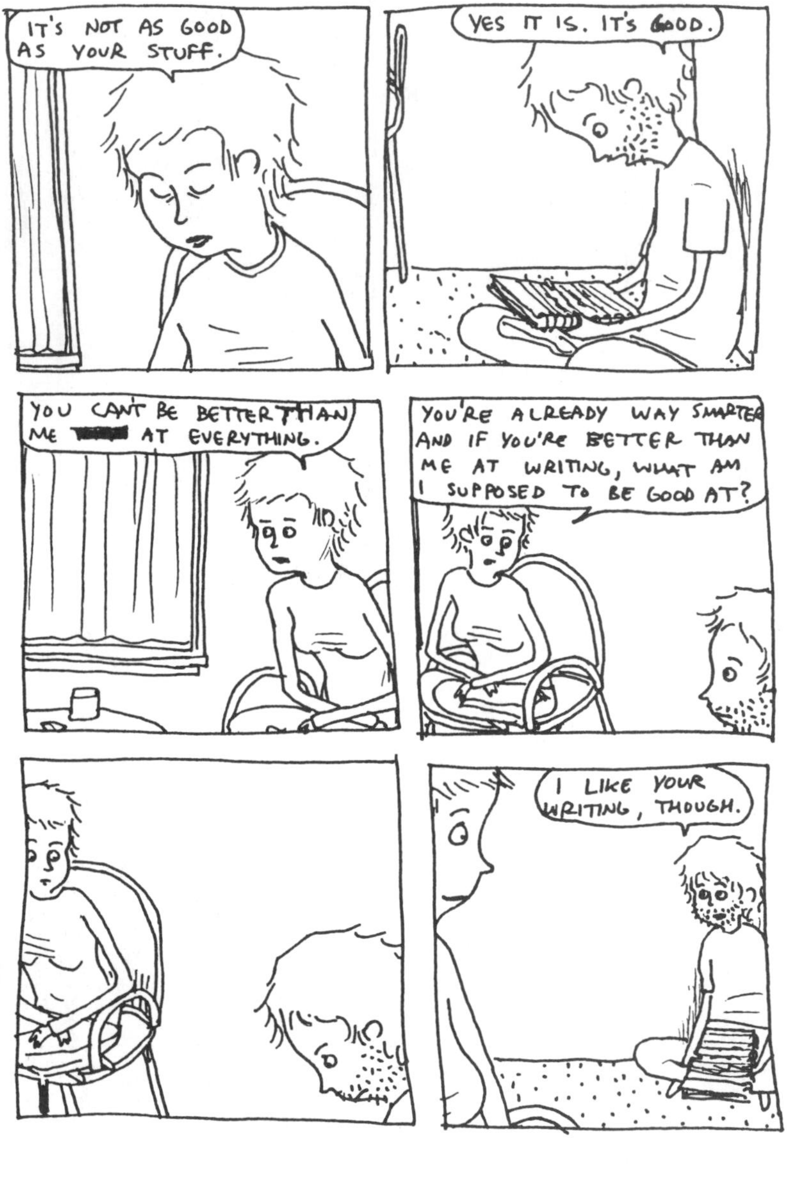
IT'S NOT AS GOOD AS YOUR STUFF.
YES IT IS. IT'S GOOD.
YOU CAN'T BE BETTER THAN ME [redacted] AT EVERYTHING.
YOU'RE ALREADY WAY SMARTER AND IF YOU'RE BETTER THAN ME AT WRITING, WHAT AM I SUPPOSED TO BE GOOD AT?
I LIKE YOUR WRITING, THOUGH.

FRIDAY

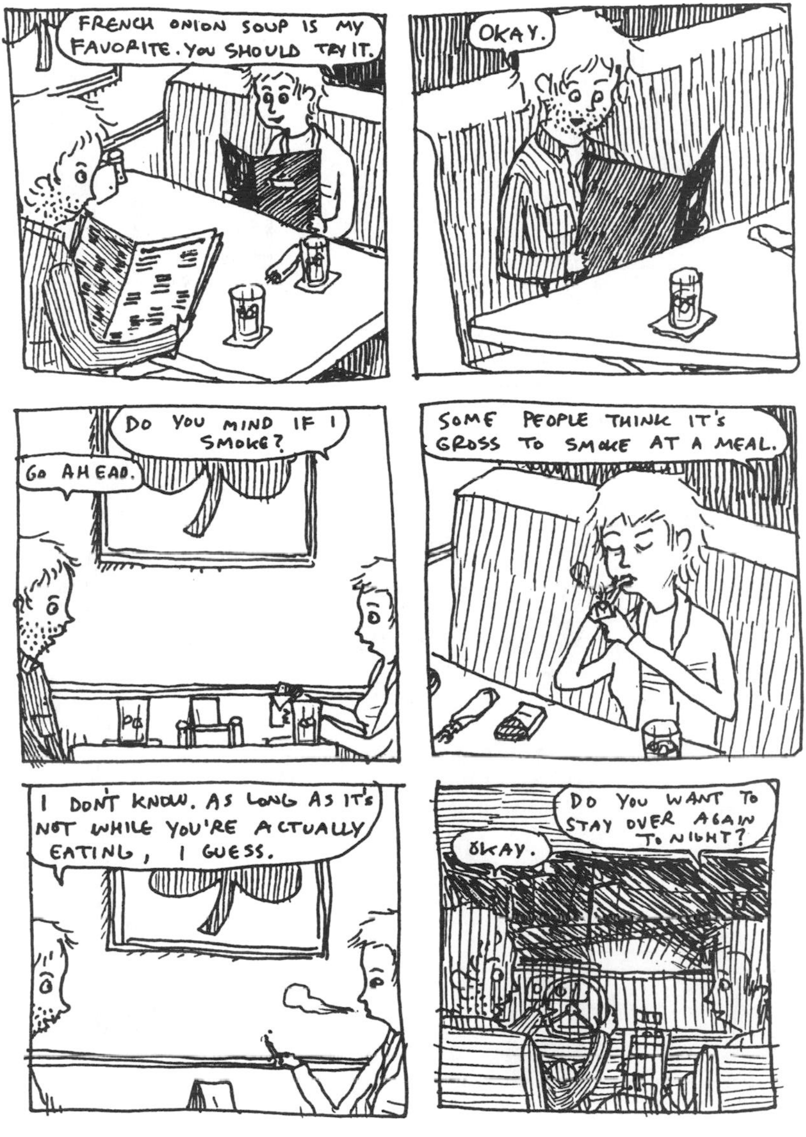

FRENCH ONION SOUP IS MY FAVORITE. YOU SHOULD TRY IT.
OKAY.
DO YOU MIND IF I SMOKE?
GO AHEAD.
SOME PEOPLE THINK IT'S GROSS TO SMOKE AT A MEAL.
I DON'T KNOW. AS LONG AS IT'S NOT WHILE YOU'RE ACTUALLY EATING, I GUESS.
DO YOU WANT TO STAY OVER AGAIN TONIGHT?
OKAY.

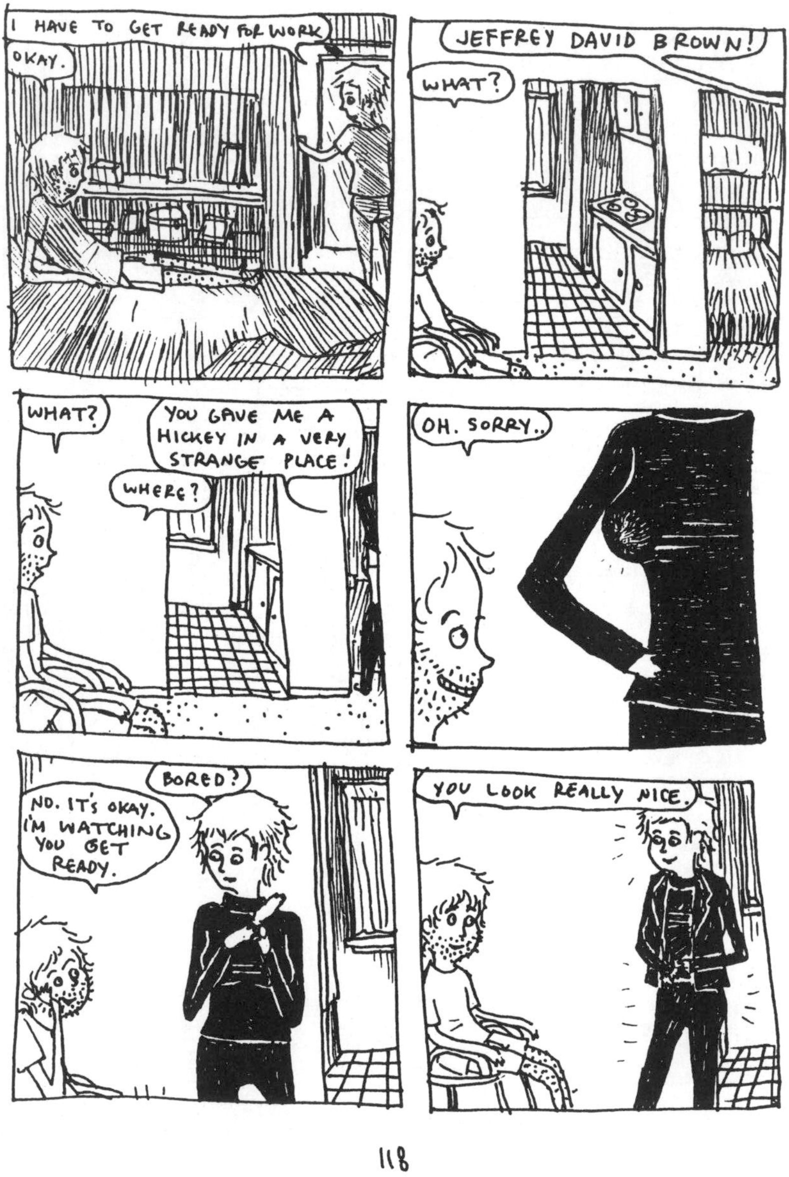
I HAVE TO GET READY FOR WORK
OKAY.
JEFFREY DAVID BROWN!
WHAT?
WHAT?
YOU GAVE ME A HICKEY IN A VERY STRANGE PLACE!
WHERE?
OH. SORRY..
BORED?
NO. IT'S OKAY. I'M WATCHING YOU GET READY.
YOU LOOK REALLY NICE.

EYE OF THE BEHOLDER

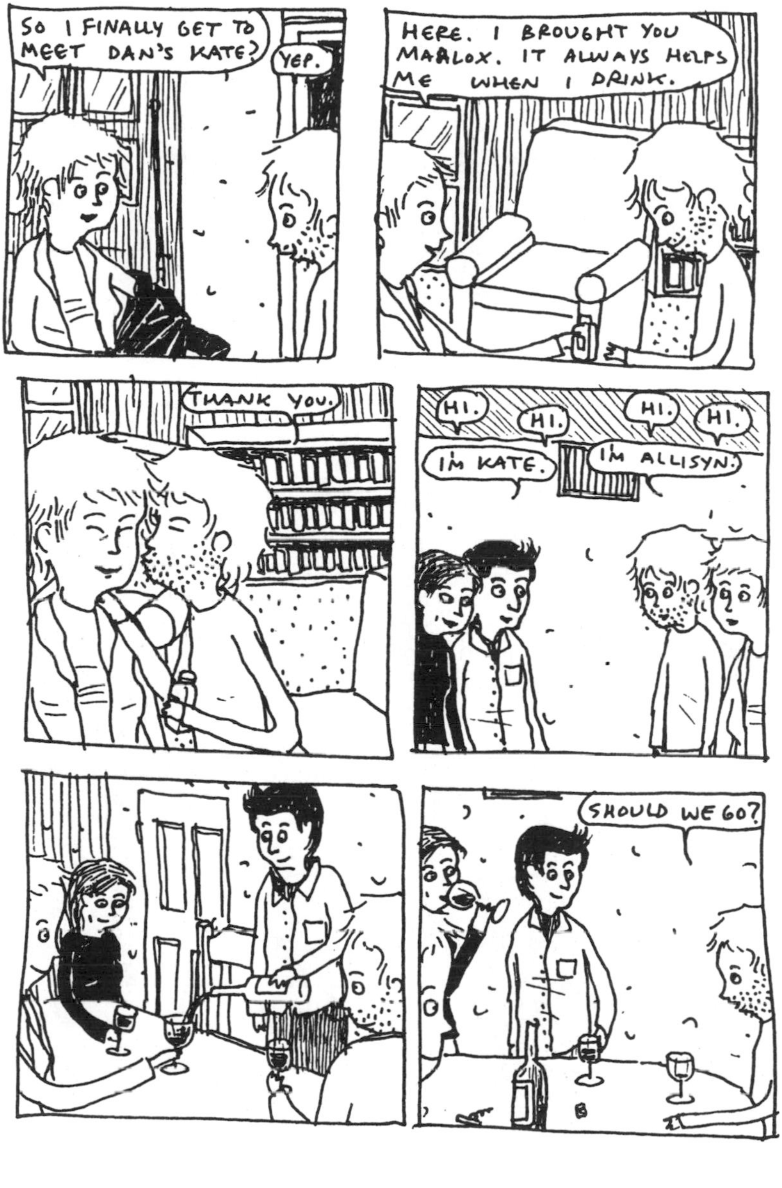

SO I FINALLY GET TO MEET DAN'S KATE?
YEP.
HERE. I BROUGHT YOU MAALOX. IT ALWAYS HELPS ME WHEN I DRINK.
THANK YOU.
HI.
HI.
HI.
HI.
I'M KATE.
I'M ALLISYN.
SHOULD WE GO?

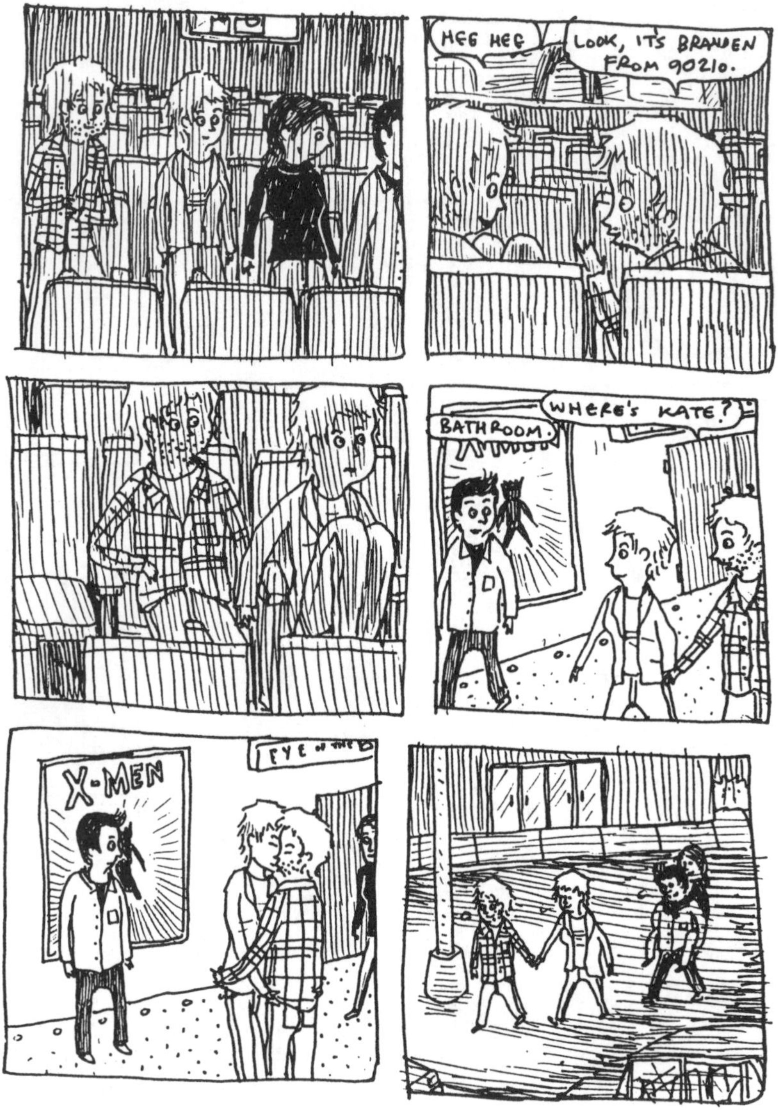
HEE HEE
LOOK, IT'S BRANDEN FROM 90210.
WHERE'S KATE?
BATHROOM.
X-MEN

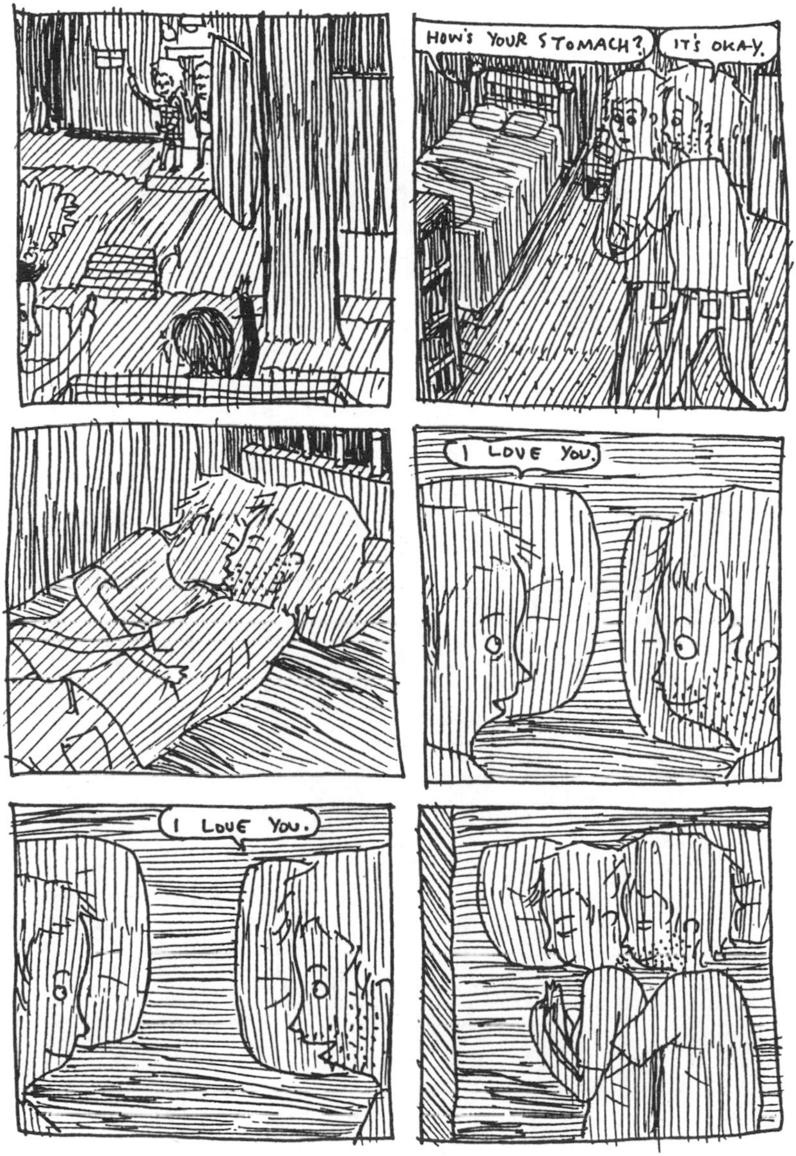
HOW'S YOUR STOMACH?
IT'S OKAY.
I LOVE YOU.
I LOVE YOU.

MISSING

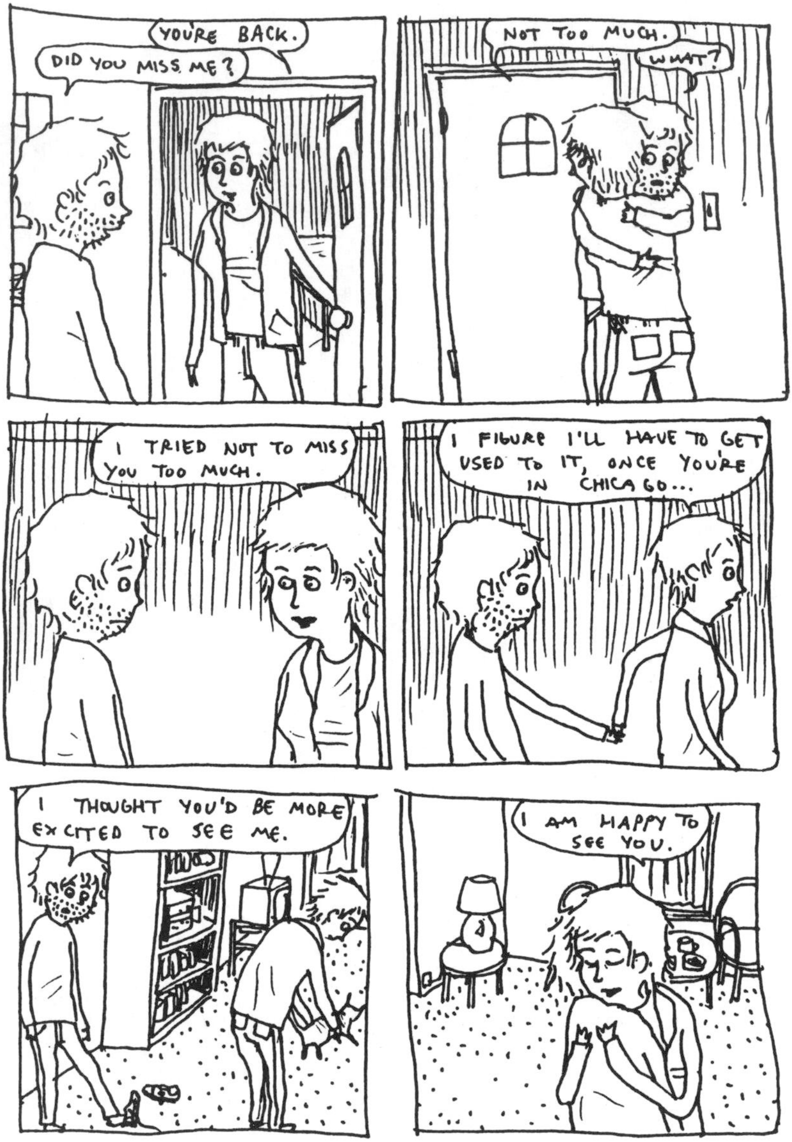
DID YOU MISS ME?
YOU'RE BACK.
NOT TOO MUCH.
WHAT?
I TRIED NOT TO MISS YOU TOO MUCH.
I FIGURE I'LL HAVE TO GET USED TO IT, ONCE YOU'RE IN CHICAGO...
I THOUGHT YOU'D BE MORE EXCITED TO SEE ME.
I AM HAPPY TO SEE YOU.

MOVING

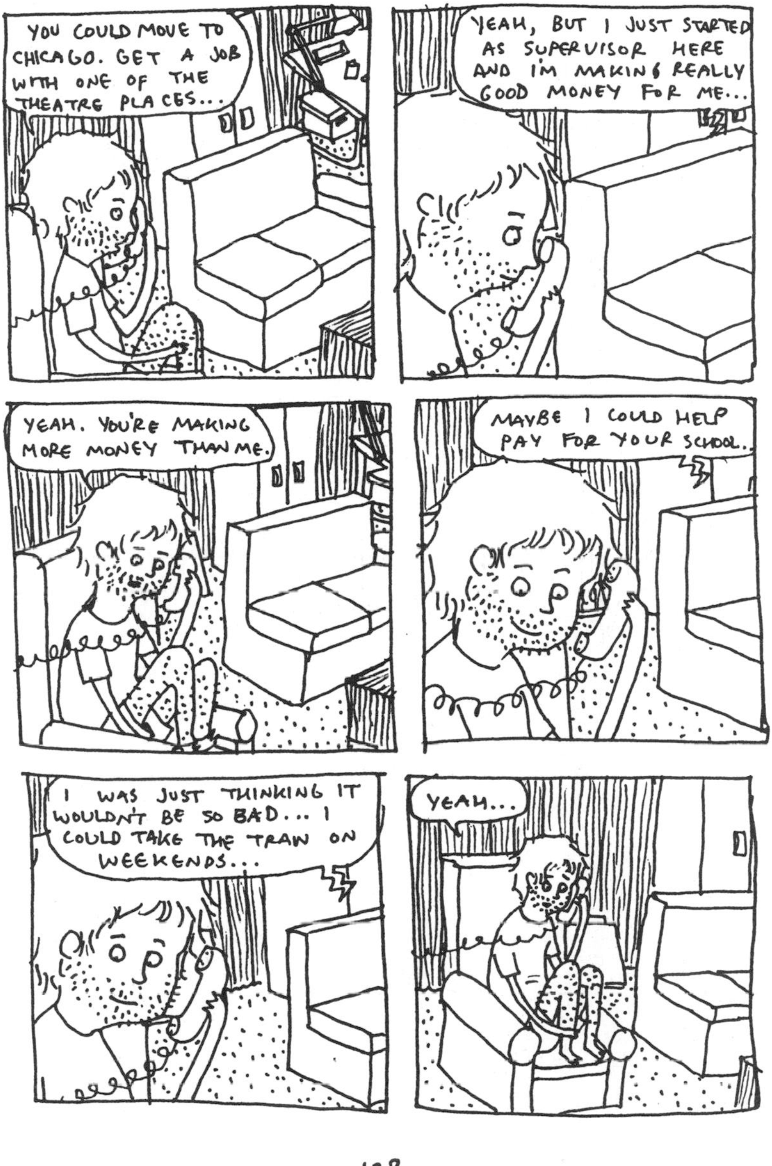
YOU COULD MOVE TO CHICAGO. GET A JOB WITH ONE OF THE THEATRE PLACES...
YEAH, BUT I JUST STARTED AS SUPERVISOR HERE AND I'M MAKING REALLY GOOD MONEY FOR ME...
YEAH. YOU'RE MAKING MORE MONEY THAN ME.
MAYBE I COULD HELP PAY FOR YOUR SCHOOL...
I WAS JUST THINKING IT WOULDN'T BE SO BAD... I COULD TAKE THE TRAIN ON WEEKENDS...
YEAH...

COFFEE

DRIVING

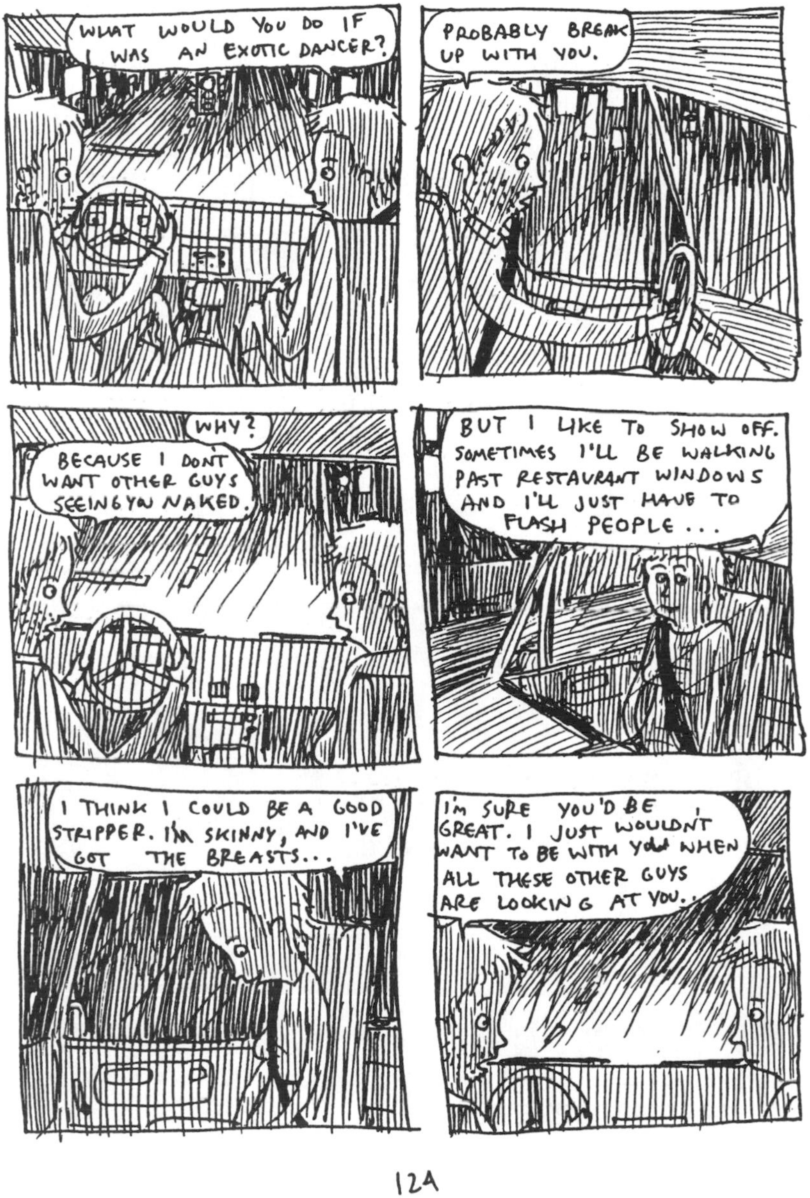
WHAT WOULD YOU DO IF I WAS AN EXOTIC DANCER?
PROBABLY BREAK UP WITH YOU.
WHY?
BECAUSE I DONT WANT OTHER GUYS SEEING YOU NAKED.
BUT I LIKE TO SHOW OFF. SOMETIMES I'LL BE WALKING PAST RESTAURANT WINDOWS AND I'LL JUST HAVE TO FLASH PEOPLE...
I THINK I COULD BE A GOOD STRIPPER. I'M SKINNY, AND I'VE GOT THE BREASTS...
I'M SURE YOU'D BE GREAT. I JUST WOULDN'T WANT TO BE WITH YOU WHEN ALL THESE OTHER GUYS ARE LOOKING AT YOU...

FAVORITE

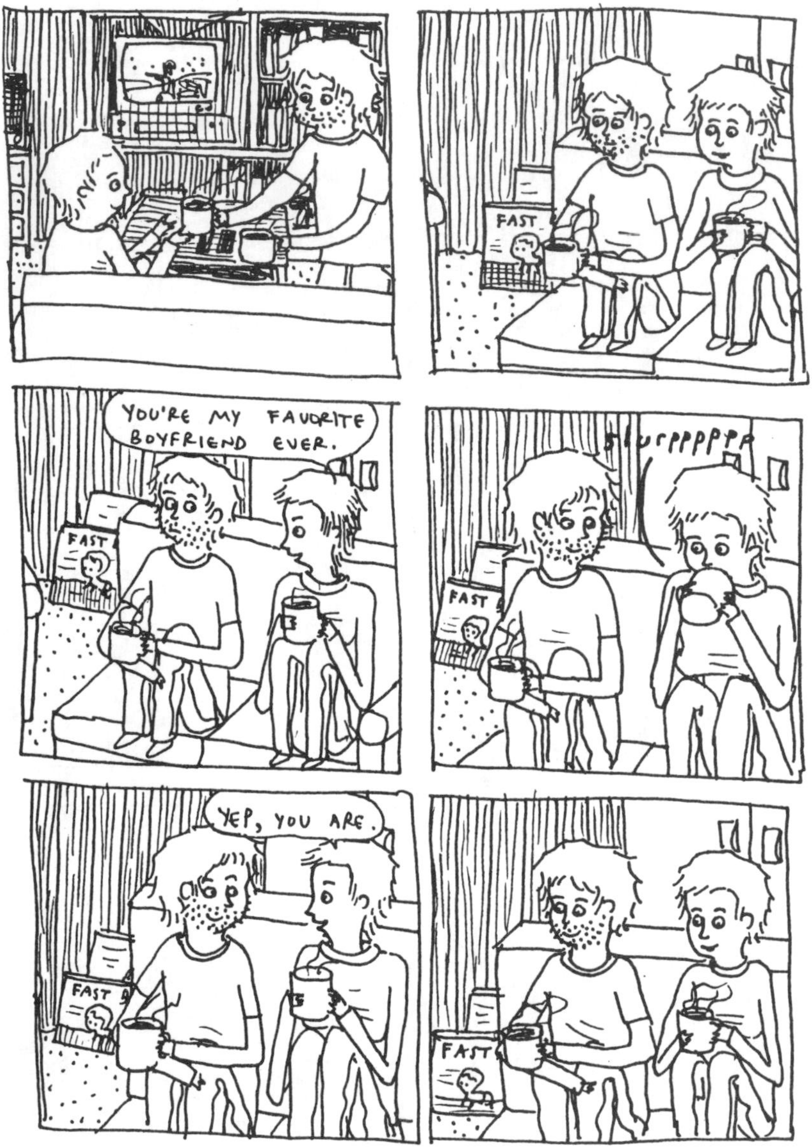
YOU'RE MY FAVORITE BOYFRIEND EVER.
FAST
YEP, YOU ARE.

WILL YOU STILL

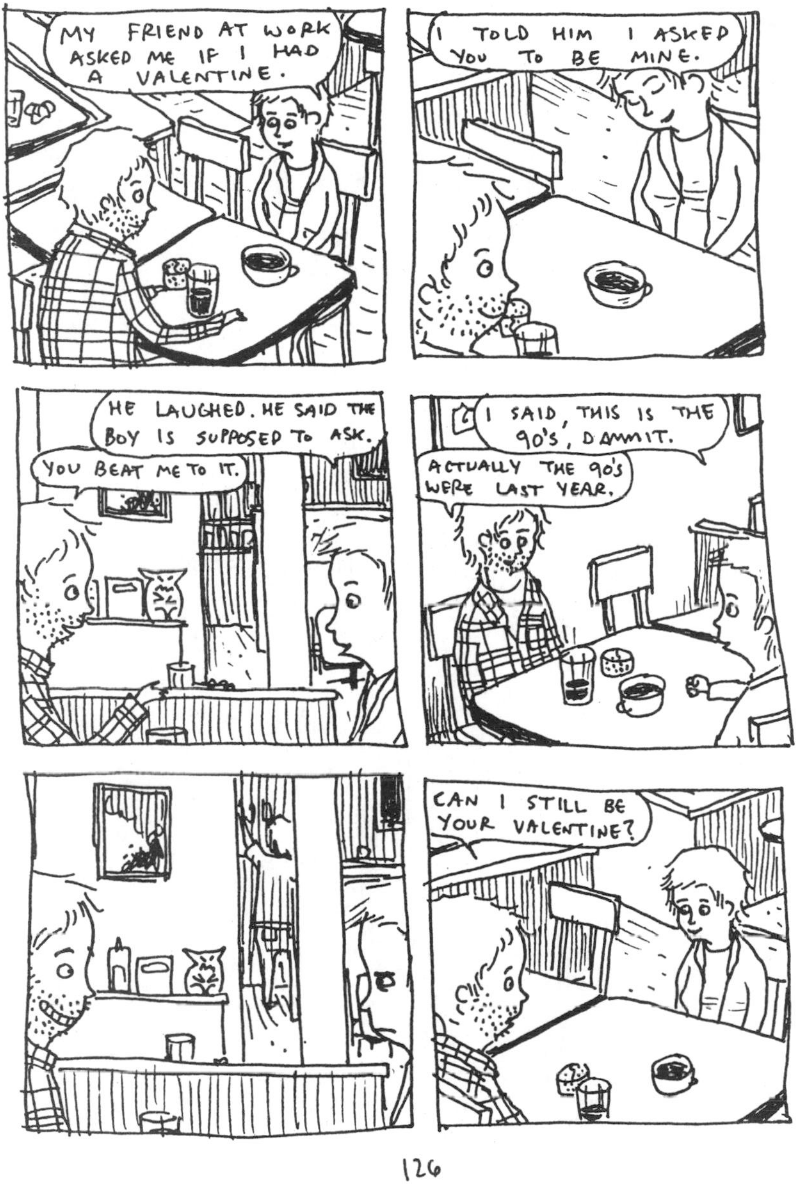
MY FRIEND AT WORK ASKED ME IF I HAD A VALENTINE.
I TOLD HIM I ASKED YOU TO BE MINE.
HE LAUGHED. HE SAID THE BOY IS SUPPOSED TO ASK.
YOU BEAT ME TO IT.
I SAID, THIS IS THE 90'S, DAMMIT.
ACTUALLY THE 90'S WERE LAST YEAR.
CAN I STILL BE YOUR VALENTINE?

COMPLETE SILENCE

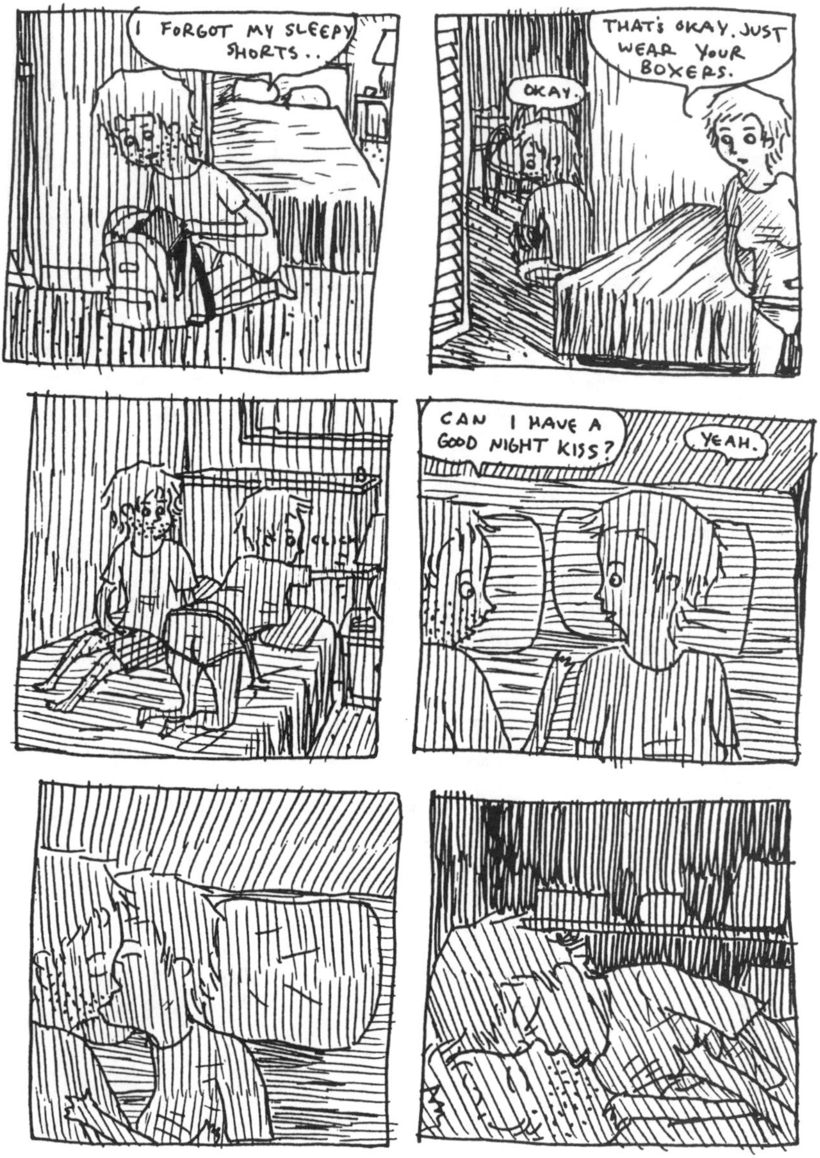
I FORGOT MY SLEEPY SHORTS..
THAT'S OKAY. JUST WEAR YOUR BOXERS.
OKAY.
CLICK
CAN I HAVE A GOOD NIGHT KISS?
YEAH.

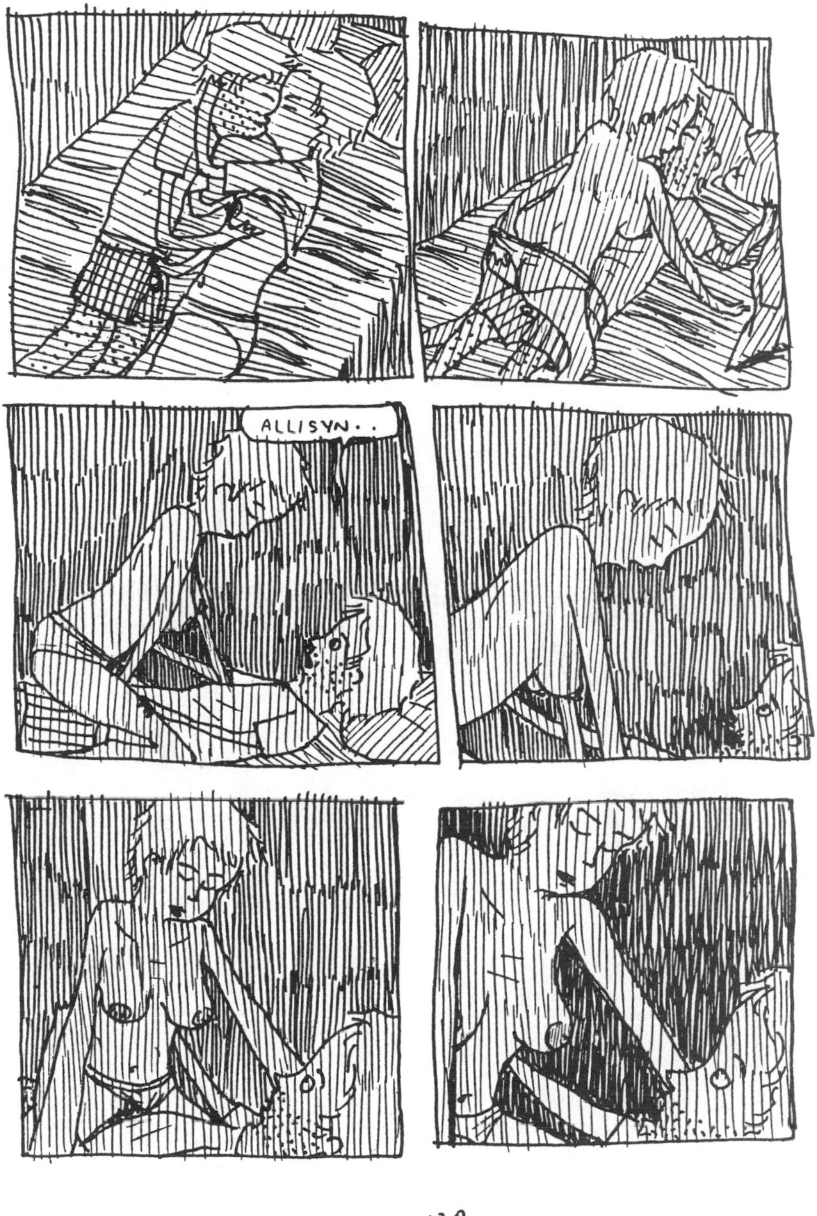
ALLISYN..

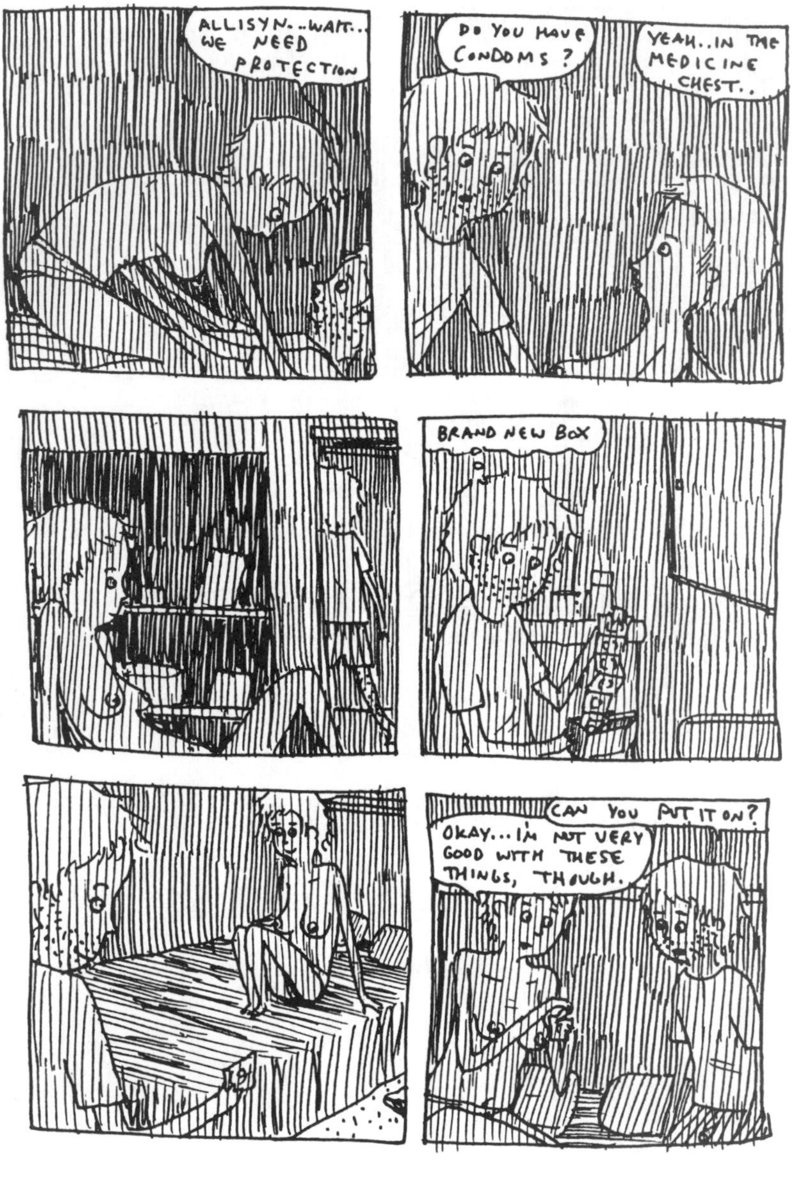
ALLISYN...WAIT... WE NEED PROTECTION
DO YOU HAVE CONDOMS?
YEAH..IN THE MEDICINE CHEST..
BRAND NEW BOX
CAN YOU PUT IT ON?
OKAY...I'M NOT VERY GOOD WITH THESE THINGS, THOUGH.

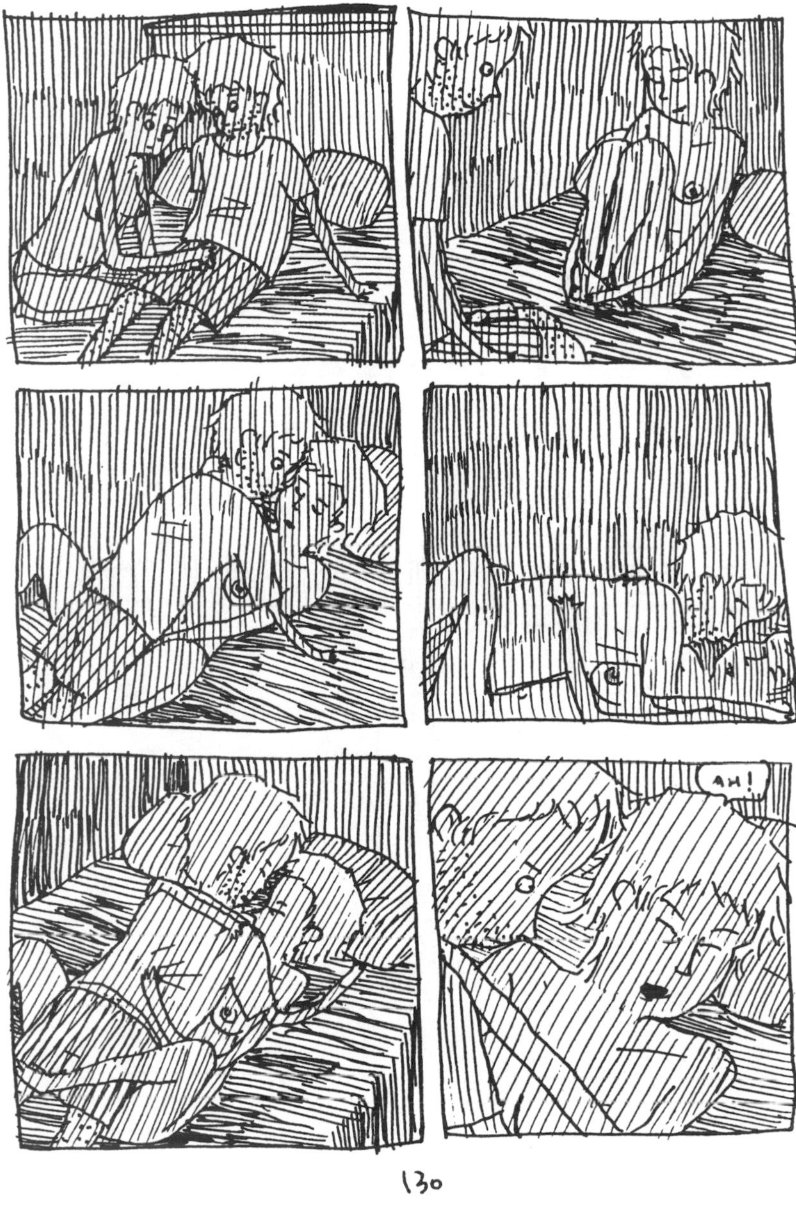
AH!

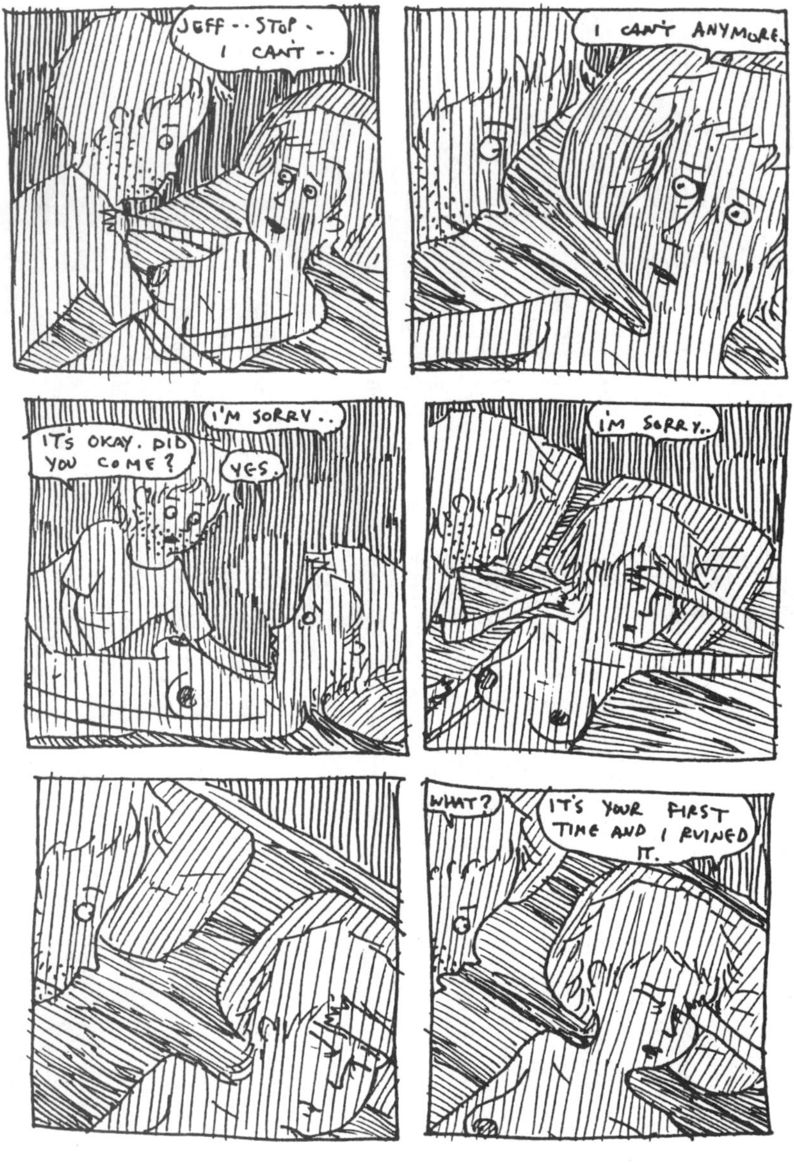
JEFF -- STOP - I CAN'T --
I CAN'T ANYMORE.
I'M SORRY..
IT'S OKAY. DID YOU COME?
YES.
I'M SORRY..
WHAT?
IT'S YOUR FIRST TIME AND I RUINED IT.

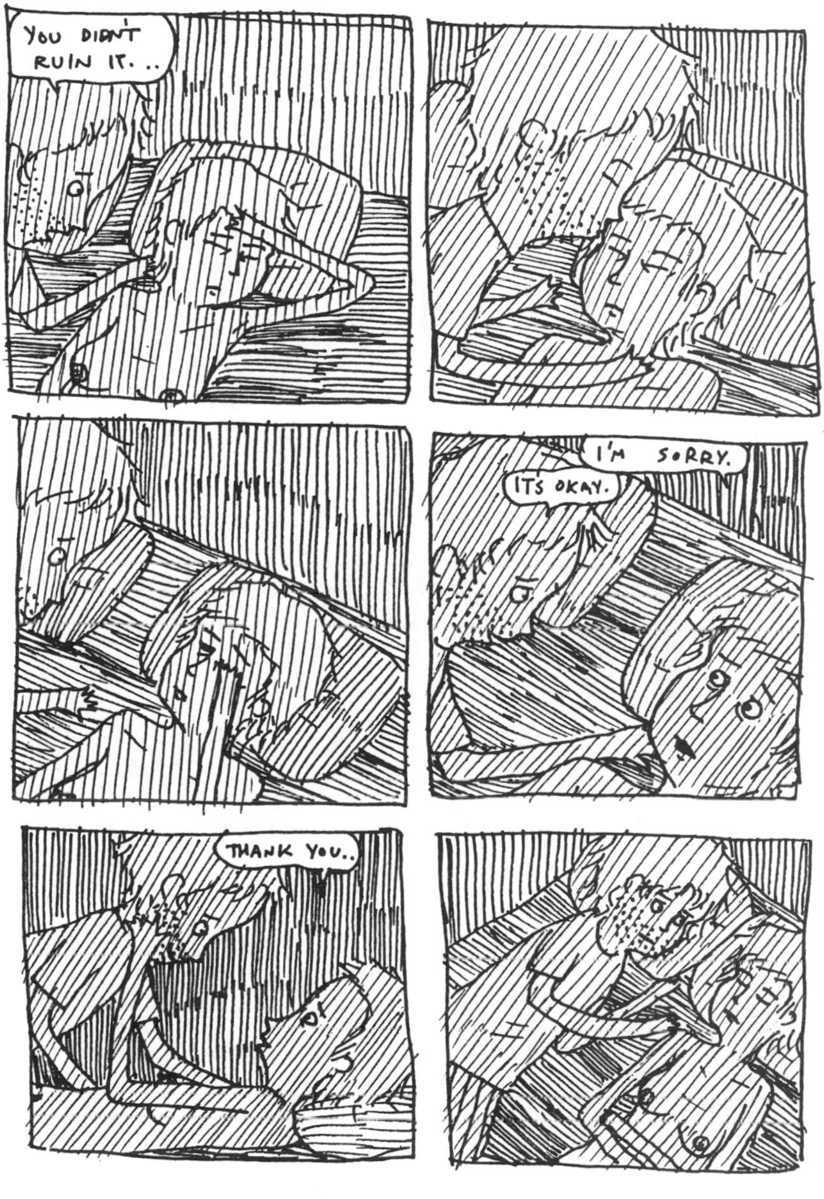
YOU DIDN'T RUIN IT. ..
I'M SORRY.
IT'S OKAY.
THANK YOU..

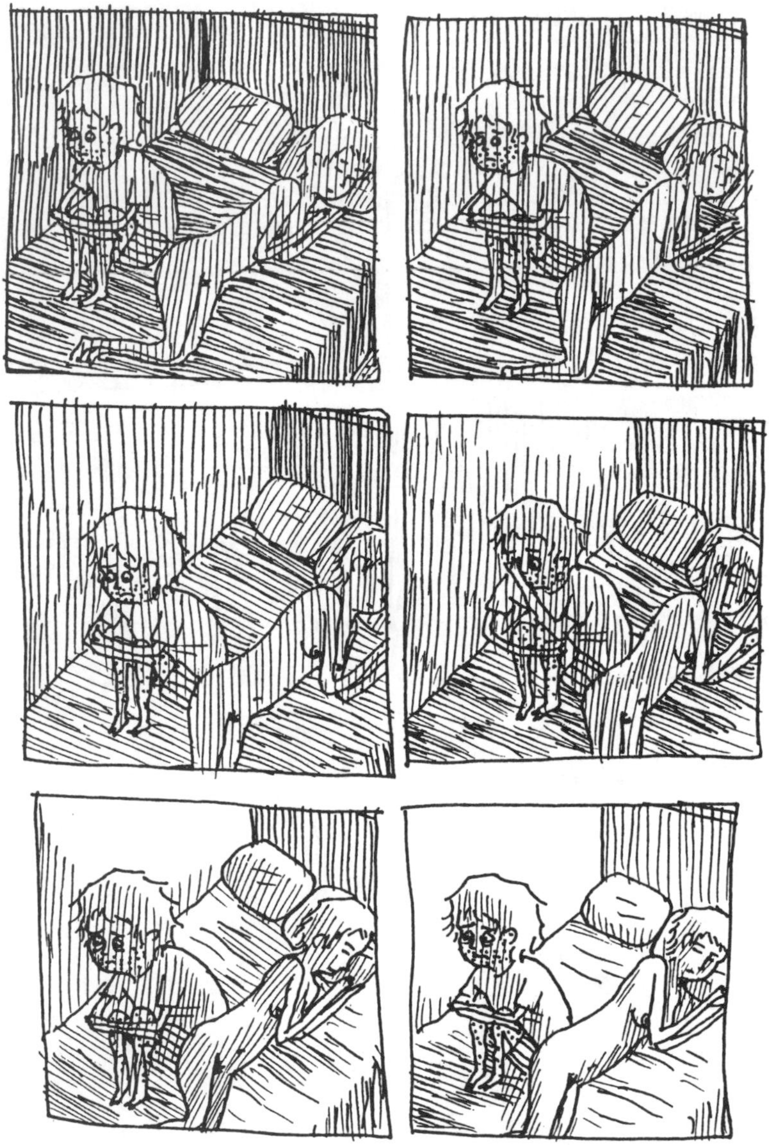

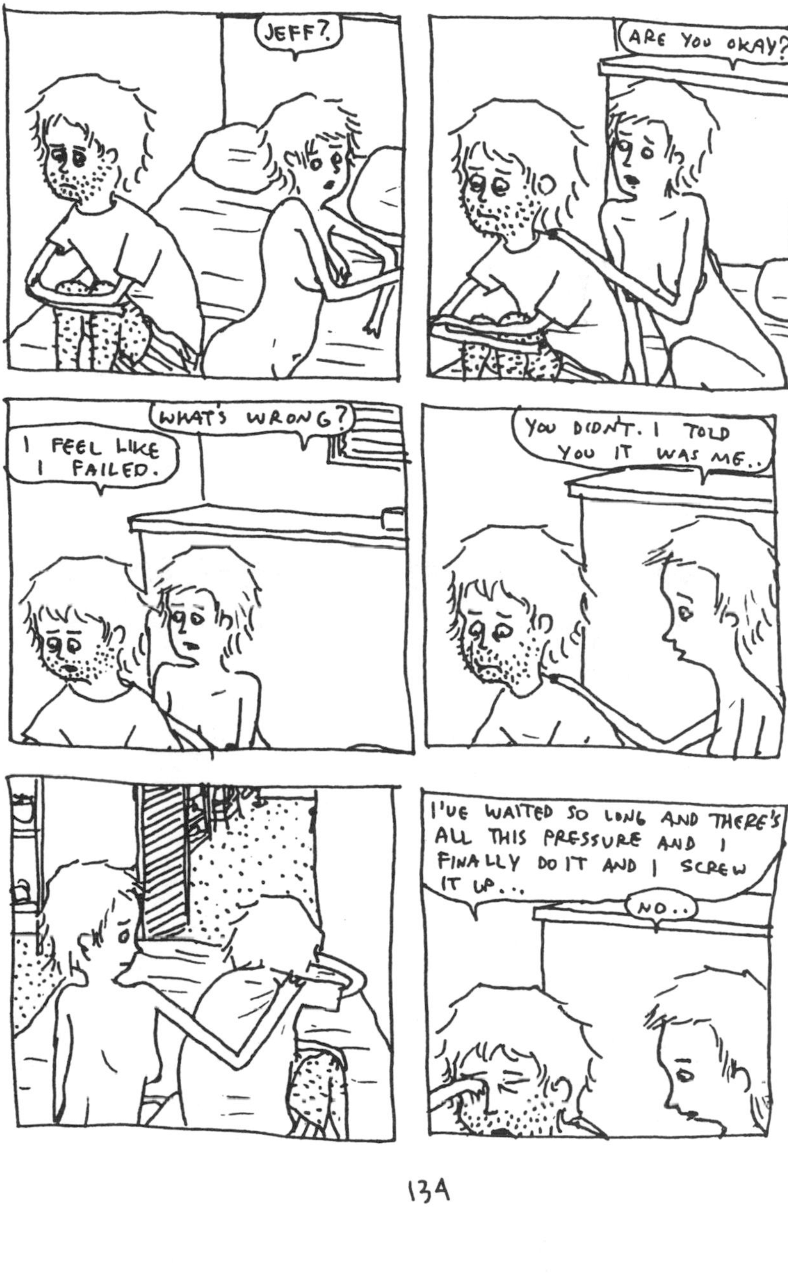
JEFF?
ARE YOU OKAY?
WHAT'S WRONG?
I FEEL LIKE I FAILED.
YOU DIDN'T. I TOLD YOU IT WAS ME..
I'VE WAITED SO LONG AND THERE'S ALL THIS PRESSURE AND I FINALLY DO IT AND I SCREW IT UP...
NO..

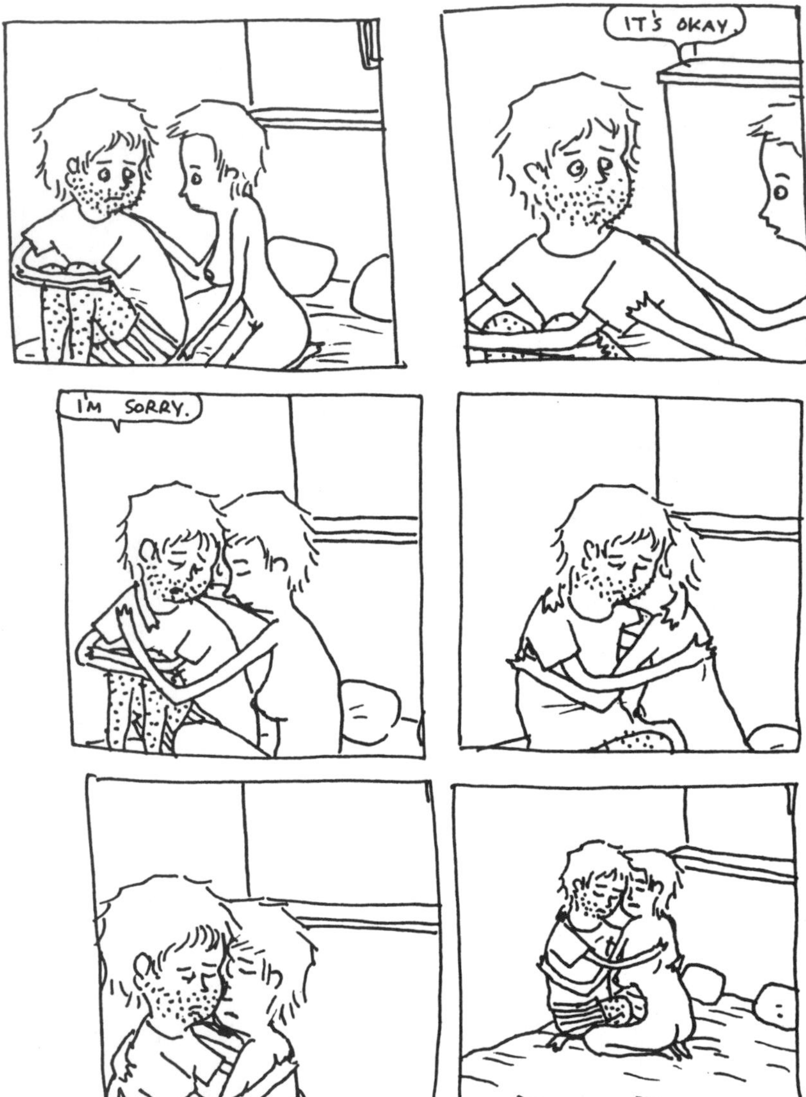
IT'S OKAY.
I'M SORRY.

FOUND

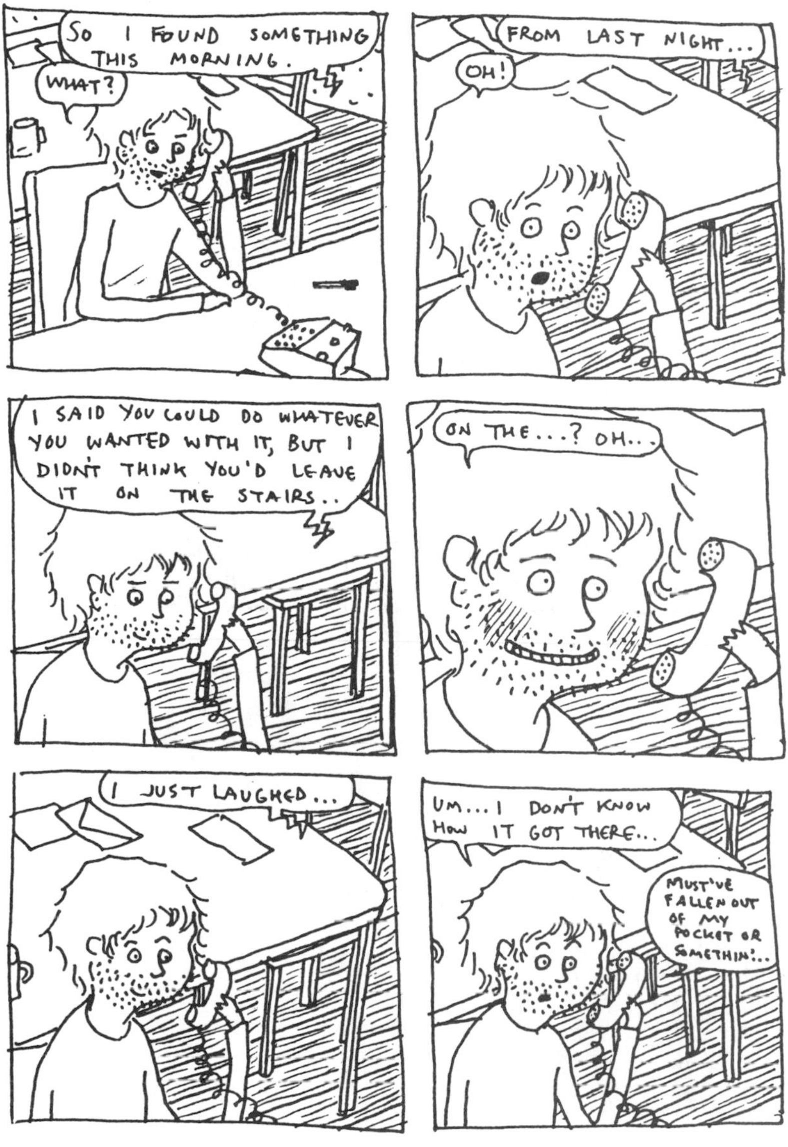
SO I FOUND SOMETHING THIS MORNING.
WHAT?
FROM LAST NIGHT...
OH!
I SAID YOU COULD DO WHATEVER YOU WANTED WITH IT, BUT I DIDN'T THINK YOU'D LEAVE IT ON THE STAIRS..
ON THE...? OH..
I JUST LAUGHED...
UM...I DON'T KNOW HOW IT GOT THERE...
MUST'VE FALLEN OUT OF MY POCKET OR SOMETHIN'...

WARMTH

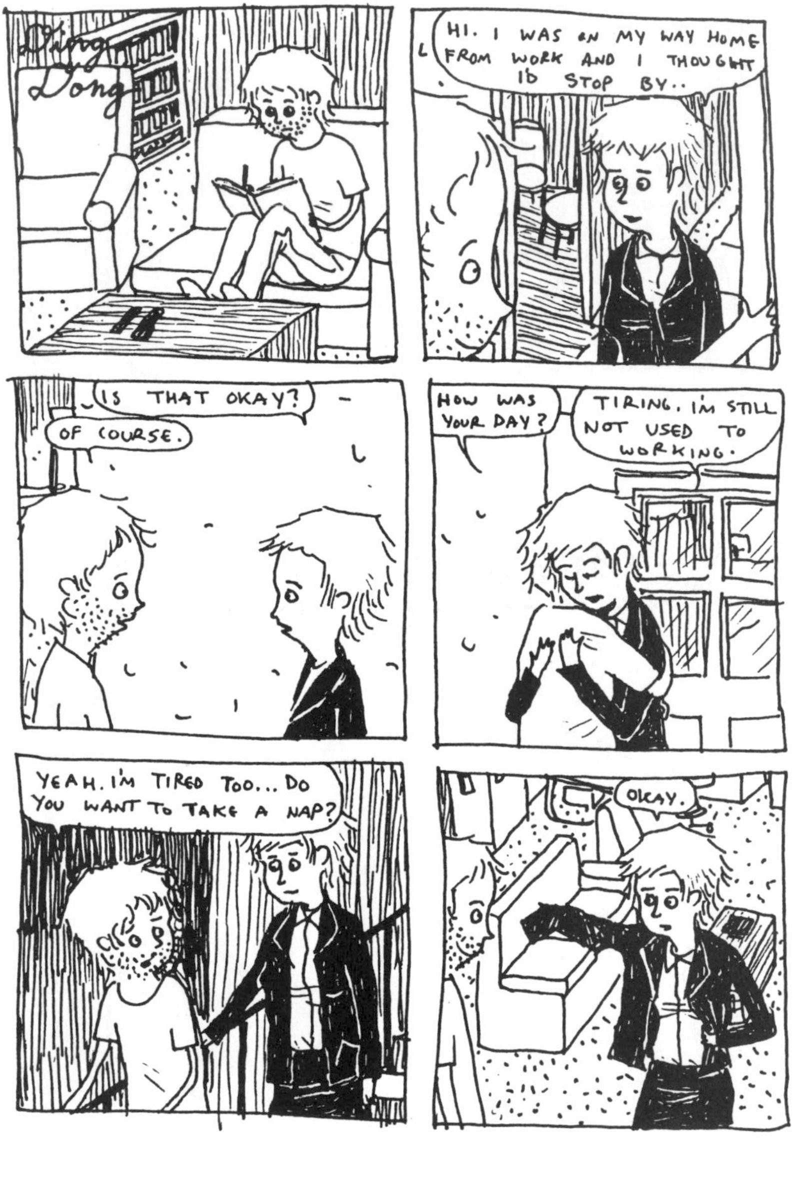
Ding Dong
HI. I WAS ON MY WAY HOME FROM WORK AND I THOUGHT I'D STOP BY..
IS THAT OKAY?
OF COURSE.
HOW WAS YOUR DAY?
TIRING. I'M STILL NOT USED TO WORKING.
YEAH. I'M TIRED TOO... DO YOU WANT TO TAKE A NAP?
OKAY.

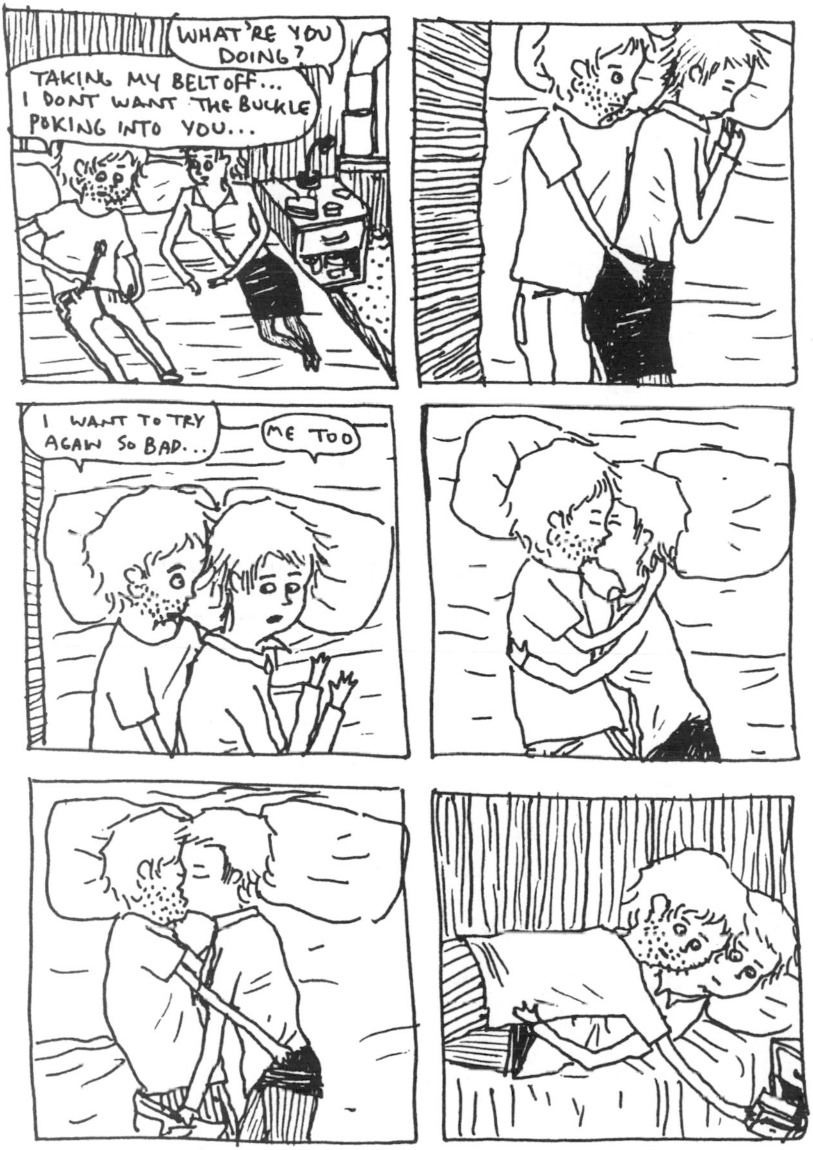
WHAT'RE YOU DOING?
TAKING MY BELT OFF... I DONT WANT THE BUCKLE POKING INTO YOU...
I WANT TO TRY AGAIN SO BAD...
ME TOO

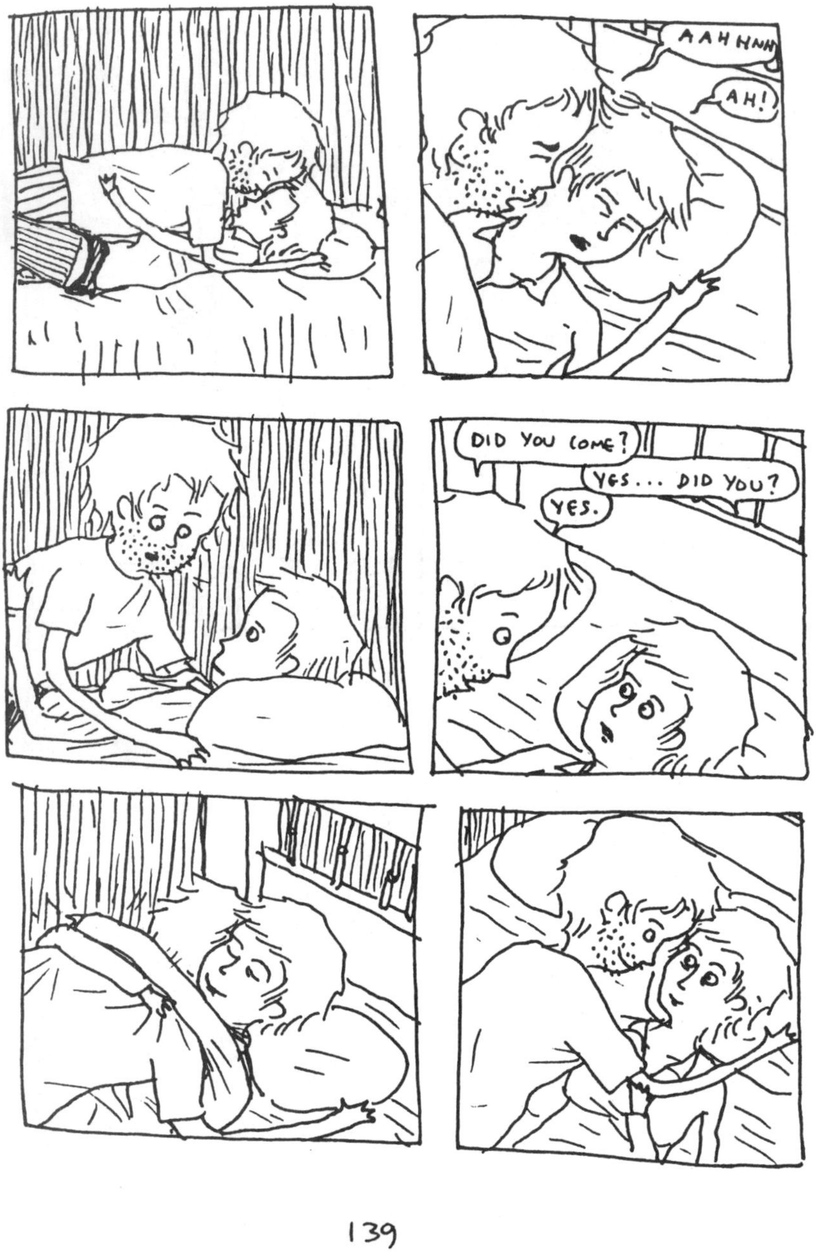
AAHHNN
AH!
DID YOU COME?
YES... DID YOU?
YES.

TATTOO

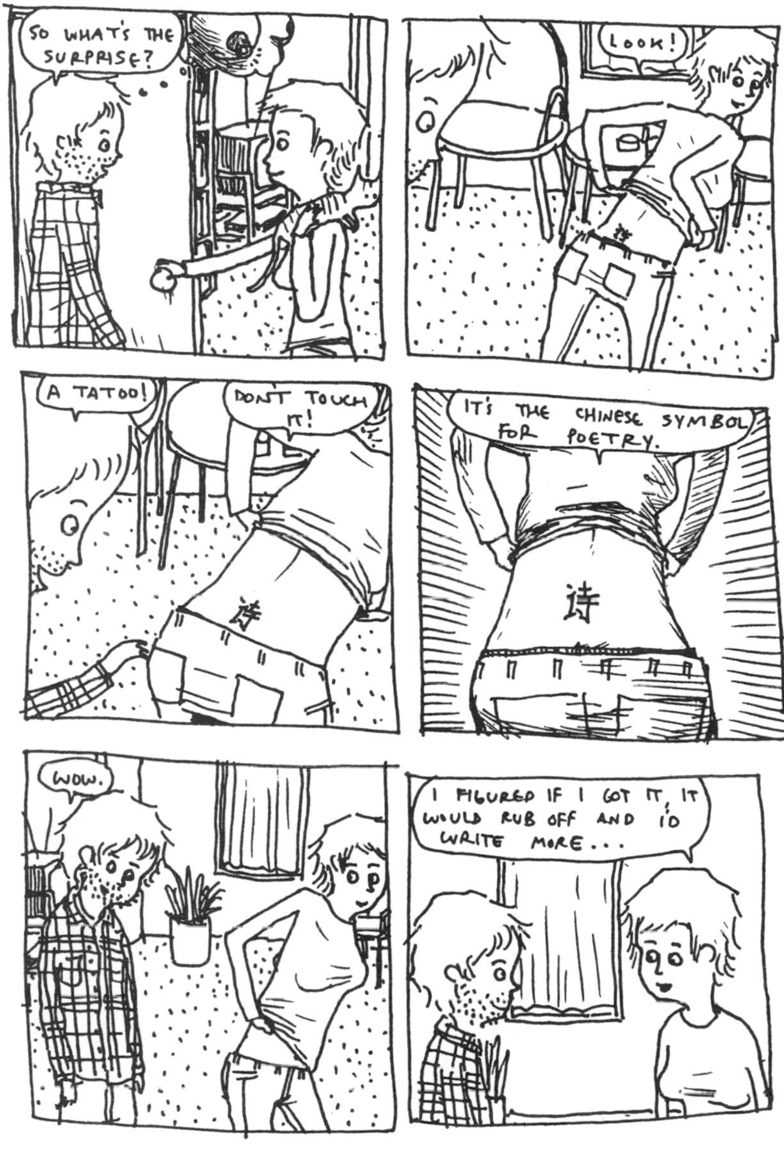
SO WHAT'S THE SURPRISE?
LOOK!
A TATOO!
DONT TOUCH IT!
IT'S THE CHINESE SYMBOL FOR POETRY.
WOW.
I FIGURED IF I GOT IT, IT WOULD RUB OFF AND I'D WRITE MORE...

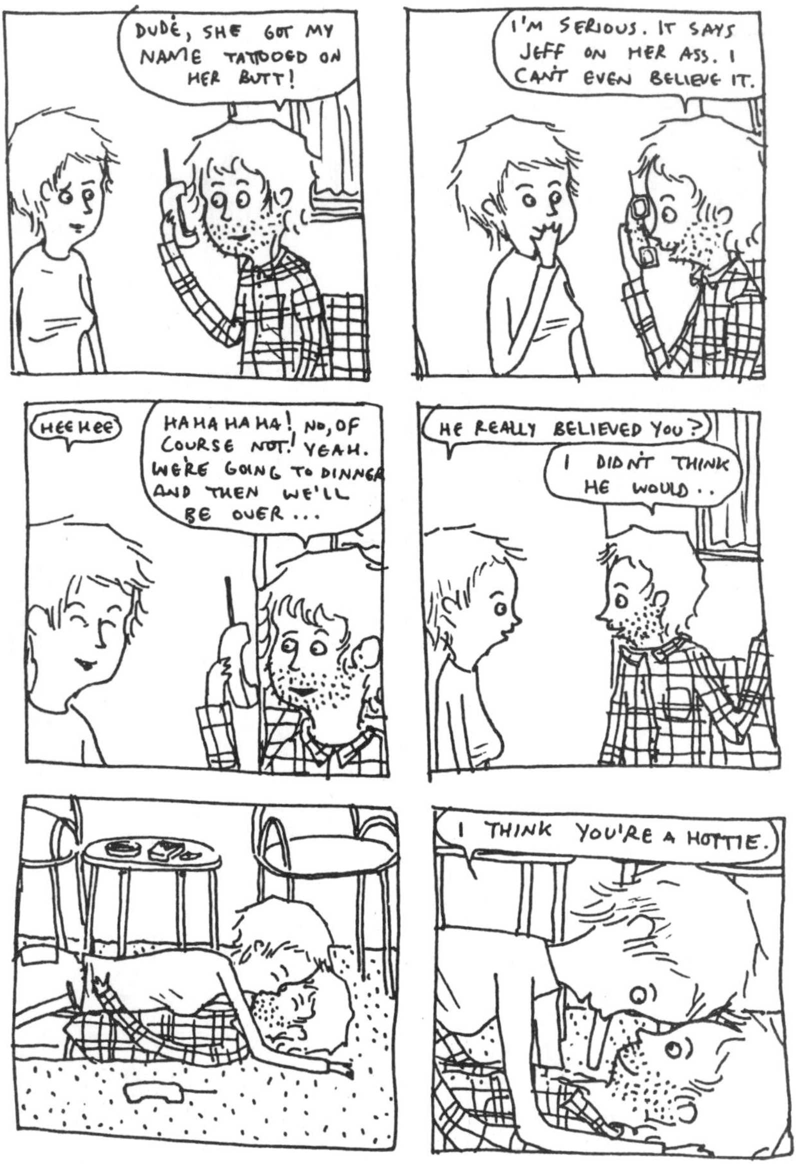
DUDE, SHE GOT MY NAME TATTOOED ON HER BUTT!
I'M SERIOUS. IT SAYS JEFF ON HER ASS. I CAN'T EVEN BELIEVE IT.
HEE HEE
HAHAHAHA! NO, OF COURSE NOT! YEAH. WE'RE GOING TO DINNER AND THEN WE'LL BE OVER...
HE REALLY BELIEVED YOU?
I DIDN'T THINK HE WOULD..
I THINK YOU'RE A HOTTIE.

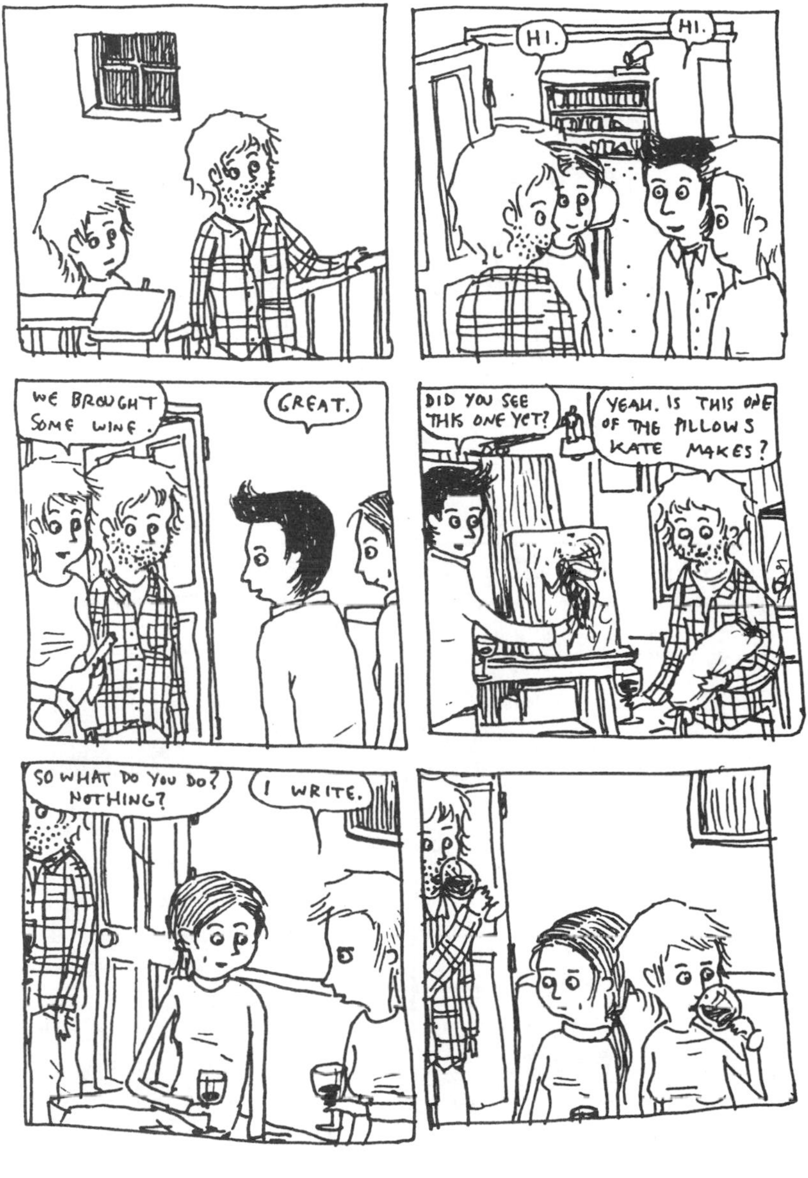
HI.
HI.
WE BROUGHT SOME WINE.
GREAT.
DID YOU SEE THIS ONE YET?
YEAH. IS THIS ONE OF THE PILLOWS KATE MAKES?
SO WHAT DO YOU DO? NOTHING?
I WRITE.

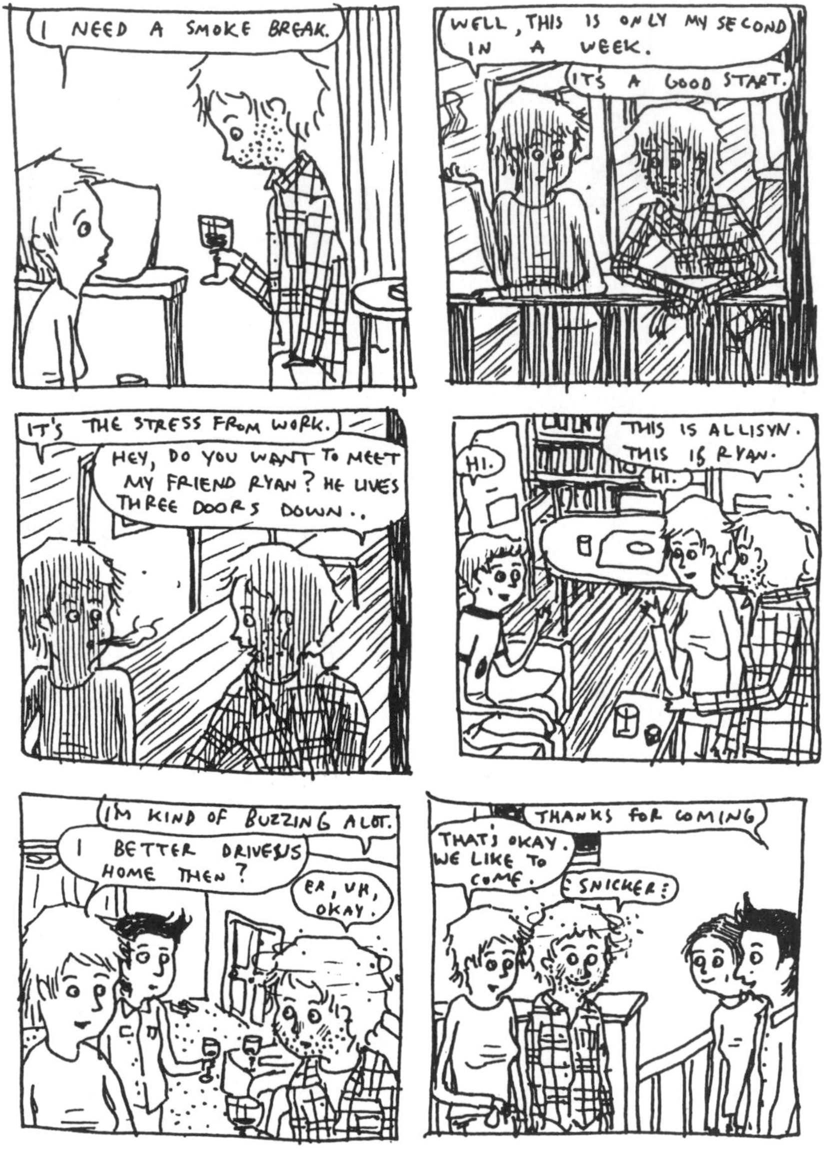
I NEED A SMOKE BREAK.
WELL, THIS IS ONLY MY SECOND IN A WEEK.
IT'S A GOOD START.
IT'S THE STRESS FROM WORK.
HEY, DO YOU WANT TO MEET MY FRIEND RYAN? HE LIVES THREE DOORS DOWN..
HI.
THIS IS ALLISYN. THIS IS RYAN.
HI.
I'M KIND OF BUZZING ALOT.
I BETTER DRIVE US HOME THEN?
ER, UH, OKAY.
THANKS FOR COMING
THAT'S OKAY. WE LIKE TO COME.
SNICKER!

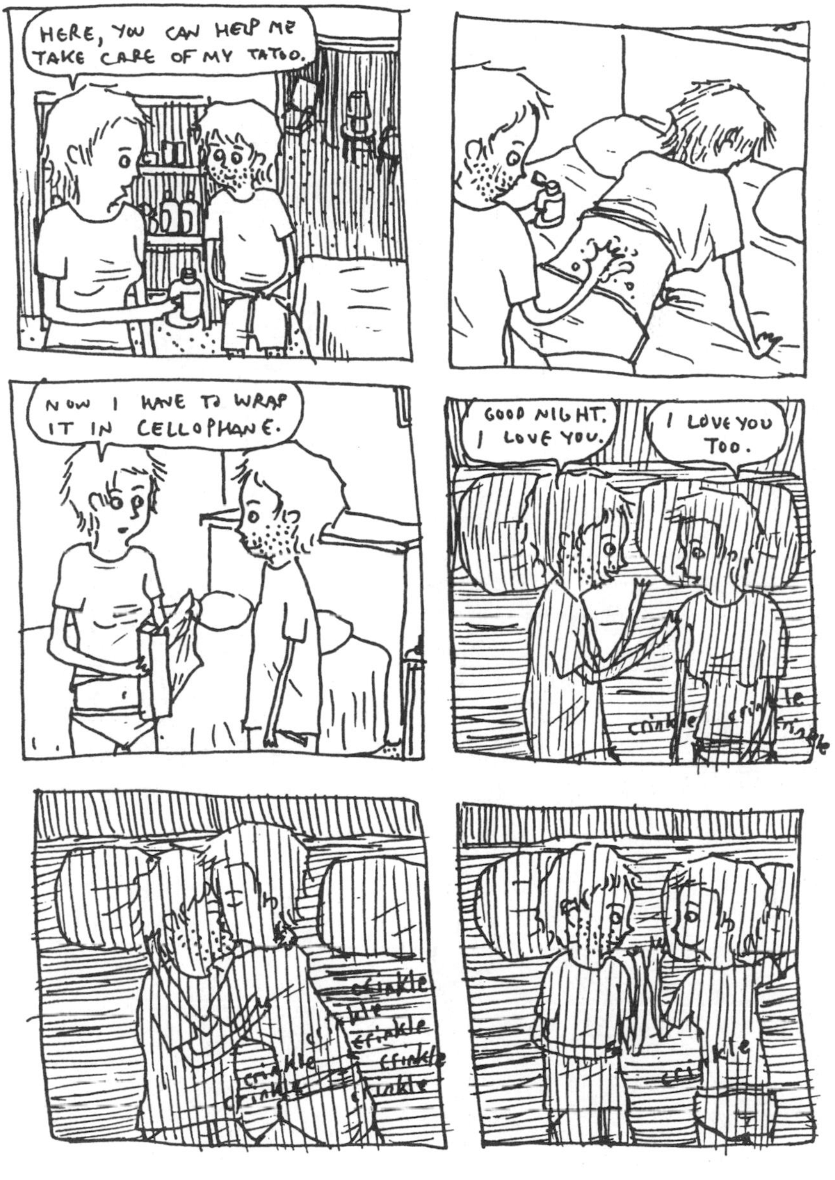
HERE, YOU CAN HELP ME TAKE CARE OF MY TATOO.
NOW I HAVE TO WRAP IT IN CELLOPHANE.
GOOD NIGHT. I LOVE YOU.
I LOVE YOU TOO.
crinkle crinkle crinkle
crinkle crinkle crinkle crinkle crinkle crinkle crinkle
crinkle

SEX

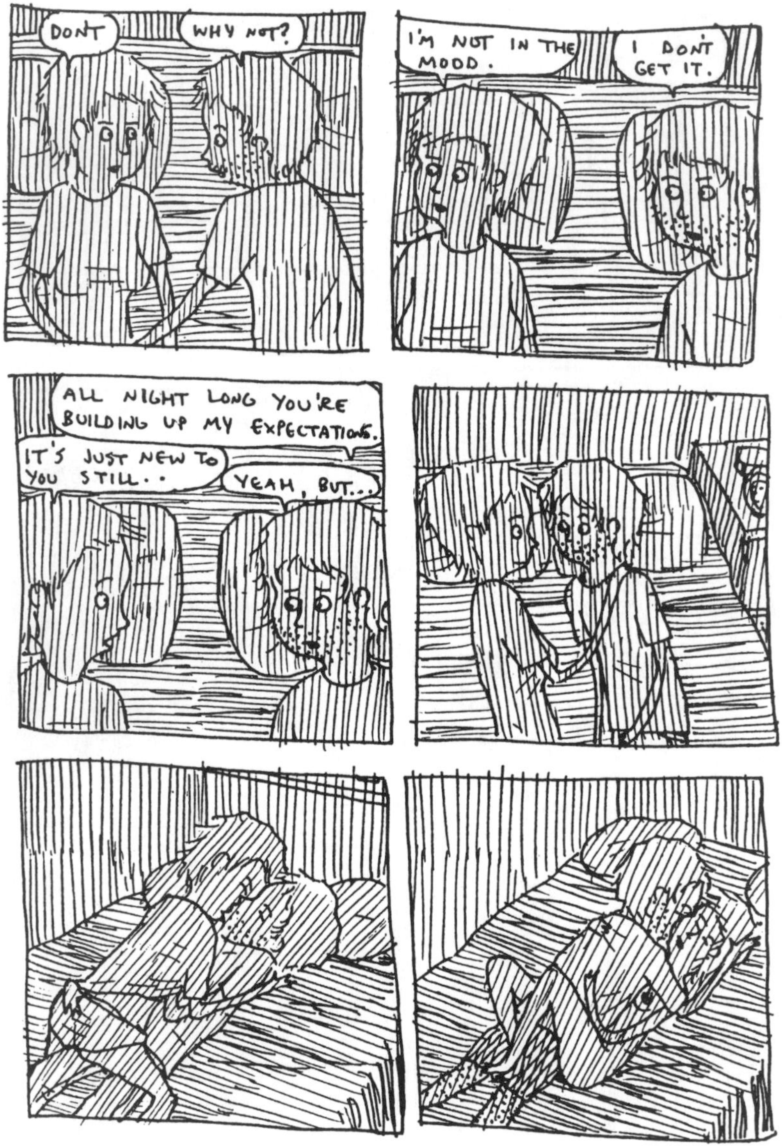
DONT
WHY NOT?
I'M NOT IN THE MOOD.
I DON'T GET IT.
ALL NIGHT LONG YOU'RE BUILDING UP MY EXPECTATIONS.
IT'S JUST NEW TO YOU STILL..
YEAH, BUT...

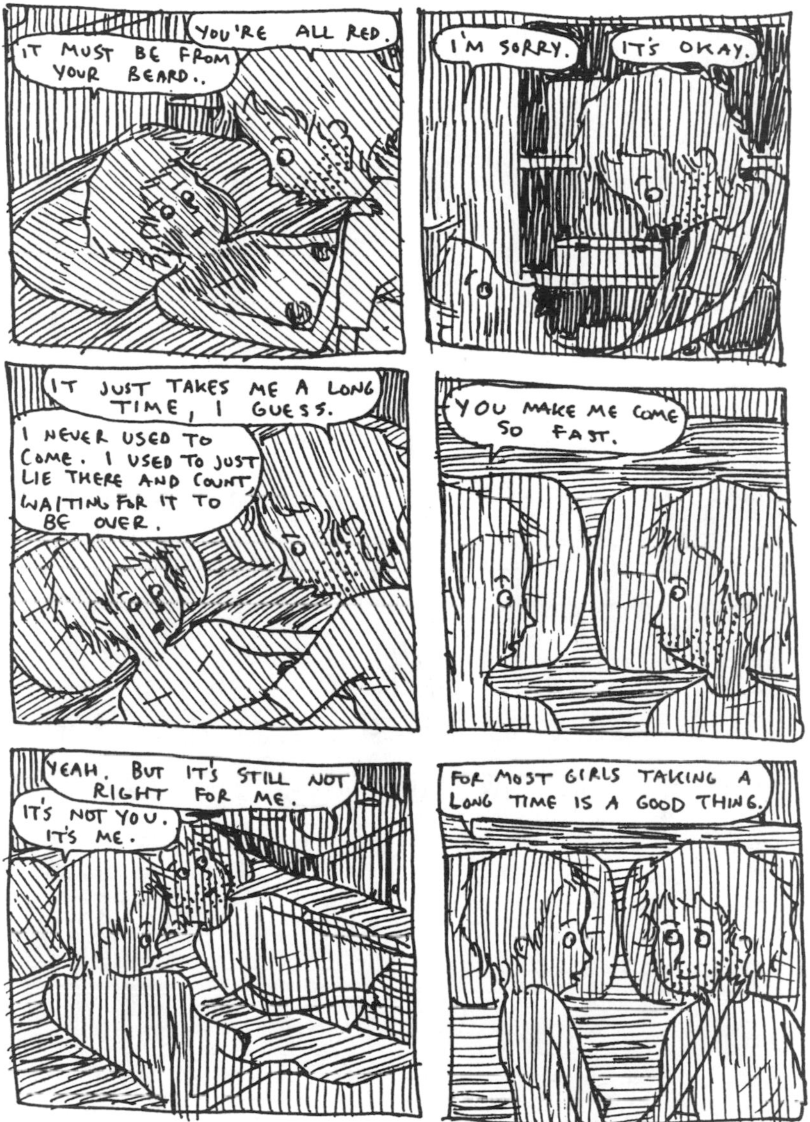
YOU'RE ALL RED.
IT MUST BE FROM YOUR BEARD..
I'M SORRY.
IT'S OKAY.
IT JUST TAKES ME A LONG TIME, I GUESS.
I NEVER USED TO COME. I USED TO JUST LIE THERE AND COUNT WAITING FOR IT TO BE OVER.
YOU MAKE ME COME SO FAST.
YEAH. BUT IT'S STILL NOT RIGHT FOR ME.
IT'S NOT YOU. IT'S ME.
FOR MOST GIRLS TAKING A LONG TIME IS A GOOD THING.

VALENTINE'S DAY

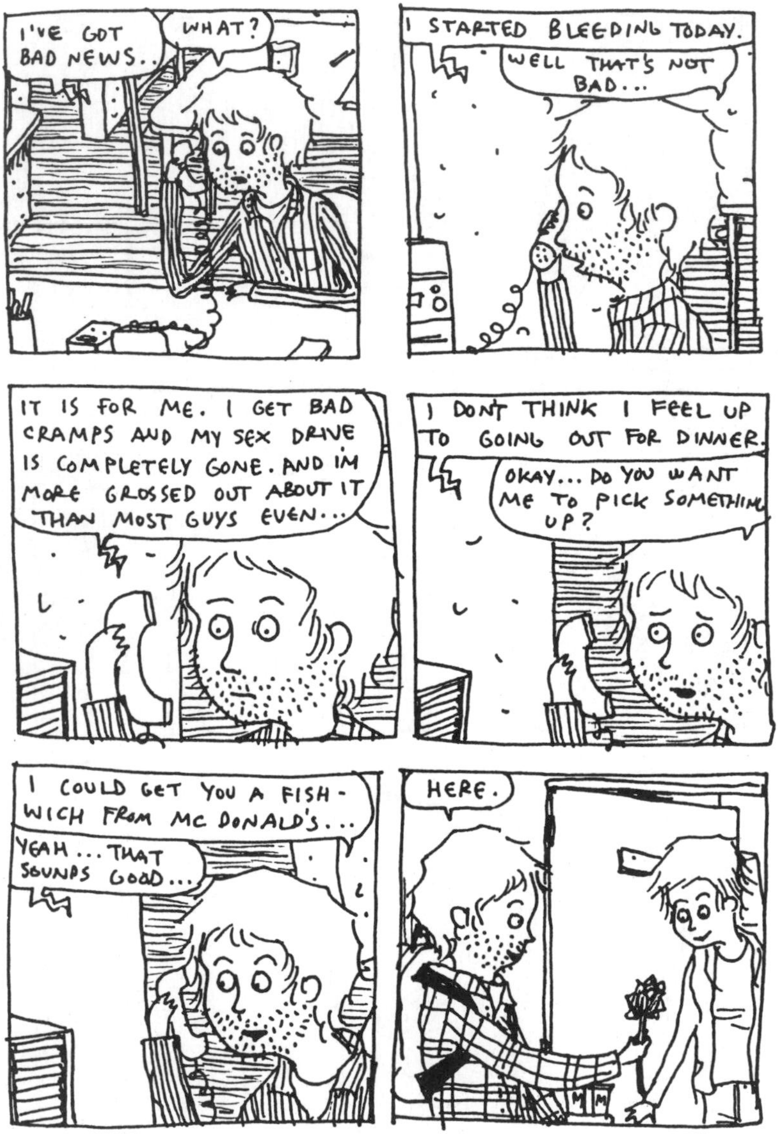
I'VE GOT BAD NEWS...
WHAT?
I STARTED BLEEDING TODAY.
WELL THAT'S NOT BAD...
IT IS FOR ME. I GET BAD CRAMPS AND MY SEX DRIVE IS COMPLETELY GONE. AND IM MORE GROSSED OUT ABOUT IT THAN MOST GUYS EVEN...
I DONT THINK I FEEL UP TO GOING OUT FOR DINNER.
OKAY... DO YOU WANT ME TO PICK SOMETHING UP?
I COULD GET YOU A FISH-WICH FROM MC DONALD'S...
YEAH... THAT SOUNDS GOOD...
HERE.

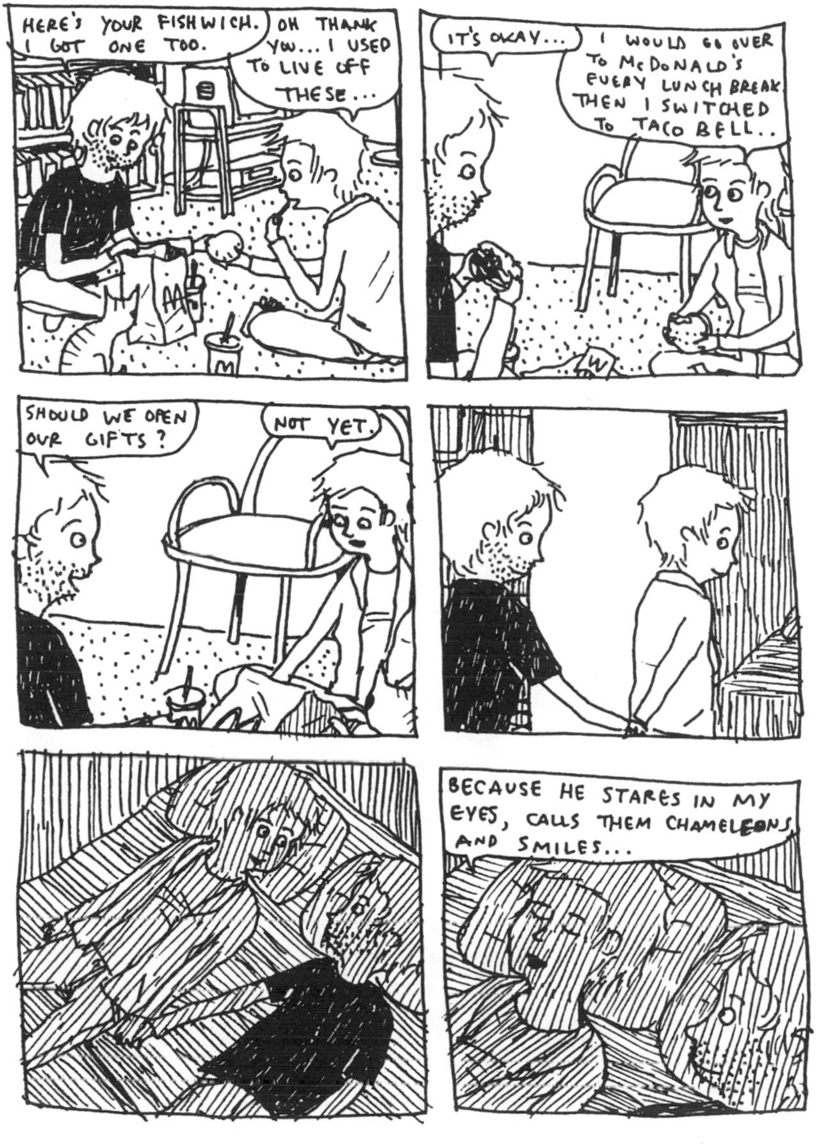
HERE'S YOUR FISHWICH. I GOT ONE TOO.
OH THANK YOU... I USED TO LIVE OFF THESE...
IT'S OKAY...
I WOULD GO OVER TO McDONALD'S EVERY LUNCH BREAK THEN I SWITCHED TO TACO BELL..
SHOULD WE OPEN OUR GIFTS?
NOT YET.
BECAUSE HE STARES IN MY EYES, CALLS THEM CHAMELEONS AND SMILES...

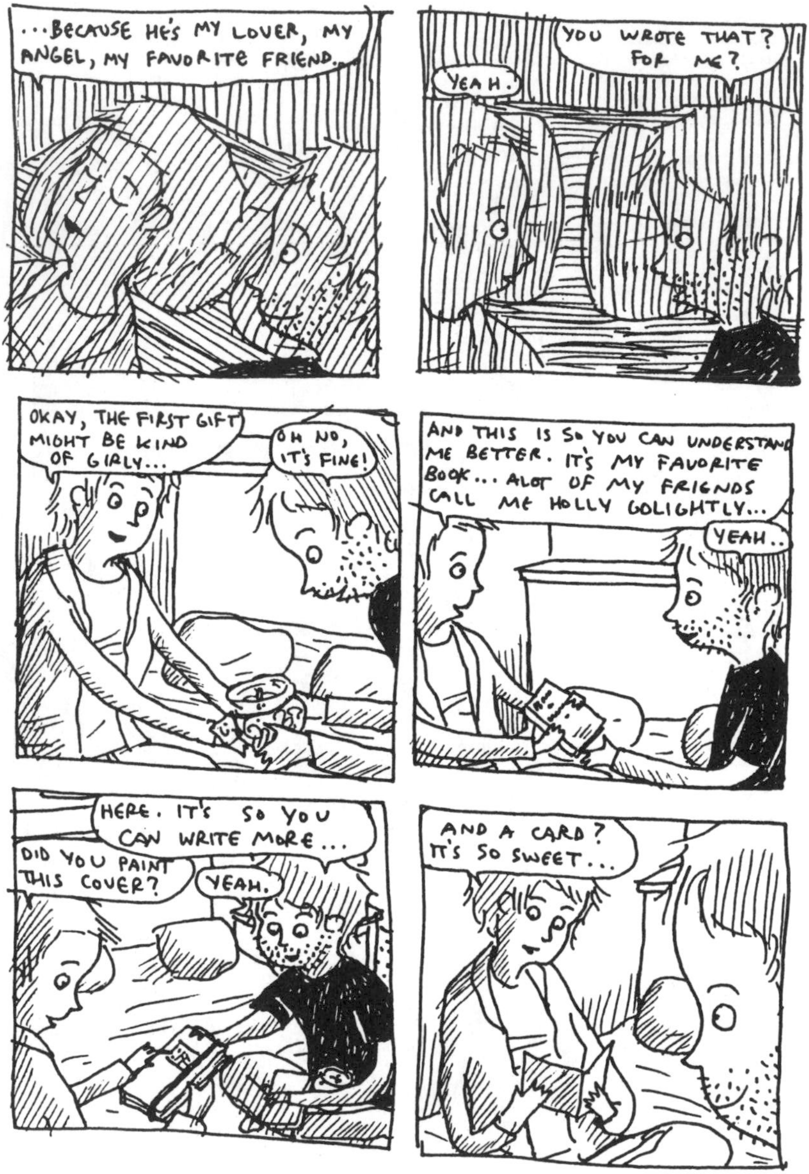
...BECAUSE HE'S MY LOVER, MY ANGEL, MY FAVORITE FRIEND...
YOU WROTE THAT? FOR ME?
YEAH.
OKAY, THE FIRST GIFT MIGHT BE KIND OF GIRLY...
OH NO, IT'S FINE!
AND THIS IS SO YOU CAN UNDERSTAND ME BETTER. IT'S MY FAVORITE BOOK... ALOT OF MY FRIENDS CALL ME HOLLY GOLIGHTLY...
YEAH..
HERE. IT'S SO YOU CAN WRITE MORE...
DID YOU PAINT THIS COVER?
YEAH.
AND A CARD? IT'S SO SWEET...

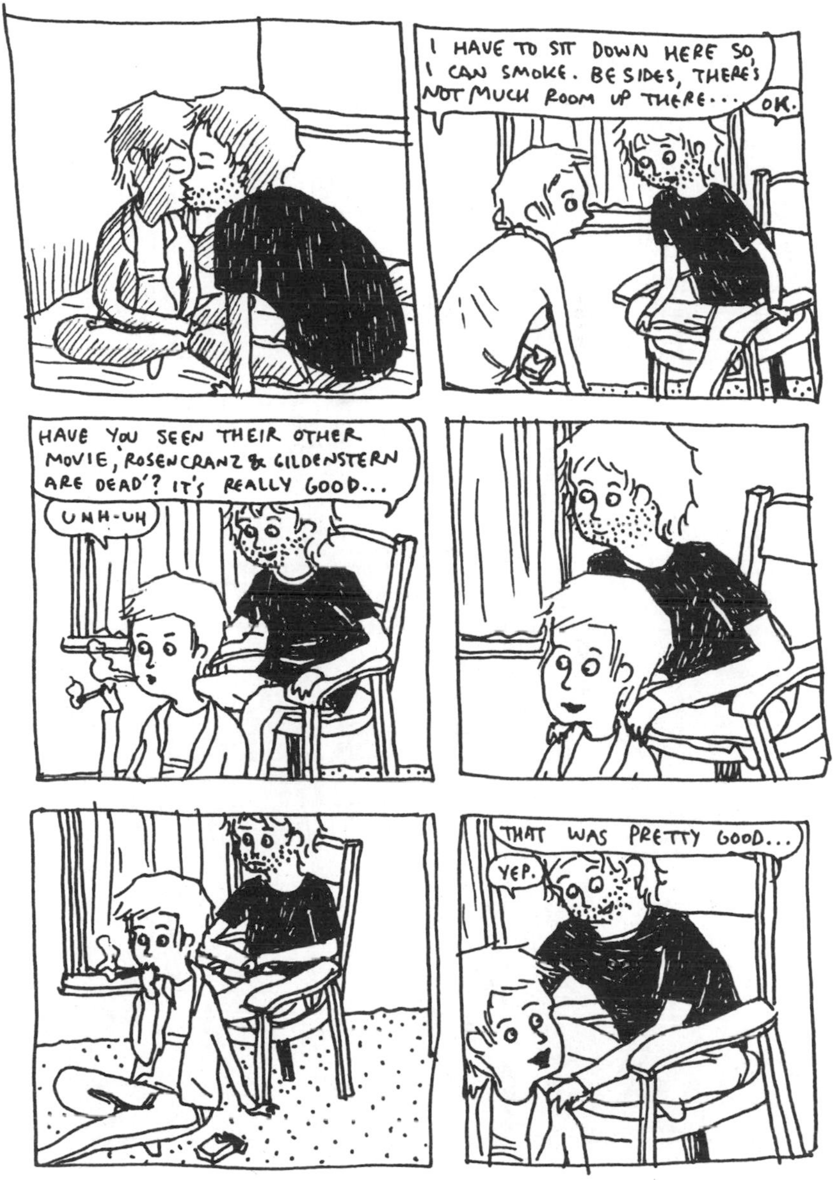
I HAVE TO SIT DOWN HERE SO, I CAN SMOKE. BESIDES, THERE'S NOT MUCH ROOM UP THERE...
OK.
HAVE YOU SEEN THEIR OTHER MOVIE, 'ROSENCRANZ & GILDENSTERN ARE DEAD'? IT'S REALLY GOOD...
UNH-UH
THAT WAS PRETTY GOOD...
YEP.

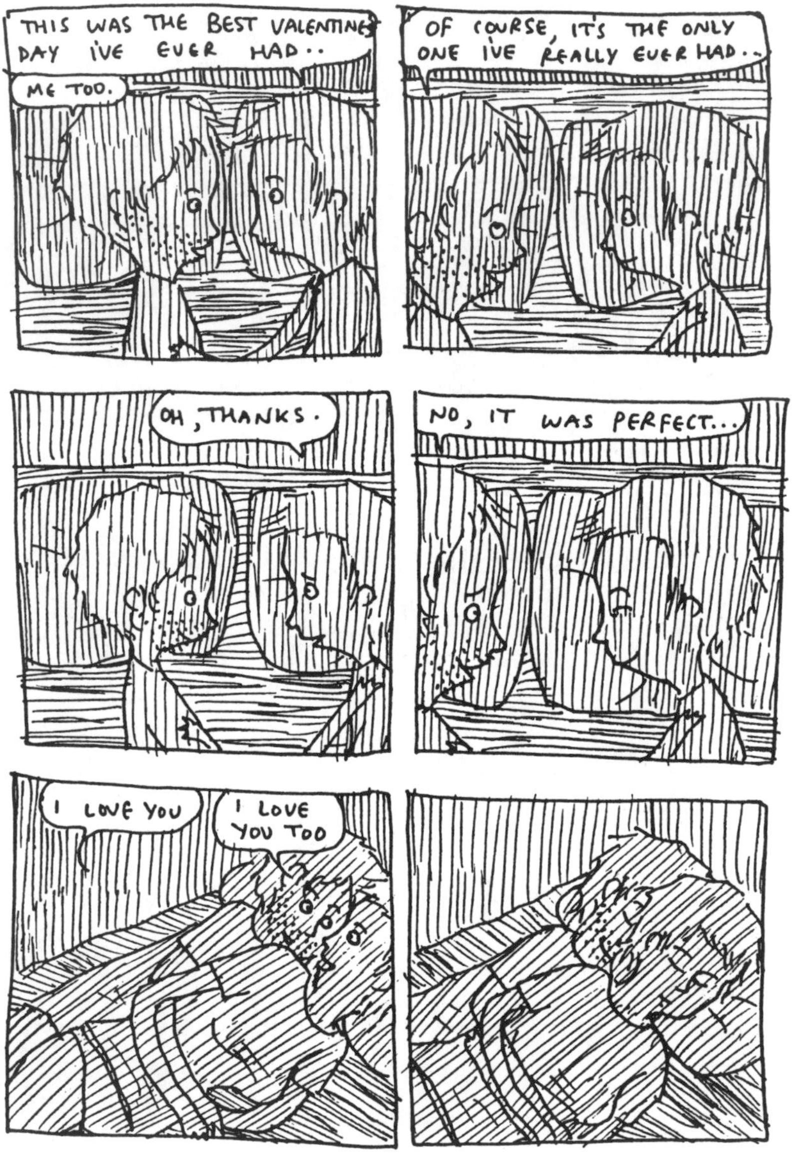
THIS WAS THE BEST VALENTINES DAY I'VE EVER HAD..
ME TOO.
OF COURSE, IT'S THE ONLY ONE I'VE REALLY EVER HAD..
OH, THANKS.
NO, IT WAS PERFECT...
I LOVE YOU
I LOVE YOU TOO

LATE

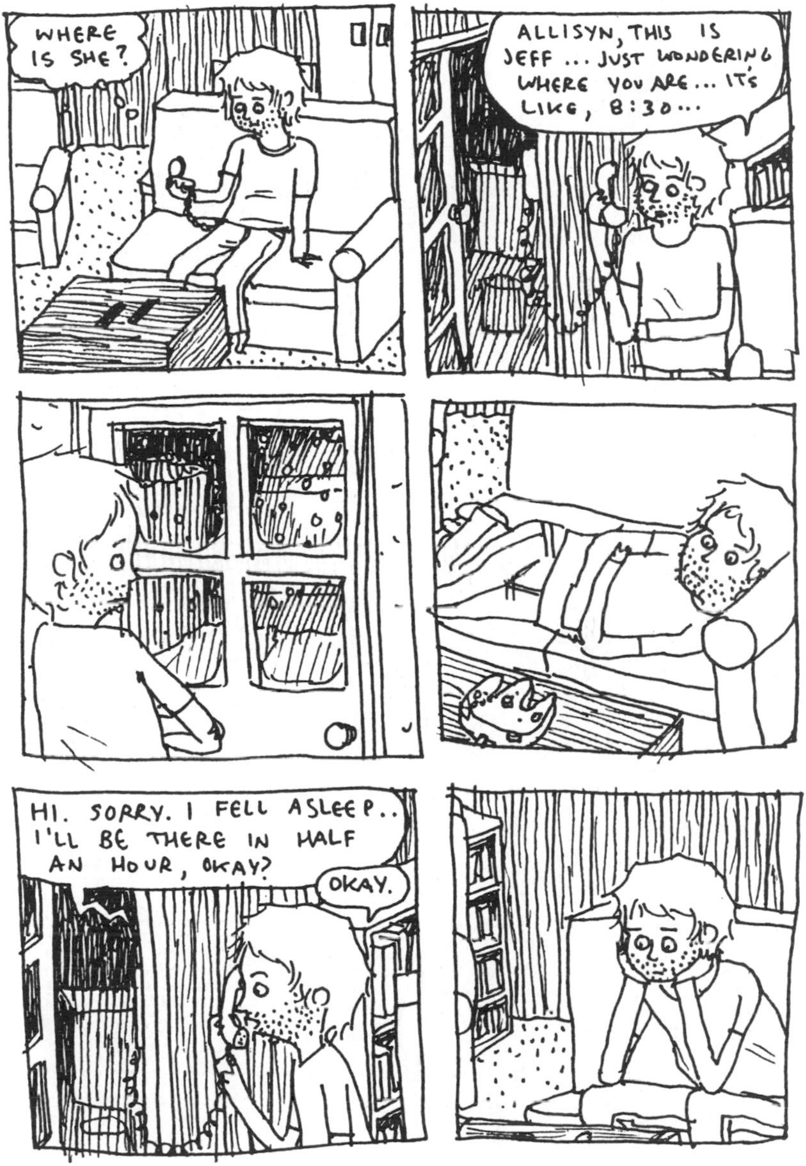
WHERE IS SHE?
ALLISYN, THIS IS JEFF ... JUST WONDERING WHERE YOU ARE... IT'S LIKE, 8:30...
HI. SORRY. I FELL ASLEEP.. I'LL BE THERE IN HALF AN HOUR, OKAY?
OKAY.

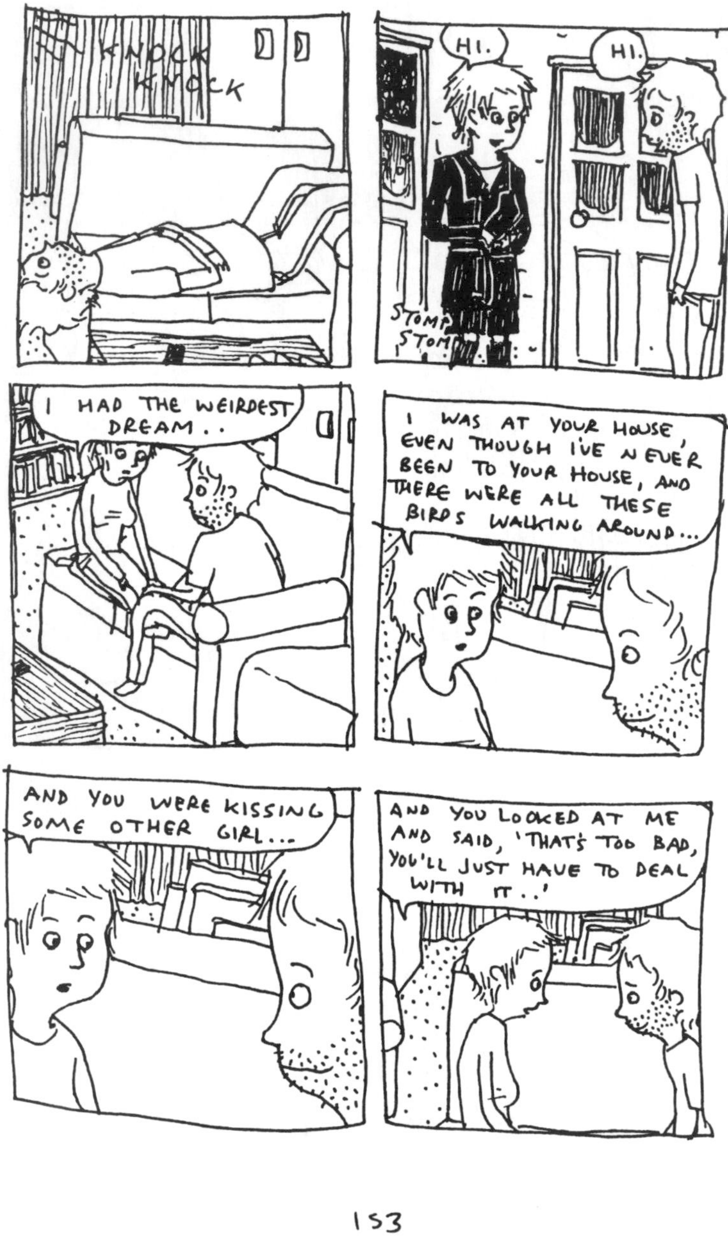
KNOCK
KNOCK
HI.
HI.
STOMP
STOMP
I HAD THE WEIRDEST DREAM..
I WAS AT YOUR HOUSE, EVEN THOUGH I'VE NEVER BEEN TO YOUR HOUSE, AND THERE WERE ALL THESE BIRDS WALKING AROUND...
AND YOU WERE KISSING SOME OTHER GIRL...
AND YOU LOOKED AT ME AND SAID, 'THAT'S TOO BAD, YOU'LL JUST HAVE TO DEAL WITH IT..'

SWEETNESS FRUSTRATION

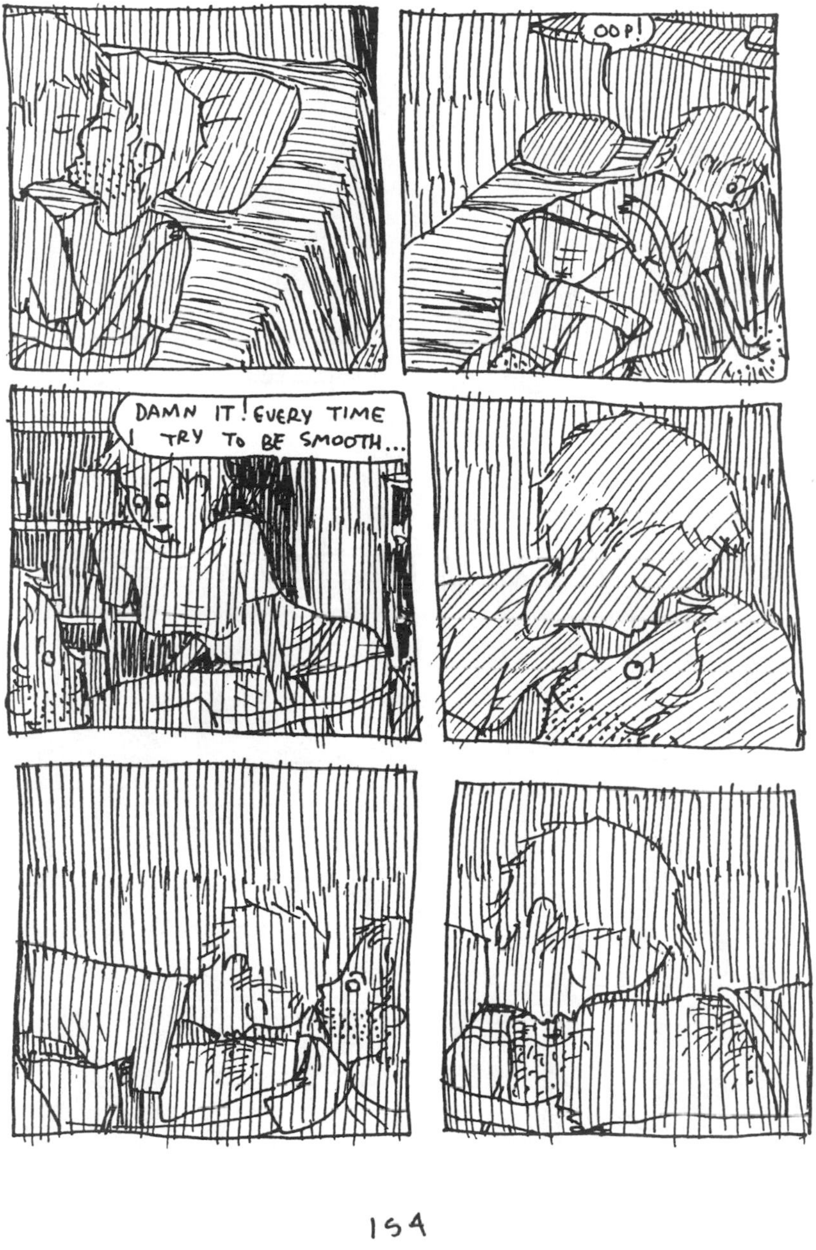
OOP!
DAMN IT! EVERY TIME I TRY TO BE SMOOTH...

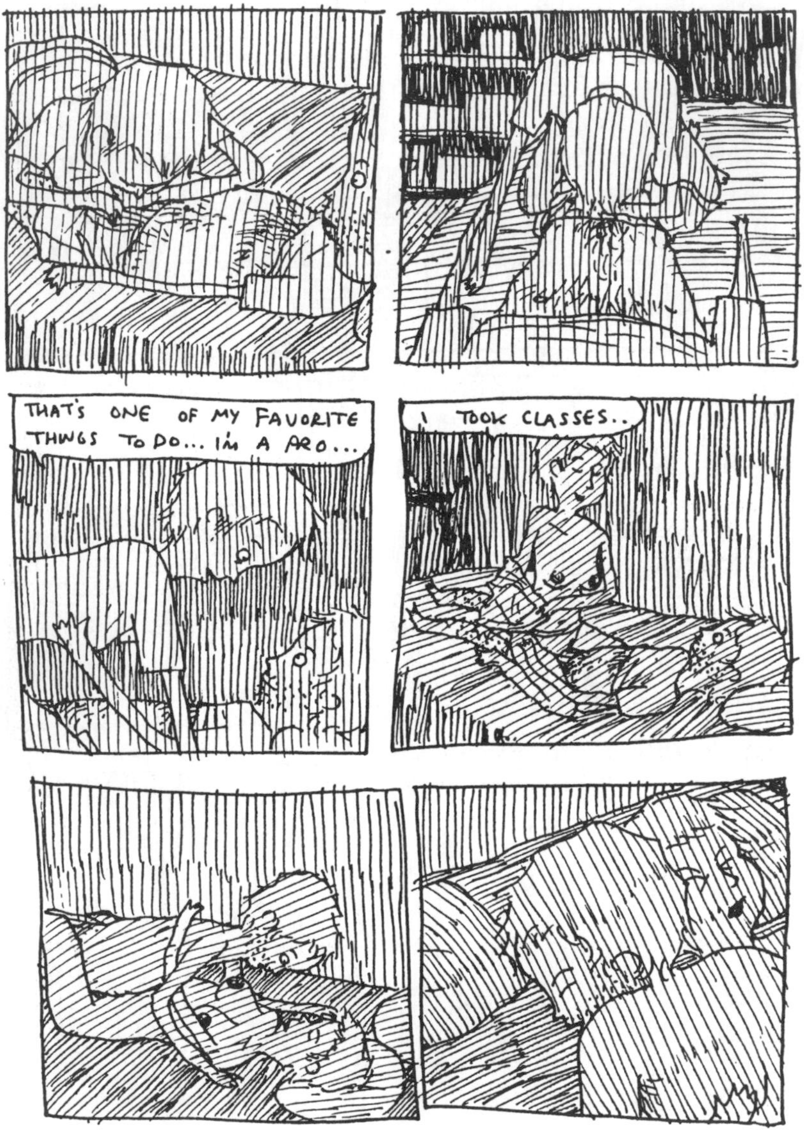
THAT'S ONE OF MY FAVORITE THINGS TO DO... I'M A PRO...
I TOOK CLASSES..

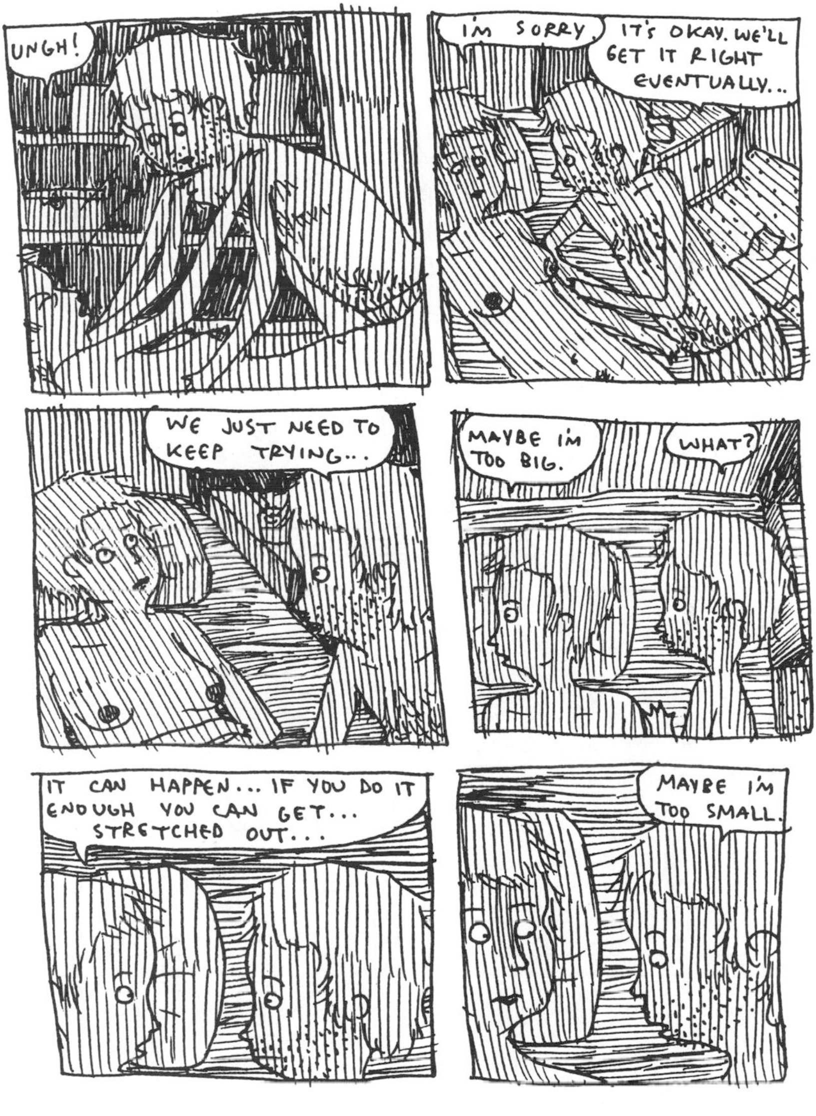
UNGH!
I'M SORRY.
IT'S OKAY. WE'LL GET IT RIGHT EVENTUALLY...
WE JUST NEED TO KEEP TRYING...
MAYBE I'M TOO BIG.
WHAT?
IT CAN HAPPEN... IF YOU DO IT ENOUGH YOU CAN GET... STRETCHED OUT...
MAYBE I'M TOO SMALL.

FLAT

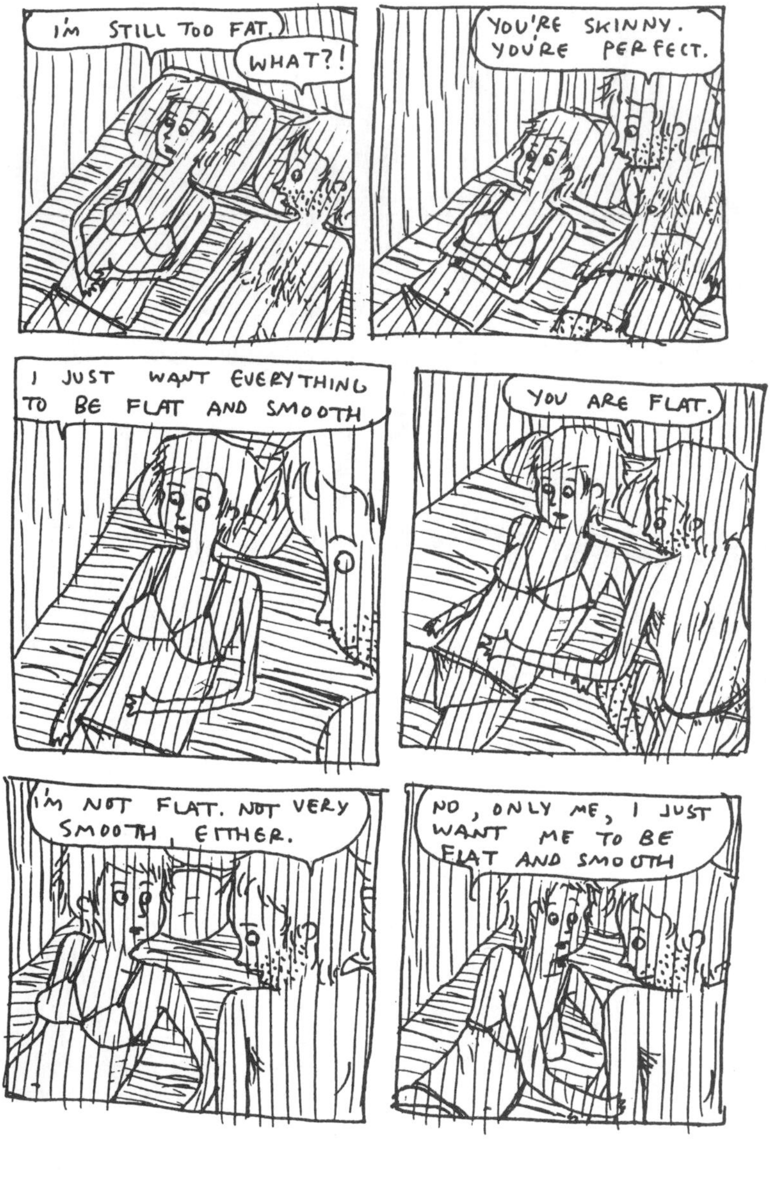
I'M STILL TOO FAT.
WHAT?!
YOU'RE SKINNY. YOU'RE PERFECT.
I JUST WANT EVERYTHING TO BE FLAT AND SMOOTH
YOU ARE FLAT.
I'M NOT FLAT. NOT VERY SMOOTH, EITHER.
NO, ONLY ME, I JUST WANT ME TO BE FLAT AND SMOOTH

GIFTS

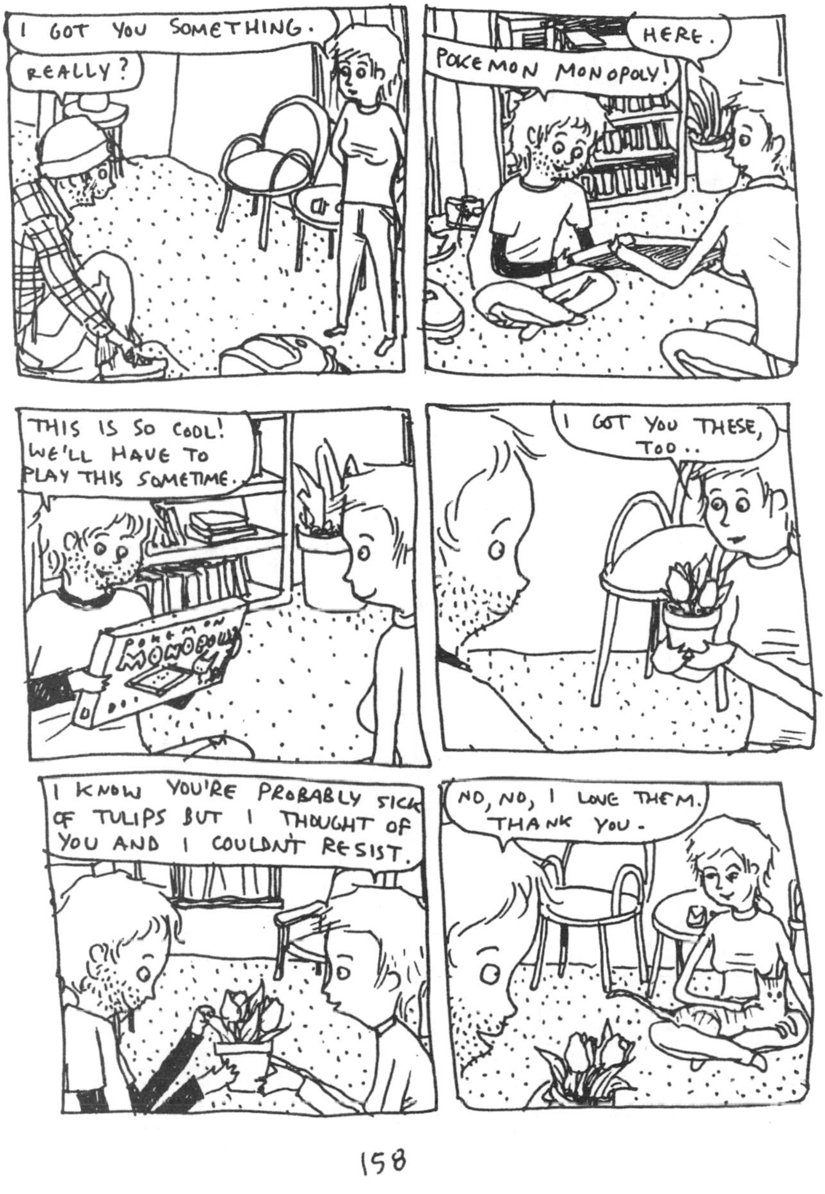
I GOT YOU SOMETHING.
REALLY?
HERE.
POKEMON MONOPOLY!
THIS IS SO COOL! WE'LL HAVE TO PLAY THIS SOMETIME.
I GOT YOU THESE, TOO..
I KNOW YOU'RE PROBABLY SICK OF TULIPS BUT I THOUGHT OF YOU AND I COULDN'T RESIST.
NO, NO, I LOVE THEM. THANK YOU.

JONES

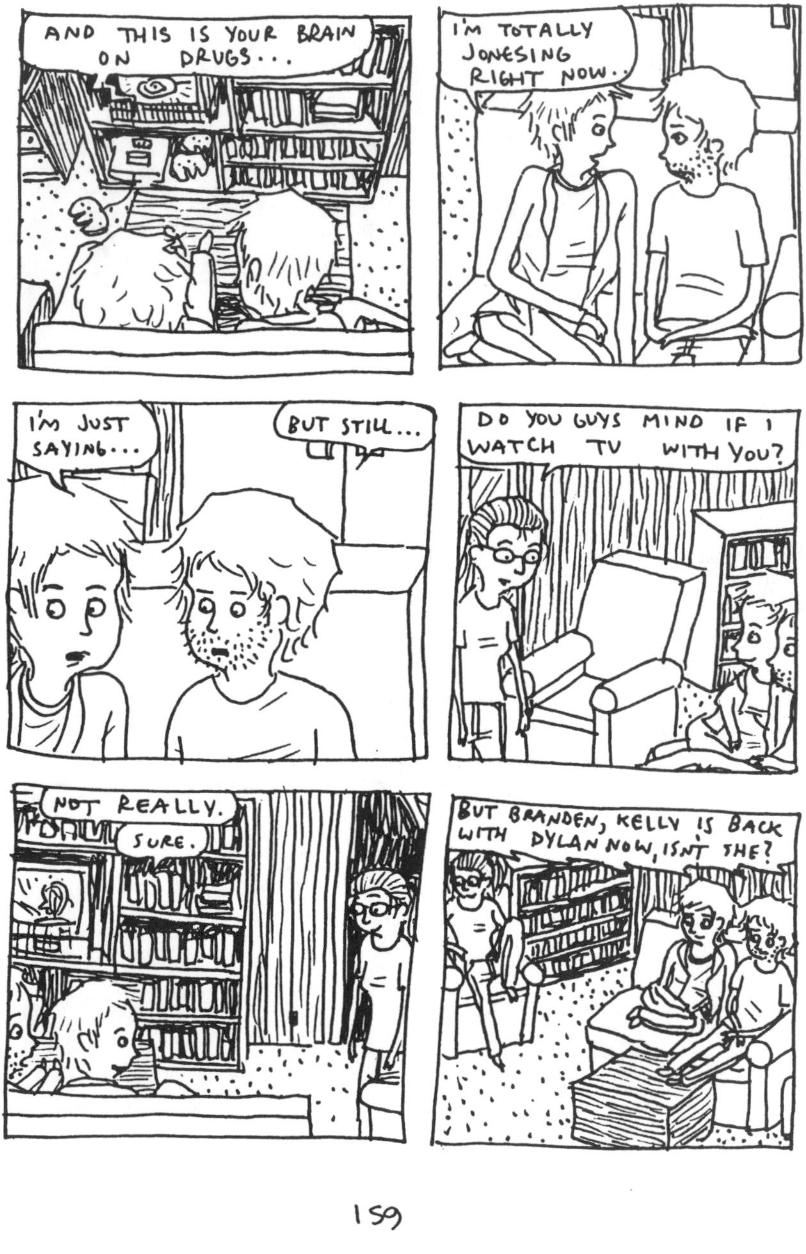
AND THIS IS YOUR BRAIN ON DRUGS...
I'M TOTALLY JONESING RIGHT NOW..
I'M JUST SAYING...
BUT STILL...
DO YOU GUYS MIND IF I WATCH TV WITH YOU?
NOT REALLY.
SURE.
BUT BRANDEN, KELLY IS BACK WITH DYLAN NOW, ISN'T SHE?

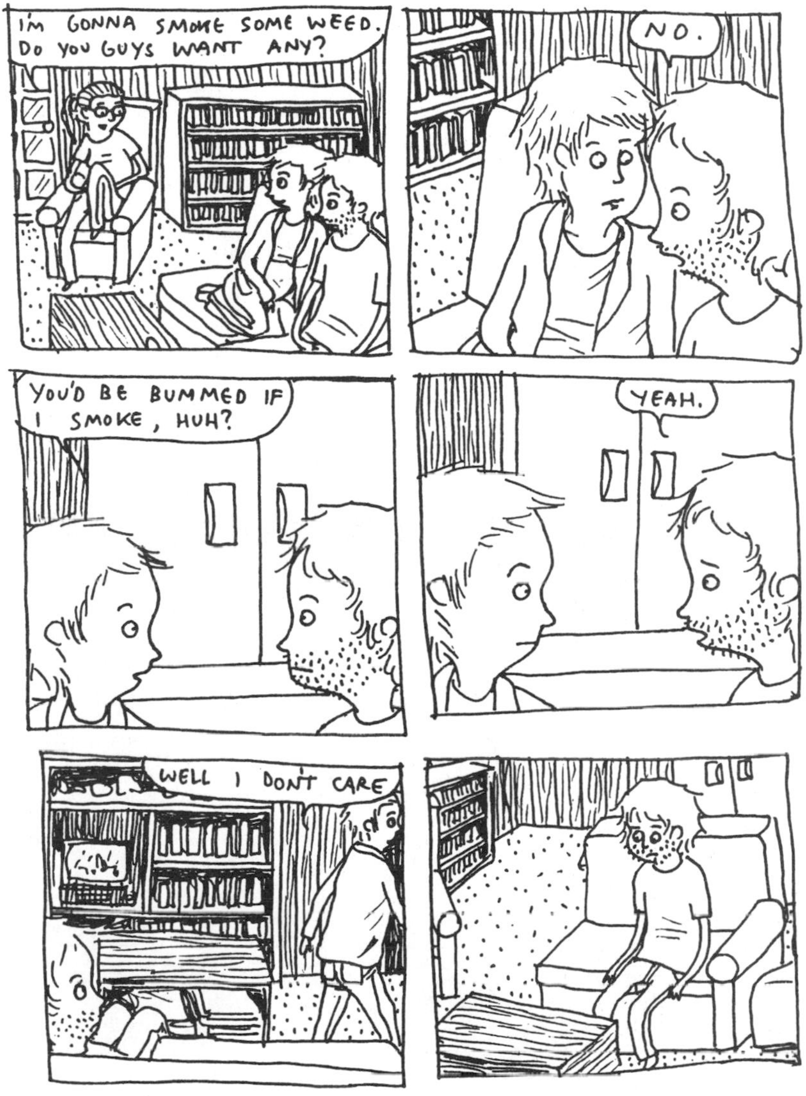
I'M GONNA SMOKE SOME WEED. DO YOU GUYS WANT ANY?
NO.
YOU'D BE BUMMED IF I SMOKE, HUH?
YEAH.
WELL I DON'T CARE

INSOMNIA

WEED

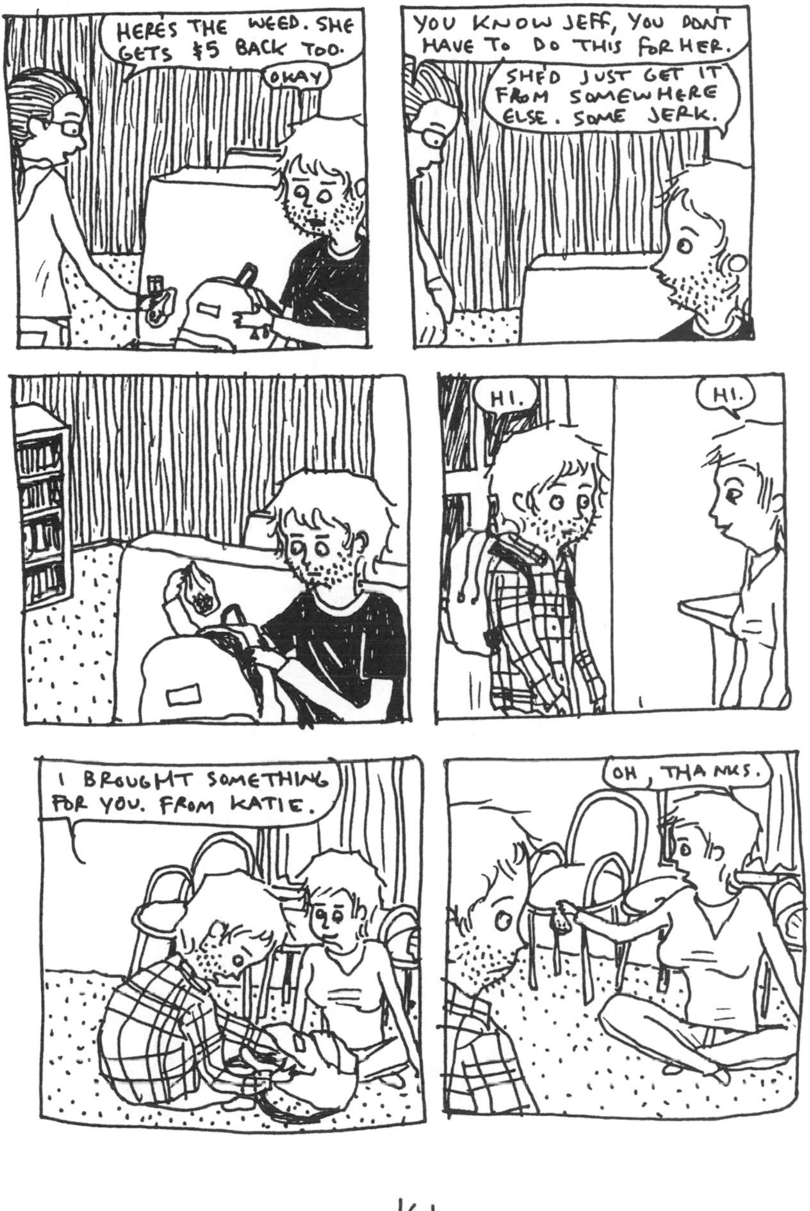
HERE'S THE WEED. SHE GETS $5 BACK TOO.
OKAY
YOU KNOW JEFF, YOU DON'T HAVE TO DO THIS FOR HER.
SHE'D JUST GET IT FROM SOMEWHERE ELSE. SOME JERK.
HI.
HI.
I BROUGHT SOMETHING FOR YOU. FROM KATIE.
OH, THANKS.

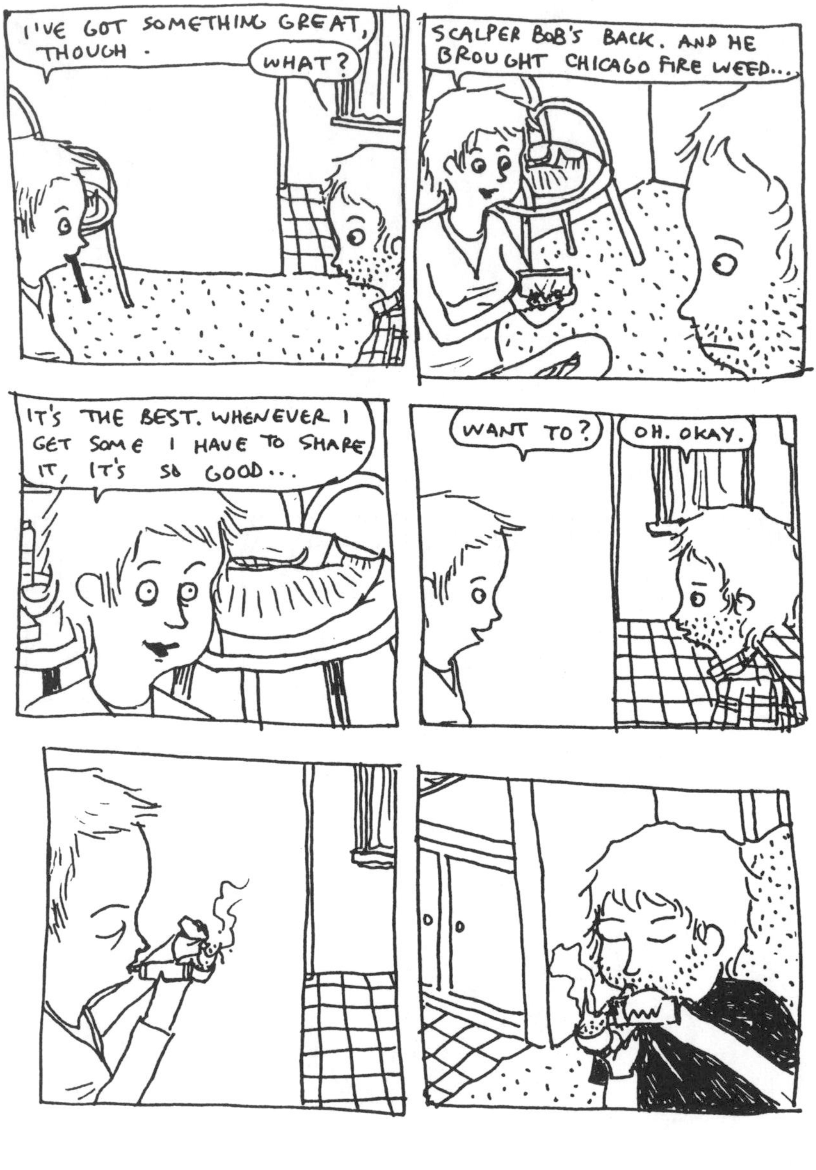
I'VE GOT SOMETHING GREAT, THOUGH.
WHAT?
SCALPER BOB'S BACK. AND HE BROUGHT CHICAGO FIRE WEED...
IT'S THE BEST. WHENEVER I GET SOME I HAVE TO SHARE IT, IT'S SO GOOD...
WANT TO?
OH. OKAY.

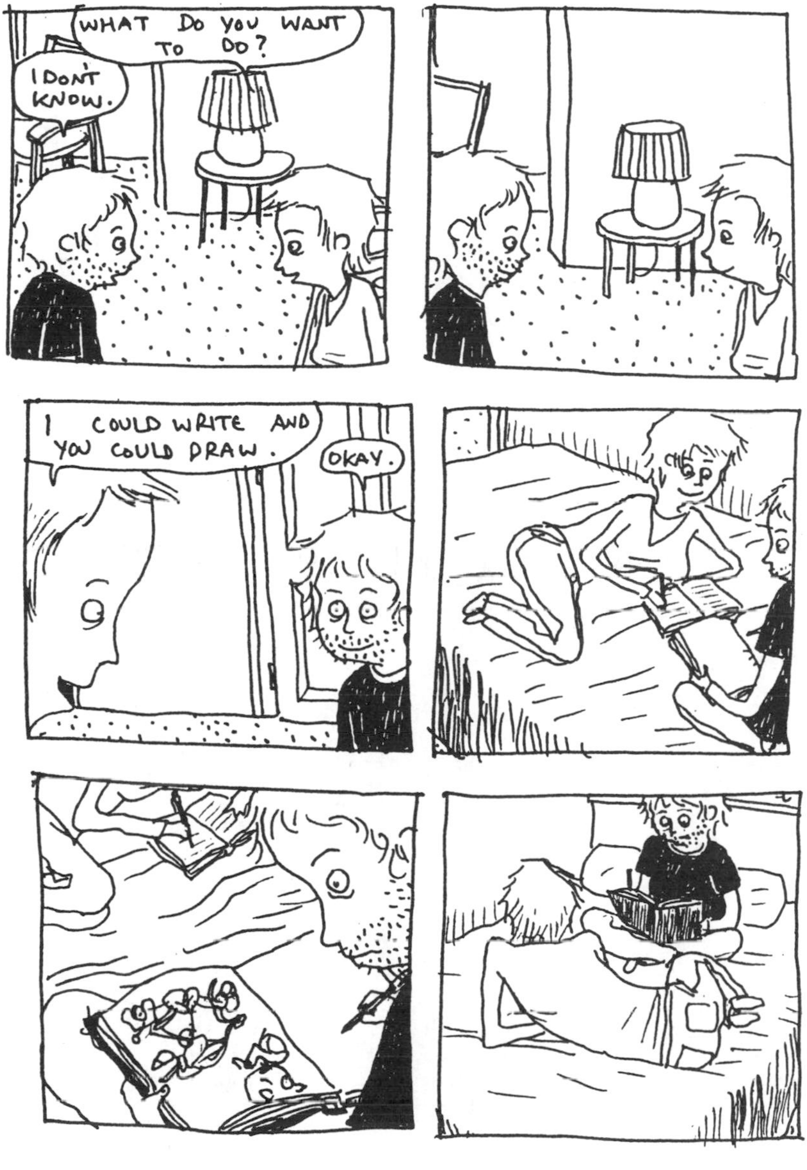
WHAT DO YOU WANT TO DO?
I DON'T KNOW.
I COULD WRITE AND YOU COULD DRAW.
OKAY.

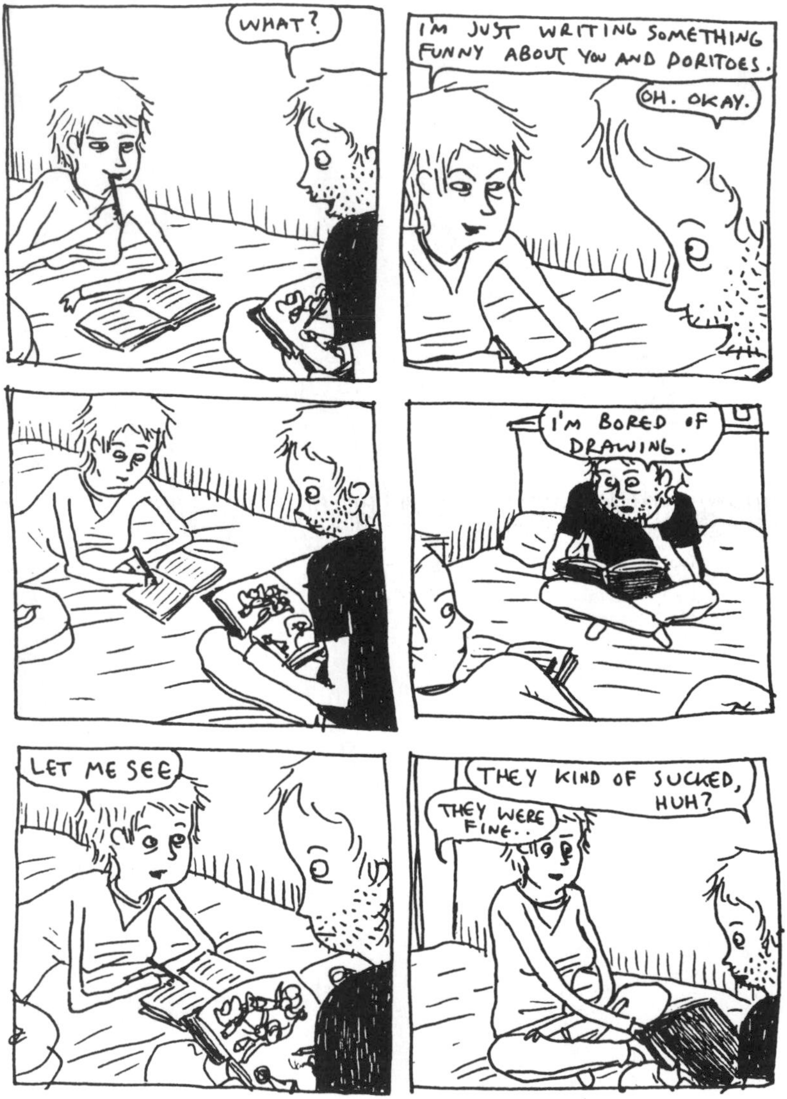
WHAT?
I'M JUST WRITING SOMETHING FUNNY ABOUT YOU AND DORITOES.
OH. OKAY.
I'M BORED OF DRAWING.
LET ME SEE
THEY KIND OF SUCKED, HUH?
THEY WERE FINE..

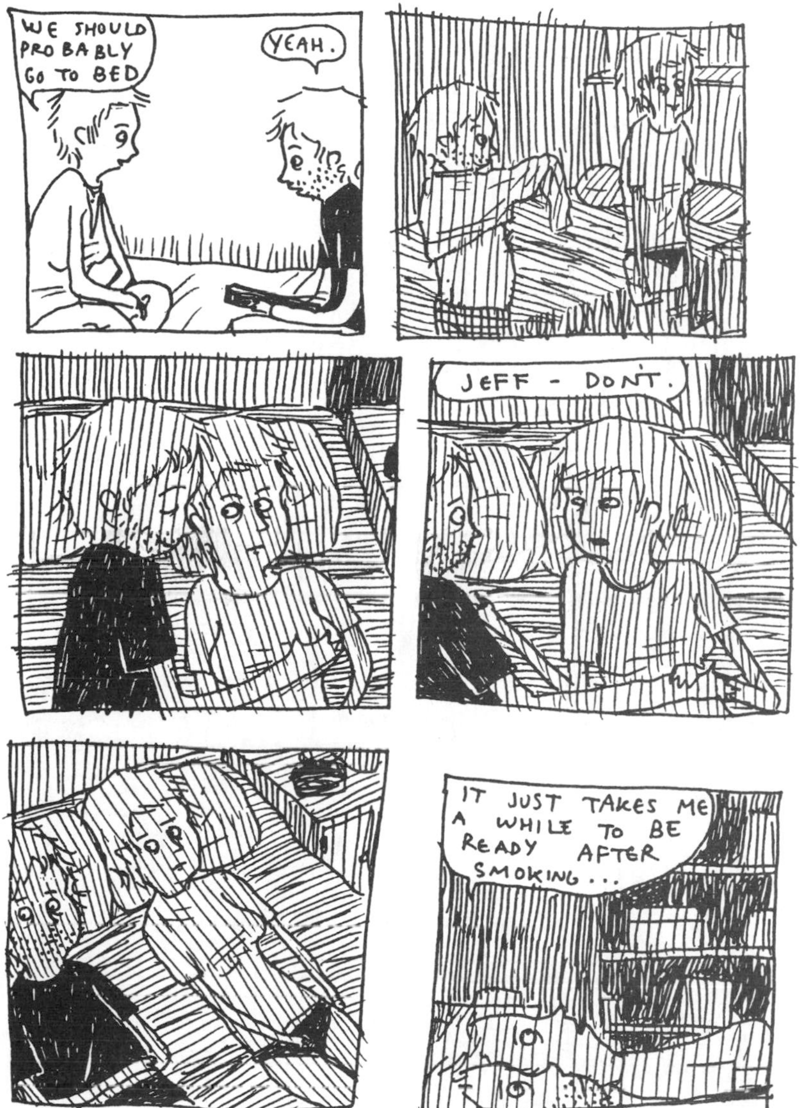
WE SHOULD PROBABLY GO TO BED
YEAH.
JEFF - DON'T.
IT JUST TAKES ME A WHILE TO BE READY AFTER SMOKING...

WRONG

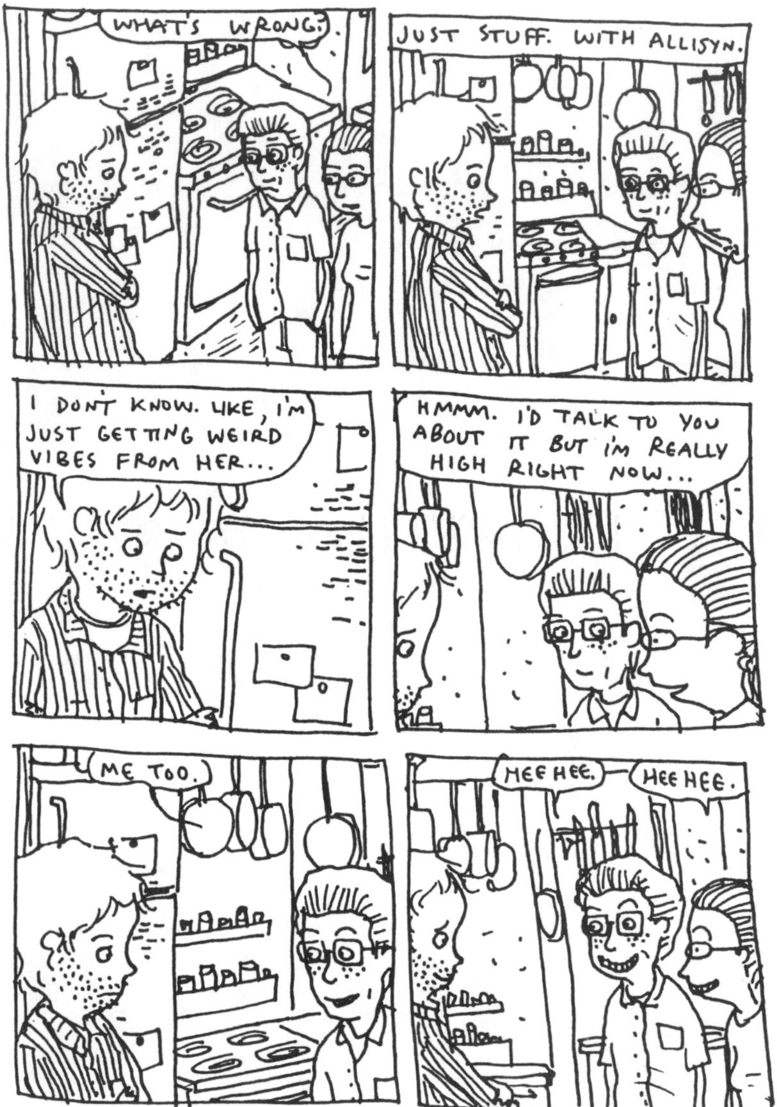
WHAT'S WRONG?
JUST STUFF. WITH ALLISYN.
I DON'T KNOW. LIKE, I'M JUST GETTING WEIRD VIBES FROM HER...
HMMM. I'D TALK TO YOU ABOUT IT BUT I'M REALLY HIGH RIGHT NOW...
ME TOO.
HEE HEE.
HEE HEE.

SLEEP

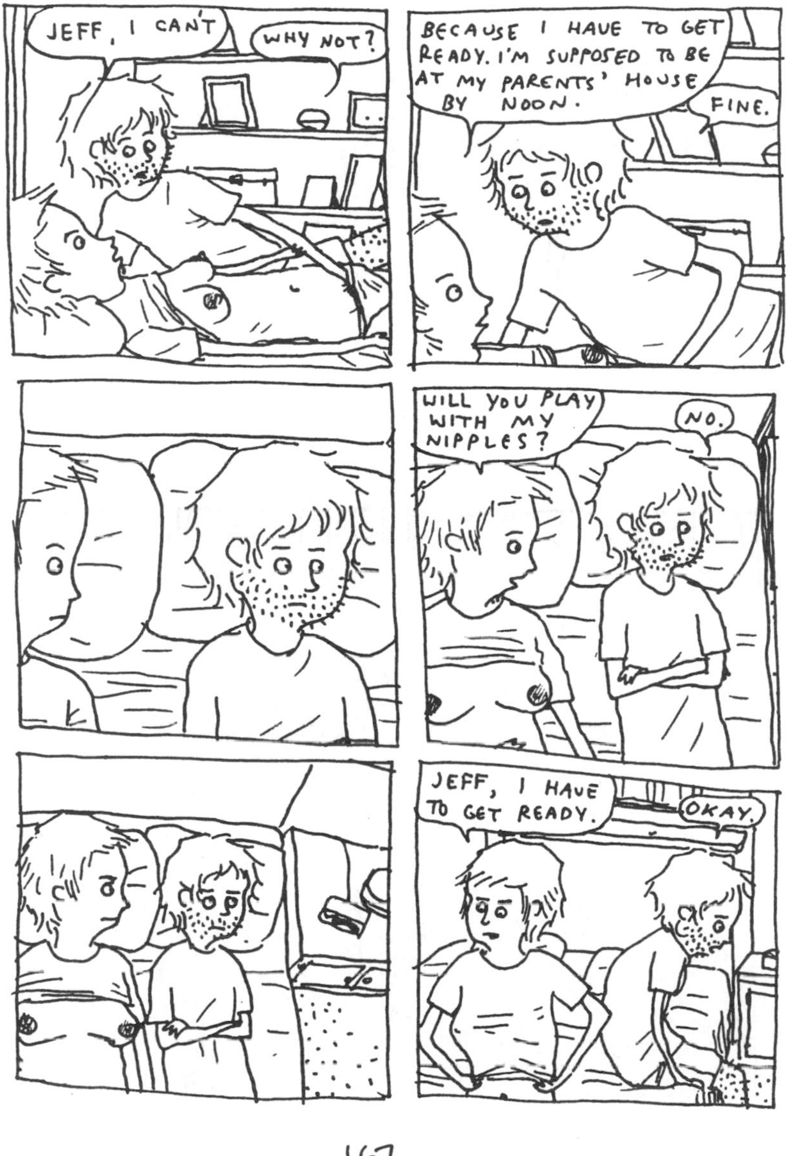
JEFF, I CAN'T
WHY NOT?
BECAUSE I HAVE TO GET READY. I'M SUPPOSED TO BE AT MY PARENTS' HOUSE BY NOON.
FINE.
WILL YOU PLAY WITH MY NIPPLES?
NO.
JEFF, I HAVE TO GET READY.
OKAY.

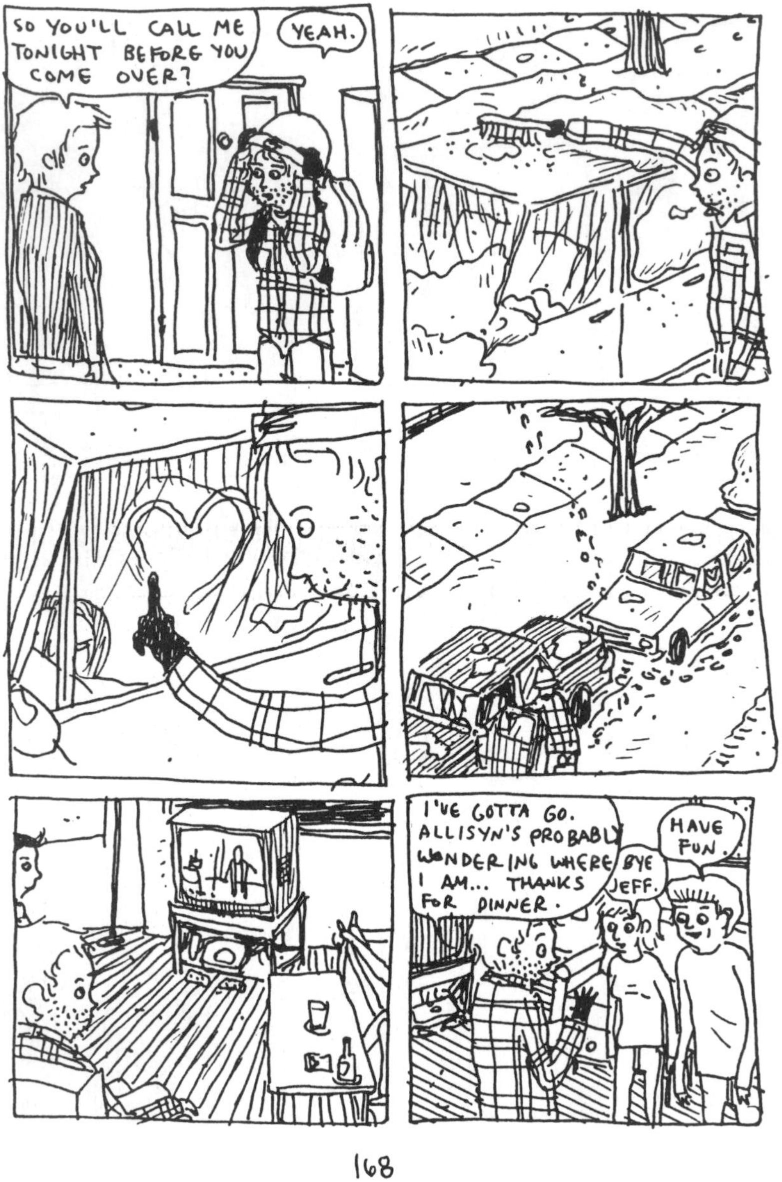
SO YOU'LL CALL ME TONIGHT BEFORE YOU COME OVER?
YEAH.
I'VE GOTTA GO. ALLISYN'S PROBABLY WONDERING WHERE I AM... THANKS FOR DINNER.
BYE JEFF.
HAVE FUN.

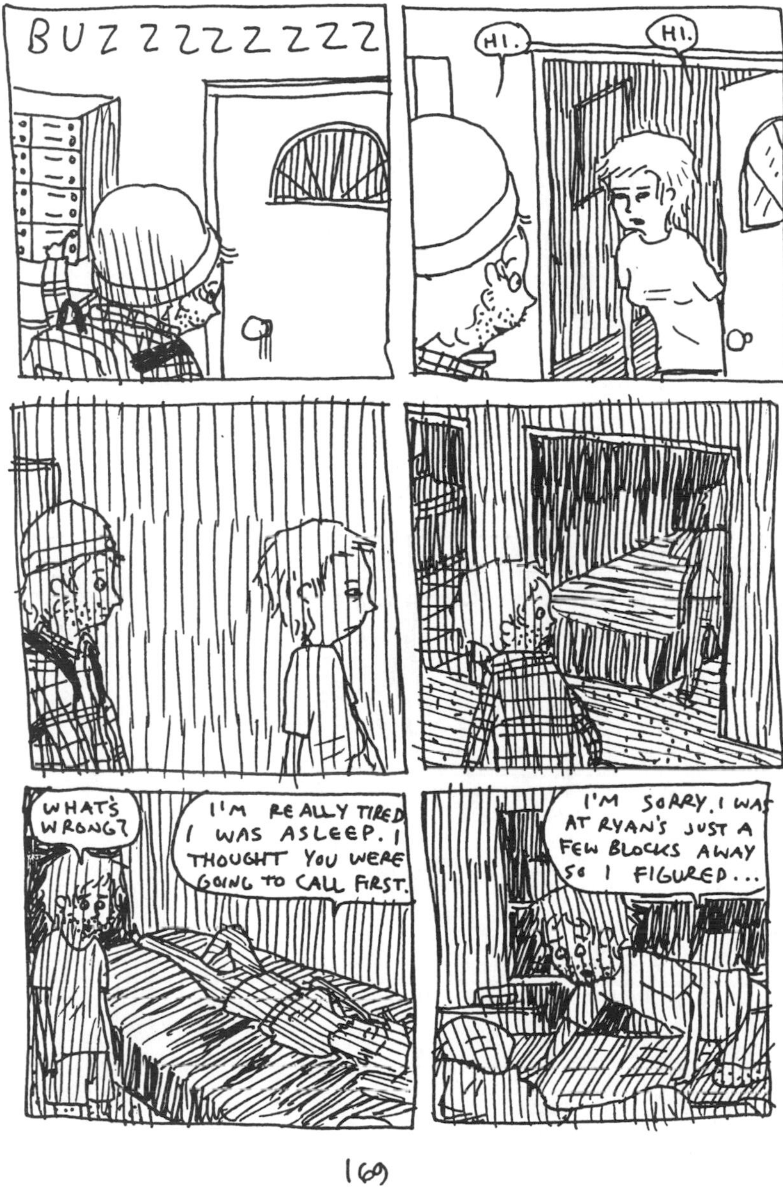
BUZZZZZZZZZ
HI.
HI.
WHAT'S WRONG?
I'M REALLY TIRED I WAS ASLEEP. I THOUGHT YOU WERE GOING TO CALL FIRST.
I'M SORRY. I WAS AT RYAN'S JUST A FEW BLOCKS AWAY SO I FIGURED...

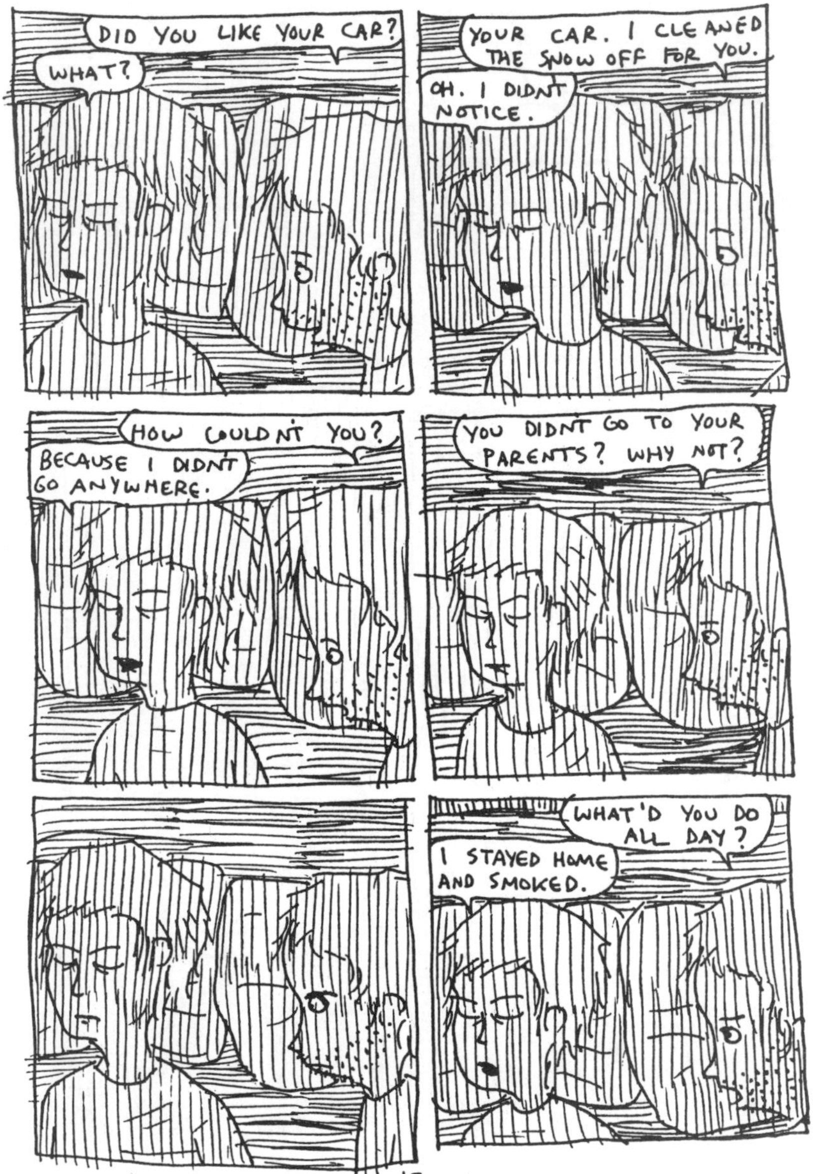
DID YOU LIKE YOUR CAR?
WHAT?
YOUR CAR. I CLEANED THE SNOW OFF FOR YOU.
OH. I DIDNT NOTICE.
HOW COULDN'T YOU?
BECAUSE I DIDN'T GO ANYWHERE.
YOU DIDNT GO TO YOUR PARENTS? WHY NOT?
WHAT'D YOU DO ALL DAY?
I STAYED HOME AND SMOKED.

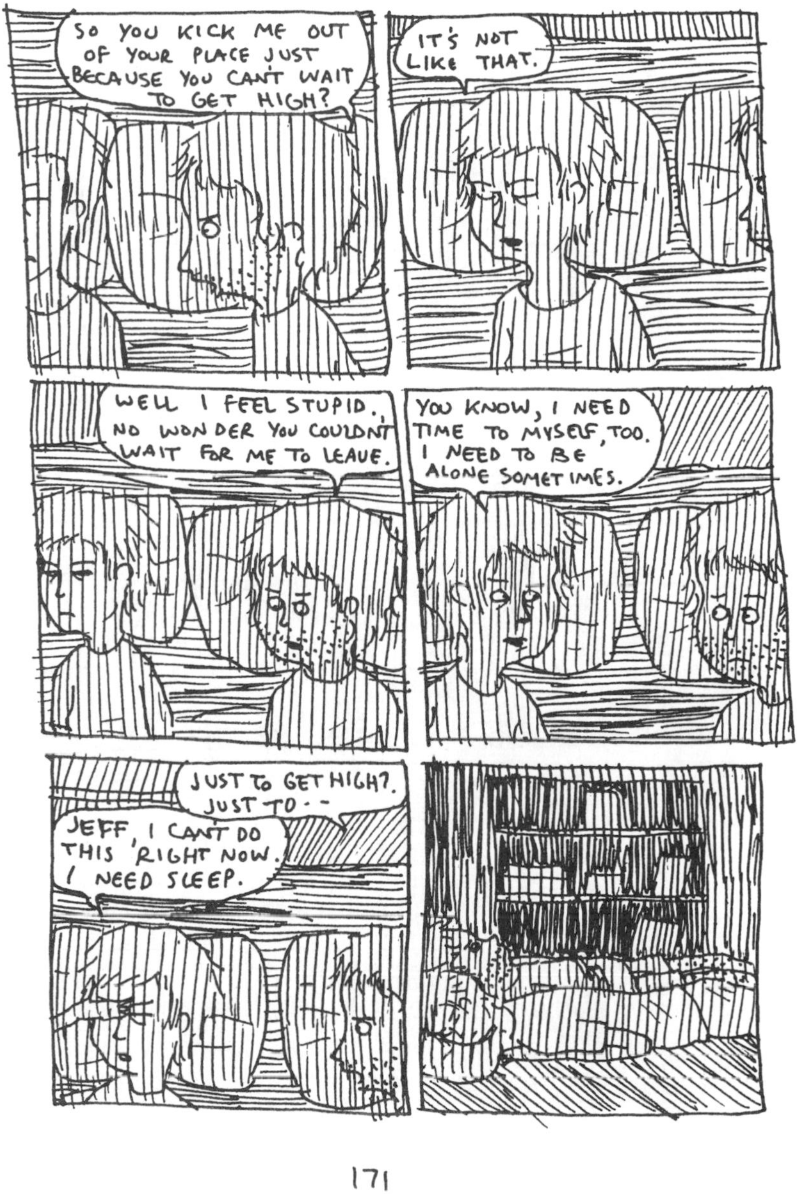
SO YOU KICK ME OUT OF YOUR PLACE JUST BECAUSE YOU CAN'T WAIT TO GET HIGH?
IT'S NOT LIKE THAT.
WELL I FEEL STUPID. NO WONDER YOU COULDN'T WAIT FOR ME TO LEAVE.
YOU KNOW, I NEED TIME TO MYSELF, TOO. I NEED TO BE ALONE SOMETIMES.
JUST TO GET HIGH? JUST TO--
JEFF, I CAN'T DO THIS RIGHT NOW. I NEED SLEEP.

FEEL RIGHT

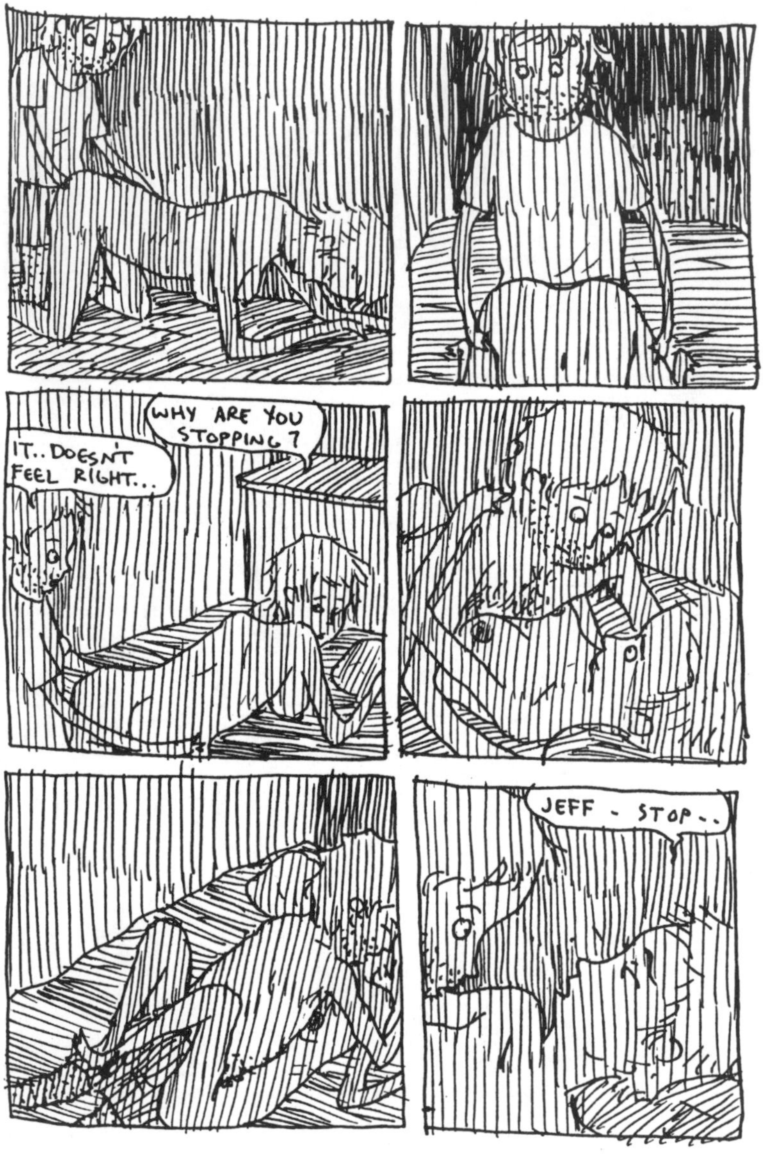
WHY ARE YOU STOPPING?
IT.. DOESN'T FEEL RIGHT...
JEFF - STOP..

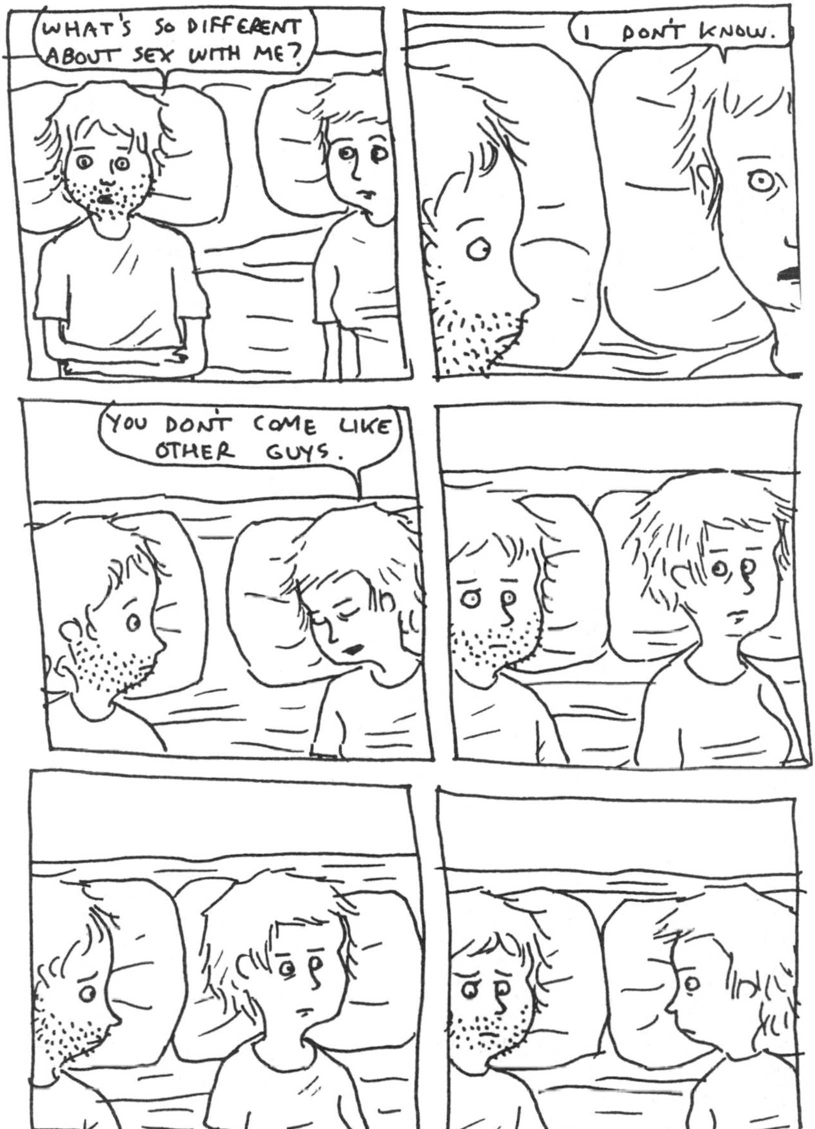
WHAT'S SO DIFFERENT ABOUT SEX WITH ME?
I DON'T KNOW.
YOU DON'T COME LIKE OTHER GUYS.

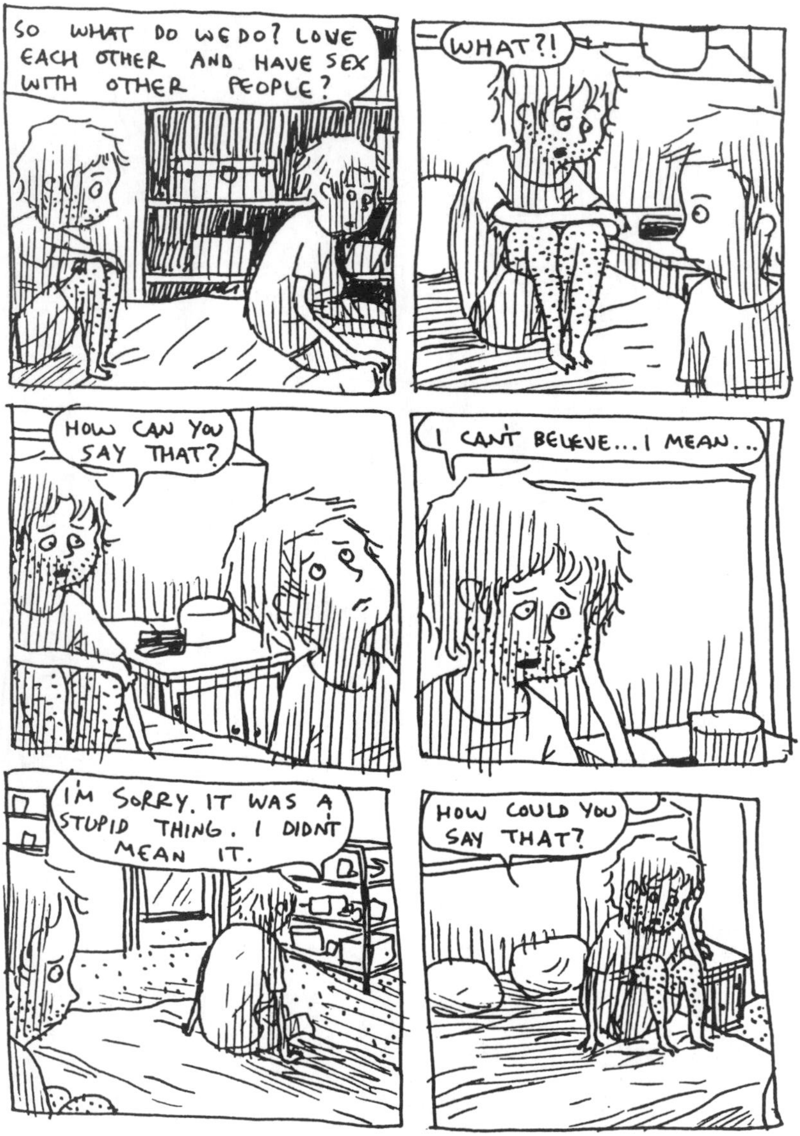
SO WHAT DO WE DO? LOVE EACH OTHER AND HAVE SEX WITH OTHER PEOPLE?
WHAT?!
HOW CAN YOU SAY THAT?
I CAN'T BELIEVE... I MEAN...
I'M SORRY. IT WAS A STUPID THING. I DIDN'T MEAN IT.
HOW COULD YOU SAY THAT?

DISTANT

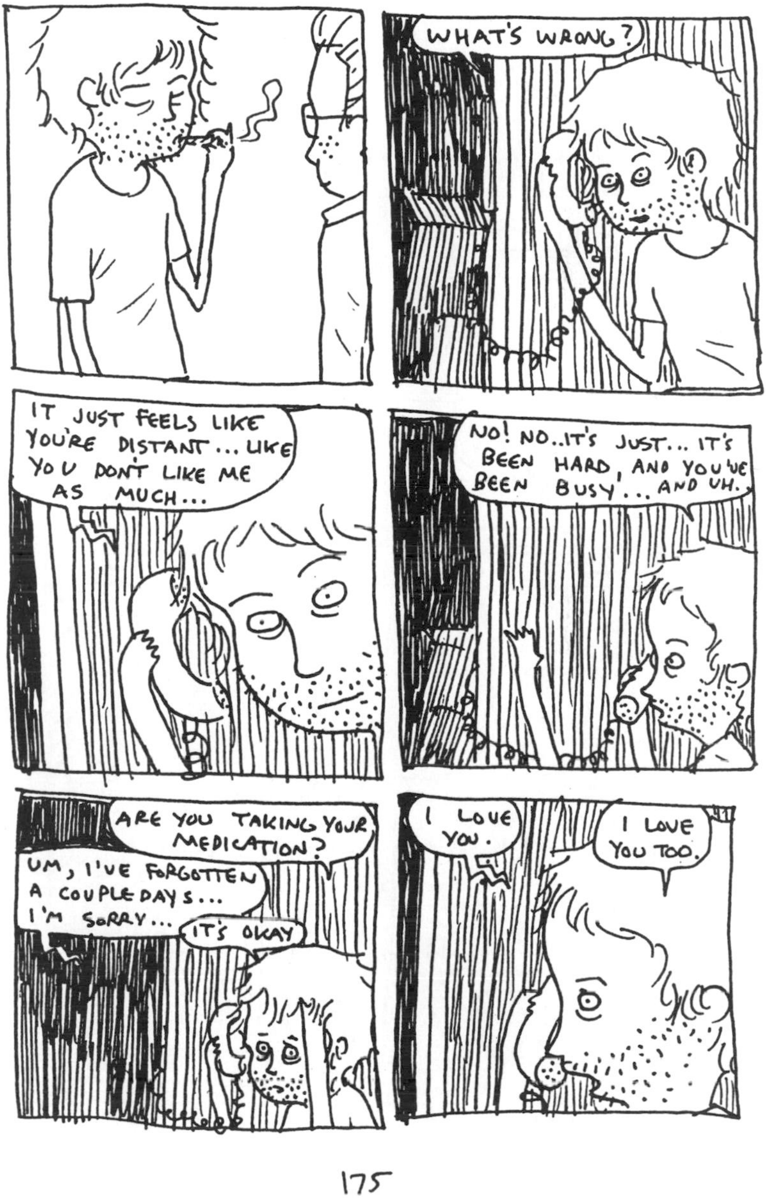

WHAT'S WRONG?
IT JUST FEELS LIKE YOU'RE DISTANT... LIKE YOU DON'T LIKE ME AS MUCH...
NO! NO..IT'S JUST... IT'S BEEN HARD, AND YOU'VE BEEN BUSY... AND UH.
ARE YOU TAKING YOUR MEDICATION?
UM, I'VE FORGOTTEN A COUPLE DAYS... I'M SORRY...
IT'S OKAY
I LOVE YOU.
I LOVE YOU TOO.

COCAINE

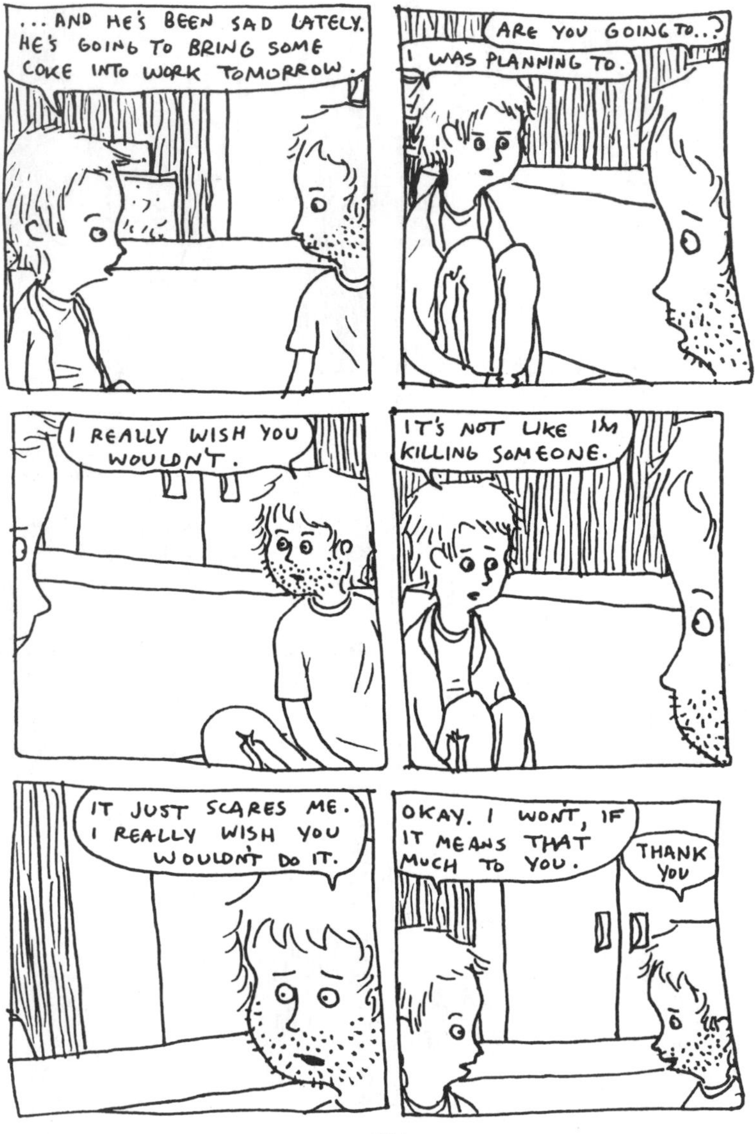
...AND HE'S BEEN SAD LATELY. HE'S GOING TO BRING SOME COKE INTO WORK TOMORROW.
ARE YOU GOING TO..?
I WAS PLANNING TO.
I REALLY WISH YOU WOULDN'T.
IT'S NOT LIKE I'M KILLING SOMEONE.
IT JUST SCARES ME. I REALLY WISH YOU WOULDN'T DO IT.
OKAY. I WON'T, IF IT MEANS THAT MUCH TO YOU.
THANK YOU

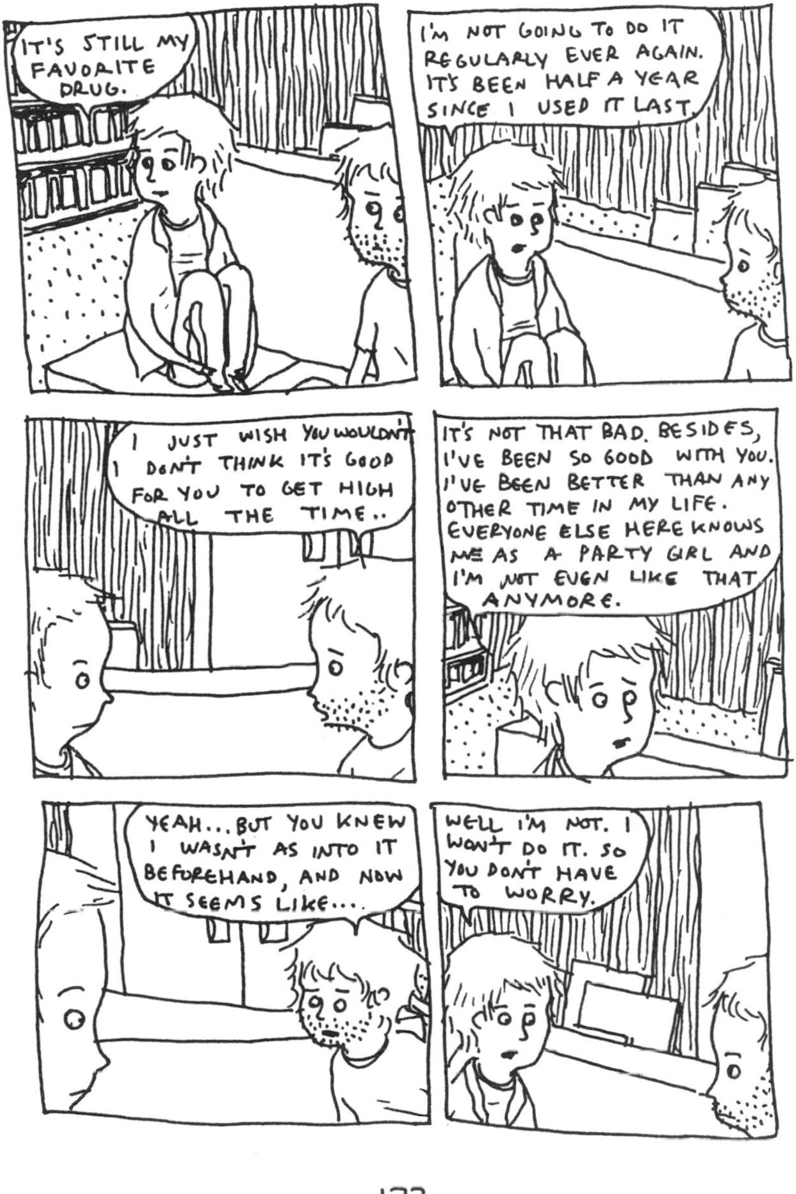
IT'S STILL MY FAVORITE DRUG.
I'M NOT GOING TO DO IT REGULARLY EVER AGAIN. IT'S BEEN HALF A YEAR SINCE I USED IT LAST.
I JUST WISH YOU WOULDN'T. I DON'T THINK IT'S GOOD FOR YOU TO GET HIGH ALL THE TIME..
IT'S NOT THAT BAD. BESIDES, I'VE BEEN SO GOOD WITH YOU. I'VE BEEN BETTER THAN ANY OTHER TIME IN MY LIFE. EVERYONE ELSE HERE KNOWS ME AS A PARTY GIRL AND I'M NOT EVEN LIKE THAT ANYMORE.
YEAH... BUT YOU KNEW I WASN'T AS INTO IT BEFOREHAND, AND NOW IT SEEMS LIKE...
WELL I'M NOT. I WON'T DO IT. SO YOU DON'T HAVE TO WORRY.

HOME ALONE

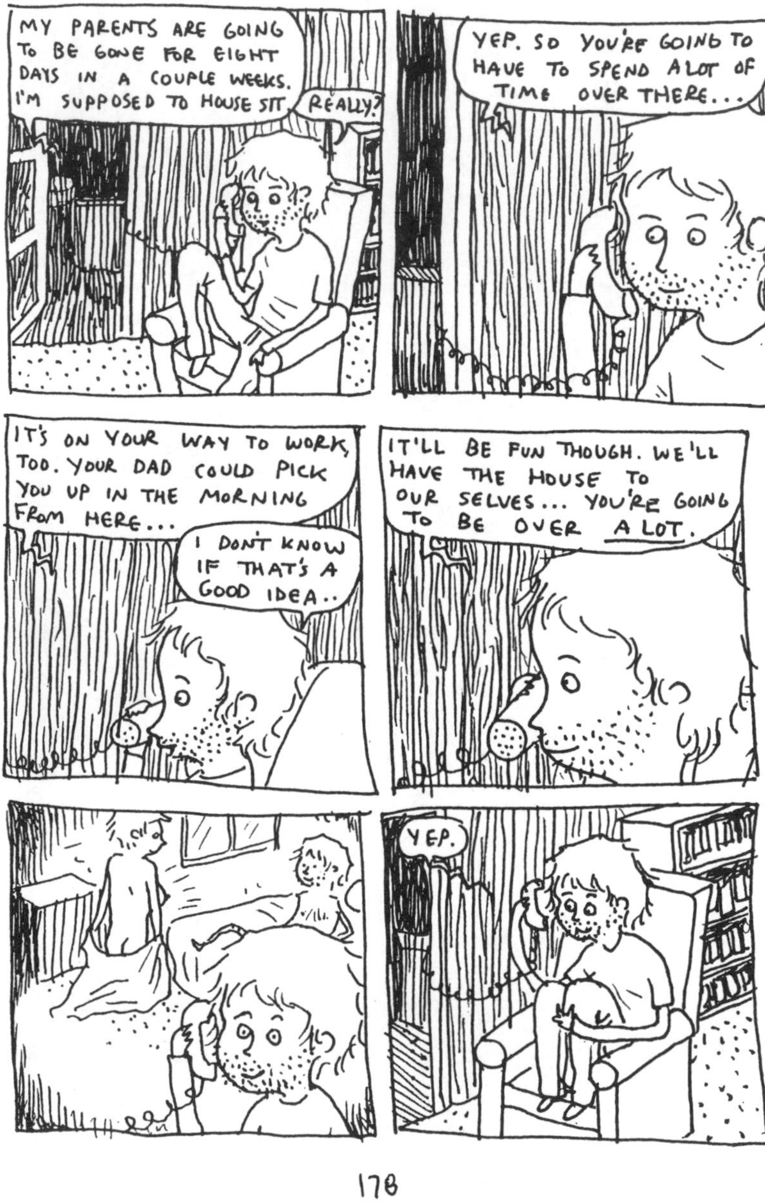
MY PARENTS ARE GOING TO BE GONE FOR EIGHT DAYS IN A COUPLE WEEKS. I'M SUPPOSED TO HOUSE SIT.
REALLY?
YEP. SO YOU'RE GOING TO HAVE TO SPEND A LOT OF TIME OVER THERE...
IT'S ON YOUR WAY TO WORK, TOO. YOUR DAD COULD PICK YOU UP IN THE MORNING FROM HERE...
I DON'T KNOW IF THAT'S A GOOD IDEA..
IT'LL BE FUN THOUGH. WE'LL HAVE THE HOUSE TO OUR SELVES... YOU'RE GOING TO BE OVER A LOT.
YEP.

"ART"

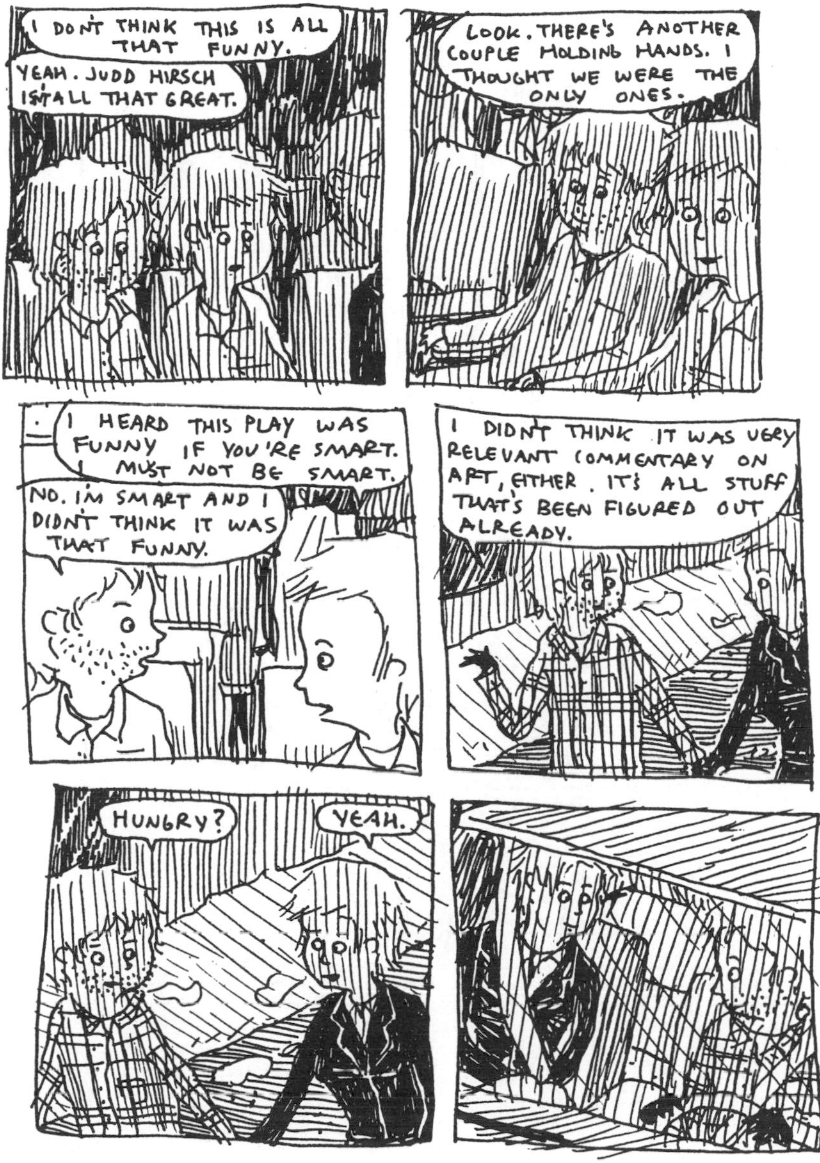
I DON'T THINK THIS IS ALL THAT FUNNY.
YEAH. JUDD HIRSCH ISN'T ALL THAT GREAT.
LOOK. THERE'S ANOTHER COUPLE HOLDING HANDS. I THOUGHT WE WERE THE ONLY ONES.
I HEARD THIS PLAY WAS FUNNY IF YOU'RE SMART. I MUST NOT BE SMART.
NO. I'M SMART AND I DIDN'T THINK IT WAS THAT FUNNY.
I DIDN'T THINK IT WAS VERY RELEVANT COMMENTARY ON ART, EITHER. IT'S ALL STUFF THAT'S BEEN FIGURED OUT ALREADY.
HUNGRY?
YEAH.

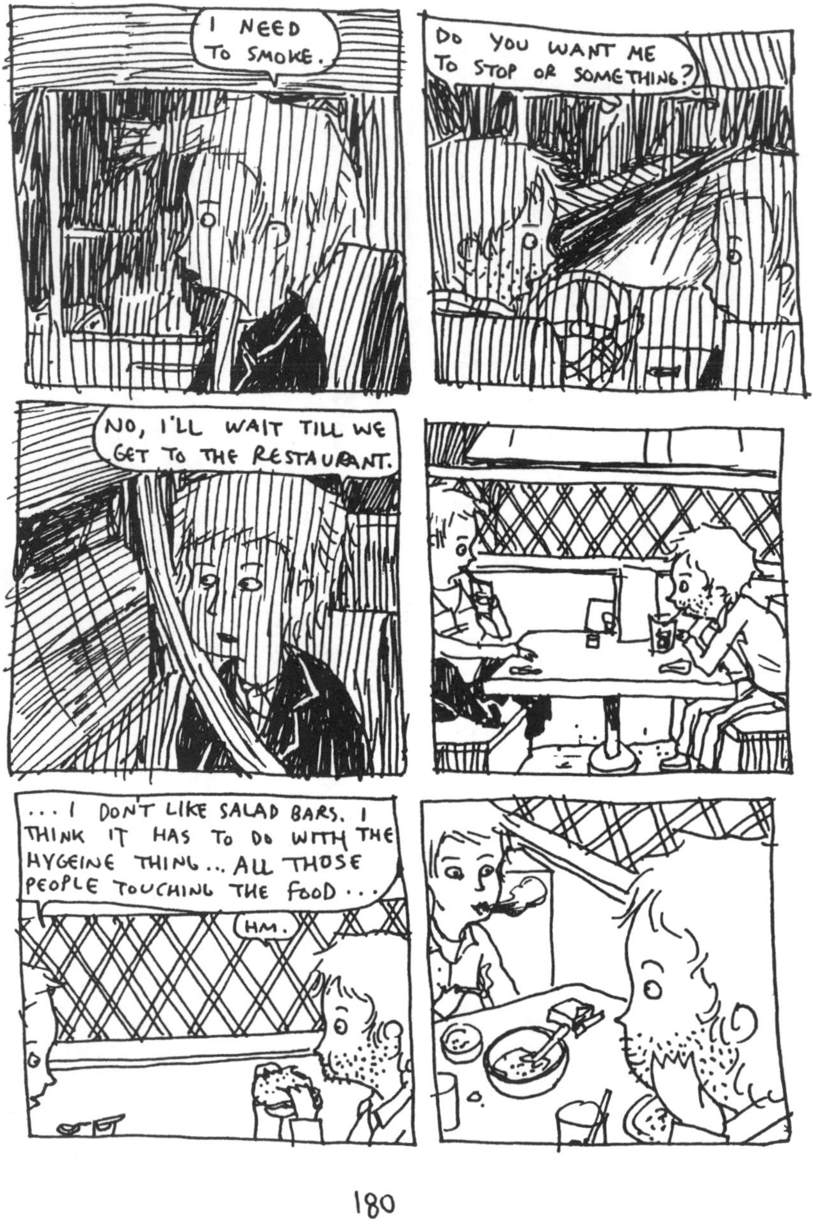
I NEED TO SMOKE.
DO YOU WANT ME TO STOP OR SOMETHING?
NO, I'LL WAIT TILL WE GET TO THE RESTAURANT.
...I DON'T LIKE SALAD BARS. I THINK IT HAS TO DO WITH THE HYGEINE THING... ALL THOSE PEOPLE TOUCHING THE FOOD...
HM.

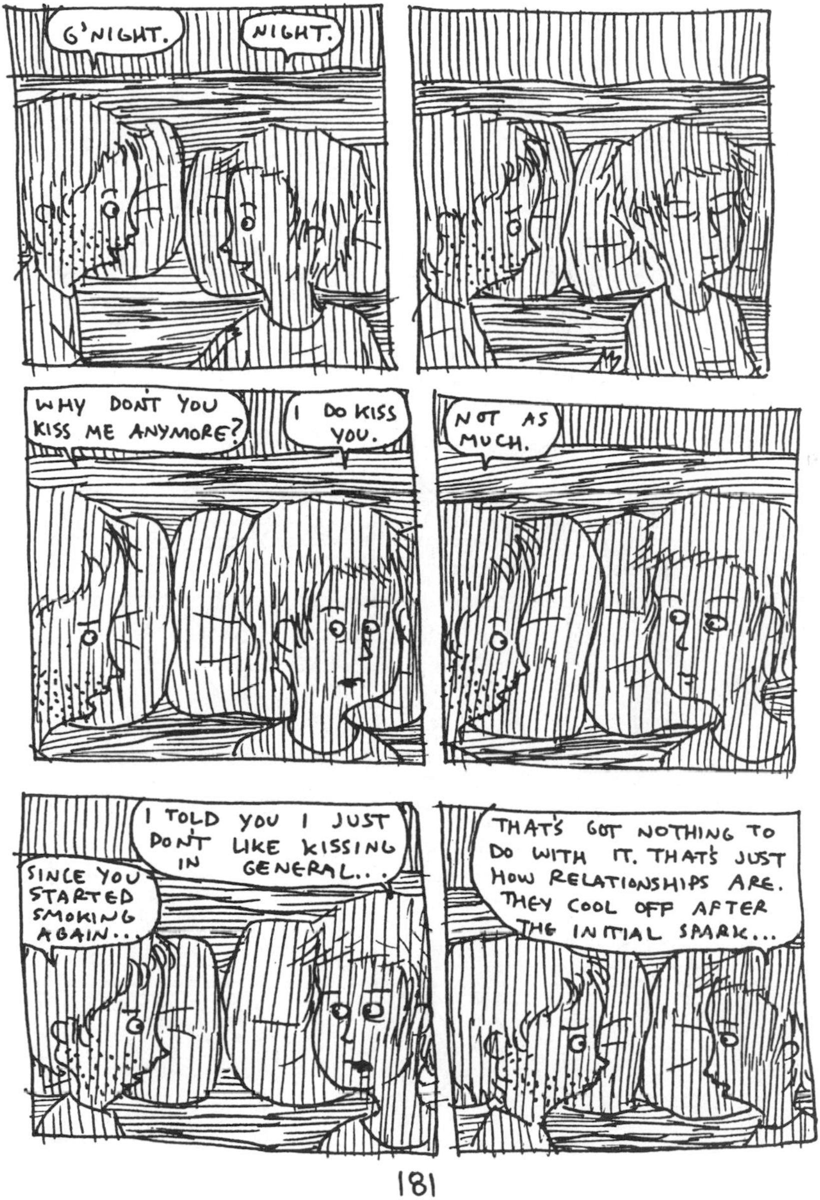
G'NIGHT.
NIGHT.
WHY DON'T YOU KISS ME ANYMORE?
I DO KISS YOU.
NOT AS MUCH.
SINCE YOU STARTED SMOKING AGAIN...
I TOLD YOU I JUST DON'T LIKE KISSING IN GENERAL...
THAT'S GOT NOTHING TO DO WITH IT. THAT'S JUST HOW RELATIONSHIPS ARE. THEY COOL OFF AFTER THE INITIAL SPARK...

UNTITLED

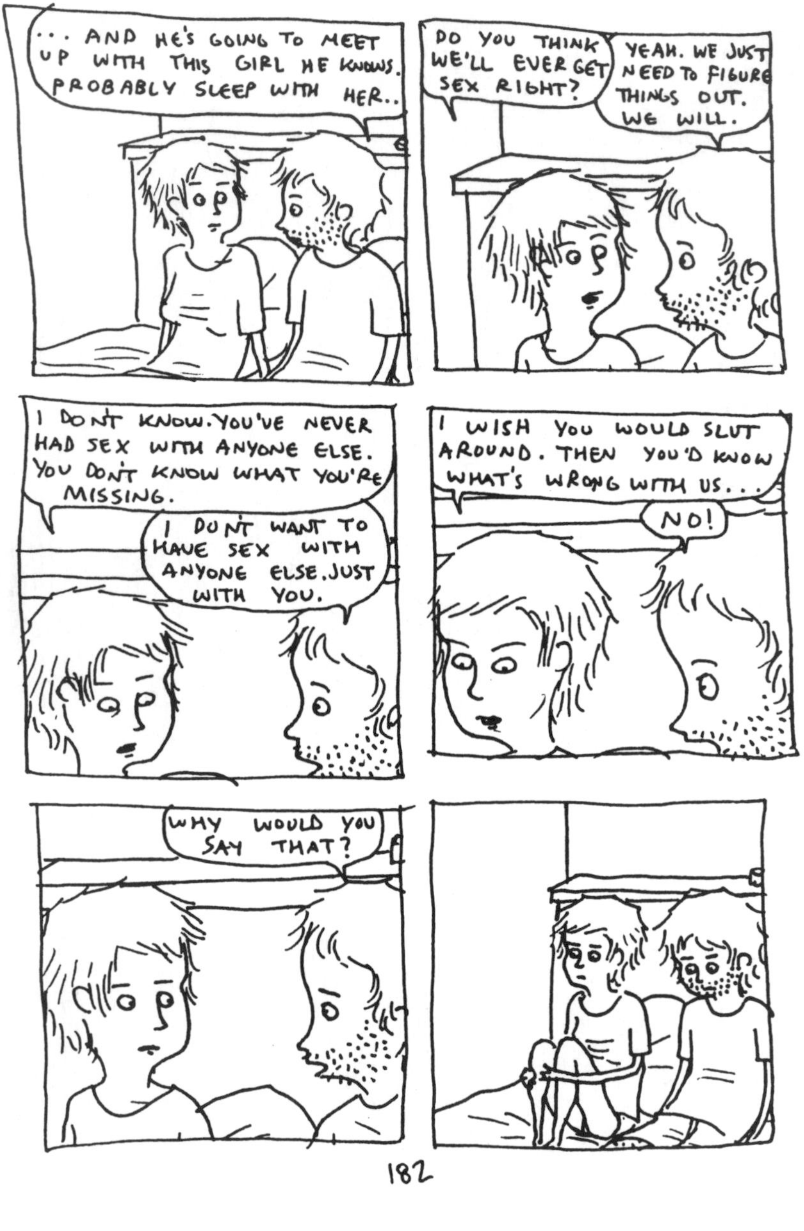

... AND HE'S GOING TO MEET UP WITH THIS GIRL HE KNOWS. PROBABLY SLEEP WITH HER..
DO YOU THINK WE'LL EVER GET SEX RIGHT?
YEAH. WE JUST NEED TO FIGURE THINGS OUT. WE WILL.
I DON'T KNOW. YOU'VE NEVER HAD SEX WITH ANYONE ELSE. YOU DON'T KNOW WHAT YOU'RE MISSING.
I DON'T WANT TO HAVE SEX WITH ANYONE ELSE. JUST WITH YOU.
I WISH YOU WOULD SLUT AROUND. THEN YOU'D KNOW WHAT'S WRONG WITH US...
NO!
WHY WOULD YOU SAY THAT?

DRINKS

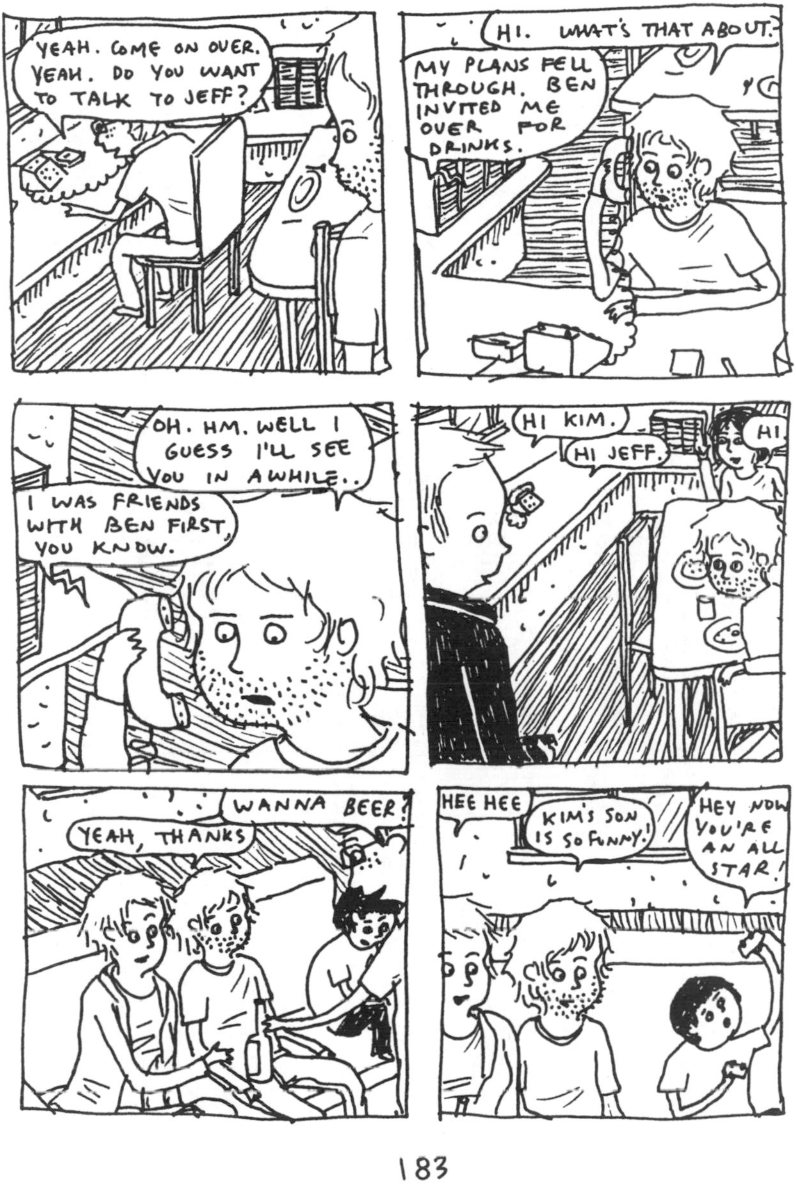
YEAH. COME ON OVER. YEAH. DO YOU WANT TO TALK TO JEFF?
HI. WHAT'S THAT ABOUT?
MY PLANS FELL THROUGH. BEN INVITED ME OVER FOR DRINKS.
OH. HM. WELL I GUESS I'LL SEE YOU IN AWHILE..
I WAS FRIENDS WITH BEN FIRST, YOU KNOW.
HI KIM.
HI JEFF.
HI.
WANNA BEER?
YEAH, THANKS
HEE HEE
KIM'S SON IS SO FUNNY!
HEY NOW YOU'RE AN ALL STAR!

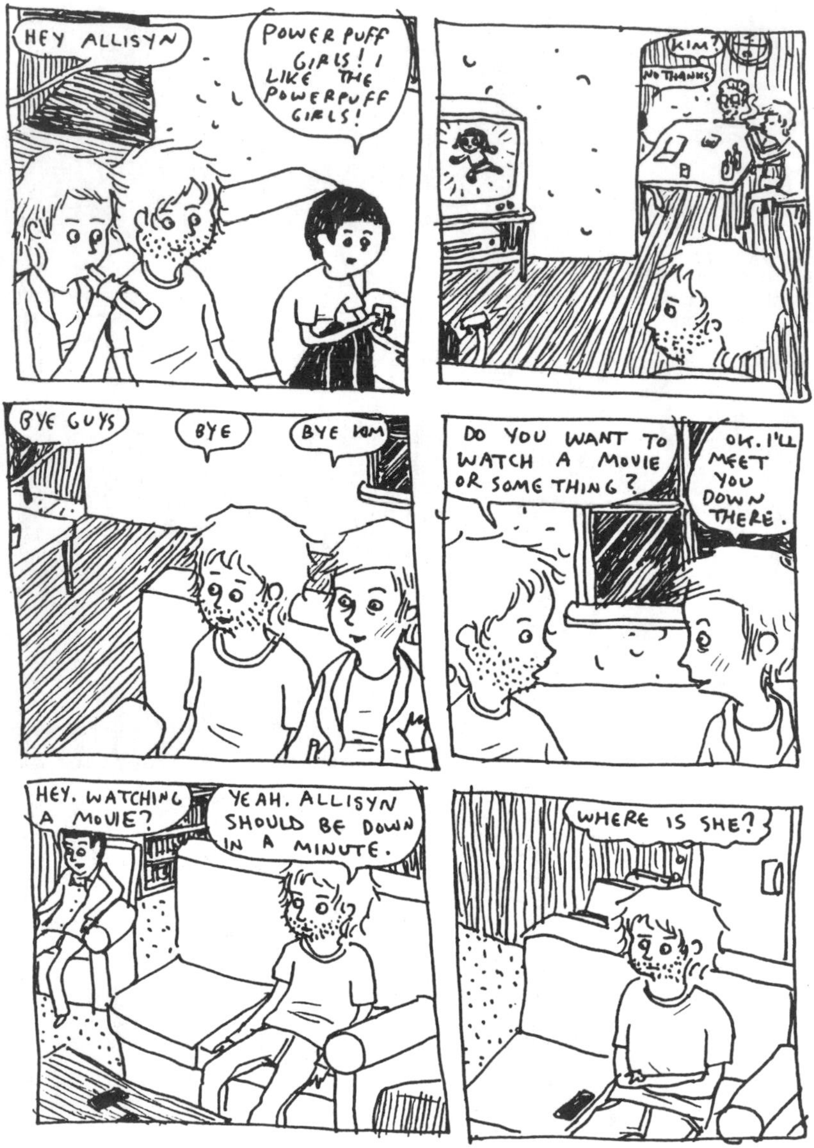
HEY ALLISYN
POWERPUFF GIRLS! I LIKE THE POWERPUFF GIRLS!
KIM?
NO THANKS
BYE GUYS
BYE
BYE KIM
DO YOU WANT TO WATCH A MOVIE OR SOMETHING?
OK. I'LL MEET YOU DOWN THERE.
HEY. WATCHING A MOVIE?
YEAH. ALLISYN SHOULD BE DOWN IN A MINUTE.
WHERE IS SHE?

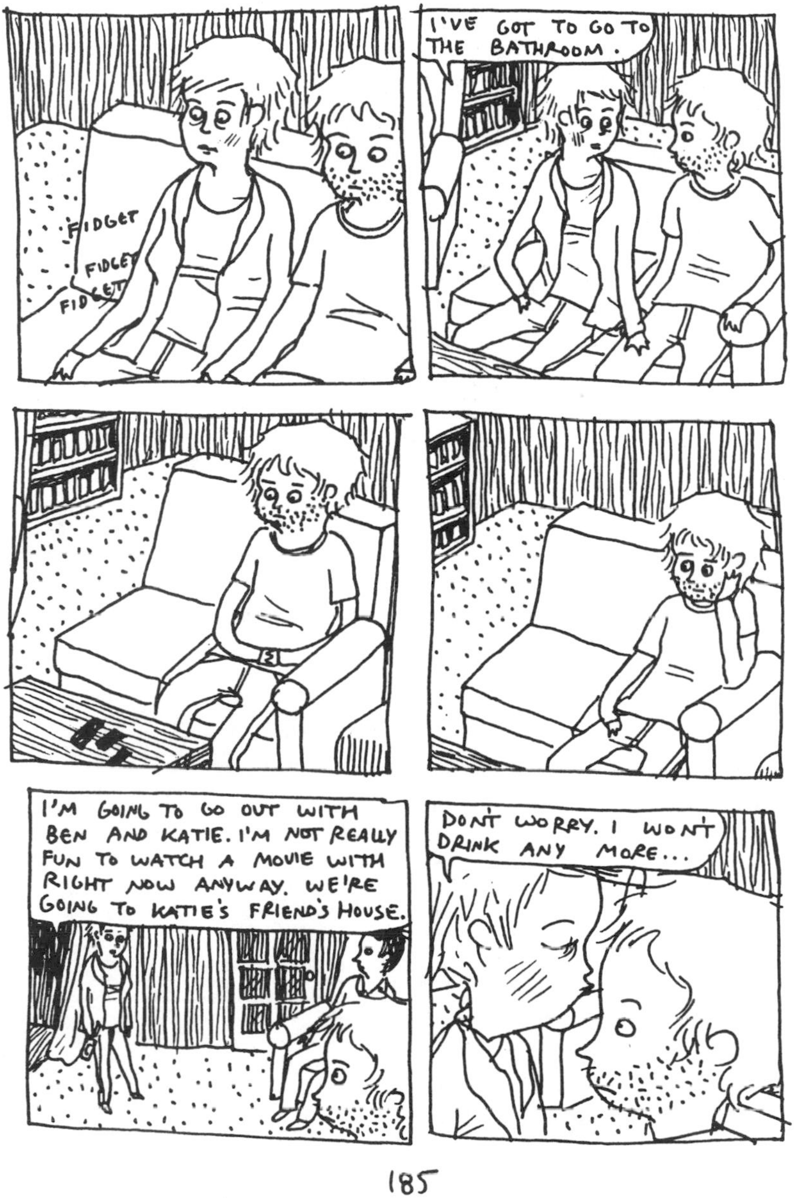
FIDGET
FIDGET
FIDGET
I'VE GOT TO GO TO THE BATHROOM.
I'M GOING TO GO OUT WITH BEN AND KATIE. I'M NOT REALLY FUN TO WATCH A MOVIE WITH RIGHT NOW ANYWAY. WE'RE GOING TO KATIE'S FRIEND'S HOUSE.
DON'T WORRY. I WON'T DRINK ANY MORE...

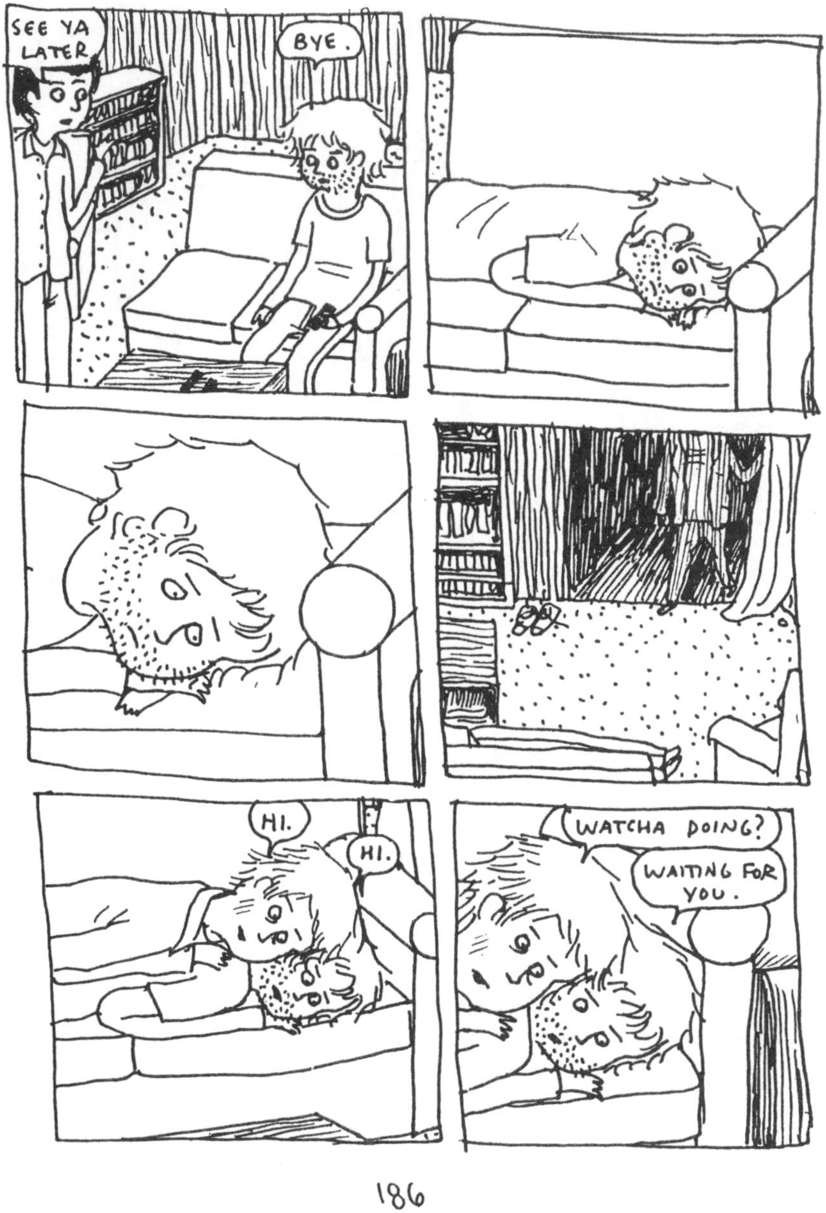
SEE YA LATER
BYE.
HI.
HI.
WATCHA DOING?
WAITING FOR YOU.

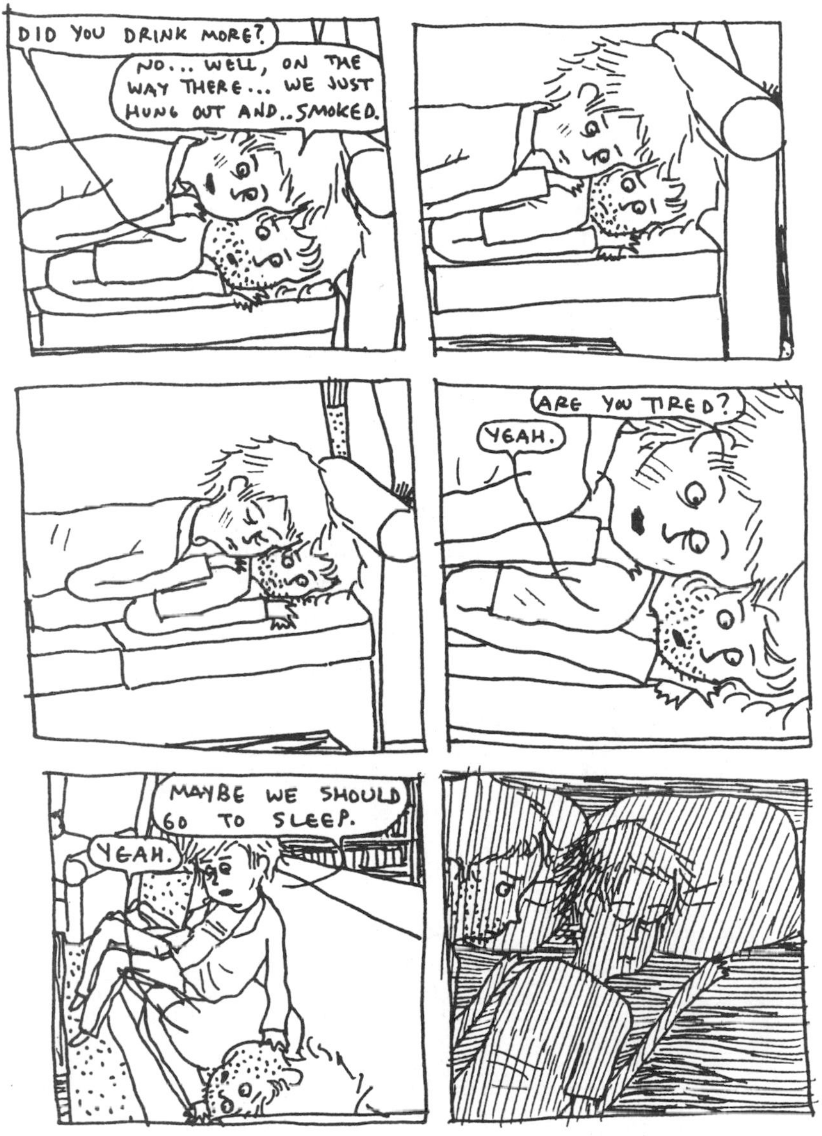
DID YOU DRINK MORE?
NO... WELL, ON THE WAY THERE... WE JUST HUNG OUT AND.. SMOKED.
ARE YOU TIRED?
YEAH.
MAYBE WE SHOULD GO TO SLEEP.
YEAH.

THE LAST TIME

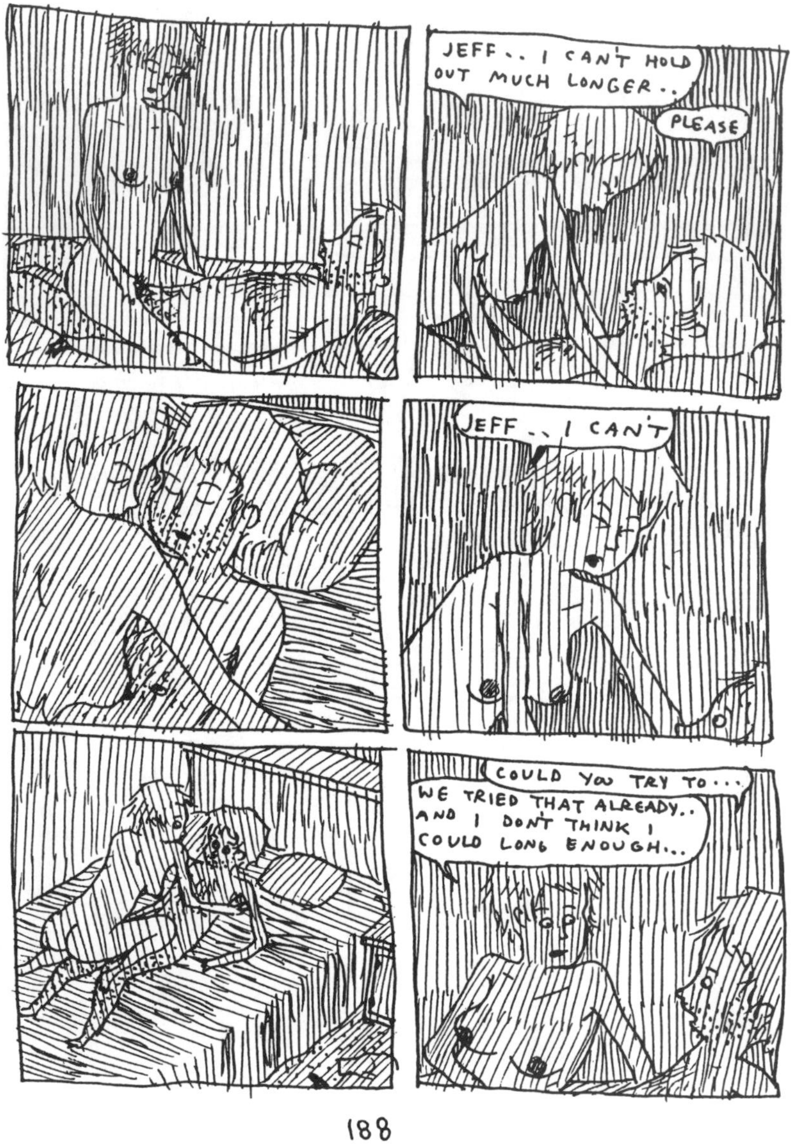

JEFF.. I CAN'T HOLD OUT MUCH LONGER..
PLEASE
JEFF.. I CAN'T
COULD YOU TRY TO...
WE TRIED THAT ALREADY.. AND I DON'T THINK I COULD LONG ENOUGH...

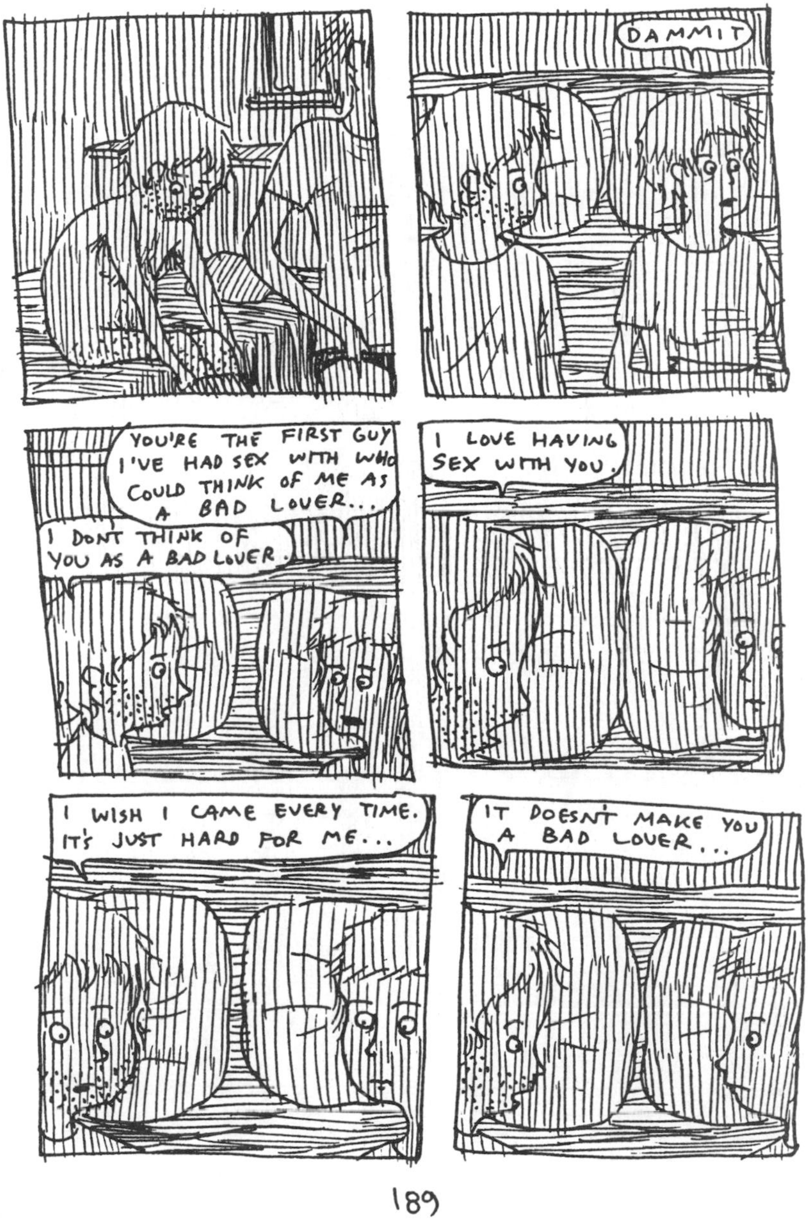
DAMMIT
YOU'RE THE FIRST GUY I'VE HAD SEX WITH WHO COULD THINK OF ME AS A BAD LOVER...
I DONT THINK OF YOU AS A BAD LOVER.
I LOVE HAVING SEX WITH YOU.
I WISH I CAME EVERY TIME. IT'S JUST HARD FOR ME...
IT DOESN'T MAKE YOU A BAD LOVER...

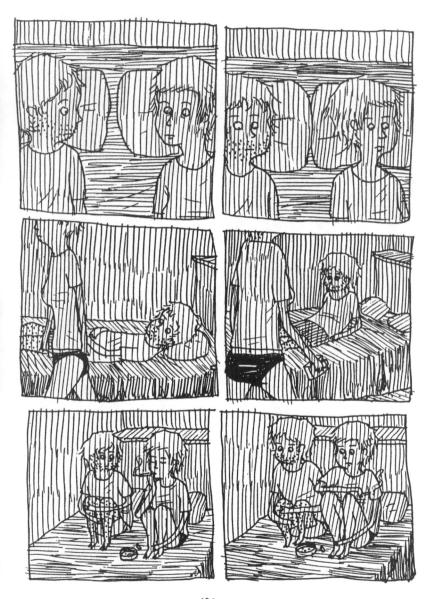

190

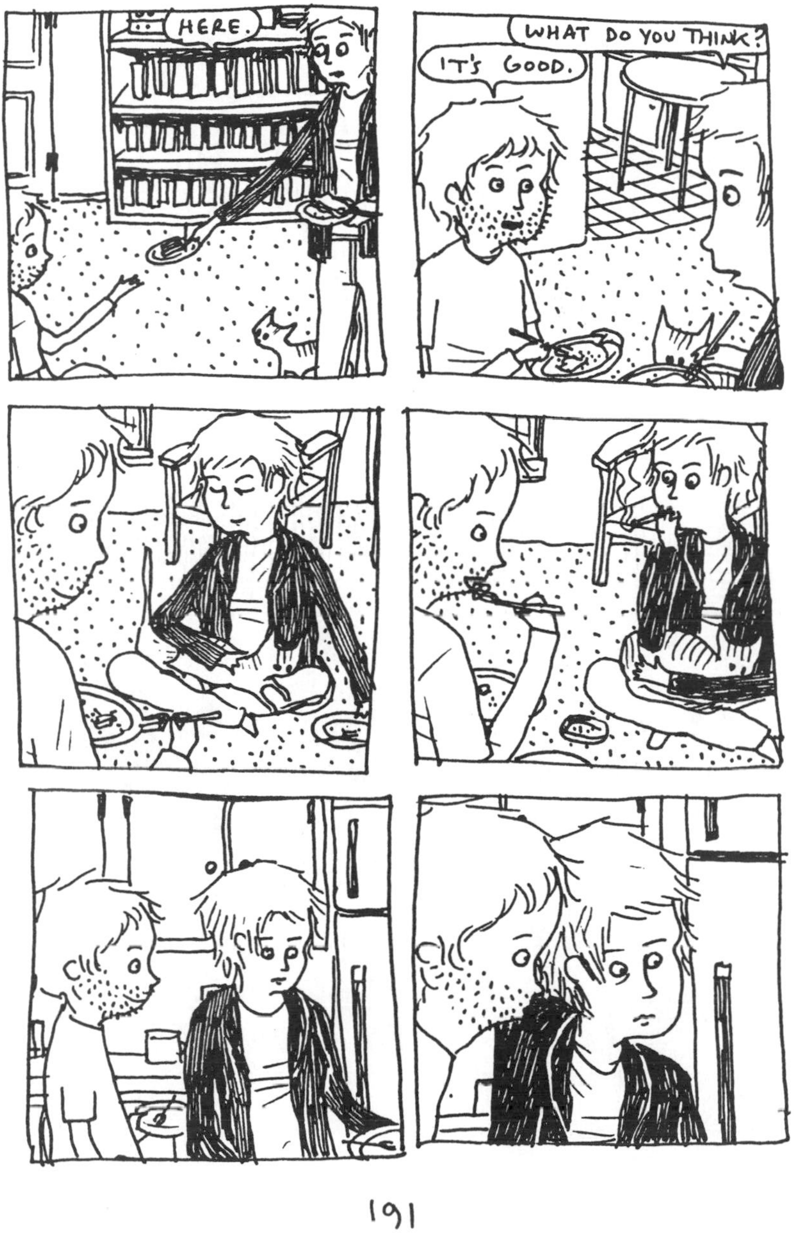
HERE.
WHAT DO YOU THINK?
IT'S GOOD.

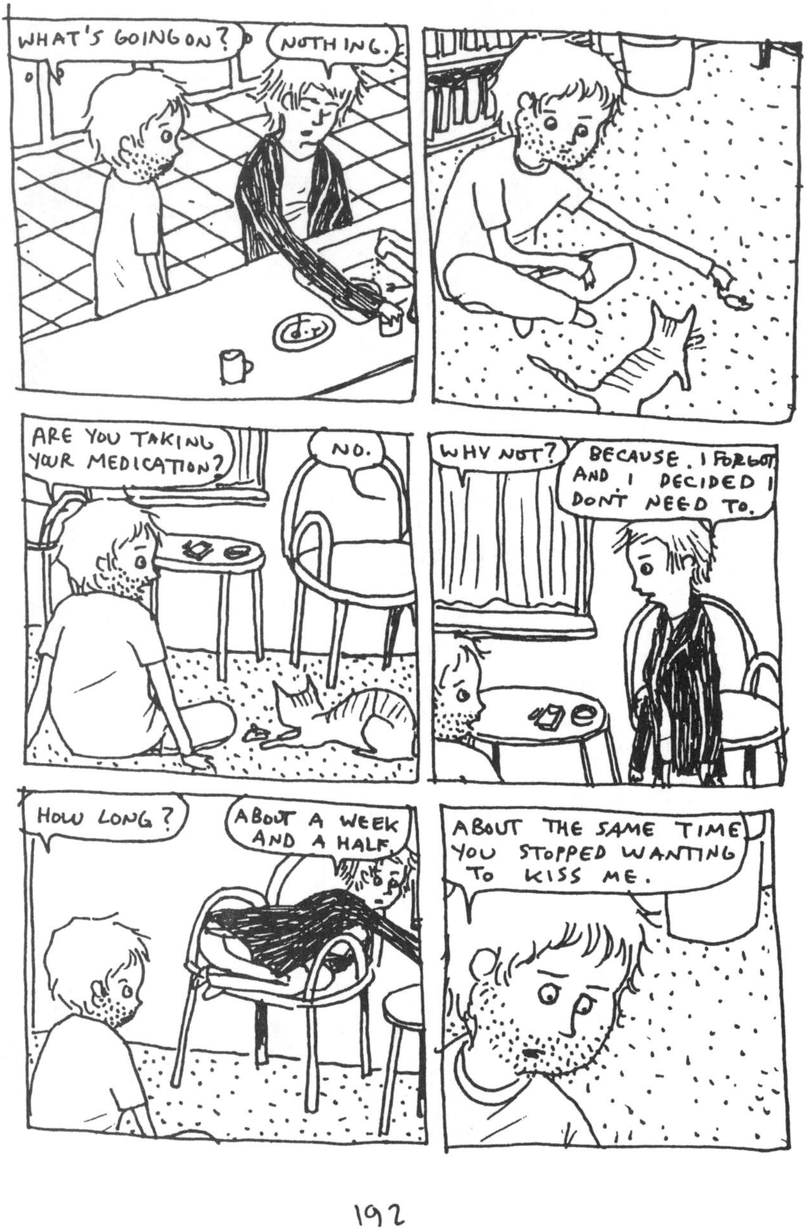
WHAT'S GOING ON?
NOTHING.
ARE YOU TAKING YOUR MEDICATION?
NO.
WHY NOT?
BECAUSE I FORGOT AND I DECIDED I DONT NEED TO.
HOW LONG?
ABOUT A WEEK AND A HALF.
ABOUT THE SAME TIME YOU STOPPED WANTING TO KISS ME.

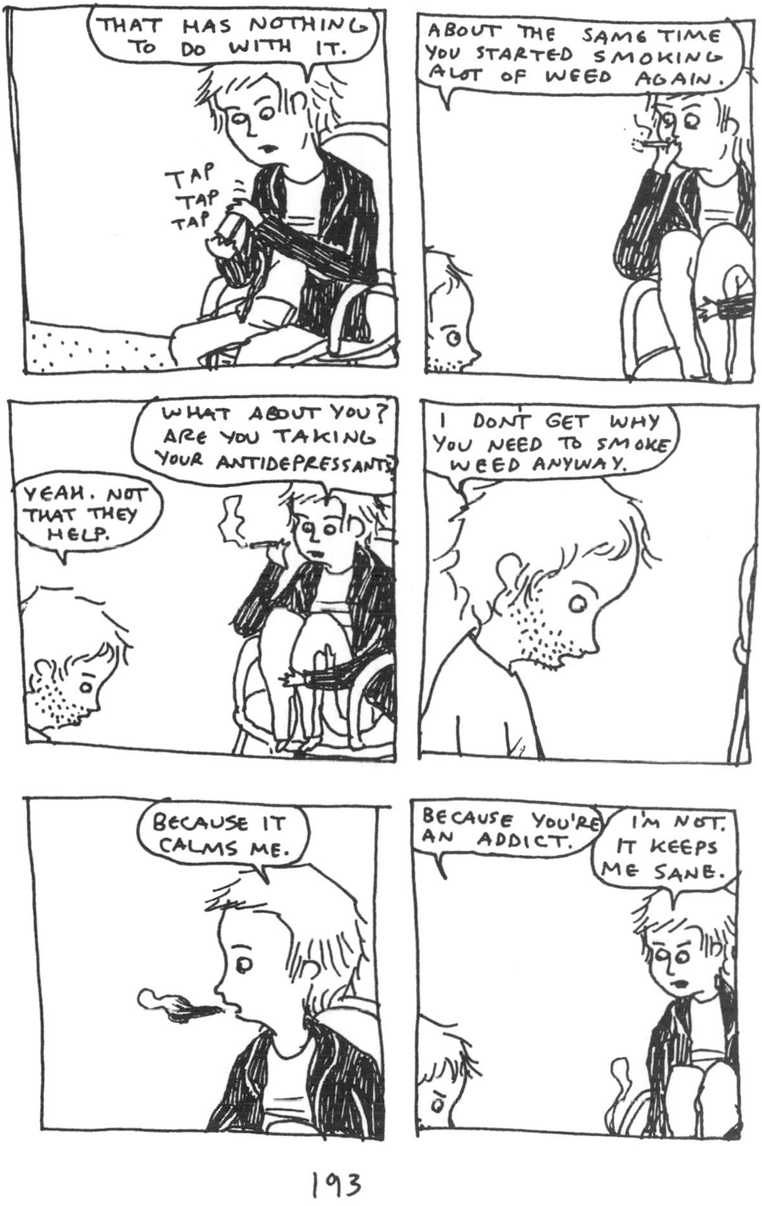
THAT HAS NOTHING TO DO WITH IT.
TAP TAP TAP
ABOUT THE SAME TIME YOU STARTED SMOKING ALOT OF WEED AGAIN.
WHAT ABOUT YOU? ARE YOU TAKING YOUR ANTIDEPRESSANTS?
YEAH. NOT THAT THEY HELP.
I DON'T GET WHY YOU NEED TO SMOKE WEED ANYWAY.
BECAUSE IT CALMS ME.
BECAUSE YOU'RE AN ADDICT.
I'M NOT. IT KEEPS ME SANE.

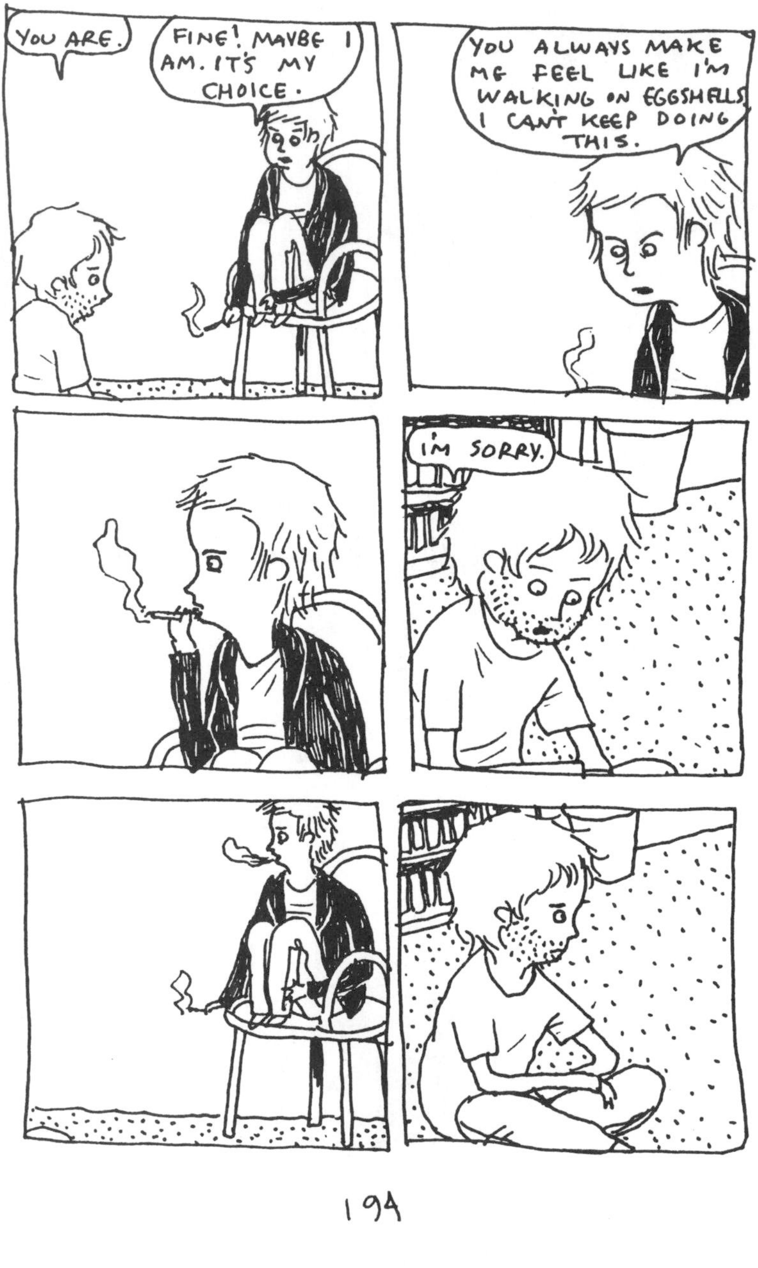
YOU ARE.
FINE! MAYBE I AM. IT'S MY CHOICE.
YOU ALWAYS MAKE ME FEEL LIKE I'M WALKING ON EGGSHELLS. I CAN'T KEEP DOING THIS.
I'M SORRY.

DARKENING

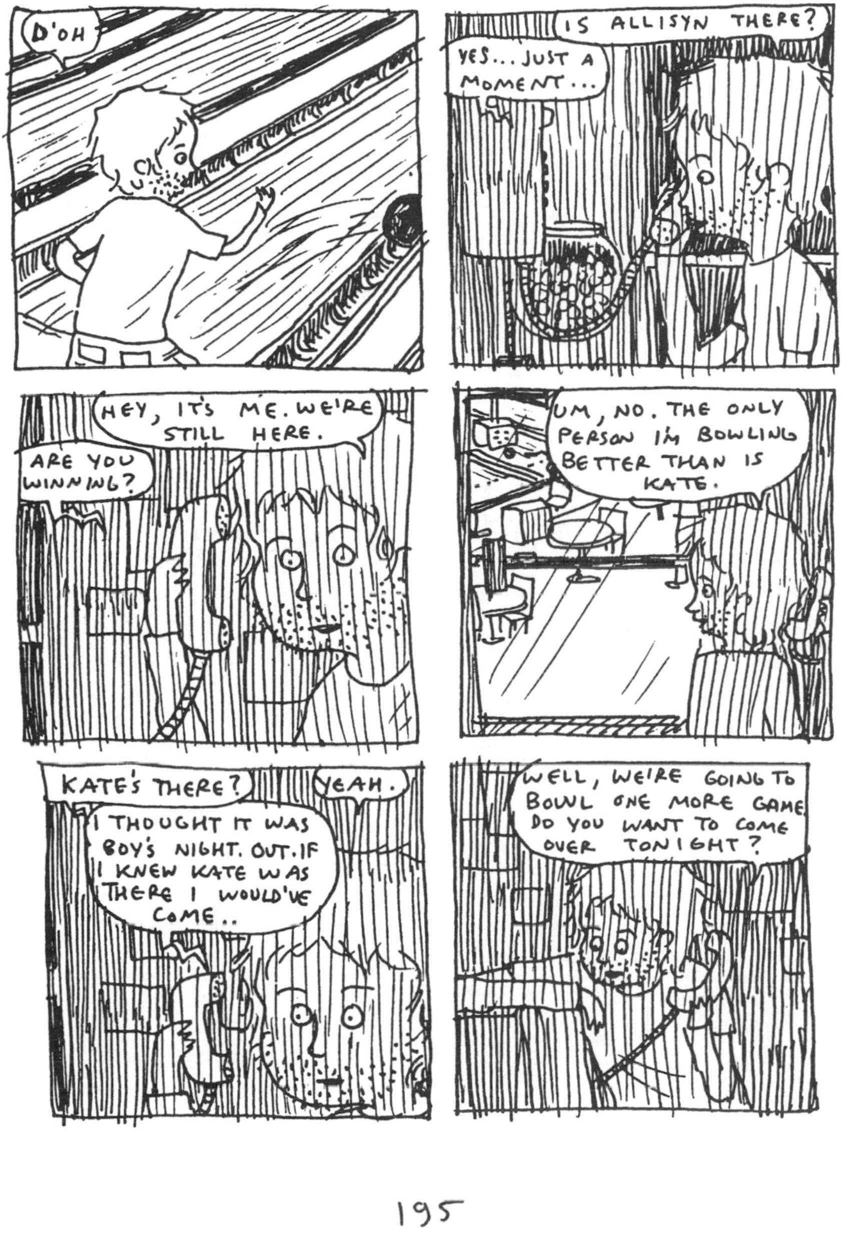
D'OH
IS ALLISYN THERE?
YES... JUST A MOMENT...
HEY, IT'S ME. WE'RE STILL HERE.
ARE YOU WINNING?
UM, NO. THE ONLY PERSON I'M BOWLING BETTER THAN IS KATE.
KATE'S THERE?
YEAH.
I THOUGHT IT WAS BOY'S NIGHT. OUT. IF I KNEW KATE WAS THERE I WOULD'VE COME..
WELL, WE'RE GOING TO BOWL ONE MORE GAME. DO YOU WANT TO COME OVER TONIGHT?

OKAY. CALL ME WHEN YOU GET HOME AND THEN IT'LL TAKE ME A HALF HOUR OR SO TO GET THERE.

OKAY.

HI. I BROUGHT SOME WINE.

HI.

I DON'T LIKE IT.

ME NEITHER. I DON'T KNOW. I DON'T REALLY LIKE WINE.

DO YOU WANT TO WATCH A MOVIE?

NO. I CAN'T STAY THAT LONG.

WHAT DO YOU MEAN? I THOUGHT YOU WERE STAYING OVER.

I NEED TO GO HOME.

I DON'T GET IT.

BECAUSE JEFF. I DON'T WANT MY PARENTS THINKING ABOUT ME HAVING SEX.

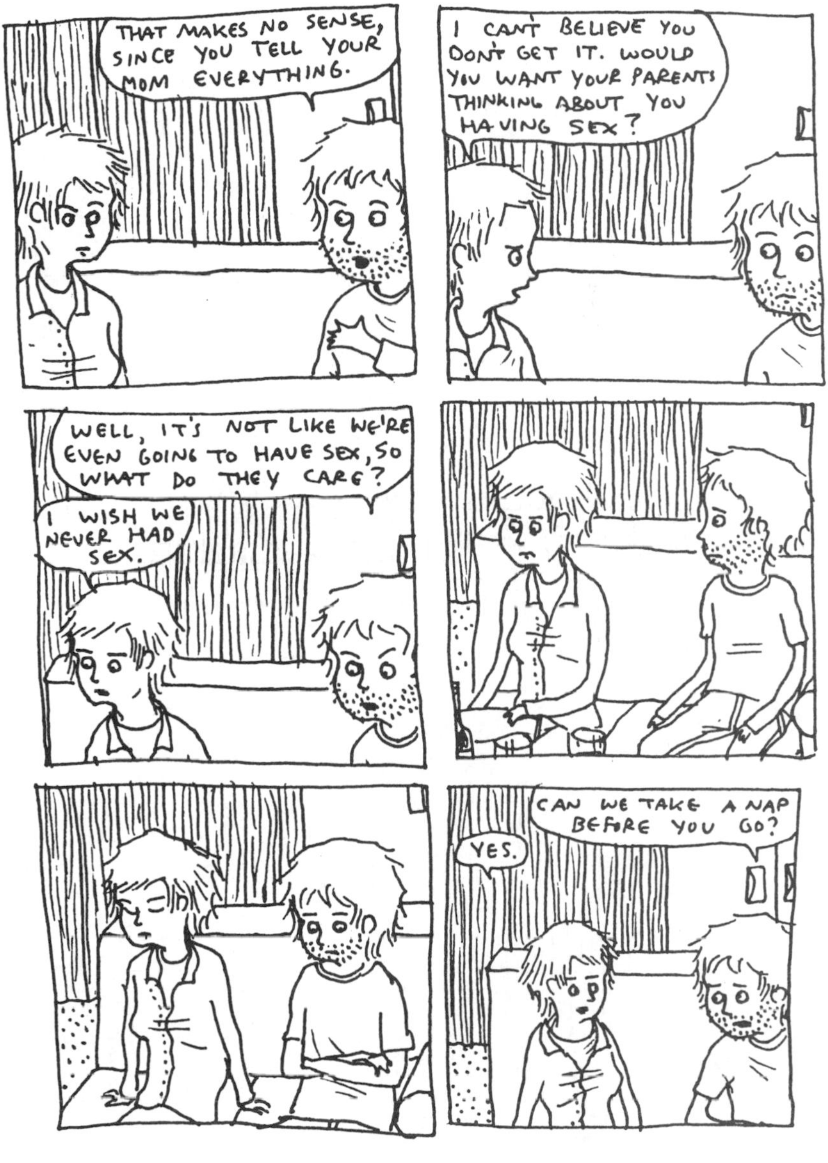
THAT MAKES NO SENSE, SINCE YOU TELL YOUR MOM EVERYTHING.
I CAN'T BELIEVE YOU DON'T GET IT. WOULD YOU WANT YOUR PARENTS THINKING ABOUT YOU HAVING SEX?
WELL, IT'S NOT LIKE WE'RE EVEN GOING TO HAVE SEX, SO WHAT DO THEY CARE?
I WISH WE NEVER HAD SEX.
CAN WE TAKE A NAP BEFORE YOU GO?
YES.

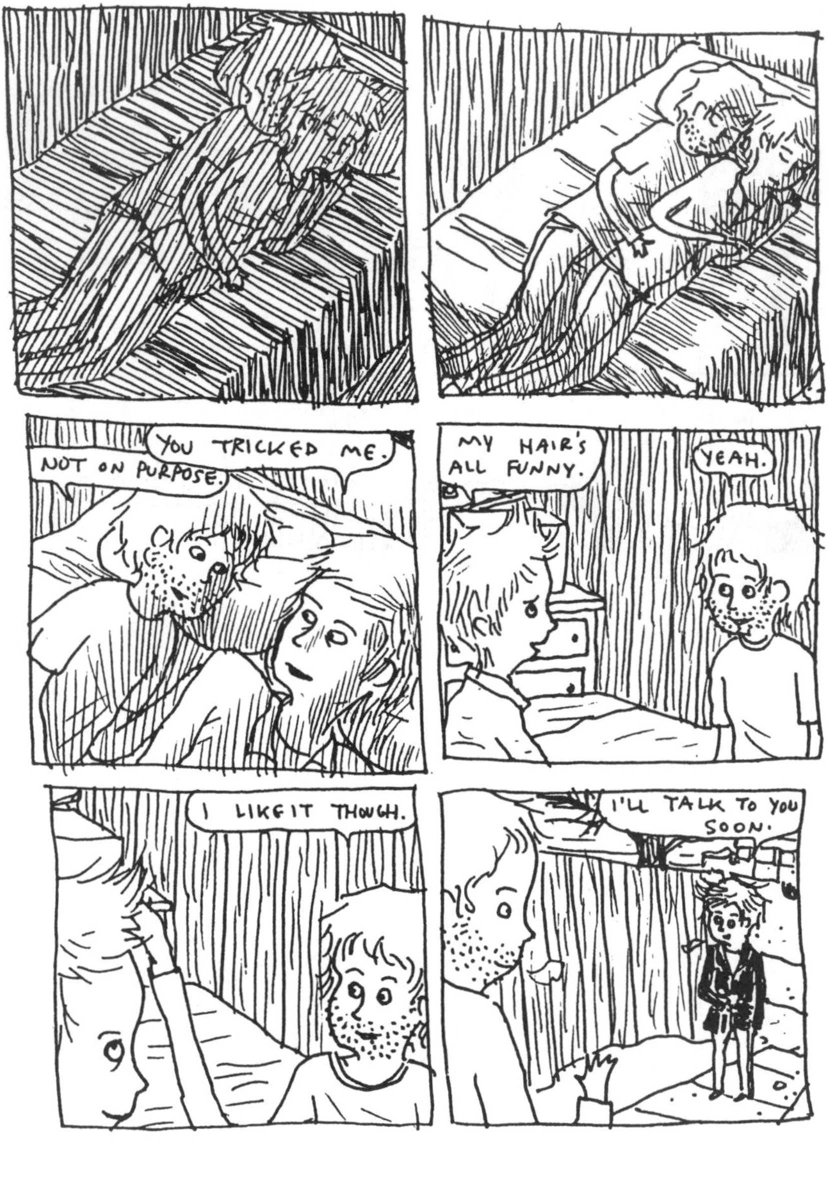
YOU TRICKED ME.
NOT ON PURPOSE.
MY HAIR'S ALL FUNNY.
YEAH.
I LIKEIT THOUGH.
I'LL TALK TO YOU SOON.

WASTED

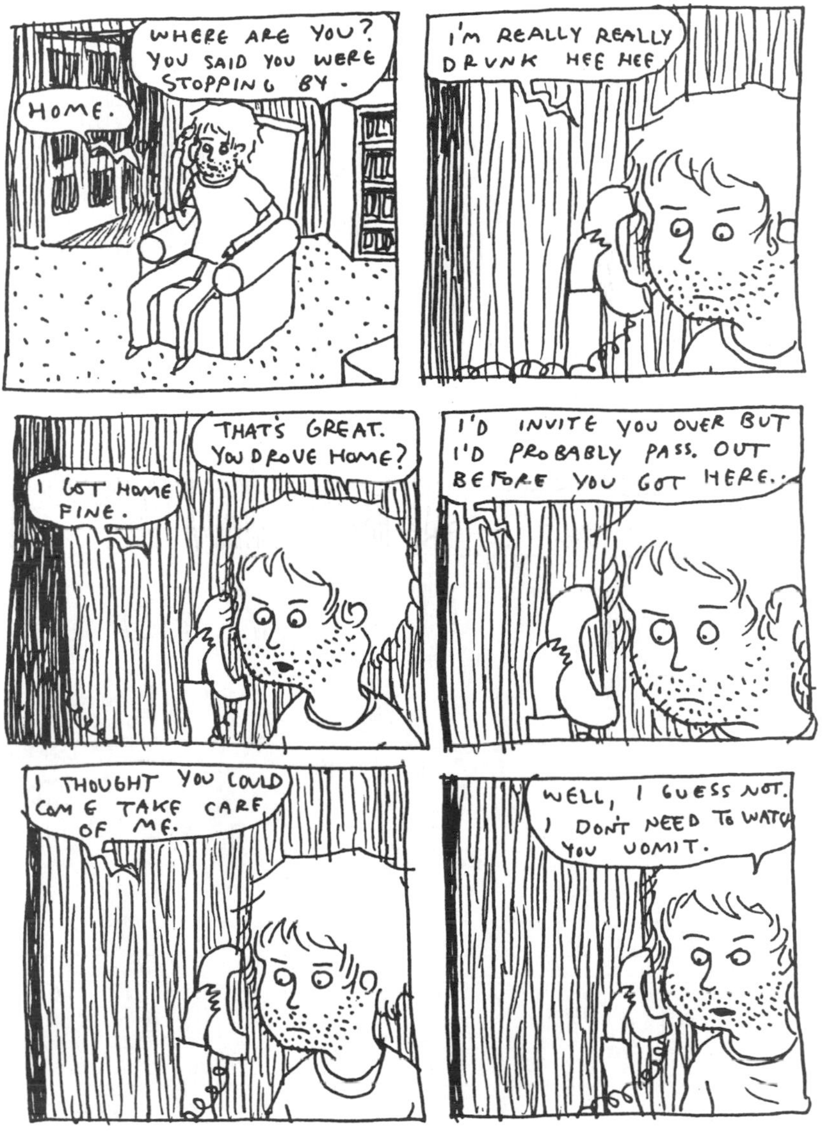

WHERE ARE YOU? YOU SAID YOU WERE STOPPING BY -
HOME.
I'M REALLY REALLY DRUNK HEE HEE
THAT'S GREAT. YOU DROVE HOME?
I GOT HOME FINE.
I'D INVITE YOU OVER BUT I'D PROBABLY PASS. OUT BEFORE YOU GOT HERE.
I THOUGHT YOU COULD COME TAKE CARE OF ME.
WELL, I GUESS NOT. I DON'T NEED TO WATCH YOU VOMIT.

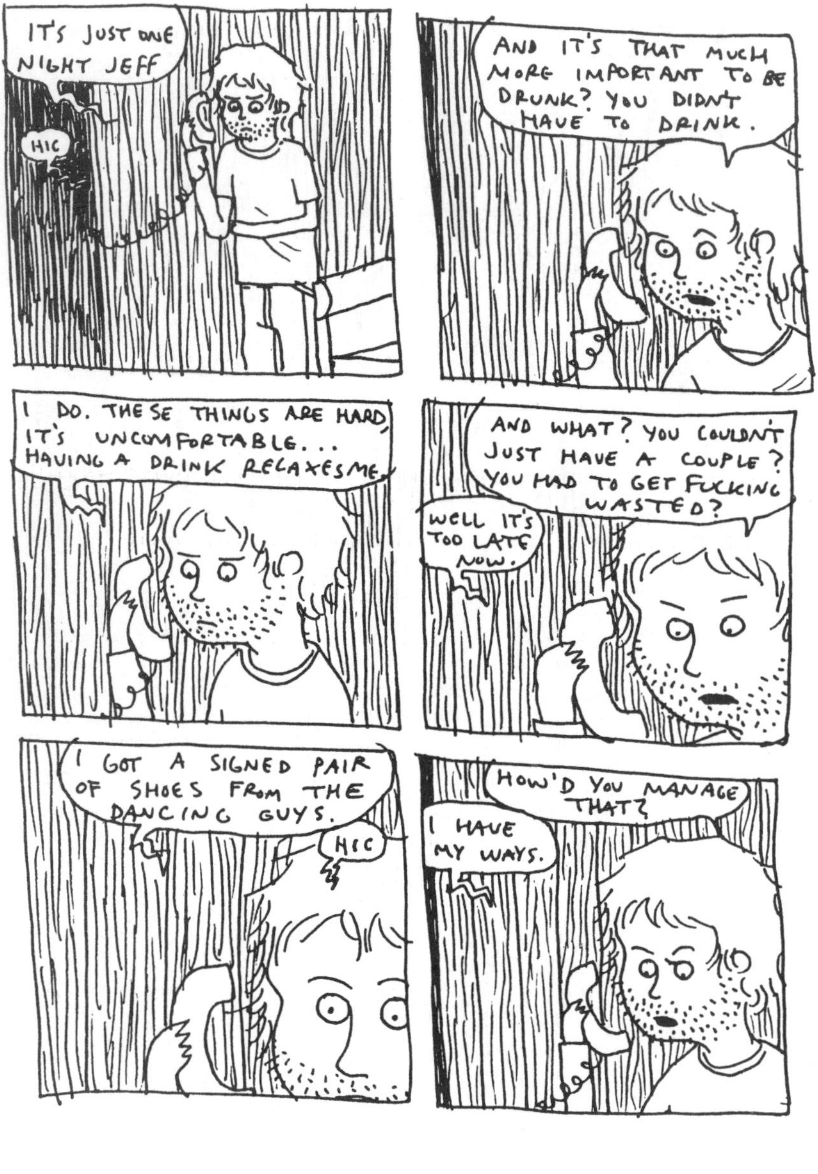
IT'S JUST ONE NIGHT JEFF
HIC
AND IT'S THAT MUCH MORE IMPORTANT TO BE DRUNK? YOU DIDN'T HAVE TO DRINK.
I DO. THESE THINGS ARE HARD, IT'S UNCOMFORTABLE... HAVING A DRINK RELAXES ME.
AND WHAT? YOU COULDN'T JUST HAVE A COUPLE? YOU HAD TO GET FUCKING WASTED?
WELL IT'S TOO LATE NOW.
I GOT A SIGNED PAIR OF SHOES FROM THE DANCING GUYS.
HIC
HOW'D YOU MANAGE THAT?
I HAVE MY WAYS.

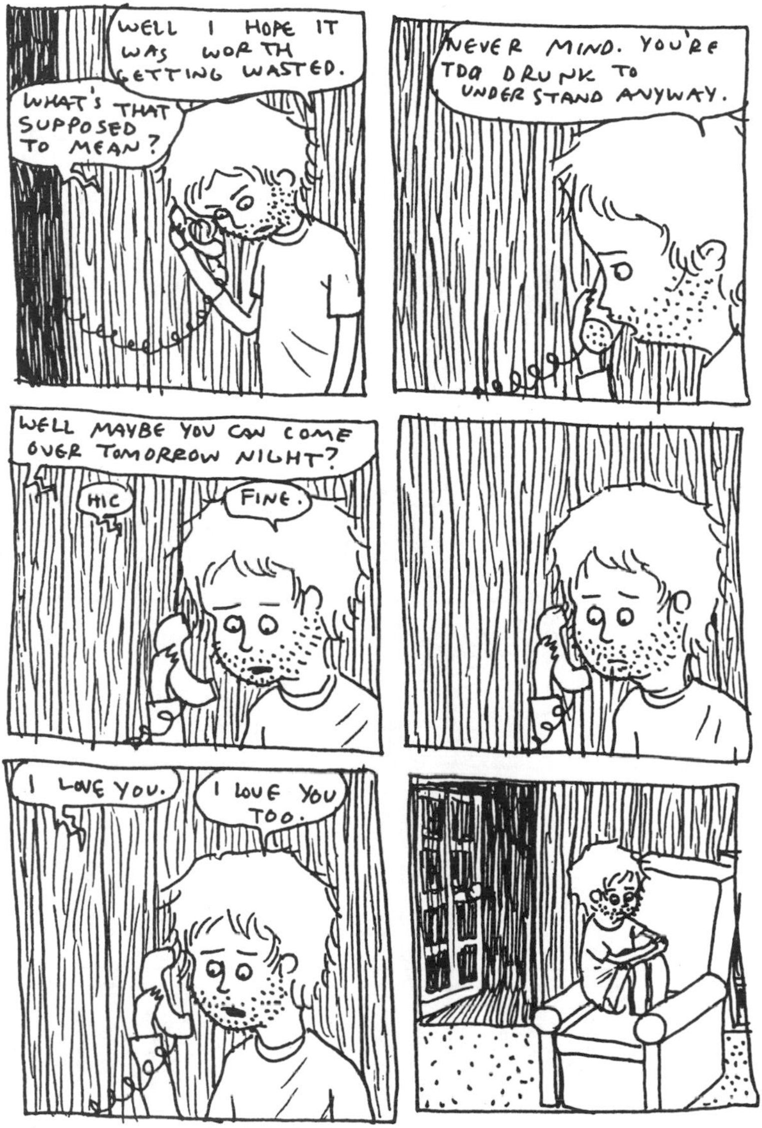
WELL I HOPE IT WAS WORTH GETTING WASTED.
WHAT'S THAT SUPPOSED TO MEAN?
NEVER MIND. YOU'RE TOO DRUNK TO UNDERSTAND ANYWAY.
WELL MAYBE YOU CAN COME OVER TOMORROW NIGHT?
HIC
FINE.
I LOVE YOU.
I LOVE YOU TOO.

THE LAST NIGHT

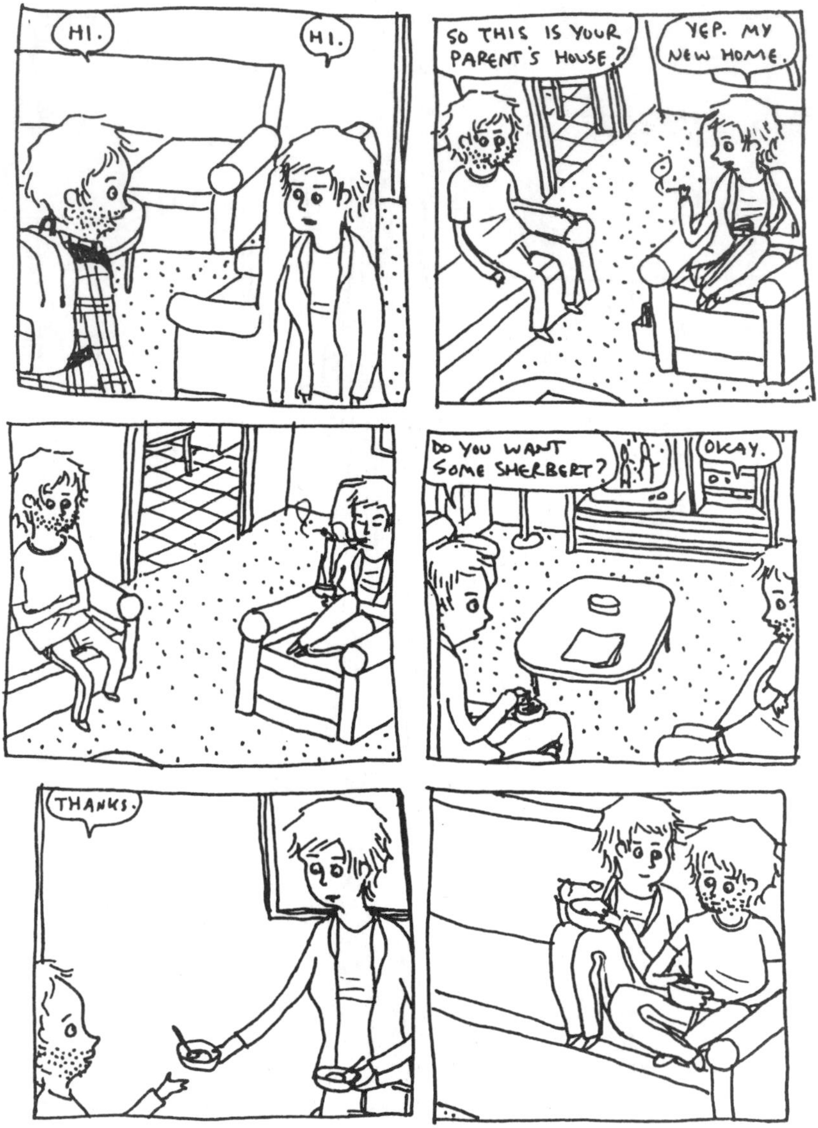

HI.
HI.
SO THIS IS YOUR PARENT'S HOUSE?
YEP. MY NEW HOME.
DO YOU WANT SOME SHERBERT?
OKAY.
THANKS.

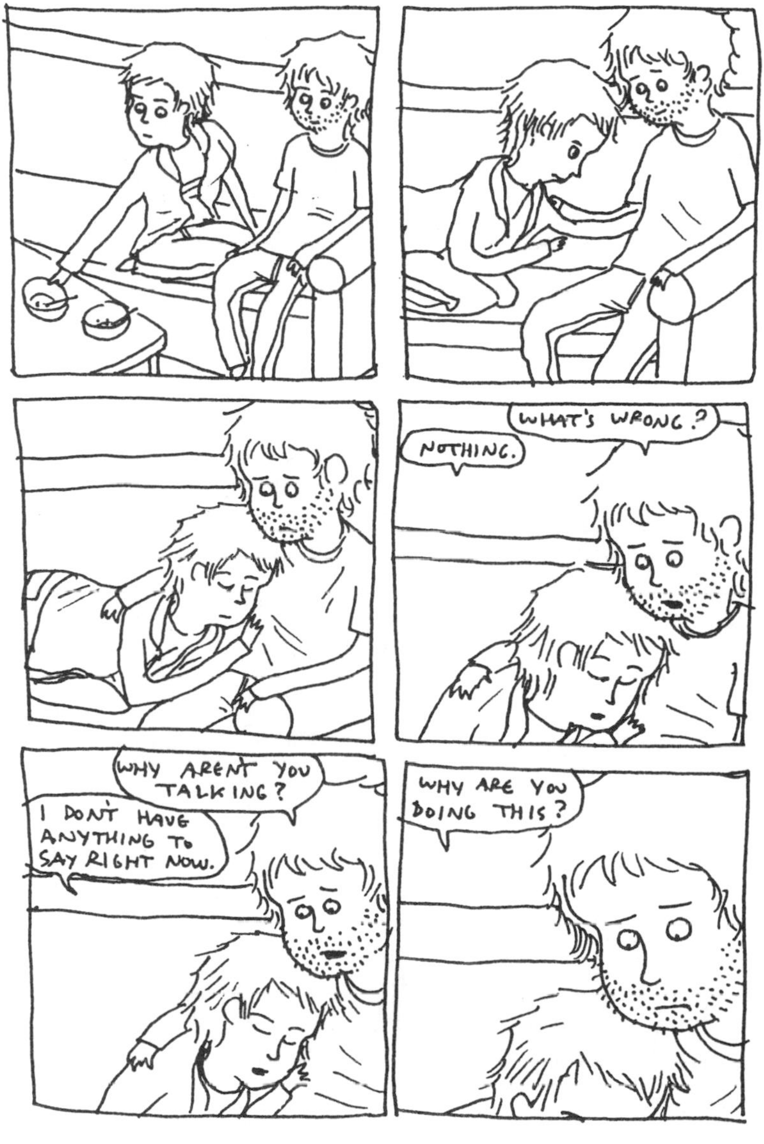
WHAT'S WRONG?
NOTHING.
WHY AREN'T YOU TALKING?
I DON'T HAVE ANYTHING TO SAY RIGHT NOW.
WHY ARE YOU DOING THIS?

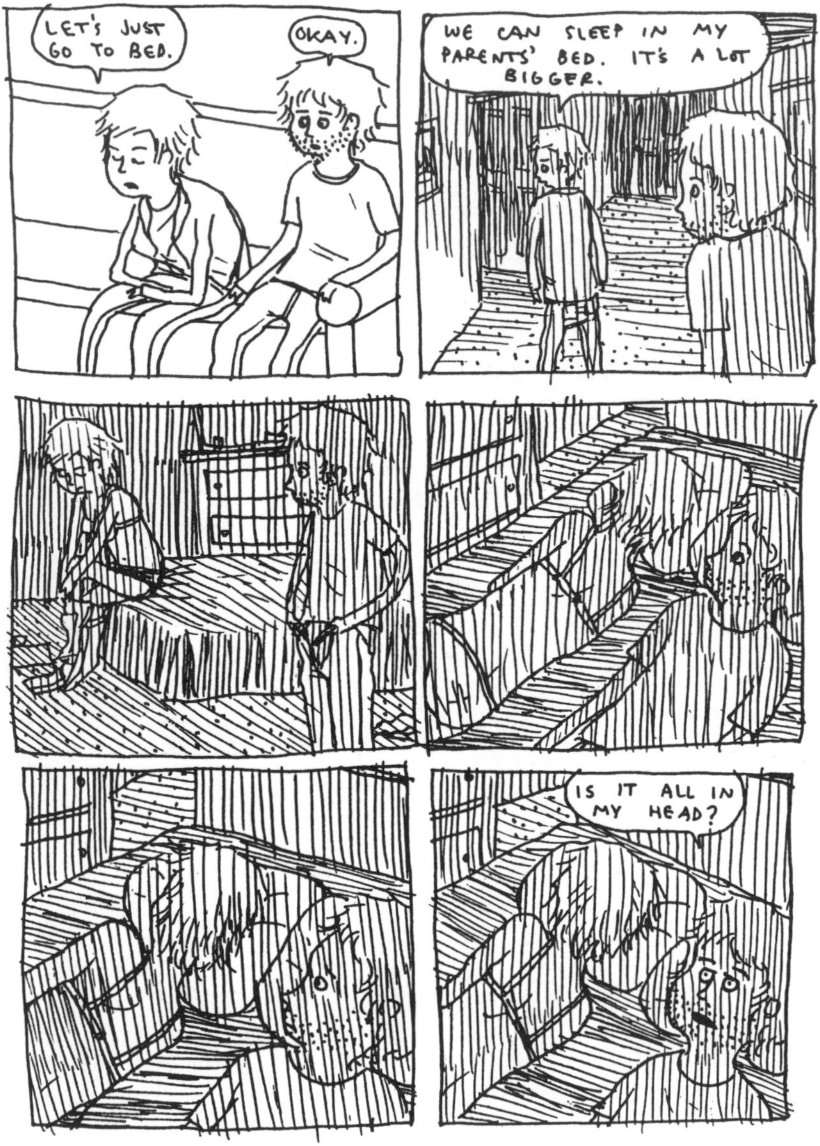
LET'S JUST GO TO BED.
OKAY.
WE CAN SLEEP IN MY PARENTS' BED. IT'S A LOT BIGGER.
IS IT ALL IN MY HEAD?

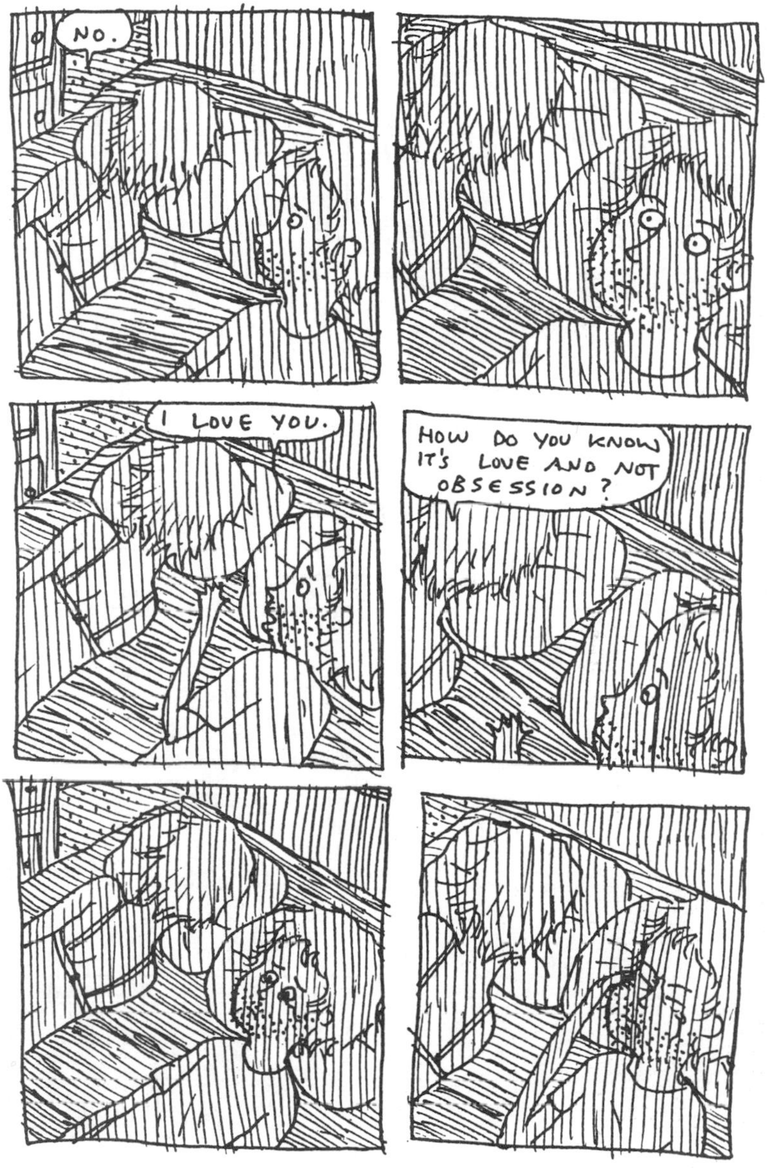
NO.
I LOVE YOU.
HOW DO YOU KNOW IT'S LOVE AND NOT OBSESSION?

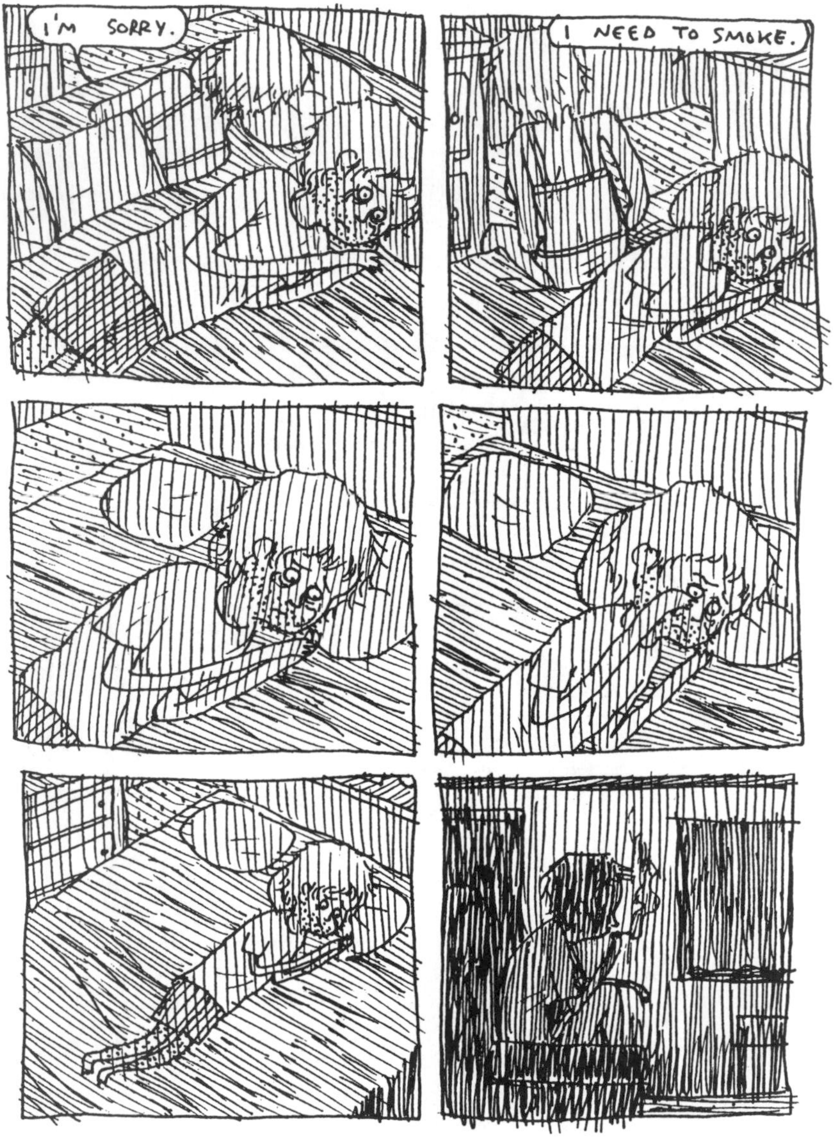
I'M SORRY.
I NEED TO SMOKE.

W O R K

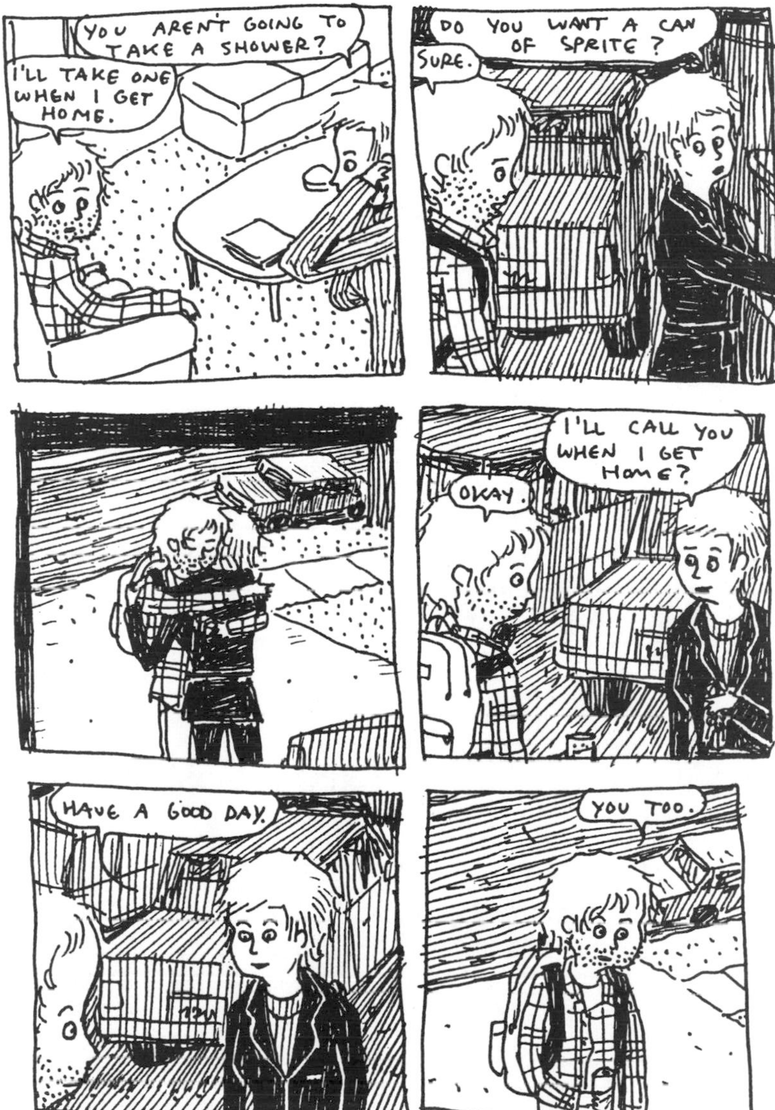
YOU AREN'T GOING TO TAKE A SHOWER?
I'LL TAKE ONE WHEN I GET HOME.
DO YOU WANT A CAN OF SPRITE?
SURE.
I'LL CALL YOU WHEN I GET HOME?
OKAY.
HAVE A GOOD DAY.
YOU TOO.

FALLEN

A NICE TALK

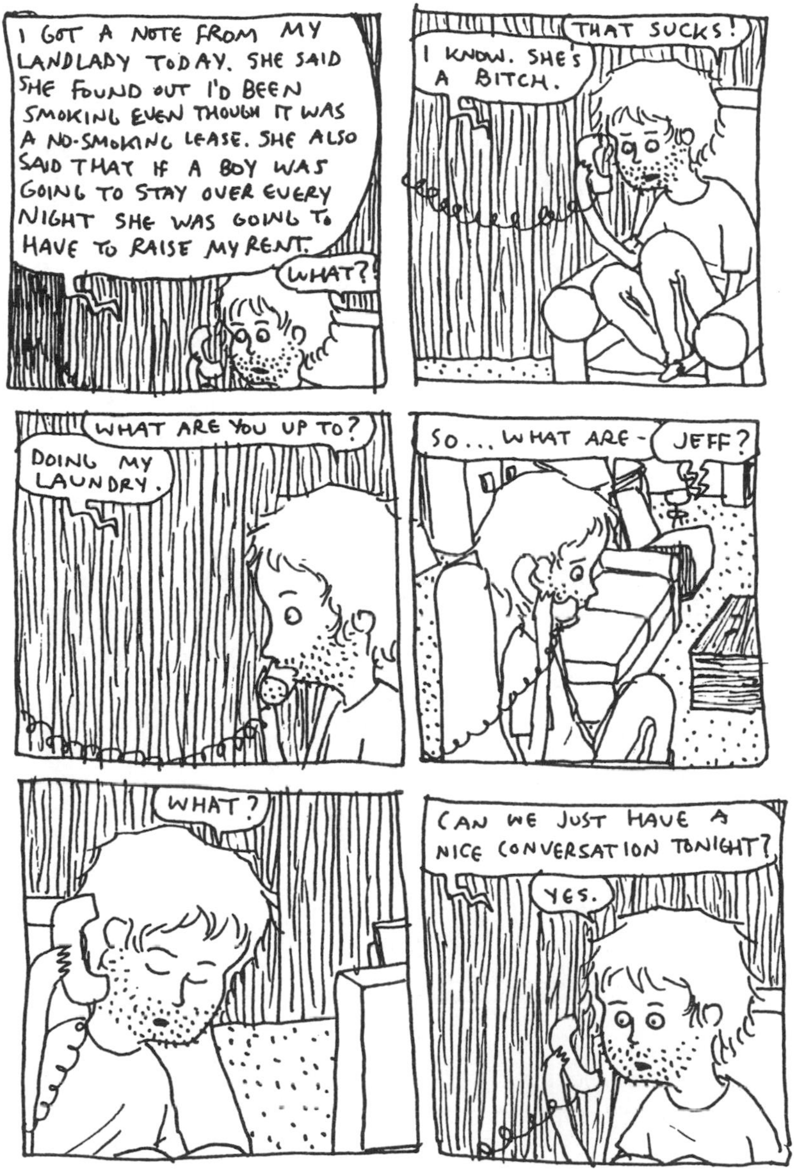
I GOT A NOTE FROM MY LANDLADY TODAY. SHE SAID SHE FOUND OUT I'D BEEN SMOKING EVEN THOUGH IT WAS A NO-SMOKING LEASE. SHE ALSO SAID THAT IF A BOY WAS GOING TO STAY OVER EVERY NIGHT SHE WAS GOING TO HAVE TO RAISE MY RENT.
WHAT?!
THAT SUCKS!
I KNOW. SHE'S A BITCH.
WHAT ARE YOU UP TO?
DOING MY LAUNDRY.
SO... WHAT ARE-
JEFF?
WHAT?
CAN WE JUST HAVE A NICE CONVERSATION TONIGHT?
YES.

SPACE

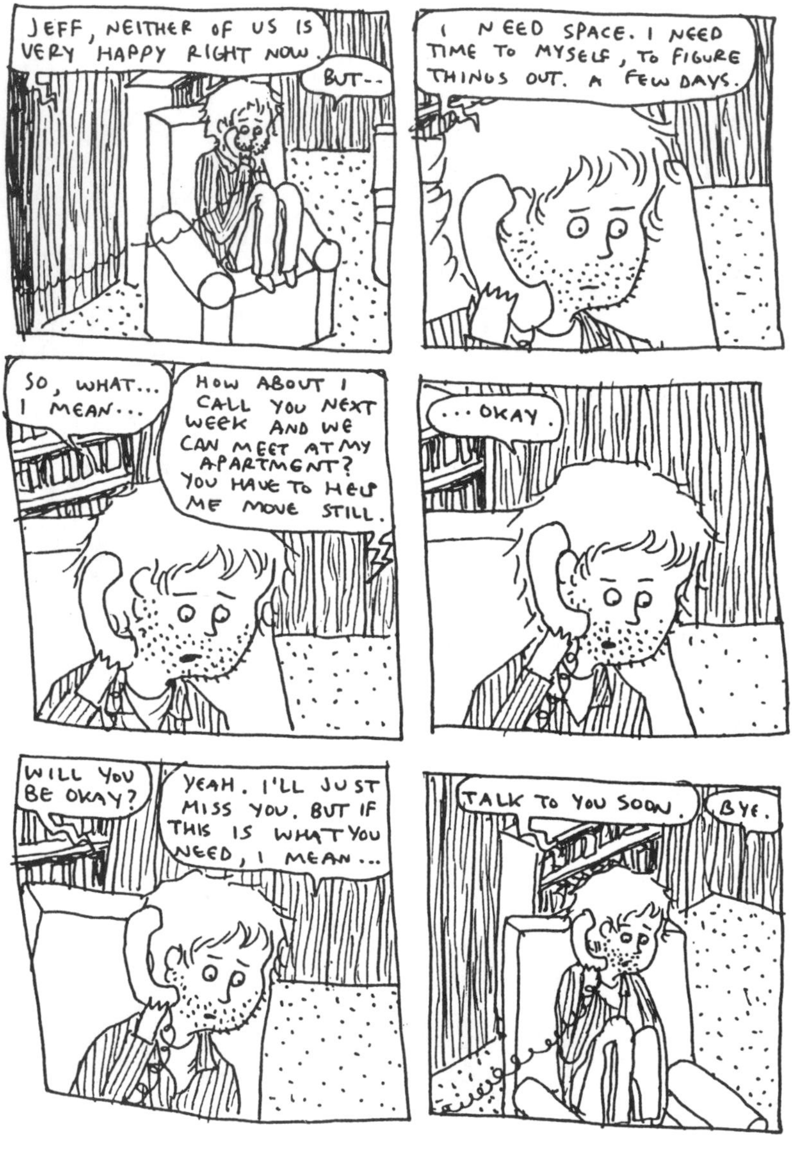
JEFF, NEITHER OF US IS VERY HAPPY RIGHT NOW.
BUT--
I NEED SPACE. I NEED TIME TO MYSELF, TO FIGURE THINGS OUT. A FEW DAYS.
SO, WHAT... I MEAN...
HOW ABOUT I CALL YOU NEXT WEEK AND WE CAN MEET AT MY APARTMENT? YOU HAVE TO HELP ME MOVE STILL.
...OKAY.
WILL YOU BE OKAY?
YEAH. I'LL JUST MISS YOU. BUT IF THIS IS WHAT YOU NEED, I MEAN...
TALK TO YOU SOON.
BYE.

BREAK

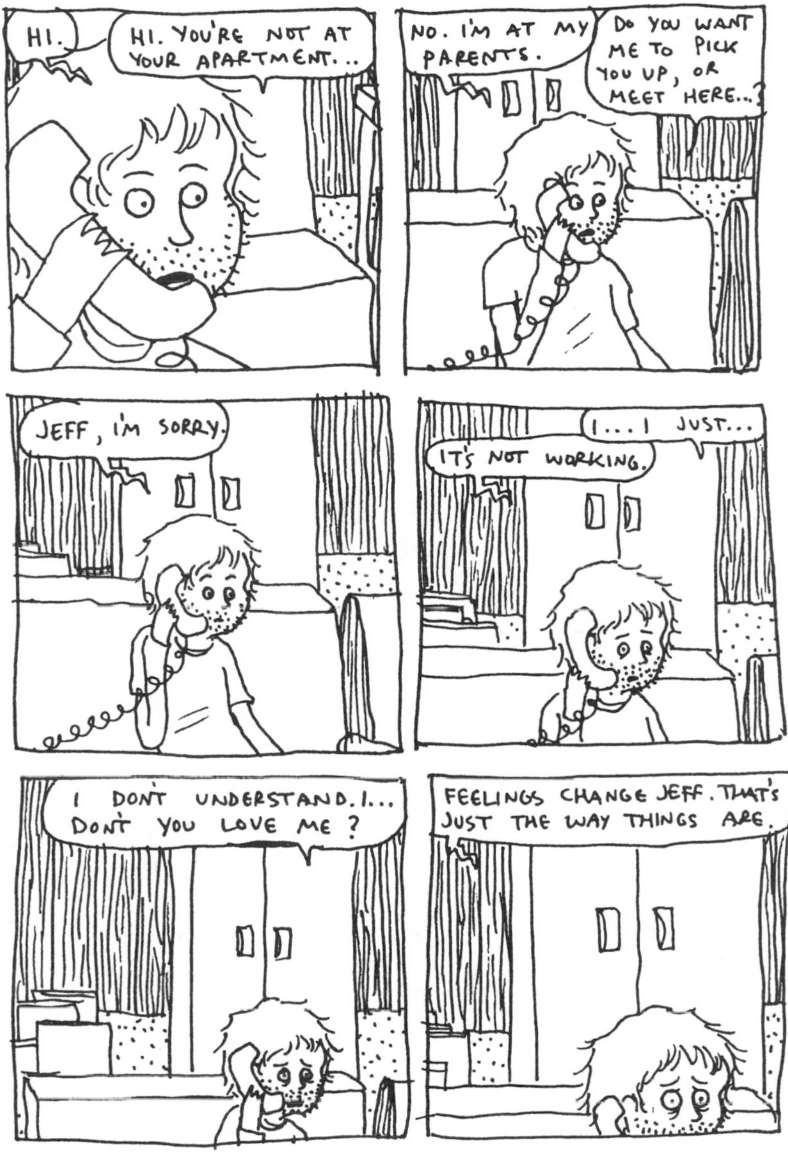
HI.
HI. YOU'RE NOT AT YOUR APARTMENT...
NO. I'M AT MY PARENTS.
DO YOU WANT ME TO PICK YOU UP, OR MEET HERE...?
JEFF, I'M SORRY.
I... I JUST...
IT'S NOT WORKING.
I DON'T UNDERSTAND. I... DON'T YOU LOVE ME ?
FEELINGS CHANGE JEFF. THAT'S JUST THE WAY THINGS ARE.

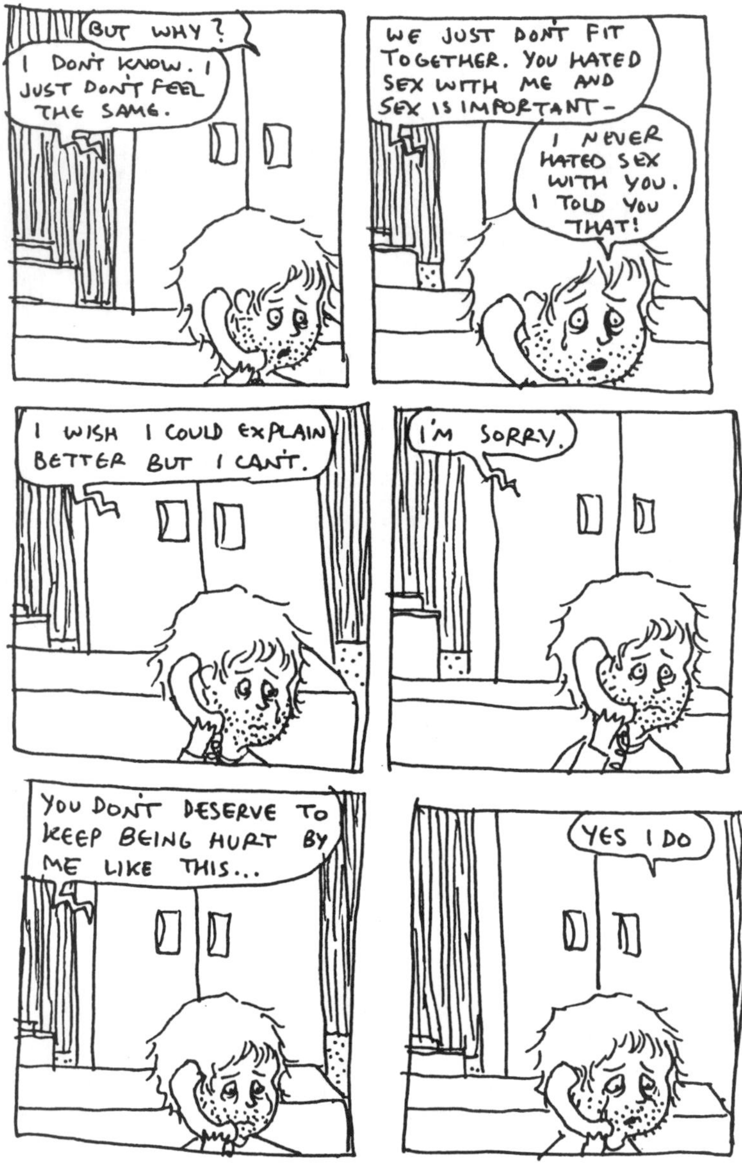
BUT WHY?
I DON'T KNOW. I JUST DON'T FEEL THE SAME.
WE JUST DON'T FIT TOGETHER. YOU HATED SEX WITH ME AND SEX IS IMPORTANT-
I NEVER HATED SEX WITH YOU. I TOLD YOU THAT!
I WISH I COULD EXPLAIN BETTER BUT I CAN'T.
I'M SORRY.
YOU DON'T DESERVE TO KEEP BEING HURT BY ME LIKE THIS...
YES I DO

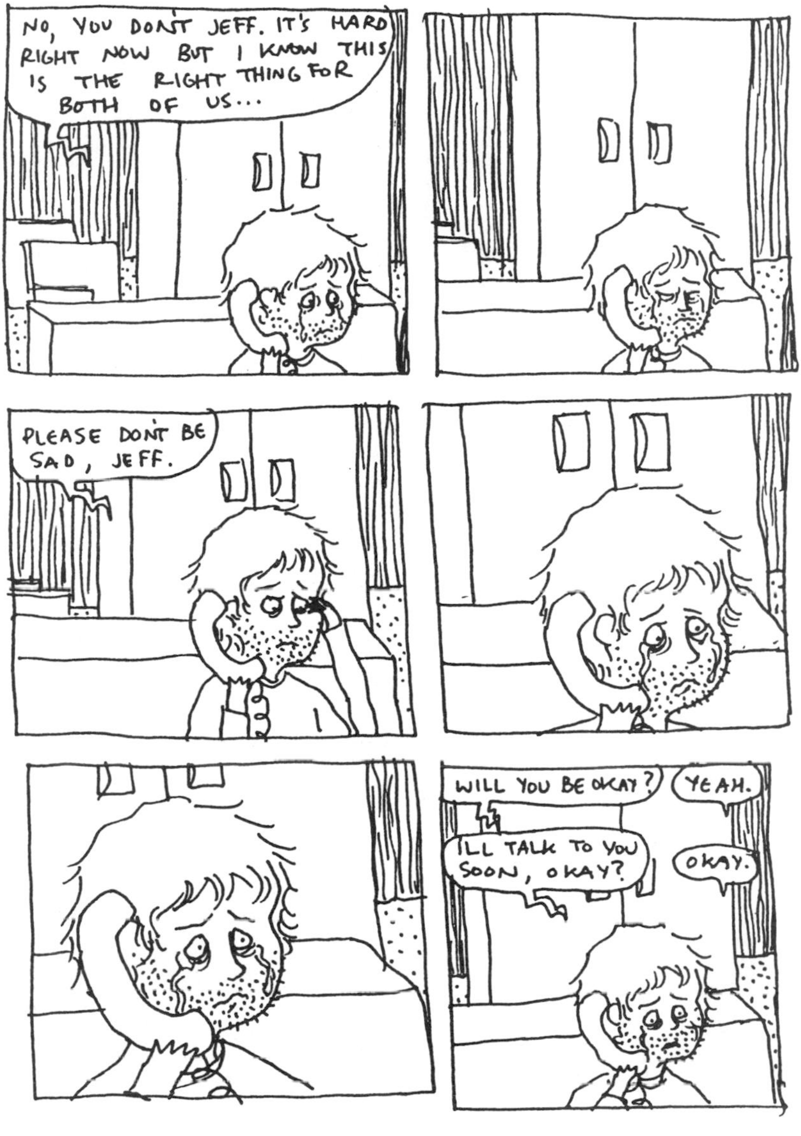
NO, YOU DON'T JEFF. IT'S HARD RIGHT NOW BUT I KNOW THIS IS THE RIGHT THING FOR BOTH OF US...
PLEASE DON'T BE SAD, JEFF.
WILL YOU BE OKAY?
YEAH.
I'LL TALK TO YOU SOON, OKAY?
OKAY.

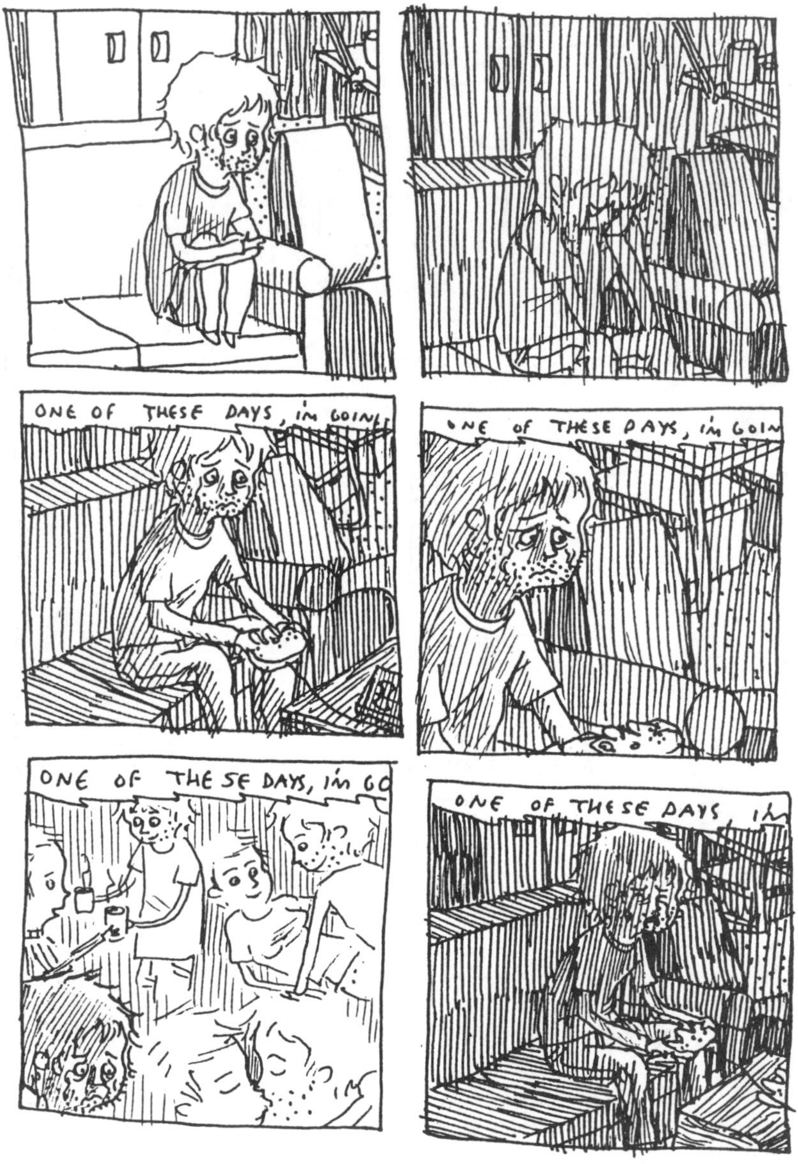

ONE OF THESE DAYS, I'M GOIN
ONE OF THESE DAYS, I'M GOIN
ONE OF THESE DAYS, I'M GO
ONE OF THESE DAYS I'M

MORNING

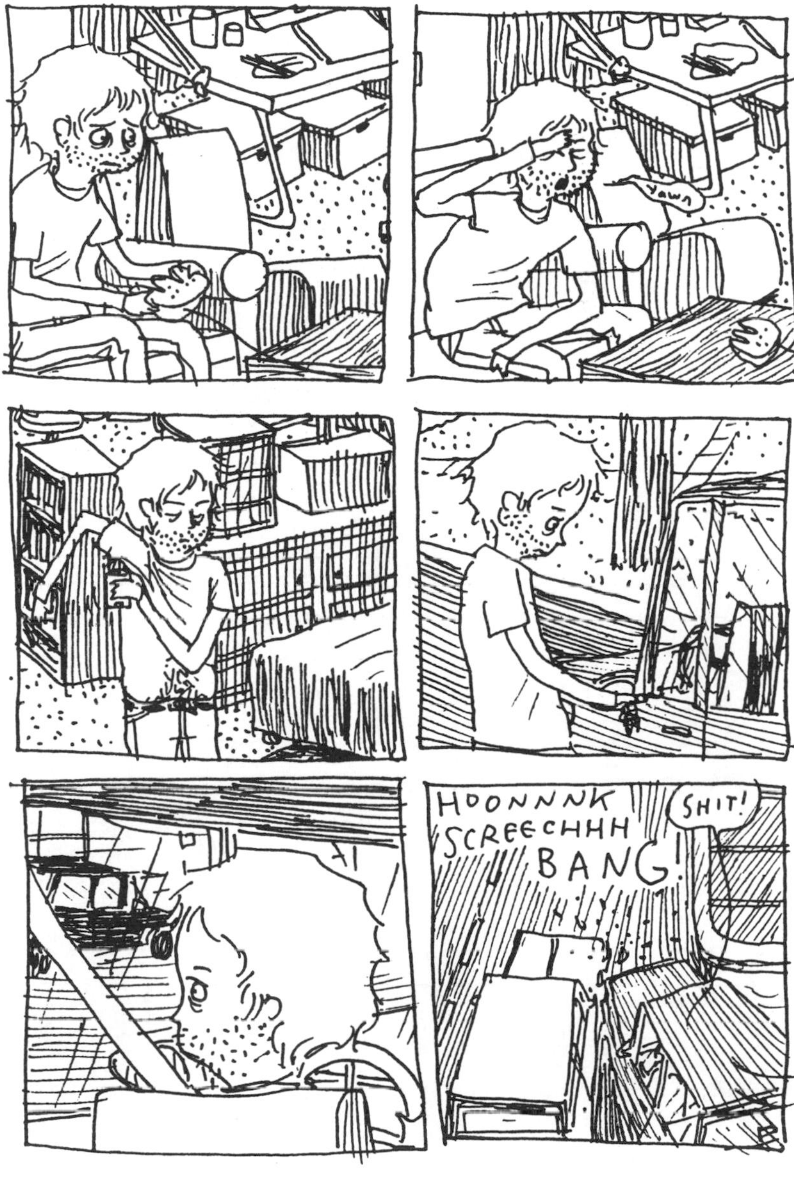
Yawn
HOONNNK
SCREECHHH
BANG!
SHIT!

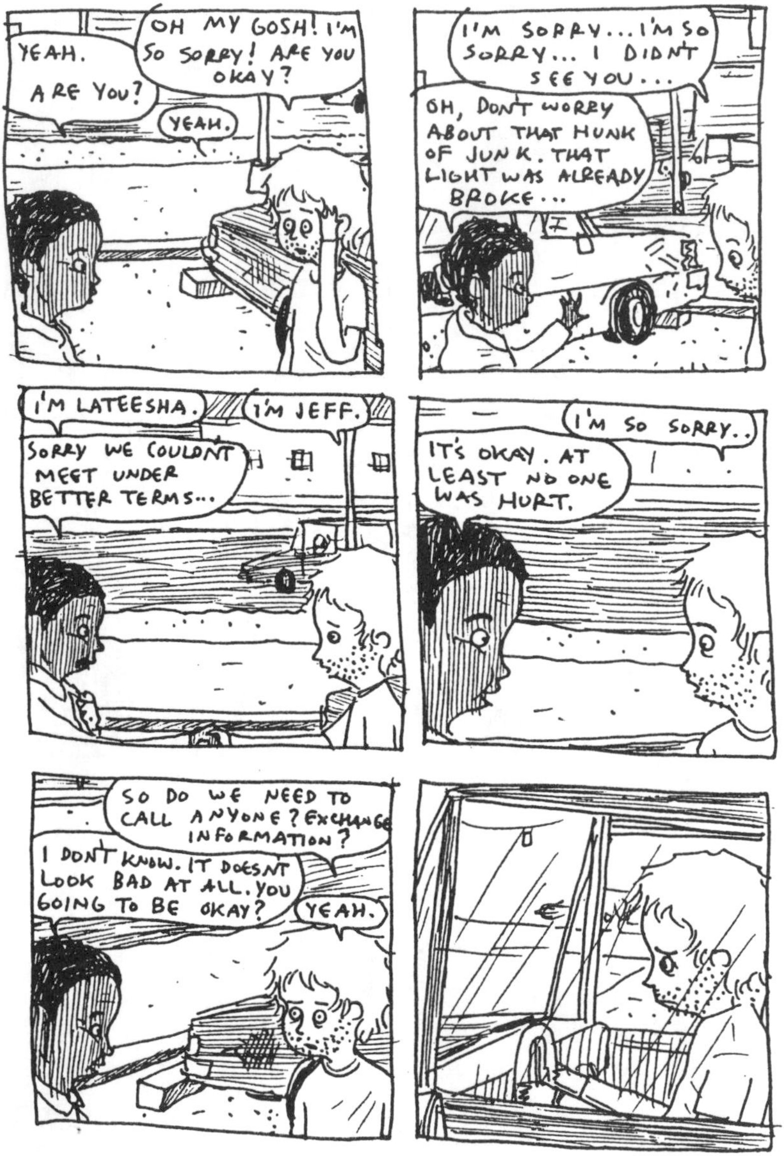
OH MY GOSH! I'M SO SORRY! ARE YOU OKAY?
YEAH.
ARE YOU?
YEAH.
I'M SORRY... I'M SO SORRY... I DIDN'T SEE YOU...
OH, DON'T WORRY ABOUT THAT HUNK OF JUNK. THAT LIGHT WAS ALREADY BROKE...
I'M LATEESHA.
I'M JEFF.
SORRY WE COULDNT MEET UNDER BETTER TERMS...
I'M SO SORRY..
IT'S OKAY. AT LEAST NO ONE WAS HURT.
SO DO WE NEED TO CALL ANYONE? EXCHANGE INFORMATION?
I DON'T KNOW. IT DOESNT LOOK BAD AT ALL. YOU GOING TO BE OKAY?
YEAH.

DRAIN

TALKING

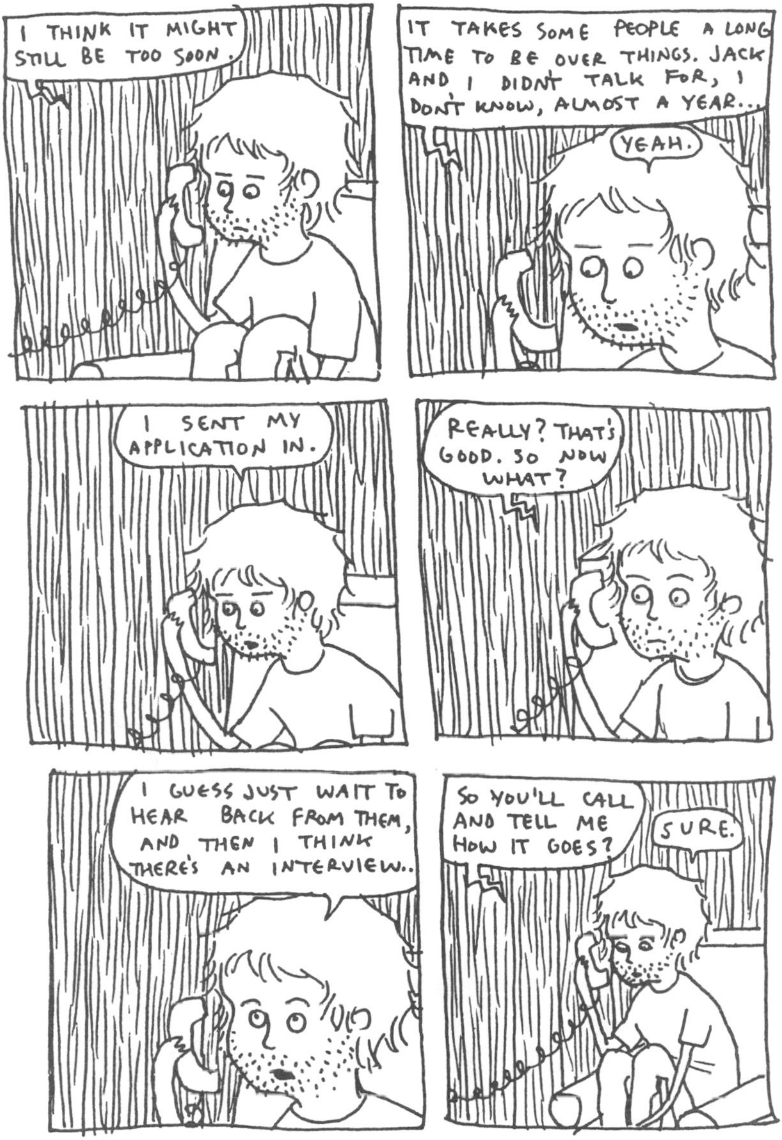
I THINK IT MIGHT STILL BE TOO SOON.
IT TAKES SOME PEOPLE A LONG TIME TO BE OVER THINGS. JACK AND I DIDN'T TALK FOR, I DON'T KNOW, ALMOST A YEAR...
YEAH.
I SENT MY APPLICATION IN.
REALLY? THAT'S GOOD. SO NOW WHAT?
I GUESS JUST WAIT TO HEAR BACK FROM THEM, AND THEN I THINK THERE'S AN INTERVIEW..
SO YOU'LL CALL AND TELL ME HOW IT GOES?
SURE.

TALKING

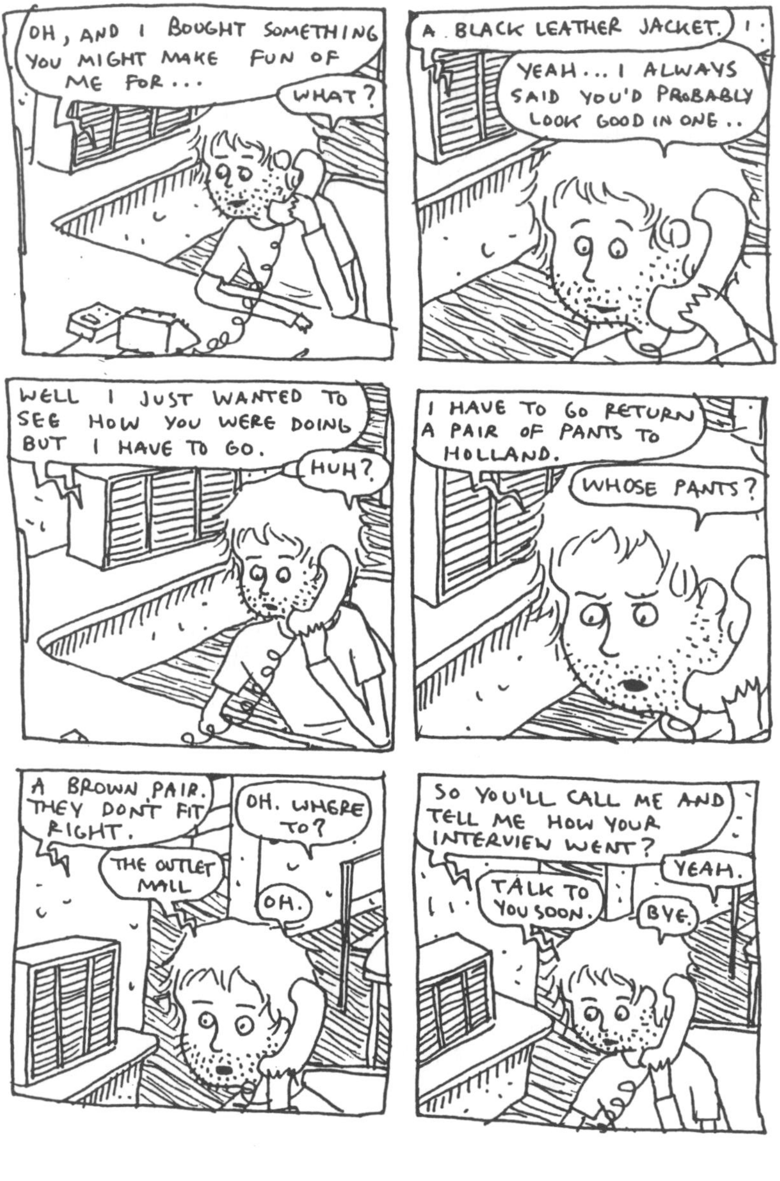

OH, AND I BOUGHT SOMETHING YOU MIGHT MAKE FUN OF ME FOR...
WHAT?
A BLACK LEATHER JACKET.
YEAH... I ALWAYS SAID YOU'D PROBABLY LOOK GOOD IN ONE..
WELL I JUST WANTED TO SEE HOW YOU WERE DOING BUT I HAVE TO GO.
HUH?
I HAVE TO GO RETURN A PAIR OF PANTS TO HOLLAND.
WHOSE PANTS?
A BROWN PAIR. THEY DON'T FIT RIGHT.
OH. WHERE TO?
THE OUTLET MALL
OH.
SO YOU'LL CALL ME AND TELL ME HOW YOUR INTERVIEW WENT?
YEAH.
TALK TO YOU SOON.
BYE.

TALKING

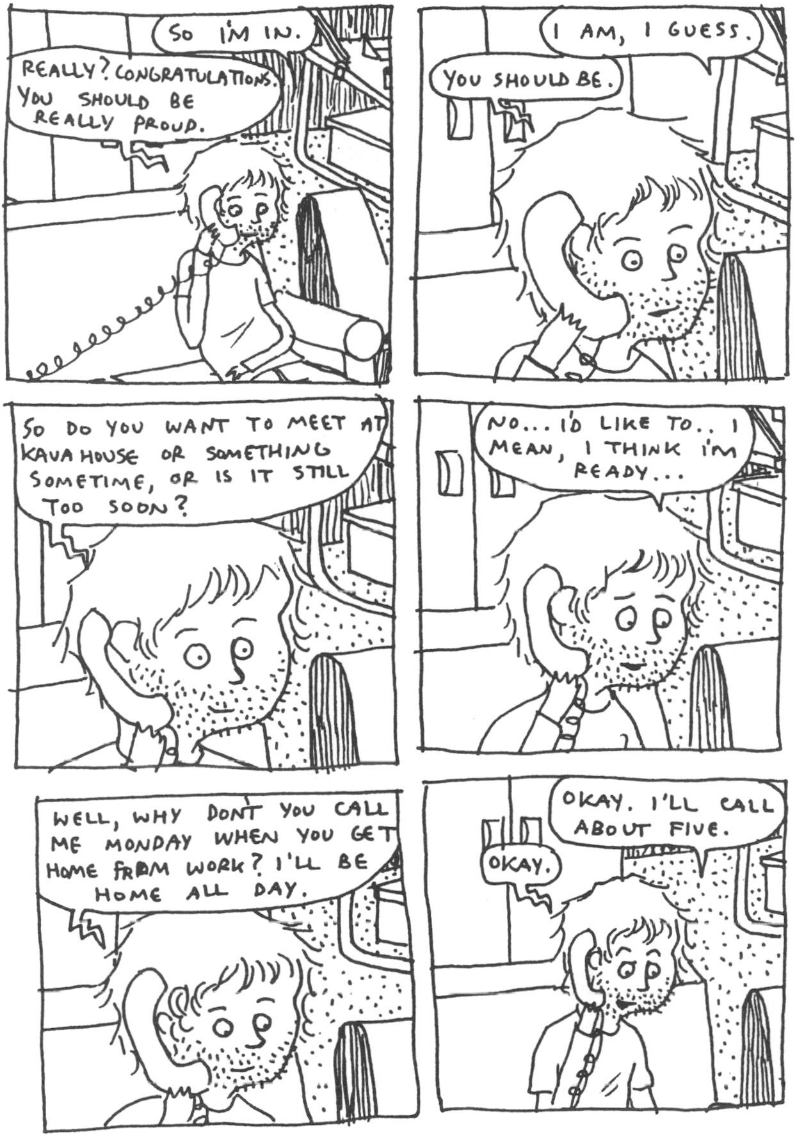
SO I'M IN.
REALLY? CONGRATULATIONS. YOU SHOULD BE REALLY PROUD.
I AM, I GUESS.
YOU SHOULD BE.
SO DO YOU WANT TO MEET AT KAVA HOUSE OR SOMETHING SOMETIME, OR IS IT STILL TOO SOON?
NO... I'D LIKE TO.. I MEAN, I THINK I'M READY...
WELL, WHY DON'T YOU CALL ME MONDAY WHEN YOU GET HOME FROM WORK? I'LL BE HOME ALL DAY.
OKAY. I'LL CALL ABOUT FIVE.
OKAY.

BLEW OFF

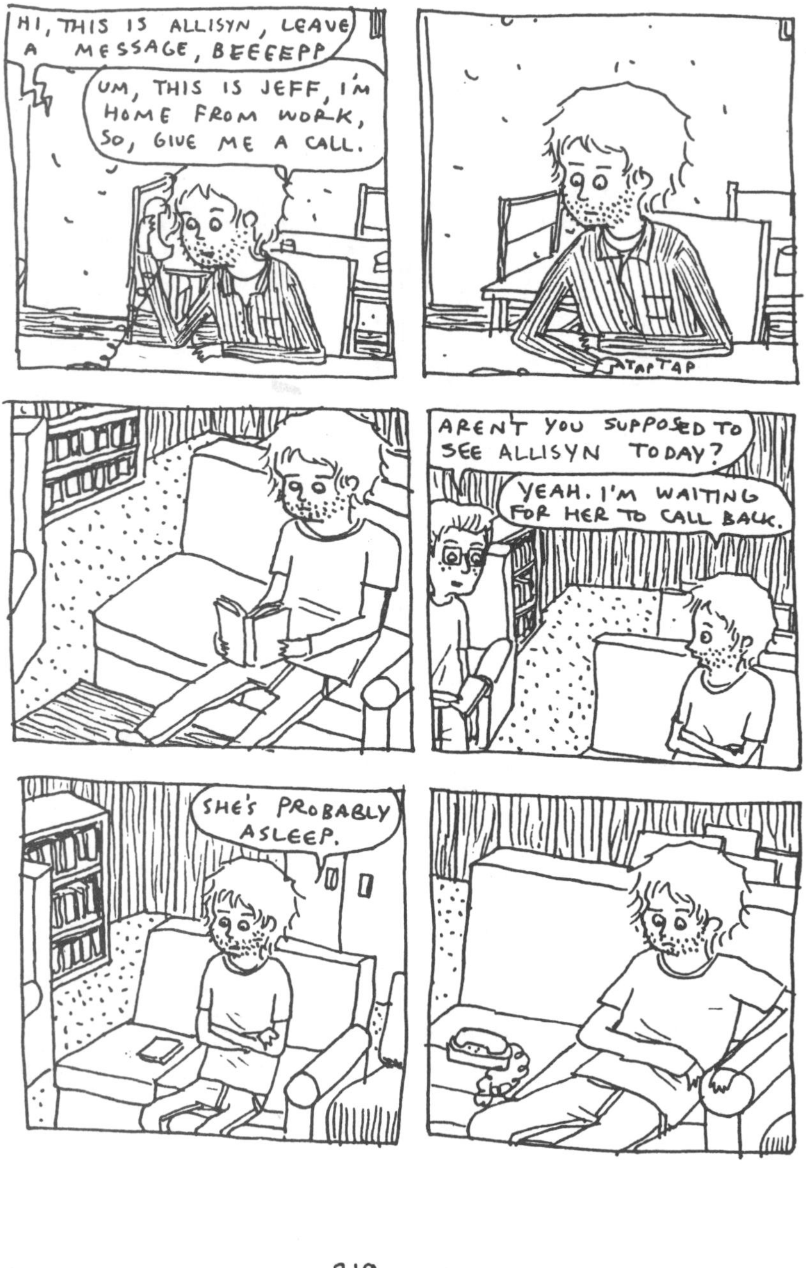
HI, THIS IS ALLISYN, LEAVE A MESSAGE, BEEEEPP
UM, THIS IS JEFF, I'M HOME FROM WORK, SO, GIVE ME A CALL.
TAPTAP
AREN'T YOU SUPPOSED TO SEE ALLISYN TODAY?
YEAH. I'M WAITING FOR HER TO CALL BACK.
SHE'S PROBABLY ASLEEP.

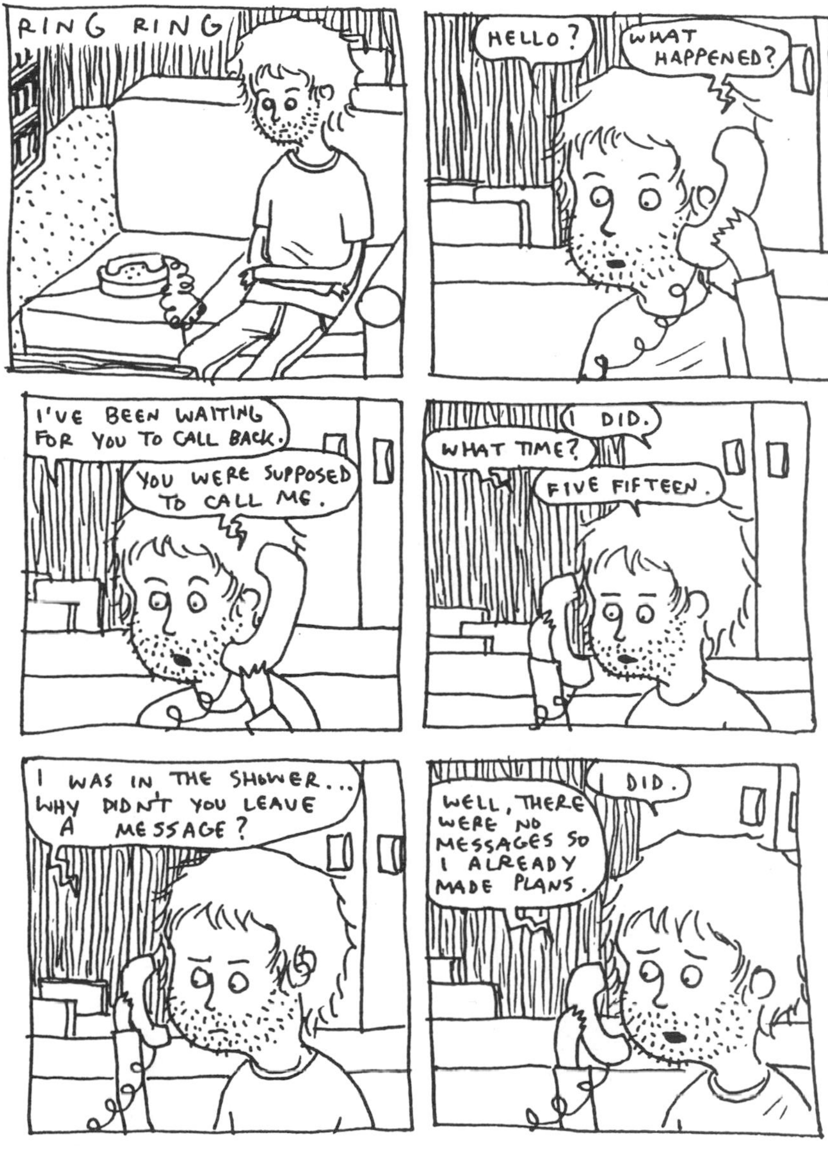
RING RING
HELLO?
WHAT HAPPENED?
I'VE BEEN WAITING FOR YOU TO CALL BACK.
YOU WERE SUPPOSED TO CALL ME.
I DID.
WHAT TIME?
FIVE FIFTEEN.
I WAS IN THE SHOWER... WHY DIDN'T YOU LEAVE A MESSAGE?
I DID.
WELL, THERE WERE NO MESSAGES SO I ALREADY MADE PLANS.

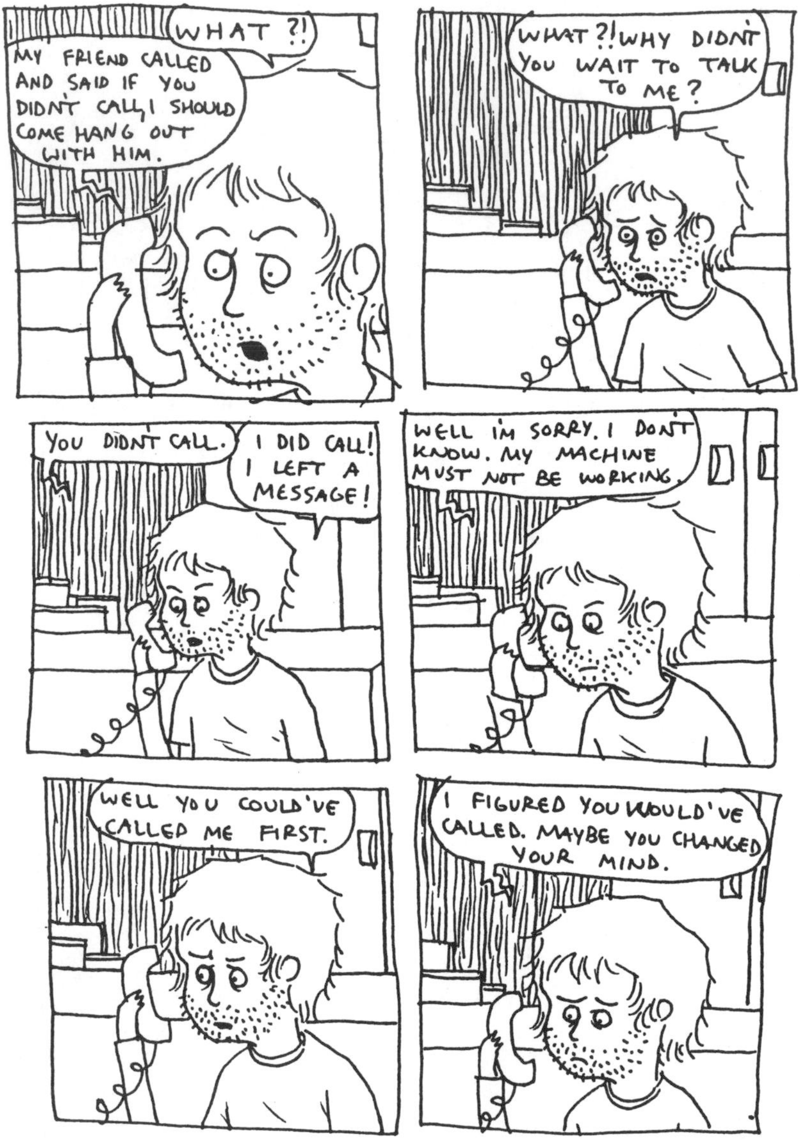
WHAT ?!
MY FRIEND CALLED AND SAID IF YOU DIDN'T CALL, I SHOULD COME HANG OUT WITH HIM.
WHAT ?! WHY DIDN'T YOU WAIT TO TALK TO ME ?
YOU DIDN'T CALL.
I DID CALL! I LEFT A MESSAGE!
WELL I'M SORRY. I DON'T KNOW. MY MACHINE MUST NOT BE WORKING.
WELL YOU COULD'VE CALLED ME FIRST.
I FIGURED YOU WOULD'VE CALLED. MAYBE YOU CHANGED YOUR MIND.

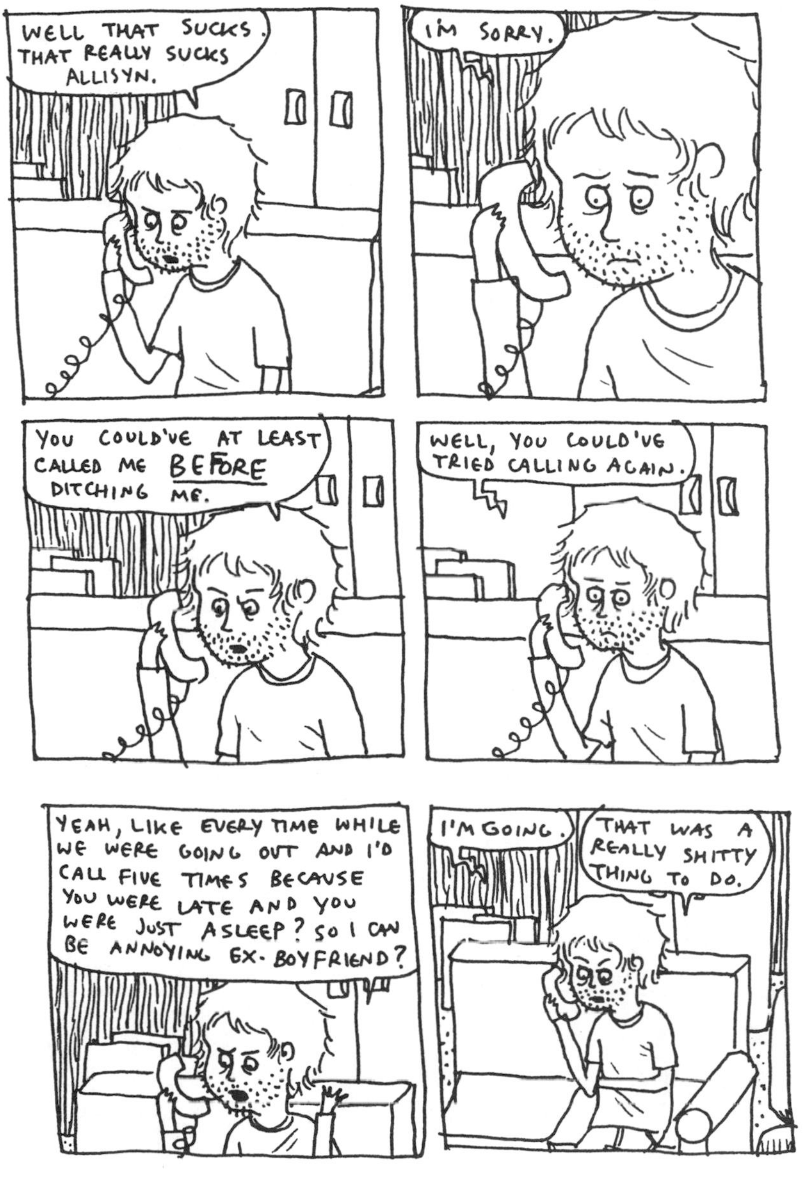
WELL THAT SUCKS. THAT REALLY SUCKS ALLISYN.
I'M SORRY.
YOU COULD'VE AT LEAST CALLED ME BEFORE DITCHING ME.
WELL, YOU COULD'VE TRIED CALLING AGAIN.
YEAH, LIKE EVERY TIME WHILE WE WERE GOING OUT AND I'D CALL FIVE TIMES BECAUSE YOU WERE LATE AND YOU WERE JUST ASLEEP? SO I CAN BE ANNOYING EX-BOYFRIEND?
I'M GOING.
THAT WAS A REALLY SHITTY THING TO DO.

NOT SO MUCH

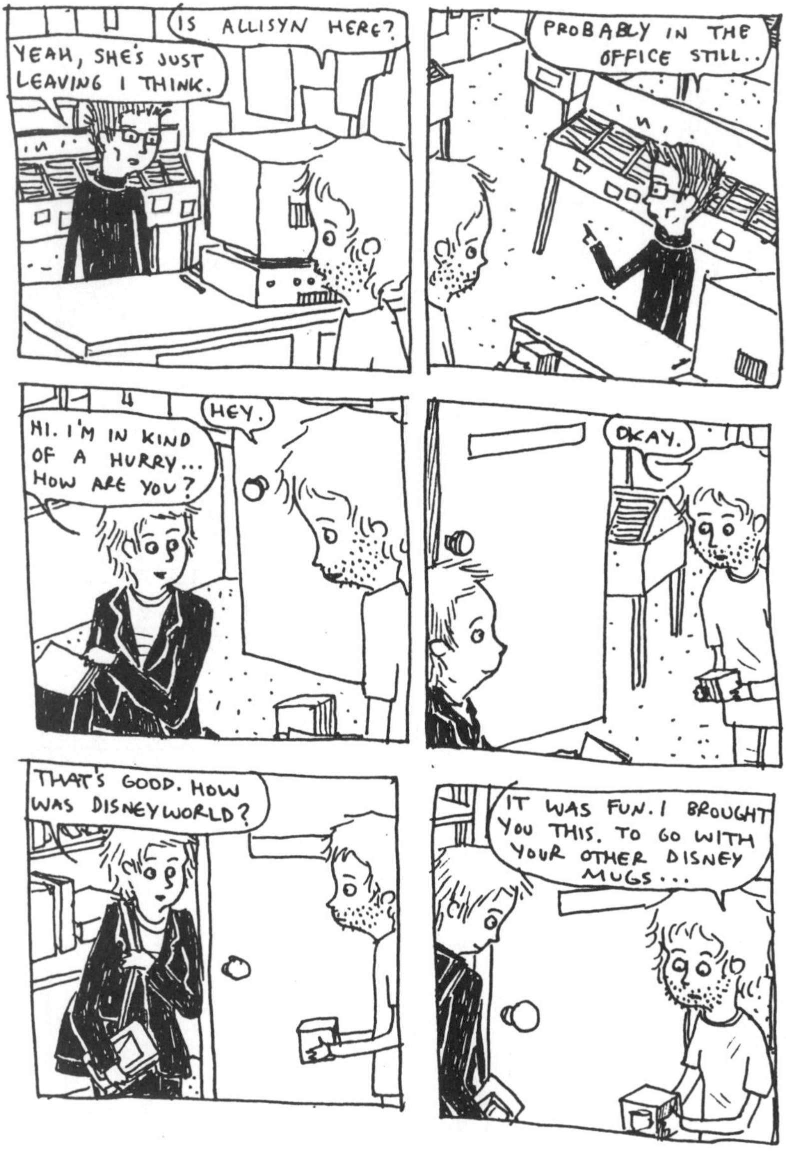
IS ALLISYN HERE?
YEAH, SHE'S JUST LEAVING I THINK.
PROBABLY IN THE OFFICE STILL..
HEY.
HI. I'M IN KIND OF A HURRY... HOW ARE YOU?
OKAY.
THAT'S GOOD. HOW WAS DISNEYWORLD?
IT WAS FUN. I BROUGHT YOU THIS. TO GO WITH YOUR OTHER DISNEY MUGS...

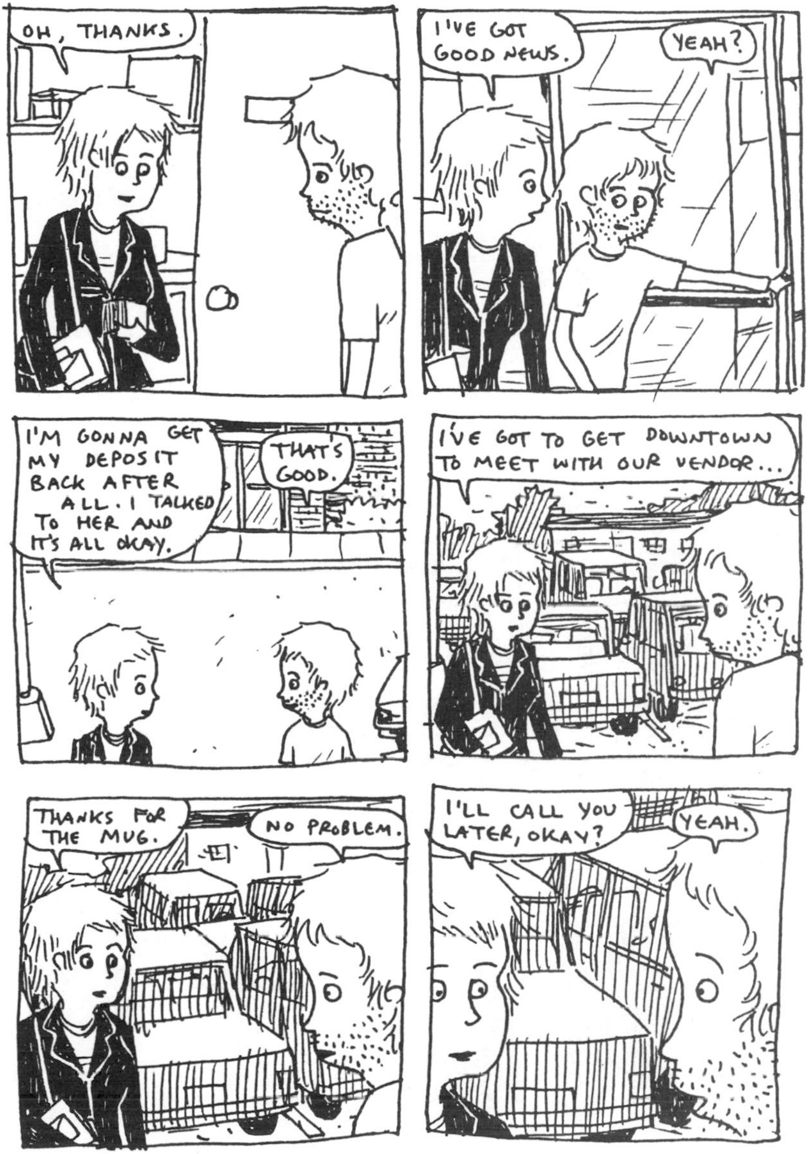
OH, THANKS.
I'VE GOT GOOD NEWS.
YEAH?
I'M GONNA GET MY DEPOSIT BACK AFTER ALL. I TALKED TO HER AND IT'S ALL OKAY.
THAT'S GOOD.
I'VE GOT TO GET DOWNTOWN TO MEET WITH OUR VENDOR...
THANKS FOR THE MUG.
NO PROBLEM.
I'LL CALL YOU LATER, OKAY?
YEAH.

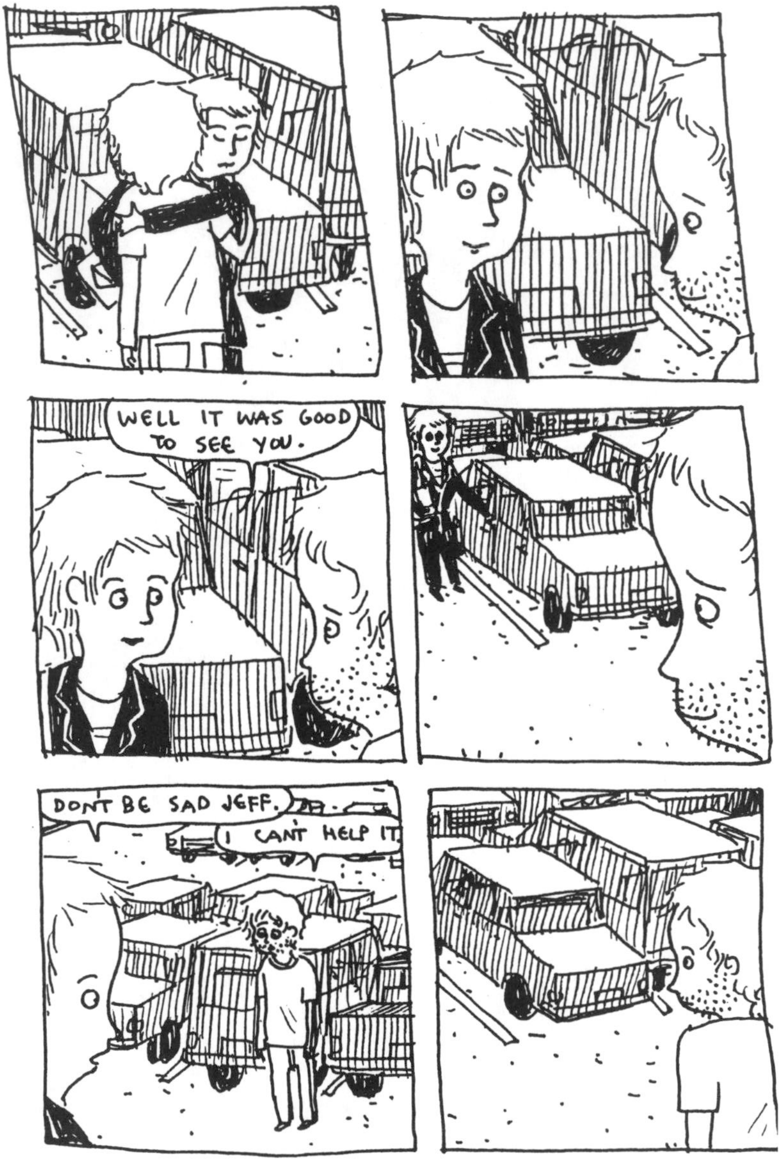
WELL IT WAS GOOD TO SEE YOU.
DONT BE SAD JEFF.
I CANT HELP IT

226

227